Conscious Discipline®

BUILDING RESILIENT CLASSROOMS

by Dr. Becky A. Bailey

800.842.2846
P.O. Box 622407, Oviedo FL 32762
ConsciousDiscipline.com

The author of this book may be contacted through Loving Guidance, Inc.
P: 800.842.2846 | ConsciousDiscipline.com

ISBN: 978-1-889609-51-5

Editor: Julie Ruffo
Cover / Page Design: Brandi Besher

This book is dedicated to personal transformation.

Personal transformation is vital for embedding resilience in our families, schools, communities, nation and the world. May we each be willing to embrace change in order to strengthen education, sustain our planet and secure a bright future for all children!

From my heart to your heart – I wish you well,
Becky Bailey

Contents

Introduction

Section 1: Safety

Section 2: Connection

Section 3: Problem Solving

Acknowledgements

All of us know friends and families who have overcome staggering challenges. Their resilience in the face of untold obstacles inspires us to believe more deeply in the power of the human spirit. I would like to thank these children and adults for inspiring me to keep imagining, envisioning and writing. Their energy drives every sentence in this book.

No book writes itself; it takes a team. Julie Ruffo is called my editor. I am honored to also call her my friend, my family, my colleague and my co-writer. Thank you, dear Julie. We've been on quite a journey together since you joined Loving Guidance as my "write hand." My gratitude goes also to the line editing talents of Jennifer Clark. Thanks to Brandi Besher who created an inspiring book cover and for the beautiful pages she designed. An extended thanks to Brandi and Keith Meyer for designing the interactive web portal that supports a deeper grasp of Conscious Discipline. My appreciation goes out to Robert Hess whose talents as a multimedia guru brings Conscious Discipline to life in film and pictures, and to Tracey Tucker for her detailed attention to all the references. Thanks to Renee Whittington whose determination and patience guided Robert, Brandi, Julie and Keith, bringing their collective talent together with a quality only she can offer.

My deep love and gratitude is extended to Linda Harris, Elizabeth Montero-Cefalo, Renee Whittington, Keith McIntyre and Paula Ashby for reading and rereading each chapter to offer their insights, clarity and wisdom. Many thanks also to the efforts of Dr. Barbara Landon, Neuropsychology Professor at the School of Medicine at St. Georges University. Her support enhanced the writing of the brain information in this book.

Conscious Discipline is based on a pay it forward transformational model. One child teaches another child an essential social skill. One teacher creates a classroom that becomes a model for others. One principal transforms a school and then helps another principal do the same. I am grateful for the thousands of Conscious Discipline enthusiasts who pay it forward in this way every day. I am particularly blessed by those who have paid it forward by providing videos, pictures and stories for this book, the interactive web portal and Shubert's School. My deepest appreciation goes to all who have transformed themselves and their classrooms, especially Vicky Hepler, Kristin Abel, Kim Jackson and Mindy Becker. My gratitude extends to visionary principals Ali Oliver, Julia Mattson, Diane Phelan, Debbie Barrett and Denise Rehm for transforming their schools and paying it forward to help others.

Finally, thanks to those who are the heart of Conscious Discipline: The Loving Guidance office staff, without whom this miracle that is Conscious Discipline could not thrive; and the Loving Guidance Associates and Certified Instructors who are the wind beneath my wings as they travel the world sharing their gifts on behalf of Conscious Discipline.

Chapter 1
INTRODUCTION

An Introduction to Conscious Discipline

> *"Be the change you want to see in the world."*
> *— Mahatma Gandhi*

All teachers demonstrate a code of conduct and a value system through their daily interactions with others. Until we become conscious of these patterns of interaction, we will be ineffective in guiding the morality of the next generation. Most of us model respect when we are calm and life is going our way. But what happens when we are stressed and life becomes complicated? How do we behave when traffic is backed up, our children forget their permission slips, our spouse forgets to go to the bank, students are horsing around instead of listening and our school's test scores are falling instead of rising to meet legislative standards?

Each classroom and school is a culture. It is time to become conscious of the culture and the behavioral patterns that are aiding or impeding learning in our schools. We must stop pretending we can effectively teach children life skills through single-issue prescriptive curriculums like Character Education, Social Skills and Bully Prevention while simultaneously using stickers, shaming, coercion and loss of privileges in attempts to force compliance. To successfully teach a life skill, we must model and demonstrate it in daily life. A lesson on respectful behavior is pointless when we regularly demonstrate disrespect by raising our voices. A bully prevention program is rendered useless when our behavior punishes, excludes or shames the children who challenge us. It is time to shift from a "Do what we say, not what we do" style of discipline to "Be the change we want to see in the world." Conscious Discipline empowers us with the mental shifts and practical skills to do just that, becoming instruments of positive transformation in our own lives and in the lives of children.

A Hidden Epidemic

Stress and trauma have been called a hidden or invisible epidemic in the United States. The truth is they are neither hidden nor invisible! About 60 percent of adults report Adverse

Childhood Experiences (trauma) such as verbal, physical or sexual abuse, or family dysfunction like incarceration, mental illness or substance abuse (Gerwin, 2013). Research indicates that traumatic stress in childhood is the leading causes of morbidity, mortality and disability in the United States (Edwards, Shipman & Brown, 2005). In addition, nearly 25 percent of children in the United States lived in poverty in 2013; that's roughly 16.1 million kids. An additional 45 percent of children live in low income homes (Jiang, Ekono & Skinner, 2014).

Stress and trauma cross all ethnic and economic lines, with grave effects on health, learning, social-emotional development and brain development. Fortunately, research suggests that caregivers can ease the negative affects of stress on children (The Center on the Developing Child at Harvard University, 2010). Caregiving does not begin and end with parents; it must be built into the cultural structure of our communities and schools because it is essential to academic and social success. Children living with stress and trauma walk through our doors every day. We generally know them by their behavioral problems (the symptoms), with the stress and trauma underlying those behaviors as a side note on their rap sheets. We tend to treat their symptoms with rewards, punishments and removal instead of meeting their needs with a culture of inclusion, healing and connection that builds resiliency. Conscious Discipline is designed to teach effective social-emotional skills, and embed resiliency into the school culture as a way to counteract the stress and trauma that are so prevalent in our society.

> I remember walking into a Conscious Discipline training saying, "Unconscious Discipline has been working just fine for me!" I was pretty resistant. I work with at-risk fifth and sixth grade children in our district-wide ACE program. The year before using Conscious Discipline I didn't have one kid pass the state test. After beginning to implement Conscious Discipline, 19 of my 23 fifth graders passed the test. It made a huge difference, and I think a big part of it is that the program helped kids feel safe and connected enough to learn. For me, I realized that before Conscious Discipline I was teaching a class; now I teach individuals.
>
> — Ted Miller, Keller Middle School, Pasadena Independent School District

 A star in the margin indicates there are resources on your web portal that support the content you are reading. In this case, visit your web portal to watch video footage of Ted Miller and other educators discussing the transformational power of Conscious Discipline. Access your portal by visiting ConsciousDiscipline.com/bookstudy

Our Hierarchical Social Brain

If we look back in our cultural history, say around 5,000 years or so, we will see why our brains are wired to be social. Our brains evolved within a small, tight community of hunters/gatherers. Our environment was demanding, resources were scarce and we were relatively weak compared to our predators, hence the need to work cooperatively. Our survival depended on the interdependence within these groups. Consequently, our brains evolved into what neuroscientists consider a social brain. In this context, "survival of the fittest" doesn't mean survival of the strongest and most forceful. It refers to those who can adapt most quickly to the demands of the moment in order to survive and thrive. Our social brain's efforts to adapt rapidly enough to meet the rate of change in a modern world stresses us all.

The disparity between our social brain and modern western society creates enormous stressors. Leadership, corporations, factories, governments and schools are generally based on a hierarchical social structure steeped in competition, individual success and authority based on power over others. Computers and telecommunications have profoundly reinvented how we communicate and socialize. We have shifted from personal interactions to texts, tweets and status updates. It is not uncommon to see a crowd of young people clumped together, all texting someone elsewhere. Social media plays an important role in our complex social society, but it cannot replace the face-to-face socialization needed for optimal brain development.

All we have to do is watch the nightly news to see people who lack the resiliency required to cope with the mismatch of a social brain in a disconnected informational age. We need a new approach for successful education (Ingvarson, Meiers, & Beavis, 2005). Conscious Discipline fulfills this need by creating a community-based learning environment called the "School Family." It asks school leadership to transform from an industrial, power-over, competitive, factory model of education to a relational-cultural leadership model with shared power, group cohesion, equality, trust and strong personal relationships in order to buffer our children from the side effects of a world full of information, stress and trauma, yet devoid of face-to-face community.

Our social brain is organized in a hierarchical manner consisting of higher and lower systems that act like two versions of ourselves. One version (the lower system) acts on impulse and seeks immediate gratification. The other version (the higher system) controls impulses and delays gratification in order to protect our long-term goals. Sometimes we are the person who wants to lose weight and sometimes we are the person who wants a cookie. The secret is being conscious of the best fit for the situation at hand. Conscious Discipline stems from this idea that conscious awareness empowers us to use our higher self-regulatory systems. Without awareness, the brain defaults to the unconscious, autopilot, knee-jerk reactions of the lower centers.

Our impulses, not our long-term goals, guide our choices when our minds are preoccupied. When we are not conscious of our actions, we can become reactive instead of proactive. We lose our ability to respond wisely to whatever curveball life throws. Someone brings out a tray of cookies and we habitually eat three. The stimulus (cookie) equals an automatic reaction (eat). Strengthening the pause between stimulus and reaction is at the core of Conscious Discipline. When we insert a pause, we free ourselves up to choose a wise response instead of a habitual reaction. We see the tray of cookies, pause to consciously consider whether eating the cookies aligns with our goals (values, beliefs, etc.) and whether the experience of eating the cookie is worth compromising those goals (values, beliefs, etc.), and then we consciously choose how to proceed.

Conscious Discipline encourages us to understand our hierarchical social brain in order to become consciously disciplined adults who can achieve long-term goals despite obstacles and distractions. We then teach this process to our children. It allows us all to be resilient, adaptable, respectful and responsible beings in a rapidly changing world. It empowers us to create our lives through choice. Some days we choose the cookies and some days we choose the veggie tray, but we always know we are the ones choosing.

From Roles to Relationships

There have been many shifts in modern society, yet none so profound as the shift from roles to relationships. Building steam in the late 1950s, society began to enter bold new territory. Collectively, we decided that the roles of the past were too limiting and the inequality built into these roles was morally oppressive. The roles of husband and wife were explicitly defined. The role of the child (to be seen and not heard) and the role of the parent (boss) were clearly articulated. Relationships were governed by these prescribed roles. As long as everyone performed his or her ordained duties, all was well. Yet, we felt something was missing in the comfort and safety of these roles, especially for those relegated to subservient roles. The powerless rebelled.

Consciousness expanded in regard to women, minorities, people with disabilities and children as people boldly demanded more. We wanted relationships that included closeness based on equal worth instead of hierarchically-prescribed roles dictating the powerful and the powerless. When we cast off our prescribed roles, we placed ourselves on new ground. Sadly, we did not have the communication skills or social-emotional competence to build a solid foundation for these new relationships. Divorce rates skyrocketed to over 50 percent. Children grew demanding and parents felt at a loss for appropriate action.

We must replace the old roles of yesteryear with a strong new foundation of social-emotional skills. As we seek meaningful relationships, we must learn to interact in ways that promote mutual respect and responsive attunement. Conscious Discipline is a skill-based program to help educators resolve conflicts, enhance brain development by creating optimal learning environments, support self-regulation in ways that strengthen relationships instead of destroying them, and help children build respectful relationships with themselves, peers, parents and each other.

Conscious Discipline as the Answer to the Hierarchical Social Brain and Changing Roles

Conscious Discipline solves the "Do as I say, not as I do" crisis that plagues communities, homes and schools. The Conscious Discipline model contrasts significantly with traditional approaches that are derived from the prescribed roles of yesteryear and fail to take our hierarchical social brain into account. Traditional classroom management systems are based on control. The teacher holds all the power and must control the students. Conscious Discipline is based on connection. It's a cultural-relationship model that serves our brain's innately social wiring and utilizes prosocial skills rather than prescribed roles. The power in the classroom is shared in the sense that all parties are responsible for their own behavior. This empowers the teacher as a self-disciplined adult who, in turn, teaches children how to become self-disciplined.

Teaching, of course, requires the adult to possess the skills he hopes to pass on to the children. One of my favorite bumper stickers says, "Can't read? Write for help." We would never expect an illiterate teacher to teach reading or a monolingual English-speaking teacher to teach Chinese. Yet, every day we ask teachers to model self-discipline, apply conflict resolution skills and work as a team with coworkers. We ask this even though most adults' default is to implode or explode under stress. Our conflict resolution "skills" often lead us to divorce, and backstabbing and gossip are the workplace norm.

Many research studies have demonstrated that the most important in-school factor for learning is the quality of the teacher/student relationship. The quality of teaching begins in the hearts and minds of the teachers, yet most of us are not conscious of the dispositions and beliefs that drive our actions. We operate from a set of preprogrammed, unexamined beliefs and unconscious values handed down from generation to generation.

Much of what we believe about school comes from our experience as students. This is in part due to the mirror neurons in our brains. Scientists have recently been decoding how mirror neurons work. They've realized humans are wired to connect with and live vicariously through others' experiences in much stronger ways than we once thought. The brain doesn't differentiate much between watching someone do something and doing it yourself (Rizzolatti & Craighero, 2004), so the years we've already spent in classrooms are probably the strongest teacher training we've experienced.

Also due to the mirror neuron system, children will use the same skills they see parents and teachers apply. I was once with a bunch of first grade children on the playground. Marissa wanted a turn on the swing. She asked Emily for a turn and Emily said, "No, I am swinging until it is time to go in." Marissa quickly shifted to her next available skill and told Emily, "I am going to turn your card to red!" Card turning, writing names on the board and caution lights create a meaningless, competitive culture that fails to teach children how to take responsibility for their actions. We are going to model skills for our students; we might as well make them useful skills.

> A dear friend once told me her lead teacher explained discipline like this: "It's important to make them cry. That means you have broken them. Don't be afraid to make an example out of one or two of them. It seems harsh, but you will thank me later." Imagine the discipline model this teacher grew up with and is passing down to the children in her care! We all possess a mental model of discipline; the question is if we're ready for an upgrade.

We have been put in the impossible situation of teaching students without possessing the necessary discipline skills to address today's complex emotional and social issues. In a culture where burnout, chronic stress and a degree of unpredictability is endemic, teachers must be resilient. We must learn to adapt well, respond wisely and recover quickly after stressful events. Conscious Discipline provides much-needed resiliency training by increasing emotional intelligence so we can develop a flexible, adaptive response to address problems constructively rather than avoiding them.

Conscious Discipline is a comprehensive, multidisciplinary self-regulation program that integrates social-emotional learning, school culture and discipline. It helps teachers and administrators build schools based on the internal resources of safety, connection and problem solving instead of external rewards and punishments. It is based on brain research that indicates our internal states dictate our behavior. Its goal is to provide systematic changes in schools by fostering the emotional intelligence of teachers first and children second. Simply put, as we become more emotionally intelligent, we are better equipped to create positive, healthy educational climates that help create and maintain optimal learning states. The three core components of Conscious Discipline are:

 Safety, through self-regulation, enhances adults' and children's ability to recognize and manage physiological and emotional upset.

Connection, through creating a compassionate School Family culture, motivates adults' and children's willingness to engage in healthy relationships, help each other be successful and change perceptions about conflict.

 Problem-solving, through changing our response to conflict and upgrading social-emotional skills, boosts adults' and children's ability to adapt to changing situations (resiliency).

With these components, everyday events and conflicts become opportunities to teach life skills. The social-emotional curriculum does not come from prescribed sequential lessons added to core standards; the curriculum emerges from daily challenges, acts of kindness, academic struggles, interpersonal conflicts, chronic rule breaking and celebrations. Our social-emotional curriculum shows up in a math lesson, in the cafeteria, on the bus or when a pet dies. Every person in the school becomes more resilient as he adapts rapidly to the needs of himself, others, circumstances and challenges in order to make wise personal choices.

Seizing conflict as an opportunity to teach life skills is integral to Conscious Discipline. When a child misspells several words on a spelling test, this provides the feedback that more practice or additional spelling instruction is needed. We do not turn his card from green to yellow or deny him five minutes of recess; we teach. This is also how we must approach daily conflict. When a child acts in hurtful ways, this provides the feedback that more practice or additional social skill instruction is needed. Attempting to remove daily conflict through administering rewards or punishments removes the opportunity for teaching social skills lessons in context. It forces schools and teachers to add yet another prescriptive curriculum to an already full workload. On your portal, read about the researched limitations of prescriptive curriculums and how they do not achieve the outcomes we truly desire.

There are two parts to discipline, the health of the relationship and the skill set of those involved. We might think of it as country western two-step dance with slow-slow steps followed by quick-quick steps. The slow-slow part of discipline is building healthy relationships that promote the willingness to cooperate. The quick-quick is the skill set needed to respond wisely in moments of conflict. We've historically ignored the relationship part of the discipline dance, focusing instead on roles and rewards. Without healthy relationships, the willingness to change a behavior is severely impaired. Conscious Discipline helps educators with both the slow-slow and the quick-quick aspects of discipline, empowering our hierarchical social brain to become a goal-directed, self-regulated, conscious and disciplined learning advocate.

Slow-slow relationship building

Quick-quick response to conflict

Teaching What We Value

Conscious Discipline leads teachers, providers, schools and programs through a transformational process that promotes permanent behavior change. The change is from an unconscious, traditional, compliance model of discipline to a conscious, relationship-based, community model.

Traditional Discipline

The traditional model of discipline is founded on rules that are upheld through reward and punishment. The goal is to obtain obedience. Those who are compliant are rewarded. Those who aren't compliant are punished and removed if disobedience persists. Fear is the tool used to empower the system as teachers attempt to control children. This system is built on three major premises:

1. It is possible to control others through environmental manipulations.
2. Rules govern behavior.
3. Conflict is a disruption to the learning process.

This type of system also creates a classroom culture and climate that teaches the following values:

Belief	Value It Teaches
It is possible to make others change.	Failure to make others change equals failure on the teacher's part.
When others don't do what we want, we must try to coerce them.	The more insubordinate they are, the more external power/force is expected and justified.
When we succeed in making others behave, we demonstrate power and authority.	Power comes from overpowering people.
When we fail to make someone obey, it's his or her fault.	If others do not do things our way, they are bad, lazy and deserving of hardship.
If others would change (do as we say), we could be happy and peaceful.	We are justified in blaming others; they are responsible for our behavior.
Children must feel bad to learn how to behave better in the future.	Revenge is the answer to life's upsets.
Conflict is bad, disruptive and must be eliminated.	If you are good enough, you can shield yourself from conflict.
Fear is the best motivator for learning.	Fear is more powerful than love.

Conscious Discipline

Conscious Discipline is built on three completely different premises:

1. Controlling and changing ourselves is possible and has a profound impact on others.
2. Connectedness governs behavior.
3. Conflict is an opportunity to teach.

Believing we must change ourselves first and model our expectations for others through self-regulation creates a classroom climate and culture that teaches the following values:

Conscious Discipline links head and heart

Belief	Value It Teaches
Changing ourselves is possible.	It is our choice whether or not to change.
We are in charge of ourselves.	We can become the person we want to be.
We are empowered by choosing to control ourselves instead of others.	Power comes from within.
When things don't go our way, we will seek solutions.	We are responsible for our feelings and actions. Our choices impact others.
We must teach children in order for them to learn to behave.	We teach others how to treat us. We cannot expect them to magically know how.
Conflict is an essential part of life.	Conflict and mistakes present us with the opportunity to learn a missing skill or let go of a limiting belief.
Love is the best motivator for learning and growth.	Love is more powerful than fear, cooperation is more effective than coercion and compassion is more powerful than competition.

Now lets look at both systems side by side.

	Traditional Discipline Compliance Model	Conscious Discipline Community Model
Motivation	Rewards and punishments	Connection and contribution
Goal	Obedience	Problem solvers
Foundation	Rules	Community
Power	External control	Internal self-regulation
Skills	Consequences	Seven Skills of Conscious Discipline
Philosophy	Rejection	Acceptance

Which model aligns the best with your own personal values? Which model aligns best with your school mission statement?

Conscious Discipline is based on a Brain State Model that empowers us to shift from educational systems grounded in controlling others to cultures of learning based on safety, connection and problem solving. Conscious Discipline is organized around the Seven Powers for Conscious Adults that help the adult to manage her internal state (safety), the creation of the School Family that utilizes connection to foster cooperation and optimal brain development (connection), and the Seven Skills of Discipline that empower the adult with strategies to teach children to self-regulate and problem solve (problem-solving).

1. **The Brain State Model** utilizes a neurodevelopmental model to help us focus our attention on internal states first and behavior second. By addressing the internal state that precedes the behavior, both adults and children learn to self-regulate and develop strong executive skills for problem solving and goal achievement.

2. **The Seven Powers for Conscious Adults** promote mindful, conscious adults who possess the ability to self-regulate. "Conscious" is a state of active, open attention in the present moment. Without conscious awareness, our ability to change old conditioned discipline practices to effective new practices is impaired. The ability to self-regulate and perceive conflict as a teaching opportunity provides the foundation for classroom safety.

3. **The School Family** provides an effective new metaphor for educational institutions. Historically, we have used the metaphor of a factory when creating our classrooms and schools. The goal of a factory is to create standardized products through a reward and punishment paradigm. Research and experience prove that we need a new metaphor if we wish to build an educational system that is successful and safe for all students. The School Family is built on a healthy family model with the goal of providing optimal development for all its members. The School Family builds connections that foster the following:

- Impulse control through co-regulation skills
- Cooperation and willingness to learn through a sense of belonging
- Executive skills through modeling, scaffolding and direct teaching

Teachers and students create a School Family through the use of routines, rituals, and classroom structures that provide the safety and connection needed for optimal development and learning.

4. **The Seven Skills of Discipline** provide the problem solving tools teachers need to transform everyday discipline issues into teaching moments. These moments are our opportunity to teach children the social-emotional and communication skills necessary to manage themselves, resolve conflict and develop pro-social behaviors. The seven skills are the foundation for a problem-solving classroom.

The image below represents the transformation change process of Conscious Discipline.

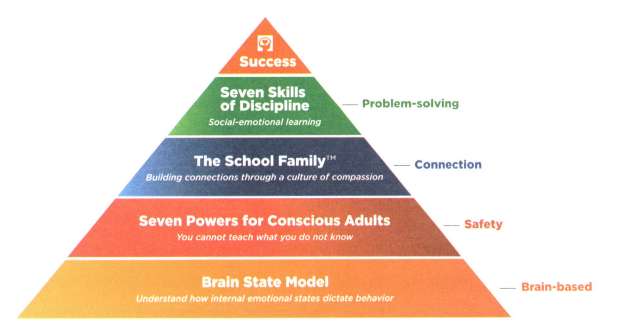

Research on the Effectiveness of Conscious Discipline

I have spent my career synthesizing life experiences and research from multiple disciplines in order to make Conscious Discipline both effective and accessible. Multiple large-scale research projects have recently demonstrated what I know to be true about Conscious Discipline: Quite simply, it works. Research assessing the effectiveness of Conscious Discipline compared classrooms using and not using Conscious Discipline, showing that Conscious Discipline does the following:

- Improves the quality of student-teacher interactions
- Improves the social and emotional behavior of students
- Reduces aggression in classrooms
- Increases student academic achievement
- Increases student academic readiness
- Decreases impulsivity and hyperactivity in difficult children
- Improves the social and emotional behavior of teachers
- Improves the organizational climate
- Improves the classroom and school climate
- Enhances parenting effectiveness
  (Barfield & Gaskill, 2005; Hoffman, Hutchinson & Reiss, 2005; Hoffman, Hutchinson & Reiss, 2009; and Rain, 2014)

> Research shows that parents with children in schools implementing Conscious Discipline view the school climate positively, even when they do not feel safe where they live. Parents in schools not using Conscious Discipline did not report this response. This demonstrates the strength of school-wide Conscious Discipline implementation in creating a positive school climate (Rain, 2014).

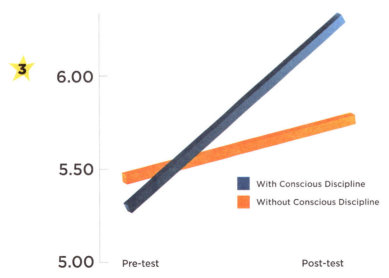

*Groups significantly different p<.01

Impact on Child Social Skills Behavior (Teacher's Report)

Teachers who used Conscious Discipline reported better social skills behavior in their students, in comparison to teachers who did not use Conscious Discipline.

Review the full research results on your portal.

Make the Most of This Book

We all have experienced discipline practices that left us belittled, shamed or rejected. We swore we would never repeat these practices on others, yet in moments of distress, that's exactly what we've done. This book is about transformation. It is a journey that, once embraced, will change how you live, how you parent and how you teach.

The first three chapters of this book lay a foundation for the transformation process you will undertake. The **Introduction** chapter you are reading now examines traditional beliefs about discipline and new information that points us toward a better way. The **Brain State Model** chapter explains the relationship between the brain and misbehavior, showing why shifting from reward and punishment to creating schools based on safety, connection and problem-solving is critical for academic success. The **School Family** chapter explains how school culture impedes or enhances optimal learning.

The remaining seven chapters are divided into three sections that each supports an overriding developmental need derived from the Conscious Discipline Brain State Model. These sections are **Safety**, **Connection** and **Problem-solving**.

Each chapter within these three sections focuses on one skill to discipline children, one power for conscious adults, current brain information and how to build your School Family. Next, we'll look at each component in greater depth.

Introduction

Chapter 1: Introduction
Chapter 2: Conscious Discipline Brain Model
Chapter 3: School Family

Section 1 • Safety

Chapter 4: Composure
Chapter 5: Assertiveness

Section 2 • Connection

Chapter 6: Encouragement
Chapter 7: Choices
Chapter 8: Empathy

Section 3 • Problem Solving

Chapter 9: Positive Intent
Chapter 10: Consequences

Section 1: Safety Through Composure and Assertiveness

Section 1 of this book focuses us on creating safe classrooms and schools. Safety meets the developmental need of a survival state in the Conscious Discipline Brain State Model. It is the foundation upon which all else is built.

The acronym N.A.R.C.S. helps us remember the combined tools required for soothing survival state stress through safety. These tools are Noticing, Assertiveness, Routines, Composure and the language of Safety. These tools are explained in the Composure and Assertiveness chapters. We can provide children with the safety embedded in these lifelong skills or they may grow to find external methods of soothing like addiction, drugs and alcohol (thus the acronym N.A.R.C.S.).

Adults who can own and regulate their upset are at the core of a sense of safety. Out-of-control adults are always a threat to children. We can no longer blame children for making us angry. We can no longer ask children to develop self-control and respectful communication skills when we model a different set of skills during our upset moments. Safety requires us to regulate our inner states and take responsibility for our thoughts, feelings and actions. Safety is not about controlling the actions of others; it is about regulating ourselves effectively. The Skill of Composure and the Skill of Assertiveness help us create a felt sense of safety in the classroom by allowing us to stay calm enough to vigilantly focus on what we want children to do.

Skill of Composure, Power of Perception

From the Power of Perception we are able to access and extend the Skill of Composure. This reminds us that we have a choice of how to see events. Seeing a child's behavior as a call for help or as a sign of disrespect will aid or derail our composure. When we choose a helpful perception, composure allows us to access the higher centers of our brain and respond with wisdom. It also teaches children that obnoxious, manipulative or aggressive behaviors have no power over us. It allows us to be calm enough to focus on what we truly value.

> Conscious Discipline provides us with a wise path to follow so we can discipline ourselves well enough to meet our goals. When we find ourselves off course, it empowers us with the conscious awareness that we have lost our way. It then gives us the skills to refocus, get back on our path and achieve our desired goals.

Skill of Assertiveness, Power of Attention

From the Power of Attention we are able to access, extend and utilize the Skill of Assertiveness. Assertiveness is the medium through which we teach respect; it is the skill that sets boundaries in a way that teaches others how we want to be treated. It is essential for limit setting, goal achievement and problem-solving. Assertiveness, the voice of no doubt, responds to the current moment with clarity, assuredness and a vigilant focus on what we want children to do. Focusing on what we want children to do wires the brain for success and sets us up to encourage children every step of the way.

One teacher who had an "aha" moment at a training looked at me and said, "You mean we must constantly think before we discipline a child? It's a lot easier just to put their names on the board. I don't know if I can be that conscious all day." Imagine a teacher saying the same thing in regard to content areas: "You mean you want me to think while teaching reading and science?" Unconsciously moving clips, giving out points, flipping cards and removing recess need to evolve. It is time for us to become conscious in our discipline approaches.

Section 2: Connection Through Encouragement, Choices and Empathy

Section 2 of the book is about connection and belonging. Connection directs the flow of information in the brain. Healthy connections promote problem-solving and thriving, while unhealthy connections promote defensive survival skills in efforts to feel safe. Humans are hardwired to be social. Our social brain develops through our relationships. Building human connections equals building neural connections. Connection meets the developmental need of an emotional state in the Conscious Discipline Brain State Model.

The acronym R.E.J.E.C.T. helps us remember the combined tools needed to meet the child's need for belonging. These tools are **R**ituals, **E**ncouragement, **J**obs, **E**mpathy, **C**hoices and **T**he School Family. Without a felt sense of connection, children often feel rejected; thus the acronym R.E.J.E.C.T.

In order to ensure optimal brain development, we must start creating compassionate classrooms where children begin caring about themselves and others on a deep level. The School Family is the ultimate representation of this compassion and commitment. The skills of Encouragement, Choices and Empathy help us build compassion and connection in our classrooms, fostering the willingness to focus on helping each other be successful. All the skills represented by R.E.J.E.C.T. are found in the chapters within Section 2.

Skill of Encouragement, Power of Unity

Composure allows us to self-regulate enough to assertively focus on what we want. This vigilant focus gives us unlimited access to the Skill of Encouragement and Power of Unity. The Power of Unity calls on us to realize we are all in this together and allows us to access and extend authentic Encouragement to others. Knowing we are all energetically connected to one another allows us to offer encouragement and develop compassionate School Families. We know on a deep level that what we offer to others, we experience within ourselves. As we encourage children, we encourage ourselves. As we discourage children, we discourage ourselves. Discouragement has its roots in focusing on what we don't want. As we attempt to manipulate children with bribes and threats, we manipulate ourselves. The Skill of Encouragement motivates children to bring the best of themselves to each moment.

Skill of Choices, Power of Free Will

No matter how much we encourage others or ourselves, we still have the free will to accept or reject the guidance being offered. From the Power of Free Will we are able to understand and utilize the Skill of Choices. Life is a constant series of choices. No one is forcing us to go to work, making us act like raving lunatics or getting us to eat more vegetables; these are all choices. When we acknowledge that children are choosing to comply with us, we honor and encourage them to use their free will for the good of all. If we continue to look for ways to make them do homework or get them to finish their chores, manipulation replaces choices and our view of free will becomes distorted. The Skill of Choices helps children choose compliance and facilitates their ability to focus on the task at hand.

Skill of Empathy, Power of Acceptance

When children reject our guidance and make poor choices, it is our job to offer empathy to help them accept personal responsibility for their choices. From the Power of Acceptance we can remove our bias of how life should be (our judgment of how others should think, feel and behave), accessing the Skill of Empathy. When we can relax into the current moment without the need to change it in any way, we can allow others to be themselves. We can see from their point of view, join with them in the moment and become a mirror for them to find clarity. This helps free them to change their perceptions, relinquish their judgments, process their feelings and take personal responsibility for their actions through reflection instead of blaming others. The Skill of Empathy helps children take personal responsibility for their choices by managing their emotions instead of acting them out.

Section 3: Problem-Solving with Positive Intent and Consequences

Section 3 of the book provides the skills for problem-solving. In this section you will learn how to empower bullies and victims, utilize conflicts to teach life skills, and solve everyday problems with confidence. Problem-solving in a social setting meets the developmental need of an integrated executive state in the Conscious Discipline Brain State Model. The tools for this section provide a healthy space for us to be all we can be; thus the acronym S.P.A.C.E. These tools are **S**olutions, **P**ositive intent, **A**cademic integration, **C**onsequences and **E**xecutive skills.

Problem-solving can only exist once we create a felt sense of safety and increase connection by building a compassionate School Family. Most of us are trying to use conflict resolution programs in school climates that actually impede problem solving, or we are asking children in survival and emotional states to resolve conflicts without access to the higher brain systems that are needed for success. Without self-control (safety) and willingness (connection), we become stuck in the problem (who did what to whom first, who is to blame, and what is unfair).

Children, as part of their developmental journey, will try as many ways as possible to get the world to go their way. The adult's job is to accept the moment as it is and respond wisely. If an adult is still trying to make the world go his way, power struggles become the norm and problem solving the exception. Section 3 instills the mind set of letting the moment exist as it is, seeing the best in each situation and focusing on solutions instead of faultfinding. The Skill of Positive Intent and the Skill of Consequences will help us toward this goal.

Skill of Positive Intent, Power of Love

From the Power of Love, we are asked to see the best in others by using the Skill of Positive Intent. Our perception of the intent behind other people's actions is completely made up. If one child pushes another child, we get to make up the aggressor's intent. Was the child's intent to be mean to others, to get the adult's attention or to access the marker the child is holding? We truly don't know. We do, however, have a choice of how we make it up. The Power of Love asks us to have the faith to make people's intent up positively. When we do this with children, we define their core as good and their behavior as needing correction. We keep our internal state calm, allowing us to access our own wisdom in the moment. If we make it up negatively, we send the message, "You are your actions and you are bad." Making up negative intent also throws us into the lower centers of our brain where we will react habitually. The Skill of Positive Intent allows us to consciously transform aggressive acts into life skills, derailing the development of bullies. Positive intent also facilitates composure, allowing us access to all the skills learned in previous chapters.

Skill of Consequences, Power of Intention

Consequences is the last skill covered, not because it is the least important, but because we need the first six skills to use consequences effectively. With the Power of Intention, we can use self-awareness to help children take responsibility for their choices through the Skill of Consequences. Consequences are often distorted and confused with punishments. Consequences happen all the time. They are not something adults make up to deliver to children who have done wrong (punishments). Every choice has an inherent consequence bound to it. Often we are not conscious of these consequences or we hide from them through blame and rationalization. For consequences to be effective we must own our feelings (instead of blaming others), reflect on our choices and become conscious of their impact (instead of judging ourselves and others as bad).

Many guidance and discipline programs focus extensively on consequences. As teachers begin learning about Conscious Discipline, they ask, "Doesn't the child ever get consequences?" The answer is a resounding, "Yes." Conscious Discipline provides teachers with a class culture and seven skills that are essential for successful conflict resolution and effective consequences. Giving consequences to children who pronounce, "I don't care," is simply an exercise in discouragement for all involved. The Skill of Consequences allows us to help children learn from their mistakes instead of repeat them.

> "The Conscious Discipline powers and skills that emerge from them became like an internal toolbox to guide me. As I use the powers and skills, they become who I am, not what I have learned. Life is a choice and it is up to us to decide what we want it to look like."
>
> — Jenny Barkac, first grade teacher, Billings Public Schools, Montana

We have each approached difficult situations in brilliant and not so brilliant ways. The powers and skills of Conscious Discipline help us increase our brilliance through upgraded skills and the conscious awareness of knowing when our actions are hurtful instead of helpful. The "conscious" part of Conscious Discipline helps us become aware of ineffective choices and the "discipline" part provides us with the skills to be effective in living our highest values and achieving our desired goals. If we want children to learn from their mistakes and make different choices in the future, we must create internal and external conditions that support this goal. The chart below shows the synergy of the seven skills and how they can be used in any combination to address any life event.

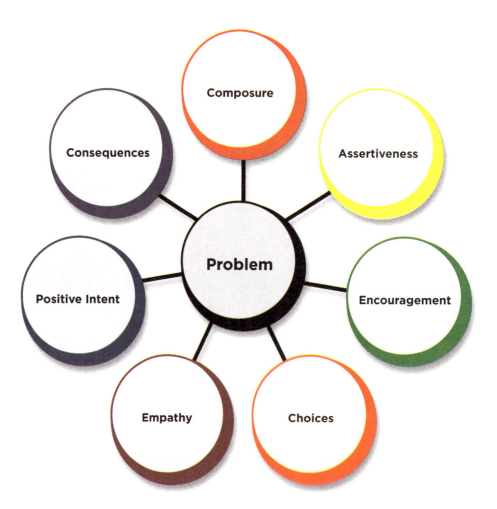

Teachers who draw upon these powers and skills create classrooms that model our highest values and prosocial skills. This happens automatically. As teachers become conscious of their intentions, and change their perceptions and responses to classroom conflict, so will the children. Our classrooms become living, breathing units of healthy socialization. No separate artificial lessons are needed for character education, bully prevention or social skills. Conscious Discipline creates authentic change from the inside out.

Successful violence prevention, safe schools, character education and conflict resolution are not separate curriculums; they are a mindset. They require self-regulation and social-emotional competence. They rely on the ability to trust, establish relationships, set limits, offer and ask for help in socially appropriate ways, and solve everyday problems constructively. Ultimately, Conscious Discipline integrates all these factors into your existing academic curriculum. It's better than a BOGO because you get more than just two for one; you get it all!

Pay It Forward Transformational Change

Conscious Discipline is transformational change, which is very different than traditional or transitional change. Traditional changes ask us to do Skill A better, faster and more effectively. Transitional change asks us to stop doing Skill A and learn Skill B. Transformational change asks us to change both our mindset and our skill set. For that to happen, we must be committed to the process, allow ourselves to make mistakes and take it slowly. It is a process that takes patience and forgiveness, but the payoff from that persistence is life changing and will impact generations to come.

This book encourages transformational change through immediate application in your life, classroom and school. Read Chapters 1-3 as you would any other book. Then, because it takes at least 21 days of consistent focus and practice to create or change a habit, you would read and implement only one skill chapter per month for Chapters 4-10. While this one chapter per month guideline is helpful, it is absolutely essential to progress at your own pace. (For example, you might progress steadily at one chapter per month for Chapters 4, 5, 6 and 7, and then spend three months fully implementing Chapter 8.) Be gentle with yourself. Reread sections that are meaningful. Reflect and implement the routines, rituals and classroom structures that support the skill and power in each chapter. Utilize the many free resources we provide online, including the book study portal. Reach out for support as needed.

Given the demanding nature of teachers', administrators' and providers' jobs, Conscious Discipline utilizes a "pay it forward" model to support transformational change. The goal is to focus on creating model classrooms with the most enthusiastic teachers who seek out a variety of training experiences and achieve full implementation in their classrooms. These teachers pay it forward by providing hands-on training for other willing teachers within the school. Once a school is implementing Conscious Discipline school-wide, the administration pays it forward by serving as a model site for other administrators and educators to learn from. Paying it forward in this manner ensures the utmost in flexibility, guarantees sustainable change, and provides ongoing motivation for personal and professional growth. One of the best ways to learn a skill is to teach it to others, and being of service provides a sense of satisfaction and self-worth that few endeavors can match. Watch a portal video of how a Pasadena, Texas school district is experiencing the many benefits of paying it forward with Conscious Discipline.

Though built on a pay it forward model of communal learning, Conscious Discipline is uniquely self-directed. You may proceed through the book alone, with a colleague, in teams or as an entire staff. If you choose to proceed alone, you will likely wish to seek assistance from your spouse, children, siblings or friends for some of the role-playing activities. They will enjoy being part of your life and your growth. Our many workshops, Loving Guidance Associates and Certified Instructors are also here to support you every step of the way.

Consider attending one of our workshops where you can deepen your learning with like-minded individuals who are also on this journey. Each year I lead the Conscious Discipline Summer Institute, a weeklong event designed to help you experience, integrate and internalize Conscious Discipline. I hope to meet you there one day.
— *Dr. Becky Bailey*

The following resources will help you as you proceed:

- Log into the interactive web portal to deepen your learning through additional information, activities and videos organized by chapter. A numbered star symbol in the text margin indicates that a supplemental item can be found on the portal. You can pause reading to interact with the portal when you see the star symbol or you can access the portal at the end of each chapter. The interactive portal is organized by chapter and by the number appearing inside each star symbol. It also contains a list of helpful resources for each chapter. Visit ConsciousDiscipline.com/bookstudy from your computer, tablet or smart phone to access the portal.

- Utilize the many free tools available at ConsciousDiscipline.com. Be certain to browse Shubert's School, where you can click to watch more than 300 videos of Conscious Discipline implemented worldwide from infancy through high school.

Shubert's School
ConsciousDiscipline.com/Shubert

- Join with others implementing Conscious Discipline on Facebook, Pinterest, Twitter, YouTube and other social media. Post questions and share your successes while benefitting from the experiences of thousands of other Conscious Discipline users.

  - Facebook.com/ConsciousDiscipline
  - Pinterest.com/ConsciousD
  - Twitter.com/ConsciousD or @ConsciousD
  - YouTube.com/user/LovingGuidance

- Consider purchasing the *Conscious Discipline Online e-Course* for additional support, especially if you are doing a school-wide book study. The Online e-Course breathes life into each chapter of the Conscious Discipline book as Dr. Becky Bailey presents each power and skill in her engaging and unique style.

- Also consider purchasing the *Creating the School Family* book for a more in depth understanding of the routines, rituals and classroom structures discussed in this book.

- Seeking to track your progress? Conscious Discipline provides a standardized rubric for self-evaluation. You'll not only see dramatic changes in your classroom, you'll be able to personally measure your results with these rubrics. ConsciousDiscipline.com/free-resources

- Seeking specific guides for implementing Conscious Discipline in your particular job, with your particular age group? Conscious Discipline provides downloadable, age-specific implementation guides for parents, educators, administrators and mental health professionals. ConsciousDiscipline.com/free-resources

As you progress through this book, you will feel deep changes. These changes manifest in your life both inside and outside of school. It is a wonderful, empowering feeling, however, change does not come without some anxiety. Old skills will die off, sometimes kicking and screaming as new skills replace them. Breathe deeply and continue your journey. As you work on one skill, run the other facets of your class as you have in the past. Each month you'll make small but significant changes. By the end of the year, you'll be reflecting on how to better structure your classroom for the upcoming year. Apply Conscious Discipline again the next year and enjoy continued growth. Due to the nature of transformational change, Conscious Discipline takes about three years to feel natural and integrated. Be patient with yourself and enjoy the process. You cannot have an unhappy ending to a happy journey!

Year One: Year one is an "add on" year. Utilize whatever discipline approach you have always used, but add on the new skills, routines, rituals and structures you feel confident in using. Conscious Discipline replaces external behavior charts with internal skills. You cannot pull down the chart or let go of the red light system until you have upgraded your skills.

Year Two: Year two is a "let go" year. As you progress in your skill set, you will find that external control and tangible reinforcements are no longer necessary. One teacher carried a clipboard around to give children checks for misbehavior. The second year with Conscious Discipline, she asked her class what would be helpful to them, and they all asked her to put down the clipboard. She emailed me with excitement and said, "I have been clipboard-free for two weeks and it is wonderful!" In year two, let old methods die a natural death as you find they are no longer needed.

Year Three: Year three is one of integration. As you become more comfortable with the language of Conscious Discipline and the School Family routines, rituals and structures, you will be free to discover the many ways Conscious Discipline can integrate into your existing curriculum. In year three, your academic and social curriculum starts to become seamless.

1-2-3, Let's Do It!

Our planet, our country, our schools and our children need us to be the change we want to see in the world. Our greatest fear is not that we are unworthy; our greatest fear is that we are worthy and powerful beyond measure. It is time to set aside your fears and become the best "you" possible. To reach your destination, you mustn't obsess about the outcome. Instead, enjoy the process of personal growth. There's a fable that illustrates this point:

A young boy journeyed far from home to study with a sage. The boy asked, "How long will it take before I am as wise as you?" The sage answered, "Five years." The boy said, "That's a long time. What if I work twice as hard?" The teacher responded, "Ten years." "That's crazy," shouted the boy, "What if I study all day and all night?" Calmly the sage replied, "Then it would take you fifteen years." "I don't understand," said the boy, "Every time I promise to work harder to reach my goal, you say it will take longer to achieve. Why?" "The answer is simple," replied the sage, "With one eye fixed on the goal, you have only one eye left to guide you on your journey."

Enjoy this journey and relax into the process of change. Be willing to let your old beliefs go and let new ideas enter. Do the exercises. Make commitments to yourself and keep them. Practice using the skills. You can do it!

> I wish you well!
> — *Dr. Becky Bailey*

Summary of Conscious Discipline

	Chapter / Skill	Power	Brain Smart
4	**Composure** Being the person you want others to become	**Perception** No one can make you angry without your permission	Composure gives you access to the higher centers of your brain
5	**Assertiveness** Saying "no" and being heard: Setting limits respectfully	**Attention** What you focus on, you get more of	Attention directs neuroplasticity and all learning
6	**Encouragement** Building the School Family	**Unity** We are all in this together	Encouragement, connection and belonging primes the brain for willingness, engagement and academic success
7	**Choices** Building self-esteem and willpower	**Free Will** The only person you can make change is yourself	Choices motivated from within, lacking coercion, improve goal achievement and self-regulation
8	**Empathy** Teaching children to manage their emotions	**Acceptance** This moment is as it is	Empathy integrates the brain for personal responsibility and self-control
9	**Positive Intent** Creating teaching moments with oppositional, shut down and aggressive children	**Love** See the best in others	Optimism produces oxytocin, increasing trust, safety and moral behavior
10	**Consequences** Helping children learn from their mistakes	**Intention** Mistakes are opportunities to learn	The brain functions differently under threat

School Family	Key Phrases
Friends and Family Board, Safe Place, Brain Smart Start, Safekeeper Ritual, Greeting/Goodbye Rituals	• **S.T.A.R.** - **S**mile, **T**ake a breath **A**nd **R**elax! • I'm safe. Keep breathing. I can handle this. • Your arm is going like this (demonstrate).
Visual Routines, Class-made Books, Time Machine, After Conflict Reconnecting Ritual	• I'm going to __. • Did you like it? • Name, Verb, Paint for assertive commands
Connecting Rituals, Ways to Be Helpful Board/Book, Job Board	• You did it! Good for you! • You ___ so ___. That was helpful.
Visual Rules, Behavior Chart	• You have a choice! You may __ or __. Which is better for you?
We Care Center	• D = Your face is going like this (demonstrate). • N = You seem __. • A = You wanted __ or you were hoping __.
Celebration Center, School Family Assemblies, Wishing Well	• You wanted __ (or you were hoping __). You may not __. When you want __, say or do __. Say it now for practice.
Time Machine, Class Meetings, Class Meeting Rituals	• Did you like it? • Are you telling me to be helpful or hurtful? • You have a choice, you can choose to __ and __ or you can choose to __ and __. • Tell me what will happen if you __ again. • I can see by your actions you are choosing to __.

Chapter 2
BRAIN STATE MODEL

Why Use a Brain State Model?

> *"Behavior management systems that focus on controlling behaviors from the outside will never build deep values and internal control."*
> — *Sir Peter David Gluckman*

While conducting a workshop in New York City, I used my greeting apron to welcome attendees. The apron has four images on it, a fish, a skunk, a butterfly and a happy face. Each of these images represents a unique handshake. I asked each individual, "Would you like a fish, skunk, butterfly or happy face greeting this morning?" About midway through my greetings, a woman looked straight at me and said, "I would like you to move so I can get some coffee!"

In that instant, this stressed-out attendee demonstrated what we all know to be true: Our internal state dictates our external behavior. When we are feeling calm and appreciative, we are more likely to let cars merge on the freeway and overlook the lady with 15 items in the "10 items or fewer" line at the grocery store. However, if we are feeling harried, frustrated or overwhelmed, we inch toward the bumper in front of us so no one can merge and ruthlessly count the items in other people's carts to determine if they deserve the express line. State dictates behavior! Yet when it comes to discipline, historically our focus has been on behaviors (usually with the goal of stopping them).

If you imagine an iceberg, there is more ice beneath the water than above it. Behavior is the part of the iceberg we see above the water. Our internal state, made up of conscious and unconscious beliefs about the world and ourselves, is the part below the surface of the water. The tip of the iceberg did not sink the Titanic; the unseen mass beneath the surface did. Discipline must start with what's beneath the surface. Adults and children must learn to manage their internal states instead of acting them out in tirades or tantrums. The Conscious Discipline Brain State Model is a simple, hierarchical model that provides a concrete way to show the relationship between internal states and external behaviors. It helps us understand the states that are driving the behaviors, so we can address them effectively before attempting to teach new skills. This model helps us meet four core objectives:

1. To remain in a relaxed, alert state while interacting with children.
2. To identify the internal state the child is experiencing so we know which responses will more likely be helpful.
3. To assist the child in achieving a relaxed, alert state of learning **before** we attempt to teach a new skill or deliver a consequence.
4. To address the behavior by teaching an effective new skill.

All behavior is a form of communication. We acknowledge and act on this belief with babies. We can hear an infant's cries as a way of communicating distress. The crying communicates a need for a diaper change, food or other need. As we help babies soothe their inner states by meeting their needs, the crying shifts to engagement. Seeing infants' behavior as a form of communication is easy for most of us. The challenge is holding onto this truth as the child matures. With older children, our perception often shifts to seeing disobedience, disrespect or defiance. As we shift our perception, we also shift our intent. Instead of trying to discern the communication behind the behavior, our goal becomes stopping it. When we expend our efforts on stopping behaviors, we ignore children's unmet needs and missing skills, sometimes with extreme results like bullying, suicide and school shootings. Zero tolerance zones and exclusionary tactics (like suspension and expulsion) simply hide the problem, compound it or make it someone else's issue to deal with. We are better served by welcoming the important communication behind the misbehavior so we can transform it from a socially unacceptable form of communication to one that is acceptable, safe and healthy.

Read the examples below. Determine which perspective makes the most sense to you.

Child Behavior Child grabs another child's toy.	**Child Communication** I want to play with the toy.
Adult Response "It's not nice to grab from others."	**Adult Implied Communication** You are not nice for wanting the toy.
"Gentle touches, gentle touches."	Take the toy gently.
"You know the rules about grabbing. Turn your card to red and you will lose recess."	Wanting the toy is a punishable act.
"You wanted to play with the toy. When you want a turn say, *May I have a turn with the toy, please?*"	You wanted to play with the toy. Saying, "May I have a turn with the toy, please?" is an acceptable way to get your needs met.

Internal State Versus Behavior

Reflect on all the time you have spent and frustration you have felt while trying (and failing) to stop a child's behavior. All conflict starts with internal emotional upset. Ultimately, our goal must be to respond to the upset first and then address the behavior in a way that transforms it rather than struggling to stop it.

A negative internal state is like a little gremlin in the forest that keeps lighting fires. Teachers spend their days running around frantically putting out fires from, "Calm down!" to "Sit down!" What if we taught the little gremlin to plant trees instead of start fires? Essentially, that is what happens when we shift our emphasis from trying to stop or otherwise control children's behavior (putting out fires) to teaching them the new skill of self-regulation (planting trees).

As mentioned earlier, almost everyone recognizes a baby's cry as a form of communication. The outward signs of upset may change as children age, but upset behavior is always a form of communication. We seem to forget this basic truth as they grow. Children's brains develop in an integrated and hierarchically layered way. A young 3-year-old child may throw his body on the floor screaming and crying for a cookie when feeling frustrated about not getting his way. We can demand he stop screaming with the threat of time out, try to distract him with another object or help him deal with the frustration that comes when the world is not going his way.

A 4-year-old child may shout, "I hate you!" to express her thwarted desire for a cookie. We can dismiss the message by saying, "Well, I love you," overlay the action with guilt by saying, "You make Mommy sad talking like that," or see the hurtful words as a communication of her frustration by saying, "You seem angry. It's hard to wait for your cookie until after dinner. Breathe with me. You can do it."

A 9-year-old child might try to debate the pros and cons of cookies before dinner. We can enter into the debate in an attempt to win the power struggle, give up the cookies to avoid the conflict, or choose to keep the limit we've set and help the child handle frustration by saying, "You seem unhappy about waiting until after dinner. It's hard to wait. You can handle it. Take a breath and then finish setting the table. You have a choice. You can do the cups or the napkins next. Which is better for you?"

As a child grows, the behavior changes from crying to hurtful actions to arguing. Take a deep breath and reflect on your own discipline style. Do your responses generally help the child learn to handle the internal state (frustration, disappointment, anger) that is at the root of the conflict? How much time do you spend putting out fires, trying to stop a behavior?

Behavior management systems that focus on controlling behaviors from the outside will never build deep values and internal control (Gluckman & Hanson, 2006). When we focus on behavior without helping children manage their inner states, we are putting out fires but leaving the little fire starter active, as demonstrated in the examples above. When we regulate our internal states and teach children to do the same, we transform behavior by creating a pause where self-regulation can occur. We (adults and children alike) can then choose the wisest response to meet the demands of the moment.

A Multidisciplinary Approach

Conscious Discipline uses a multidisciplinary brain model for discipline. It goes beyond behavioral approaches, which work to extinguish or reinforce specific behaviors by offering a neurodevelopmental model of the brain based on and adapted from the work of Drs. Bruce Perry, Daniel Siegel, Allan Schore, Louis Cozolino, Joseph LeDoux, Paul MacLean and Alexander Luria. This model, called the Conscious Discipline Brain State Model, becomes a general frame that helps us understand the internal states of mind, brain and body that are most likely to produce certain behaviors. Once we understand this relationship, we can learn how to respond in a way that helps children change from an upset state to one that is conducive to lasting behavioral changes. We can then cultivate self-regulation and teach new skills effectively.

Conscious Discipline's comprehensive approach helps us understand the whys and hows of the internal state behind behavior. This understanding guides our management of our own internal states and our responses to children's inner states so we can teach appropriate social skills and conflict resolution strategies. It empowers us to maintain a sense of connection during upset, thereby strengthening relationships instead of damaging them with constant power struggles. Imagine being able to manage your own upset, connect with children during their behavioral outbursts and then transforming these difficult moments into life lessons for all involved. Conscious Discipline makes all this possible.

States of Mind

My mother used to say to me, "Becky, you have worked yourself into a state. Now what are you going to do about it?" I thought she was crazy. In my mind, my internal state of upset had nothing to do with me and everything to do with her not allowing Mary Beth to sleep over. It was a simple fix: Mom says, "Yes," instead of, "No," Mary Beth comes over, my internal state shifts from angry to happy, and all is well! It never dawned on my 10-year-old self that I had control over my internal state. I was righteous in my upset. Mom made me mad and should pay for the upset she caused! I remember huffing and puffing. None of it fazed my mom, which infuriated me. How dare she not fix this pain inside of me? If she loved me, she would let Mary Beth sleep over and take away this horrible feeling! It took years for me to truly understand that I am responsible for managing my own feelings. My mother lovingly taught me this lesson every time she refused to accept blame for my upset: I can change my inner state by becoming conscious of it and owning it. Wow! Thank you, Mom.

Many researchers have studied and shed light on the states of mind associated with stress, fear and helplessness (LeDoux, 1996; McEwen, 2001; Sapolsky, 1998; Siegel, 2010). Many of us understand the relationship between state and behavior on a physical level. If we are hungry, we eat. If we are thirsty, we drink. However, most of us are unconscious of how emotional state dictates how we perceive events and react to children, and how they react back to us. The Conscious Discipline Brain State Model provides a conscious guide for practical interventions. This Brain State Model is not intended to make educators into neuroscientists or therapists; it is designed to help teachers know what discipline strategy might be helpful in assisting children progress from a disorganized internal state to an organized, regulated internal state so they can wisely solve problems. (We commonly call this shift from disorganized to organized "self-regulation" or "self-control.") This process requires extensive adult coaching at first, but the goal is for children to do it by themselves.

The Conscious Discipline Brain States

> **_Knowing about the brain can help us move from self-judgement to self-acceptance._**

The Conscious Discipline Brain State Model recognizes three basic brain/body/mind states. Instead of referring to them as states of brain/body/mind each time, we simply call them "brain states" or "internal states." The purpose of learning about these states is to help identify the internal state a child is most likely experiencing, and then assist him in achieving an optimal state for learning new skills before attempting to address his behavior. The model shows these states as specific regions within the brain; however, it is imperative to understand that each state includes the integration of brain, body and mind.

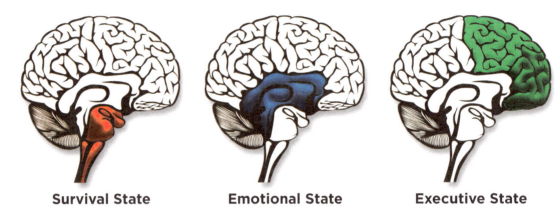

| Survival State | Emotional State | Executive State |

As you can see above, the three states of the Brain State Model are a survival state, an emotional state and an executive state. Each internal state carries with it a certain skill set. When we understand which state the child is operating from, we can choose strategies that will help him achieve a more integrated internal state with a more advanced skill set. The Brain State Model also empowers adults with the knowledge and skills to maintain better control over our internal states. Addressing our own internal state is always the first step in addressing the child's internal state and, ultimately, external behavior.

Survival State: The survival state represents our animal, genetic past. The survival state is activated under threat. It is a reactive state in which self-defense is the primary goal and intention. The model represents all the varied systems that regulate survival functions as the brain stem because it is phylogenetically the oldest, most primitive part of the brain. When activated, it results in some of our most primitive behaviors: fight, flight and freeze.

Emotional State: When we talk about the emotional state in Conscious Discipline, we are talking about an upset emotional state activated by the world not going our way and our personal past conditioning. It represents what happens when our buttons are pushed and our conditioned reactions emerge. The Brain State Model depicts all the varied systems that activate these upset emotional functions as the limbic system. The limbic system consists of several interconnected brain structures (amygdala, hippocampus, etc.) that process memories, activate our emotions and tell us what is worth remembering. The brain would be overwhelmed if there were not some method of prioritizing, and so the amygdala serves as the gatekeeper of the emotional state. If the experience is tagged as threatening, the amygdala is activated, and self-defense (not learning) becomes the goal of the exchange.

Executive State: The executive state represents the optimal integrated learning state, one of relaxed alertness. The Brain State Model depicts all the integrated systems that regulate executive functions as the prefrontal lobes of the cortex. The prefrontal lobes have been called the CEO of the brain due to the regulatory function they serve. When integrated, they allow us to inhibit preprogrammed reactions, see from others' points of view, manage our emotions, and access goal achievement and problem-solving skills. The executive state is a state of mindful, conscious integration where feelings and thoughts align, where we can access our intuitive knowledge and brilliance, and hear the voice of our "wise advocate" within. In this integrated, responsive state, we can direct our thoughts and feelings rather than be driven by them. We are integrated within ourselves and attuned with others in a way that allows us to look for solutions instead of ruminate on problems and blame.

Let's look a little closer at each of these brain states.

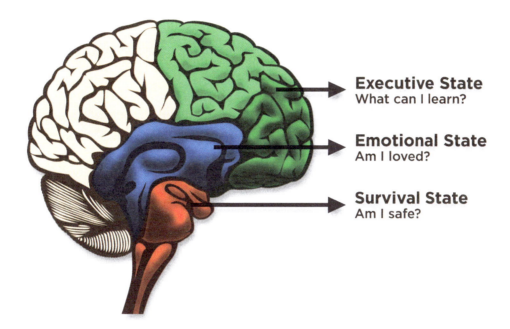

Executive State
What can I learn?

Emotional State
Am I loved?

Survival State
Am I safe?

The Survival State: "Am I Safe?"

The survival state represents our body's alarm and arousal system. Humans are hard-wired with a set of fast-reacting skills that automatically emerge when a survival state is triggered. Our genetic past has wired our brains to access these skills when we find ourselves threatened. We access these skills unconsciously, nonverbally and automatically. The intent behind these skills is self-defense at all cost.

If someone throws a rock at your head, immediately ducking is the best course of action. It would be somewhat ridiculous to appraise the situation, go over the pros and cons of ducking, and prepare your future response to the attacker. By the time you do all this, you would need stitches where the rock hit you. The survival state is beneficial in this case because it allows us to avoid the oncoming rock without conscious thought. However, when a child spills her milk and we become triggered into a survival state, our unconscious reaction might be to yank her arm. In this case, it would be helpful to be able to access a brain state where we could appraise the situation and choose a wiser course of action.

The Alarm System Wolf Metaphor

Our alarm system is embedded in our survival system. The goal is for the alarm to sound, causing us to take fast and immediate action, and then for the alarm to shut off. In prehistoric times, when our fight, flight or freeze response evolved, fight was manifested in aggressive, combative behavior; flight was manifested by fleeing potentially threatening situations; and freeze meant being quiet so we could not be seen. In the Conscious Discipline model freezing also represents surrendering. Surrendering is a form of giving in or giving up because of adults' threats.

A healthy survival system sounds the alarm when the real or imagined wolf comes. It reacts by fighting, fleeing or freezing, and then shuts the alarm off once the wolf is gone. This system that worked so well for prehistoric humans was not created to withstand the lengthy, repeated imagined threats we experience today. In modern times few of us are literally being chased by wolves, yet our perception of an everyday irritation can trigger a survival state. One friend of mine perceived things like her husband's laundry in a pile next to the hamper as a wolf (a threat to their love). She reacted by fighting at first and then fleeing (she divorced him). Many adults perceive drivers on the road as wolves. Their reaction is often to drive aggressively. Children react similarly when triggered into a survival state. Some children see a wolf as soon as you say, "Open your math book," or, "It's clean up time." These situations can automatically throw us back to a prehistoric fight, flight or freeze reaction unless we learn to consciously choose a different response.

When children are in a survival state, they possess the fight, flight or freeze skill set our ancestors and all animals possess. It is difficult to fight with or run from someone four times your size, so young children will often freeze or surrender to the adult's demands more often than older children. Young girls tend to surrender more than young boys, and firstborn children tend to surrender more than children born second. The behaviors you will see from a child in a survival state are:

Fight: Hit, push, scream, bite
Flight: Withdraw, run away, hide
Freeze: Surrender by complying, apathy by giving in or giving up by crying.

The Arousal System Clacker Metaphor

Arousal is generally defined as our level of alertness. Arousal is largely a survival state function of the autonomic nervous system (though the emotional state also plays a role). In Conscious Discipline, we use the metaphor of a clacker to demonstrate the function of our arousal system. My neighbor's child had a birthday party. The party favor was a plastic toy hand clacker for the children to use to give the birthday boy a "hand." After he opened each present, the children would give their clackers a shake and the plastic hands would clap together. Some party attendees clacked appropriately and some shook their little clackers until I was ready to scream.

We can think of an over-aroused autonomic nervous system like a clacker going crazy all day long. How hard it would be to pay attention, sit still or focus on the task at hand? We can think of an under-aroused autonomic nervous system as one with an internal clacker that only claps its hands every five minutes or so. Imagine how this slow, spaced-out state of lethargy would make learning difficult.

Some children are born over-aroused or under-aroused due to genetic abnormalities, prenatal or perinatal experiences, or difficult temperaments. Others experience environmental stressors that yield the same results. We know the frustration of trying to reach and teach these children. Their brains sacrifice learning in favor of defending against new information, defending against (yet yearning for) connection with others and defending against class rules. Though most children do not fall into this category, all children experience stressors that result in an over or under-activated arousal. When the arousal system isn't functioning optimally, it doesn't matter how wonderful our curriculum is or what standards we expect them to achieve; it is impossible for the child to be successful with a clacker that's out of whack. In order to facilitate learning, we must first help them manage their arousal and alarm systems optimally. We do this by providing physical and psychological safety.

The Developmental Question, "Am I Safe"

For the optimal development of the systems activating and managing the survival state, the child must be raised in safe environments and go to safe schools. The developmental question being asked by the survival state is, "Am I safe?" (I call these "developmental questions" because an affirmative answer is needed for the brain to continue to develop in optimal ways.) We must experience enough physical and emotional safety for the body to move out of surviving and into being receptive. The developmental question "Am I safe?" is basically an adaptation of pioneering developmental psychologist Erik Erikson's first stage of psychosocial development, asking, "Is the world a trustworthy place?"

Years ago I was asked to go to the United Nations to develop a document about the rights of children. The other two people invited, T. Berry Brazelton and Penelope Leach, were like demigods to me. I had no idea why I was invited, felt severely non-deserving and experienced an overwhelming sense of threat. Metaphorically I saw wolves everywhere. I felt like I was walking through the streets screaming, "Am I safe?" Of course, the answer in my mind was, "NO!" I absolutely did not feel safe. In my survival state, it was impossible for me to focus on the intellectual task at hand; I was focused on simple survival. My hope was to get through the meeting without destroying my career or making a complete idiot of myself. Eventually, I reached a slightly calmer state where I could come up with a plan to help deal with the terror raging inside me. My solution was to go to New York, attend the meeting and not say a word. At least this plan turned down my alarm system enough that I could get some sleep and hold down food. As to what happened at the meeting, I cannot recall because I was basically unconscious (but I did survive).

Think of the most difficult children you have had in your classroom or school. They come to school aggressive and defiant, or, like me in the United Nations project, they show up completely shut down. Luke came to school, nonverbally refusing to be greeted by anyone. His eyes were downcast and his body pulled away from the adult's welcoming hand on his back. He would enter the classroom, pushing people out of his way, slinging his backpack down and preparing to fight. It would take only the slightest provocation for him to go ballistic and be hauled out of the classroom. Most teachers do not look at children like Luke and see a child who is asking, "Am I safe?" We see a defiant, aggressive child who makes it hard to for us to teach and for others to learn. However, no one comes to school ready to defend or attack unless he or she believes the world is not safe. How many children do you know who armor themselves to start their day in a world where, in their mind, they are surrounded by wolves?

For the brain to develop optimally, children need to feel emotionally, socially and physically safe. This felt sense of safety provides a strong foundation for your Conscious Discipline classroom or school.

Survival State Summary Chart

State:	Survival
Perception/trigger:	Threat
Conscious awareness:	Unconscious automatic
Accessible skills:	Fight, flight, freeze / surrender
Behaviors you might see:	Physical aggressive: Hit, kick, push, bite Tantrums: Screaming, head banging Withdrawing: Running away, hiding, shut down, daydreaming in a world of their own
Developmental question:	Am I safe?
Developmental need:	Safety
Intention:	Self-defense (dog-eat-dog world)
Combined tools for creating safety in our classrooms that helps to optimally regulate our survival states:	Noticing Assertiveness Routines Composure Safe Place / Safekeeper

A clacker represents a survival state, specifically, the autonomic nervous system.

The Emotional State: "Am I Loved?"

Imagine you are driving to the store with a carload of children when a car cuts in front of you. Your survival state kicks in, and you automatically swerve to avoid an accident. As you begin to relax, the survival system turns off and your upset emotional state turns on. You yell, "You idiot! What are you trying to do, kill us? What were you thinking? No one thinks about anyone but themselves." As the children in the backseat watch the event unfold, you are teaching them it's okay to call people names and yell harsh judgments when the world does not go your way. Imagine how this lesson might transfer to the checkout line at the store when the children ask, "Can we have a piece of candy?" and you say, "No." From the children's point of view, you have just cut them off in traffic. It's not surprising that they might yell, "You're stupid. You don't care about anyone but yourself. I hate you."

In addition to the genetic past that's hard-wired into our survival state, our emotional state provides us with some interesting software by recording our personal past. As we form memories, our emotional state tags them with both the verbal content and the emotional experience. Our brains store memories in this state-dependent way, creating mental models of how we believe things should be. If things don't go according to these conditioned models, the brain signals red alert as if a wolf is coming.

If our parents yelled at others and looked for someone to blame during moments of frustration, that script is coded into our frustrated emotional state like a file on a CD-Rom. All we have to do is find ourselves in a physiological and emotional state of frustration, and the CD-Rom within us begins to yell at others and look for blame. Of course, our parents are not the only voices recorded on our personal CD-Rom under the file named "frustration." We also have friends, family members, teachers and television.

At one time or another, most of us have said, "When I have my own children, I will never _____ them!" Yet how many of us have already _____-ed them? It's as if we open our mouths and out come the words of our mother (father, aunt, grandmother). It can feel like a CD-Rom of unhealthy beliefs and skills is recorded in our brains, and the right trigger presses the play button automatically.

In the simplest terms, we become triggered into an upset emotional state when we perceive the world is not going our way. We often say someone or something is "pushing our buttons." If we observe ourselves in a triggered state, we will hear the internal chatter of our CD-Roms playing in our heads. This negative self-talk relentlessly plays the false messages generated from the programmed mental models on our CD-Roms. These mental models, which are really networks of neurons firing together, were handed down through our relationships with our early caregivers (which in turn were handed down from their early caregivers, who got them from their caregivers, etc.).

We are not our CD-Roms. Our CD-Roms generally contain inaccurate stories and explanations that cause us to act in ways that aren't necessarily beneficial. Over time, we start believing the false messages on the CD-Roms are true. One of the stories I tell myself is, "If I'm not responsible for everything, it will all fall apart." When I get triggered by a problem at work, my CD-Rom kicks in and the voice in my head righteously recites worst case scenarios and reasons I need to stay ultra-involved in every aspect of my business. "After all, here's another example of exactly why…" the CD-Rom barks in my head. I can see the family pattern of workaholics who have believed this thinking, when in reality it's just another false message recorded on my CD-Rom! (FYI: I'm not involved in every aspect of my business and yet it does run quite successfully.)

See if you can recognize and identify with any of these false messages:

- I'm not good enough.
- There's something wrong with me.
- I shouldn't have _____.
- I'll be rejected. Everyone thinks I'm _____
- I don't deserve to be happy.
- My worth comes from taking care of others.

What CD-Rom stories do you use to explain life events, especially in regard to misbehaving children? See if you can recognize or identify with any of these false messages:

- Give children an inch and they will take a mile.
- Children are manipulative and can't be trusted.
- Some children are just plain mean.
- Children are spoiled or brats.
- My mother would never let me get away with that. She would have spanked me in a heartbeat.
- Their parents shouldn't put up with that.

Though they seem to be about others, these false messages are really about our perceptions and us. If we believe them and automatically react from them, we pass the same CD-Rom messages down to the next generation of children. These messages are not helpful; they thwart optimal development. When we become triggered, our attention shifts from the child to the CD-Rom messages chattering in our heads. Several things occur during this process:

- We wound the next generation of children in exactly the same ways we were wounded at the same age.
- The trigger thoughts that play in our heads blind us to the real problems and needs of children, making their behavior about us instead of them.
- We unconsciously model the exact same behaviors we are trying to eliminate.
- We perpetuate the "Do as I say, not as I do" syndrome.

> It is important to note that some people have a private CD-Rom, preferring to verbally beat themselves up. Others have a public CD-Rom, preferring to verbally beat up others. We call these "internalizing" and "externalizing" behaviors. Most of us use both types of behavior, but one of them is generally our preferred method. I personally tend to begin by blaming others and then move into berating myself.

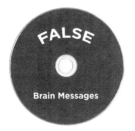

A CD-Rom represents the emotional state's preprogrammed false messages from childhood.

Activity to Discover the Discipline Skills on Your CD-Rom

Take a moment and think about how significant adults in your life reacted when the world did not go their way. Write the name of one significant adult in column one and another in column two. Then list the skills they each utilized (yelling, the silent treatment, name-calling, etc.) and the story behind the skill.

Adult 1	Adult 2
Name: _____	**Name:** _____
Skills: _____	**Skills:** _____
_____	_____
Story: _____	**Story:** _____

Even though we each have unique false messages on our personal CD-Rom, there are some commonalities. Our false messages generally revolve around name-calling and blaming others for our distress, denial, guilt and manipulation; the false messages are built into lectures, tirades and justifications supporting their truth. In an upset emotional state, we generally perceive others as the cause of our upset and seek to blame them for our distress: "You are in charge of my inner state, and you are not doing your job of making me happy!" We often enter a spiral in which we attempt to make the other person feel bad for making us feel bad, just like I tried with my mom and the sleepover. The chart on the next page shows common things we say from an upset emotional state and what these statements teach our children.

Emotional State	Adult	Child
Name-calling	What is the matter with you? (i.e. You stupid child.)	You stupid idiot.
Blaming	Now look what you made me do. Are you happy now?	He made me do it.
Denial	I am NOT angry. Now get out of my sight.	I didn't do it.
Inflicting guilt	Can't you help? Don't you see my hands are full?	Dad would let me go.
Manipulating relationships	You're just doing this to hurt me. I like the way Matthew is sitting. Do you want me to leave this house without you?	I hate you. You can't come to my birthday party. We don't like her, do we?
Making everything about you	I can't teach if you are going to continue to act like that.	You don't care about me. You're just picking on me.
Lecturing / tirades	I have told you over and over again to bring in your homework. Do you want to fail?	This isn't fair; everyone else gets to go. You don't listen to me.
Generalizing human nature	You children are all being disrespectful.	All girls are idiots.

A survival state implies a life or death perception with a physical response. An emotional state relies on the judgment of good and bad, implies a victim/villain perception toward life and attempts to make others responsible for our upset. An emotional state is actually an improvement as we move from the physical aggression and defense of a survival state, to the verbal aggression and defense of an emotional state. In real life, it can be hard to see a child saying, "F-you," as an upgrade. However, when we realize the alternative is a fist fight or we think of the devastation of school shootings, some profanity (or even a lot of profanity) would be a welcome alternative.

Emotional State - Child

Emotional State - Adult

The Developmental Question, "Am I Loved?"

The developmental question asked by someone in an emotional state is, "Am I loved?" We need to know we are loved, loving and lovable for healthy brain development. Our brains are built to link us together in families, societies and humankind as a whole (Cozolino, 2006). Being excluded or unloved is a universal fear and huge emotional trigger.

Optimal development of our relationship system requires secure attachment formed through attunement with our caregivers, especially during the first three years of life. Emotional upset creates a clacker imbalance. The way an adult responds to a child's distress determines whether their attachment bond is secure or insecure. Secure attachment requires us to be seen, be soothed and feel safe. A toddler may feel distress due to hunger, not getting what he wants or feeling tired. An attuned adult would respond to this distress in a soothing way that encourages the toddler's clacker to return to balance with a steady beat. This would promote secure attachment. A lack of attunement means the adult's response (or failure to respond) offers no relief, increasing the clacker imbalance. This would promote insecure attachment.

Just as the brain allows us to see, smell, taste, think, talk and move, it is also the organ that allows us to love (or not). While we are born with a natural capacity to nurture and be nurtured, our bonds with caregivers wire our brain systems for building and sustaining relationships. The first three years of life are critical in shaping our capacity to form healthy relationships and etching our core answer to "Am I loved" on our CD-roms. An adult with an unloveable message from childhood recorded on her CD-Rom may enter a relationship with a very loving person, yet be unable to accept that love because her mental model for attachment says, "This can't be real because I'm not that lovable."

We can easily recognize securely attached children: they are able to use friends or adults to help them through stressful situations. We can also recognize children with insecure attachments: they withdraw from the help they desperately need and/or actively fight when offered soothing nurturance during difficult times. Children with insecure attachment can seem like wounded animals. Even when we approach with loving intentions and a compassionate heart, they may metaphorically (or literally) bite us if we try to get too close.

The brain grows and develops through social interactions. A young child's brain asks, "Am I loved?" constantly as it seeks life-giving connections with caregivers, teachers and peers. "Am I loved" is the gatekeeper for the flow of information and energy. As information enters the brain through the emotional state, the gatekeeper responds, "No, I feel threatened," sending the information down to the survival centers, or "Yes, I am loved," sending the information up to the higher centers of the brain. Using a building metaphor, it would be like entering through a door on the ground floor emotional state. When we feel threatened by the person at the door, we slam it shut and hide in the basement (survival state) as we call the police. When we feel good about the person at the door, we invite him in to learn and engage (executive state).

The answer to "Am I loved" determines whether we use our energy for processing information in the higher centers of the brain or for self-protection in the lower centers of the brain. To transform our education system, each child must be able to to say, "Yes, I am loved, loving and lovable. I belong." This "yes" answer impacts the brain in two very important ways:

"Yes, I Am Loved" Creates Healthy Set Points and Skills for Managing Stress.
Everyone reading this book has experienced a coworker, administrator or child who does not deal well with life's challenges. Emotional connections, especially in our early years, are essential to creating our "set points" and mental models on our CD-Roms. Essentially, we can think of set points as optimal operating ranges to the brain. Set points inform us about our needs (i.e. hunger, thirst, safety) and are key to determining how we respond to life. They are maintained in the limbic structures of the brain, which are continually comparing our actual physiological state to our preferred state. The preferred state, especially the preferred emotional state, of any given human is established early in life and is based on how our needs were met. Anything outside of our narrow set points feels unfamiliar and dangerous, and our bodies respond accordingly (Berridge, 2004).

As an adult, I moved from Florida to New Mexico to Montana and back to Florida. Each move required huge climate adjustments. Growing up on the east coast, I was used to humidity. You could say I had a humidity set point of about 80 percent. In other words, days with 80 percent humidity felt comfortable and normal to me. When I moved to New Mexico, the average humidity was seven percent. It took a solid year of gasping for air with moisture in it, nosebleeds and humidifiers before I slowly began to adapt. I lived there six years, and even though I adapted some, it never felt right to me. Biologically I felt a yearning. My humidity set point was established early in my life; resetting it 30 years later was a challenge. The summer I moved to Montana, which has an average of 14 percent humidity (doubling that of New Mexico), I had a huge biological exhale. Just seeing the green trees and grass felt more like home! It felt good to be closer to my set point of 80 percent humidity. All this goodness quickly dissipated in winter when 20-below-zero temperatures challenged my temperature set point. I thought I would die and they would find my frozen body perfectly preserved months later. I had three job offers when I left Montana. I took the job in Florida and adjusted back to high humidity and high temperatures within about three months. Even though I don't particularly like the climate, Florida does feel familiar because of my set point.

Because the brain is a social organ, we create and change our set points through relationships. Early experience has a powerful and lasting influence on how the brain develops. Relationships, especially early relationships, establish our set points for handling stress. These experiences set up physiological expectations as to what "normal" levels of biochemicals are. These levels become written into our physiology. They also impact the amounts of chemicals we produce in response to particular situations. A child living with stressors creates an alarm set point that is on high. It feels normal for this child to be overwhelmed. In future relationships, stress and crisis will feel more familiar than caring and calmness. At school, she will prefer chaos to order. She may try to create a chaotic environment that is more comfortable to her biochemical set point.

Some people love to watch those reality TV shows where everyone bickers and backstabs; they are too crazy for me. Some people enjoy horror and suspense movies; my set point simply doesn't allow me to be entertained. I had a friend who I thought often yelled at me. I would say, "It's hard for me to listen with you yelling." She would insist she was not yelling, nor was she angry. The yelling set point was much higher in her family of origin. To her brain, she was enjoying a lively discussion. To my brain, the volume level had the same frightful effect as the wolf in our surival state metaphor. Our set points were very different. Consistently being able to answer the question, "Am I loved?" with a resounding, "Yes!" establishes healthy set points for life.

Cameron is a child with special needs. He had been on a point system for behavioral issues since he was very young. When I met him, he had recently transferred to a self-contained third grade classroom in Arizona that was using Conscious Discipline. When he entered the School

Family, his teacher spent a good deal of time helping him answer the questions, "Am I safe?" and, "Am I loved?" in the affirmative. I asked him, "Which feels better to you, being able to calm yourself down and problem solve in a way that helps you feel closer to others or earning enough points to get something really special from the treasure box at your old school?" He said, "I like being able to calm myself down. Sometimes it's scary inside me, and the toys never helped that." Then he said something I will never forget, "I guess no one at my old school thought I was able to be the boss of me." How many children do we shortchange each day by having them move a clip, pull a card or get a happy sticker instead of creating relationship-based cultures where they can learn to manage themselves? When we provide an environment and skills to help children say, "Yes, I am safe; yes, I am loved," we help them create healthy set points for life and the self-regulation required for success.

"Yes, I Am Loved" Encourages the Flow of Energy Toward an Executive State. The emotional state is the gatekeeper of the brain, regulating the flow of information and energy. Our emotions are the lens through which we see the world. When that lens perceives a consistent, "Yes," to the question, "Am I loved?" the flow of information and energy is more likely to go up toward an integrated state for problem solving and self-regulation. When our emotional state perceives a, "No," or a chronically inconsistent answer, the information and energy tends to flow down to the lower centers where we become preoccupied with safety and are unable to learn a better way of managing our behavior.

Emotional State Summary Chart

State:	Emotional
Perception/trigger:	World is not going my way
Conscious awareness:	Unconscious
Accessible skills:	CD-Rom
Behaviors you might see:	Attention seeking, relationship resistance, clinginess, perfectionism, name calling, social exclusion
Developmental question:	Am I loved?
Developmental need:	Connection
Intention:	Make me feel better and have the world go my way
Combined tools for creating connection in our classrooms to optimally regulate our emotional states:	Rituals Encouragement Jobs Empathy Choices The School Family

The Executive State: "What Can I Learn?"

I talk to a lot of people each year. Sometimes I am in the zone, and my presentation is sensational. Sometimes my presentations seem average to me and the information doesn't seem to flow. I will never forget the night in Tennessee when I received a call from my brother telling me my mother had passed away. Alone in the hotel room, I had to decide whether to do the keynote address in the morning or catch the earliest flight out. I decided I would keep my news quiet and do the keynote for Mom. In my mind, she would be able to see and hear me for the first time due to years of Alzheimer's disease that had kept her away. I nailed that keynote, one of the best I have ever done. Words flew effortlessly out of my mouth. Theory and practice weaved together like a beautiful tapestry, and everyone seemed to understand the message clearly. The last slide in my presentation was a picture of my mom. As I dedicated this presentation to her and in honor of her love that has inspired me daily, I broke down and sobbed.

During that keynote to over 2,500 people, I had set a goal and achieved it. I regulated my thoughts, emotions and actions. My belief that Mom could hear and see me was so strong that gratitude was my only feeling while I was presenting. When the presentation was over, sadness and grief flooded me.

Every person has experienced being in the zone, accessing brilliant moments when all things come together. That is the power of the integration of an executive state. The executive state is a state of relaxed alertness where we have the capacity to notice our thoughts, notice our emotions, be conscious of our actions, and possess the ability to pause and plan a wise response. We can make choices free from insecurities and impulses. We can see conflicts from multiple perspectives, offer empathy to others and solve problems. Essentially, we have the opportunity to be our best selves. In this way, the executive state puts us in touch with our wise advocate (Schwartz & Gladding, 2011). Our wise advocate can see the bigger picture, which includes our inherent worth.

The executive state represents the chief executive officer (CEO) of the brain, a magnificent integrated system within us that allows us to regulate our thoughts, emotions and behavior, and override the impulses of the lower centers of the brain. Instead of physically fighting, fleeing or verbally overreacting from an old CD-Rom, the executive state allows us to pause and plan a wise response. This pause is also where self-regulation occurs.

The Voice of Your Wise Advocate

Most of us are aware that we talk to ourselves. Adults have independent inner speech they can use as a source of self-regulation (Vygotsky, 1986). This inner voice can also be used for dysregulation. A dysregulating inner voice might say, "If one more person tells me how tired I look today, I'm going to smack him." In the same situation, the voice of self-regulation might say, "Take it easy. You had a tough night. Just two more hours and you're out of here."

Children do not generally develop mature inner speech until around age seven. So, how do young children self-regulate? They don't! Adults are children's regulators and co-regulators. How we respond to children's upset will inhibit or enhance their self-regulatory skills.

Responding to a child's emotional upset isn't usually our strong suit. Unless we actively intervene to calm ourselves, a child's upset tends to trigger our own CD-Rom and our emotional gatekeeper funnels our energy to the lower centers of the brain. When we allow ourselves to persist in a lower brain state like this, we pass down the false messages associated with the trigger, burning the same trigger and reaction onto the child's CD-Rom. It's a "gift" that keeps on giving from one generation to the next. The voice we use to discipline children is a reflection of the voice we use to discipline ourselves and it will be the voice children use to discipline themselves in the future. We have a choice to use the voice of our wise advocate or the voice on our preprogrammed CD-Rom. The voice we choose will direct our behavior.

> *We have a choice to use the voice of our wise advocate or the voice on our preprogrammed CD-Rom. The one we choose will direct our behavior.*

Most of us who have been in the workforce a while have had at least one supportive and encouraging boss, a critical and micromanaging boss, and an absentee boss who does very little. Now take a moment to read the following question slowly and reflect upon the answer: What type of boss do you have in your head most of the time?

If you have a critical internal CEO who berates you for not being good enough, is that the type of boss you want running the minds of the future generations? What about an absentee boss? We are going to pass a voice down to the children in our care. Unless we consciously choose to change it, the kind of CEOs we have managing our thoughts, feelings and actions are also the kinds of CEOs we will instill in the minds of our children.

Being an exceptional boss or manager requires a certain skill set. Effective CEOs must be organized individuals who are able to set goals, make plans, prioritize, manage their time effectively, focus attention despite distraction and be flexible enough to shift their attention when needed. They must be able to communicate effectively with all other departments in the company. They must be able to problem-solve under pressure, empathetically understand employees' needs, have the impulse and emotional control to weather all sorts of challenges, and possess the ability to reflect on their actions and change course as needed.

Both neuroimaging research and clinical research with brain-injured individuals have demonstrated that the prefrontal lobes of the cortex (which lie roughly behind your forehead) are the epicenter for all the skills mentioned above, collectively termed "the executive skills." When this skill set is online and active, our internal voice can be the supportive, efficient, flexible, encouraging, wise and successful boss of our dreams. When this skill set is offline, our CEO bows to the voice on the CD-Rom of our emotional state.

Our executive skills liberate us from the CD-Rom of false messages and our metaphorical wolves. They help us create a plan and hold strong to it regardless of outside temptations and empower us to make mindful new choices. The executive state frees us to move beyond the "Do what I say, not what I do" syndrome that plagues our homes and schools. It allows us to consciously choose our response instead of simply reacting to life and it widens our view, enabling us to see from many perspectives. For this reason, we use the symbol of heart glasses to represent an executive state.

Our executive state allows us to find our unique gifts and share them with others, reaching our true potential. In my case, it allows me to be Becky... not a set of preprogrammed, false messages and reactions from my early upbringing and genetic past, but the Becky I choose to be now in this moment.

Accessing our executive skills is only possible when we reach an optimal integrated state of relaxed alertness fostered by positive emotions. From this state of consciousness, there are two voices, one acting on the other. We are able to be a witness to our thoughts, feelings and actions rather than becoming them. As the witness (the wise advocate) we are able to make choices about which thoughts, feelings and actions support our highest goals in a certain situation. We no longer demand the world go our way; we respond wisely to whatever comes our way through new eyes. We have a choice to see things differently.

Heart glasses represent the executive state's ability to see from many perspectives.

A TOP WIFE Makes Good TEa

The executive tool set, when functioning properly and online, allows us to meet any situation with wisdom. So what exactly comprises this wonderful yet elusive set of skills? Many researchers and theorists have attempted to define them, and there are several variations of agreed upon "executive skills." In general, they empower us to do the following:

1. Set and achieve goals despite distractions
2. Regulate our emotions and inhibit impulsive behaviors
3. Self-monitor and reflect
4. Develop empathy and problem solve

Drs. Peg Dawson and Richard Guare (2009) distill these global abilities into a more defined skill set that is helpful in a classroom application, so Conscious Discipline uses an adaptation of their work. It is essential to understand that the executive skills listed below are highly interrelated. The list is simply a tool to help us understand the many complex functions of an executive state so we can more easily improve these skills in ourselves and teach these skills to children. All the skills on the list integrate with all of the others, ultimately enabling us to adapt our behavior to meet the needs of our social environment. Visit the portal to read about each of these skills and complete a self-assessment.

Conscious Discipline uses the acronym "A TOP WIFE Makes Good TEa" to help us remember the executive skills. As you read the list below, ask yourself, "Is this skill a strong suit of mine or a weak suit?"

Attention
Time Management
Organization
Prioritization
Working Memory
Impulse Control
Flexibility
Empathy
Metacognition
Goal Achievement
Task Initiation
Emotional Regulation

Jason and Matthew tape a page back into the book so their friends can read it. That was helpful.

Helping others

If you look closely, you will discover a connection between the development of executive skills and what is typically referred to as "discipline problems." Most discipline problems are simply an indication of missing and/or underdeveloped executive skills.

Think of all the time you spend helping children do the following tasks:

Attention: "Leo, it's time to clean up." "Tyler, put down the pencils and focus on your math." "Gianna, it is Brandon's turn to talk. Let's give him our full attention." "Leo, it is time to clean up. Stop playing with the toy cars and start putting them away. Leo! What did I tell you? Do you want to play with the toy cars tomorrow? Then put them away NOW!"

Time Management: "Boys and girls, you have five more minutes before clean up time." "Jonathan, you have only two more minutes to finish your math. I am not going to tell you again." "It is time for recess; you need to have finished cleaning up and be sitting on the carpet. If the class is not ready by the time I count to three, then we will just have to miss recess! 1-2----."

Organization: "Leo, the toy cars go in the tub marked cars. Pick them up out of the dollhouse and put them in the toy car tub." "Gianna, write down your homework into your planner. Did you write it down? No, you did not. Now what books do you need to take home to complete the assignment? Where are they? Are they in your backpack? No, they are not."

Working Memory: "It is time to line up for lunch. Remember, if you brought lunch to carry it. Ready? Table One, push in your chairs and line up. Brandon, you are Table Two, not Table One. Where is your lunch box?"

Impulse Control: "Leo, no hitting! Tyler is trying to help you put away the cars. Tyler is name-calling helpful or hurtful? I have had it with you two. Just leave the cars and go down to Mr. McIntyre's office. Move it boys!"

Emotional Regulation: "All right, class, let's calm down. Did you hear me? I said, CALM DOWN!" "Your mommy will be back. She always comes to pick you up." "There is no need to throw your book. I can help you with the math." "Jaquanda did not mean to step on you. It was an accident." "There is no need to speak to me in that tone of voice."

Historically, we've punished children for not having executive skills at certain ages, even though these skills are not fully developed until about age 24! (Yes, 24 years old.) Traditionally, we've approached discipline under a moral model where it is the adult's job to teach children right from wrong and good from bad. I have seen preschool teachers lose their composure over children who lack the executive skill of flexibility. We've all heard a 3-year-old scream, "I want that one," as he fixates on the red marker in another child's hand, refusing to get an identical red marker out of the bin. We could see this as a misbehaving, spoiled child or we could see it as a child who needs help to learn the executive skill of flexibility. Which approach do you think is more helpful to the child? Which do you think is more helpful for your inner state?

Homework requires almost all of the executive skills, yet many teachers regularly give homework without scaffolding the skills needed for children to complete the endeavor. Children must focus their attention on the goal given to them, be able to initiate the task that evening, organize their work into a system, remember the steps needed in the work required, prioritize what to do first, second and so on, and stick with it despite obstacles, distractions and frustrations. We require children to use executive skills, knowing they're not yet mature. This means a child's success with homework is dependent on her teachers and parents lending their prefrontal lobes as needed to scaffold her development until her prefrontal lobes have matured enough to reliably accomplish the tasks independently.

Developmental neuroimaging shows that the prefrontal cortex develops rapidly in early childhood, with important changes occurring at particular ages (at 12 months, between 3 and 6 years, and around puberty) and then continues to develop into adulthood (Zelezo, 2002). A chart on the portal shows the approximate times when different executive skills begin their developmental journey.

The skill of impulse control comes online around five months old, meaning our response at this age can begin to enhance its development. Consider the situations below. Which one scaffolds the development of impulse control?

Situation 1: Baby Tyra is hungry. She begins to cry. Her mother takes a few slow breaths to calm herself and responds soothingly, "I hear you, sweetie. I'm making your bottle now. It is coming very soon." Breathing deeply, she continues, "Your face is going like this (she mirrors Tyra's face). Your body is saying, 'Hurry up, Mom, I'm hungry.'" Mom describes what she's doing out loud as she prepares the bottle, "The milk is warm now! I'm pouring it in. It's almost ready. You can handle this. Look at you waiting! Breathe with me (Mom takes a deep breath). Here it comes!" Mom gives Tyra her bottle and says, "You did it! You waited until Mommy got the bottle ready."

Situation 2: Shelley is hungry. She begins to cry. Her mother is anxiously working to make a bottle. "Shhshhshh," she says, continuing to work as fast as possible. As Shelley cries harder, Mom says, "Shelley, please, I'm going as fast as I can. Ssshhh!"

The first interaction scaffolds impulse control development by helping the baby make tiny bits of progress toward delaying gratification. The second interaction inhibits executive skill development and derails the mother-child relationship. Responsive, attuned relationships fulfill the need for safety and connection, making them key for executive skill development.

The power of scaffolding the prefrontal lobes is evident all around us. Each holiday season, our office adopts a local family in an effort to experience our oneness and give of our goodness. We provide groceries and gifts, and enjoy a small celebration with the family. This tradition includes responsibilities for the family like writing letters to Santa so we know what gifts to purchase for the children, a visit with an office member, setting a time for the celebration and securing transportation to the celebration. This seems pretty straightforward to those of us who possess reliable access to our "A TOP WIFE Makes Good TEa" skills, but it can be daunting for a family living in a prolonged survival state. To help them be successful, an office member must lend his or her prefrontal lobes to the family by structuring everything from basic communication to arranging transportation to the celebration. One year, even with our scaffolding, the family was so overwhelmed by meeting the responsibilities that they declined our help two weeks into the endeavor. It's not that they didn't want or appreciate our efforts; they simply lacked the prefrontal lobe skills necessary to meet this handful of expectations, and we lacked the ability to scaffold them sufficiently. The added stress of the situation prompted the family to decline our efforts. This served as a powerful reminder to the office of the power of the executive skills!

Lending our prefrontal lobes does not mean doing the work for someone. It means prompting, helping and structuring their executive skills in a way that empowers them to do it for themselves. Teachers lending their prefrontal lobes and structuring the environment to actively support emerging skills are the only ways to ensure children will experience social, emotional and academic success. In Conscious Discipline, we use classroom structures that act as external prefrontal lobes to support the emerging skills. Moving a child's clip, changing the color of her card from green to red, offering trips to a treasure box and giving out referrals do not help develop the higher centers of a child's brain. Yet, often teachers and administrators insist these behavioral systems work. The children sit still and the classroom appears orderly. I would offer the following food for thought in regard to simple behavioral systems based on rewards and punishments like those mentioned above:

- These systems **do** temporarily work for children who come to school already knowing they are safe and loved. These children will comply with the rules; however, these systems hinder their executive skill development. We are trading these children's long-term ability to set and achieve goals for short-term compliance and obedience.

- These systems **do not** work for children who come to school without the security of feeling safe or loved. These children will lose whatever privilege is at stake and will fail to earn whatever privilege there is to earn. They become increasingly discouraged as their years in school progress. Their view of themselves becomes one of incompetence, their view of the world becomes one of increasing injustice, and their view of their future becomes distorted into self-sabotage or revenge against society.

- These external control systems have been shown to reduce discipline referrals, however, they also increase the negativity of the school culture. Negative school cultures impede learning, foster bullying, increase dropout rates and increase teacher turnover (Hoffman, 2008).

The Developmental Question, "What Can I Learn?"

The executive state leaves us receptive to learning. When we are in an executive state, we are metaphorically asking, "What can I learn from this encounter, this lesson or this problem?"

Answering "Am I safe" and "Am I loved" in the affirmative creates willingness. Learning new social-emotional skills is futile without the willingness to change existing behaviors. Our most difficult children are not just missing skills, they are unwilling to learn new ones due to their self-preservation goals. Children in an executive state are more willing to let go of primitive skills, impulsivity and defensive strategies in favor of learning advanced new skills. They are willing to use words instead of hit, to ask for help instead of quietly fail and to learn how to calm down instead of throw fits. They just require us to scaffold their emerging executive skills by being their teachers, coaches and mentors.

Conscious Discipline asks teachers to shift from the traditional task of making children behave to an enlightened vision of helping children be successful. Instead of asking ourselves, "What will make/get this child _____?" we must ask the new question, "What will help this child more likely be successful at _____?" Then we can look at the list of executive skills and see where the child needs scaffolding. By approaching classroom management in this fashion, we sustain a positive school climate called the School Family, develop higher order thinking skills, and encourage children to learn how to set and achieve their own goals.

> *Instead of asking, "What will make/get this child to _____?" we must ask the new question, "What will help this child more likely be successful at _____?"*

In order to make this shift from attempting to control children's behaviors to helping them consciously choose to change, we must lend our prefrontal lobes to our children. We do this by using the seven skills in this book (composure, encouragement, assertiveness, choices, positive intent, empathy and consequences), and structuring the environment in a way that helps children internalize these skills for the future. Lending our prefrontal lobes is as easy as A, B, C:

Accessing our executive state through active calming.
Being willing to perceive children's misbehavior as a communication or call for help.
Coaching new skills as necessary.

There are two huge challenges to this plan that must be addressed:

1. **The prefrontal lobe goes offline when we become stressed, and we cannot lend skills we don't have access to.** If we remain in a state of chronic stress and refuse to consciously calm ourselves and change our perceptions, we cannot be present with our children. It is easier to write a child's name on the board or give out treats from the treasure box than it is to manage our stress so we can lend children our prefrontal lobes. At some point (and I believe that point has arrived), we must consciously say, "There is a better way and I want to be part of it!"

2. **We can't lend prefrontal lobe skills to children if they are weak suits of ours, nor can we do it from a distance.** Even when we're not stressed, some of our executive skills are more developed than others. I am always amazed at teacher/parent conferences. The parent conference for a child who has attention issues often results in twenty minutes of rerouting the conversation back toward the goal. The children who can't seem to do their homework on time often have parents who forget the meeting or show up late. Every person is born with a certain set of genetic predispositions. These tendencies can be compounded or alleviated by caregivers' ability to teach and coach us through the missing skills. Parents are often deficient in the same skills as their children and therefore struggle to scaffold those skills for them. On your portal, you can view a powerful video in which a former gang leader's grandmother shares how she did her best to help him and how his Conscious Discipline-trained teacher was able to lend her prefrontal lobe skills to scaffold his success.

We cannot lend our prefrontal lobes from a distance or when we lack the skills children need help with. Imagine your neighbor needs to borrow a wrench so she can stop a leaky faucet. Try to lend her your wrench without walking over and delivering it. How helpful is that wrench? Now imagine you are standing next to her, but neither of you know how to use a wrench. How helpful is your presence? Each of us has a unique set of strengths and weaknesses when it comes to executive skills. Conscious Discipline purposefully scaffolds these skills with classroom structures. This empowers adults to strengthen our weak suits while helping children develop their own emerging skills.

Activity to See Misbehavior Differently

Part 1

Are you willing to see misbehavior as missing or emerging social, emotional and executive skills? After each situation, decide how you are willing to see the child by circling the word "yes" for the perception that would best represent yours.

A child throws a fit in the grocery store.

Missing the ability to handle frustration?   Yes

Spoiled child who won't listen to her mother when she says no?   Yes

A child does not follow directions when told.

Missing the ability to pay attention and keep out distractions?   Yes

Non-compliant child who tests the teacher?   Yes

A child intentionally hits another child.

Missing the ability to manage frustration?   Yes

Mean disrespectful child?   Yes

A child constantly pushes or elbows other children.

Missing the ability to control impulses?   Yes

Disrespectful child who refuses to keep hands and feet to self?   Yes

Part 2

Building on the same idea as in Part 1, let's add some additional perceptual challenges to see if you are still willing to see the call for help. After each situation, decide if you are willing to see the child as:

A. Being mean or rude   B. Missing skills

Child appears to accidentally push another child out of the way to get a seat next to his friend.   A   B

Child appears to intentionally push another child out of the way to get a seat next to his friend.   A   B

Child appears to intentionally push another child out of the way to get a seat next to his friend. When the teacher tells him to stop, he does it again.   A   B

Executive State Summary Chart

State:	Executive
Perception/trigger:	Curious, investigative, reflective, what help is needed?
Conscious awareness:	Conscious
Accessible skills:	Wise advocate, internal brilliance based on needs of the moment, seeing from many perspectives
Behaviors you might see:	Willingness, reflection, empathy, conflict resolution, problem-solving, managing emotions, setting goals and achievement
Developmental question:	What can I learn from this?
Developmental need:	Problem-solving in social settings
Intention:	To wisely adapt and respond to the situation at hand
Tools for creating problem-solving opportunities in our classrooms to optimally utilize our executive states:	Solutions Positive Intent Academic Integration Consequences Executive Skills

 A simple way to represent the brain is to use the palm of your hand. Visit your web portal to watch Dr. Bailey demonstrate!

An executive state allows us to see from different perspectives.

Safety, Connection and Problem-Solving: Building Brain Smart Classrooms and Schools

Children come to school asking, "Am I safe," "Am I loved," or, "What can I learn." Effective schools create cultures that answer the first two questions in the affirmative, and then provide the academic and social-emotional skills necessary for optimal growth. The graphic below summarizes helpful skills Conscious Discipline uses with each brain state.

Survival State: Safety

Combined Tools	Characteristics	Conscious Discipline Skills
N = Noticing **A** = Assertiveness (adults) **R** = Routines with pictures **C** = Composure **S** = Safe Place and Safekeeper	• No eye contact • Resistance to questions, touch and understanding • Tense face/body • Feels cornered and powerless	• Composure: S.T.A.R., upload, breathe with me • Noticing: Your arm is going like this • Language of safety: You are safe • Assertiveness: Voice of no doubt

Emotional State: Connection

Combined Tools	Characteristics	Conscious Discipline Skills
R = Rituals **E** = Encouragement **J** = Jobs **E** = Empathy **C** = Choices **T** = The School Family	• Body relaxes • Eye contact and touch are helpful • Seeking connection, understanding and/or power	• Encouragement: You can do it • Choices: You have a choice • Empathy: You seem __.

Executive State: Problem-Solving

Combined Tools	Characteristics	Conscious Discipline Skills
S = Solutions (class meetings) **P** = Positive Intent **A** = Academic Integration **C** = Consequences **E** = Executive Skills	• Tend to focus on what you don't want first • Willing and ready to learn a new skill • Able to reflect and plan • Sees impact on others	• Positive intent: You wanted __ or you were hoping __. • Natural Consequences: Did you like it? • Logical Consequences: You have a choice! You can choose to (helpful skill) and (positive consequence) or (hurtful skill) and (negative consequence). • Problem-solving: P.E.A.C.E., class meetings

Now, let's take a few moments to review our original goals for learning about the Brain State Model: 1. Remain in an executive state ourselves while interacting with children, 2. Identify the internal state a child is most likely experiencing, 3. Address the internal state by assisting the child in achieving an optimal state for learning new skills and 4. Address the behavior by teaching a new skill.

1. **Remaining in an executive state ourselves.** Our perception will shift as our internal state changes. If we feel frustrated and are experiencing an emotional state, we tend to see the child as mean or rude instead of a child who is missing a skill. From this viewpoint, we cannot access the skills we need to teach rather than punish. If we can remain relaxed and alert without judgment, we begin to see that the child does not possess or cannot access the skill needed, regardless of his intention. When we change our state, we change our perception, which changes our intent, which changes our response to the child. One of the principles of Conscious Discipline is adults must discipline themselves first and children second. This means we must change our internal state from upset to calm before attempting to help children change theirs.

2. **Identifying the child's internal state.** Once we have calmed ourselves, it is imperative that we identify the brain state the child is most likely experiencing. Use the chart below to review.

State	Behaviors (Most Likely)
Survival state skills tend to be physical	Fight by hitting, pushing, kicking, spitting, screaming; Flight by running, hiding, withdrawing; Freezing by surrendering, crying, giving in, giving up
Emotional state skills tend to be verbal	Blaming, back-talking, name-calling, social exclusion, social aggression, guilt, attention-seeking, clinging, neediness
Executive state skills	Wise advocate, problem-solving, empathy, win-win solutions

Survival State

Emotional State

Executive State

Activity to Assess the Child's Internal State

Check the brain state the person is most likely experiencing and then write the person's need (safety, connection, problem-solving) in the blank.

	Brain State	Need
Maria screams, "I hate you!"	❏ Survival ❏ Emotional ❏ Executive	_____
Jacob hit his sister in the head with a foam bat and takes his ball back.	❏ Survival ❏ Emotional ❏ Executive	_____
Carlos suddenly swerves the car to avoid a dog running across the street.	❏ Survival ❏ Emotional ❏ Executive	_____
Dylan is potty training. After his tenth unproductive trip to the potty this morning, his Pre-K teacher snaps, "This might be okay at home, but don't you play these games with me!"	❏ Survival ❏ Emotional ❏ Executive	_____
Marcus raises his hand and says, "Help me. I can't do this." His teacher says, "You raised your hand and asked for help. Good for you Marcus!"	❏ Survival ❏ Emotional ❏ Executive	_____

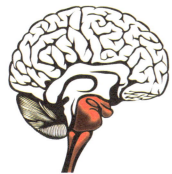

Brain State: Survival
Need: Safety

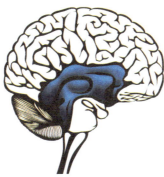

Brain State: Emotional
Need: Connection

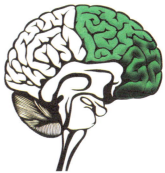

Brain State: Executive
Need: Problem-solving

3. **Assisting the child in achieving an executive state for optimal learning.** Safety calms the survival state, connection soothes the emotional state and problem-solving in social settings maximizes the executive state. As you proceed through this book, each chapter provides specific tools and interventions to facilitate the move from a lower to a higher brain state. Each chapter also contains a Brain Smart section that deepens your understanding of the relationship between our brains and behavior. Once we have assisted the child in achieving an optimal state for learning, we are ready for a fourth endeavor: Teaching a new skill.

> *Much like adults scaffold emerging executive skills for children, Conscious Discipline scaffolds the skills adults need to transform their own skill set.*

4. **Addressing the behavior by teaching the new skill.** The fourth and final stage of transforming behavior is teaching a new skill. You will accomplish this by scaffolding children's emerging executive skills using the tools, interventions and structures found throughout this book. Successful teaching can only happen once you have completed the first three steps of the process.

Development proceeds from the bottom up. How we manage one developmental level impacts the success of the next. If we think of a building, safety is the basement/foundation, connection is the ground floor and problem-solving is the top floor. When we start with a strong foundation of safety and build each floor securely upon the next, both children and adults gain access to their brilliance and are able to make the wisest choices possible in a situation. When our foundations and/or ground floors are insecure or damaged, it behooves us all (homes, schools and communities) to do the repair work needed to secure our buildings.

Now that we have a substantial understanding of the brain as it relates to social-emotional learning, we will hone in on shifting from traditional role-based, fear-based discipline models to creating the inclusive, compassionate school climate we call a "School Family." As we prepare to delve into the School Family chapter, let's take a deep breath together and say, "I'm safe. I am in charge of the process of change. How much or how little I choose to change is my decision. I will continue reading with an open mind and open heart, and embrace this journey to the best of my ability."

	Survival State	Emotional State	Executive State
Belief	I am under attack. I am not safe.	I am not loved/valued/ respected/appreciated.	I am safe enough/loved enough/capable enough. I am enough.
Emotions	Anxiety, anger, fear, terror, hopelessness, depression	Sadness, hurt, frustration, irritation, disappointment, guilt, helpless	Calm, peaceful, coherent, grateful, content, relaxed, attentive, present, alert, confident, competent
Behaviors	Physical aggression, screaming, withdrawal, run, surrender, disassociate	Social aggression, name calling, victim, martyr, guilt, manipulation	Goal directed, problem-solving, solution oriented, caring and motivated, responsible
Awareness	Unconscious	Unconscious	Conscious
Free Will	Physically reactive, instinctual DNA program, stimulus-reaction	Verbally reactive, preprogrammed CD-Rom, stimulus-reaction	Conscious choice of response Stimulus-pause-response
Questions	Am I safe?	Am I loved?	What can I learn from this?
Need	Safety	Connection	Problem-solving in social settings
Discipline Style	Threats, spanking, fear me	Egoic, bribes, manipulation, rewards and punishments, guilt, withdrawal of love, reasoning, please me	Cultural-relational based intrinsic motivation model, e.g. Conscious Discipline
Regulation	Arousal, clacker	Emotions	Behavior, thoughts, emotions, arousal

Chapter 3
SCHOOL FAMILY

The School Family: Creating Compassionate School Climates

> *"After seeing the crying parents of the girl he murdered, a teenager muttered these words: I don't know why they're crying; I'm the one going to jail."*
>
> — *Dr. Bruce Perry*

Shocking. We all have wondered how children can commit such acts of violence against each other. And then we hear words like, "I don't know why they're crying; I'm the one going to jail." Or, "This sure beats the hell out of algebra," from a 14-year-old who killed a teacher and two students. Or, "Aren't you all dead yet?" in a chemistry classroom during a rampage that killed 15 people. We wonder how these individuals can grow up without empathy, without compassion, without understanding their personal significance in the world, without feeling they belong and without knowing they are adored beyond measure. After each act of violence, we ask ourselves what we could have done differently to provide these attributes and prevent such devastating outcomes.

I don't know anyone who believes higher standardized test scores, more differentiated curricula, better lesson plans or more active learning would have helped these troubled individuals and prevented these tragedies. I believe the key that unlocks this mystery lies in the realm of family, both our families of origin and the families of choice we create with the people we see every day. Our relationships, and lack thereof, have the power to exalt us to the highest of who we are or plummet us into the depths of despair.

Conscious Discipline is based on two closely linked ideas: First, a healthy family is the ultimate cultural model for optimal development and learning; second, intrinsic motivation is the only means for achieving of life-long learning and healthy values.

A Healthy Family Model Versus the Traditional Factory Model

Conscious Discipline uses a healthy family as the template for creating an optimal school culture that answers the questions, "Am I safe?" and "Am I loved?" in the affirmative. The School Family does not replace a child's home family, but uses a healthy family model to create optimal learning environments that support the continued development of all children (those with exceptional needs, English as a second language, defiant/out-of-control and shut down/withdrawn) and all adults (administrators, teachers, staff, caregivers and parents) involved.

Historically and in many schools today, classrooms are designed on a factory model of education that has been around since the early 1900s. Take a moment and conjure an image of a factory, what it manufactures, its goals and the working environment. In this image, you might see obedient workers performing rote, repetitive tasks with little personal meaning. The factory's goal is to make as many standardized widgets as efficiently as possible, using quality control standards. Management relies on external motivators such as removing or punishing those who do not meet the daily standards and rewarding those who exceed them. Widgets that do not conform are rejected. The overarching feeling often is one of apathy, boredom and fear of not meeting today's quota or standards or losing the bonuses possible.

In the factory model of education, educators are factory workers and children are widgets. The goal is to pack a standardized curriculum into each widget's head on a specific timeline. Nonconforming child widgets are seen as blocks to production, efficiency and accountability. Often, they are repeatedly punished or expelled for their disruption to the system. Some of us are parents to nonconforming children. These children are creative, movement-oriented or simply cannot tolerate the boredom of an assembly-line approach to education.

The factory model of education is destined to leave some children behind. Some of the children left behind are marginalized for their differences and become targets for bullying or become bullies themselves. Other children excel in school, but overly-pressure themselves; anything less than a hundred percent accuracy and the top award throws them into a tailspin.

It has become widely accepted that the standardized competitive factory model is not an effective learning model, and so we must begin undoing decades of programming and reinvent our schools. We must create a new model for building school cultures, one that accepts differences, builds unity and brings all children into the fold as caring, contributing members. One that answers the questions "Am I safe" and "Am I loved" in the affirmative. Conscious Discipline believes this model is that of a healthy family. Research suggests a sustainable, caring school climate increases academic achievement, mental health, graduation rates, school connectedness, teacher retention and risk prevention (Cohen & Geier, 2010). Common sense and research inform us that social emotional skills and school climate are interdependent (Zins & Elias, 2006). Just as our ability to manage emotions, have empathy for others, constructively handle difficult situations and effectively solve problems impacts the health of a family, the same holds true at school.

Intrinsic Motivation Versus External Manipulation

Historically in the United States, the goal of discipline was to scare children into compliance. Growing up in the south, I often heard "putting the fear of God in them" was a viable discipline strategy. When children failed to complete tasks as commanded, we threatened them with loss of recess, time out, calling their parents and trips to the principal's office in the hopes they would say, "Oh, thank you, wonderful teacher! I'm going to hop right on over and take care of that task."

Many educators are acutely aware that threats and punishments are counterproductive. The power-over model they employ ruptures relationships, inhibits self-regulation, relies on fear, and generates anger, defiance and revenge rather than learning and cooperation. More recently, many shifted to a positive discipline model based on rewards and "catching kids being good." Although these approaches seem opposite from punishment, they are actually two sides of the same coin: both try to manipulate someone else's behavior and rely on fear as the tool of choice. In punishing environments children ask, "What do you want me to do, and what happens to me if I don't do it?" In rewarding environments children ask, "What do you want me to do, and what do I get for doing it?" Neither of these questions prompts children to ponder, "What kind of person do I want to be?" (Kohn, 1999). Both punishment and reward approaches are counterproductive due to their reliance on fear. There is now a broad and diverse body of research that shows fear shuts down the higher centers of the brain, rendering them ineffective and leaving us at the mercy of our impulses and insecurities (Cozolino, 2013). So, it doesn't matter whether the child is afraid of receiving a punishment or afraid he won't receive a reward. Either way his brain is preoccupied with fear (survival state) rather than learning (executive state). We must work in cooperation with the brain, not against it.

I was working at a school in California that was using Conscious Discipline. On this particular day, a group of third-grade boys were solving some bullying issues. One exasperated boy finally said, "Can't you just take a privilege away from me? Or how 'bout a paddling? This problem solving is hard!" The other boys nodded in agreement. Requiring children to be conscious of their internal states, change them, reflect on their behavior and come up with skills to replace the original behavior is much more challenging (and rewarding) than receiving a punishment. Like many children, the boys were accustomed to discipline being something that was done to them instead of something they must do for themselves.

There is a persistent and heated debate in educational literature about the use of extrinsic rewards as a motivational strategy (Sansone & Harackiewicz, 2000); however, the research is unanimous in regard to the benefits of intrinsic motivation. Schools relying on extrinsic motivation reap compliance, at best. Schools that enhance students' intrinsic motivation also enhance brain function, increasing social and academic performance, and decreasing aggressive and risky behaviors. Intrinsic motivation requires us to promote personal autonomy and interdependence, provide schoolwork that is meaningful and challenging, encourage relationships that both nurture and structure, and structure the environment to be physically and psychologically safe. Conscious Discipline does this with you, your children, your classroom and your school by shifting from reward and punishment to safety, connection and problem-solving.

Transforming School Culture with the School Family

The brain is a social organ, making interdependence the keystone of optimal learning. Conscious Discipline asks us to create a compassionate school climate called the "School Family" to meet the brain's requirement for interdependence. Compassion moves beyond being positive or cooperative, relying instead on the understanding that all living things are interrelated. Belonging is defined as "a sense of personal valued involvement in a social system so that the person feels indispensable and integral to the whole and accepted by other members" (Anant, 1966). The School Family systematically bonds all members to each other with a sense of belonging. This felt sense of belonging opens the door to problem solving, permanent behavior change, and social-emotional and academic success.

Creating compassionate school cultures is much bigger than team building during in-service trainings, making school T-shirts and calling ourselves "The McKinley Tigers." Rhetoric and upgraded terminology do not create a sense of belonging. We must go back to the most basic building blocks of all relationships: safety and trust. When we use daily interactions, especially difficult moments, to build safety and trust, we begin to create a School Family where members are willing to let down their guard and truly connect. This authentic connection wires the brain for impulse control and embodies our highest values.

Creating enough social trust to build a compassionate School Family requires significant upgrades to our skill set. Most of us rely on external means of attempting to control others' behaviors because that is how we were raised and how we were taught to "discipline" children. Control-based systems don't build internal motivation and self-regulatory skills necessary for a life of purpose. It is impossible to build a compassionate climate if the principal uses control (power) over teachers instead of shared power and relationship-building with teachers, or teachers use control (power) over students instead of shared power and relationship-building with students.

Our style of relationship-building was shaped early in life by our parents and other caregivers called "attachment figures." Early attachment figures helped us create mental models that define how we manage our emotions, express our thoughts, and resolve or avoid conflict. As mentioned in Chapter 2, secure and non-secure are the two main types of attachment models. A secure model allows us to live with flexibility, self-understanding, ease of connection with others and quick recovery from emotional upset. Non-secure models come in several forms, all of which decrease our ability to be flexible, to reflect inwardly, to connect with others, and to recover from hurt feelings and frustrations.

The attachment model we possess is dependent on how we were seen, how safe we felt and how we were soothed by our significant caregivers during times of distress in the first years of life. "Being seen" refers to how well caregivers sense the inner world behind our behaviors in order to help us self-regulate. Could caregivers relate crying to the disappointment and fear we felt when left with the sitter, or were we handed off and simply told, "Shush now, you're fine, Mommy will be back." Feeling safe means we felt protected from harm and didn't feel fearful of our own caregivers. Did caregivers threaten, scream or use guilt to manipulate us, or was our safety in their presence assured? "Being soothed" means caregivers' responses during moments of distress eased our discomfort rather than dismissing or amplifying it.

Our brain relies on relationships to shape its growth. As we say many different ways in this book, "The brain is a social organ that develops through relationships." Most mammals have only one attachment figure. Luckily, humans have a number of attachment models in our youth, and if our models are non-secure early in life, we can adjust them through later relationships and choosing to make the necessary changes. The powers and skills of Conscious Discipline, when used within the compassionate School Family culture, empower us to successfully make those changes.

The Seven Powers of Conscious Adults, the Seven Skills of Discipline and the School Family are synergistically related. The School Family provides a climate that is safe and connected, fostering the willingness to make behavioral changes and the impulse control necessary to make those changes. The powers of Conscious Discipline change our perception of conflict and the skills change our response to conflict. The School Family and the powers and skills of Conscious Discipline have a reciprocal relationship, each building on and strengthening the other.

Every chapter in this book relates a power and a skill to the formation of your School Family. As we put the skills and powers into practice, we strengthen the School Family. As we strengthen the School Family, we strengthen the effectiveness of our seven skills and powers. This allows us to be the change we wish to see in the world, and allows us to create a healthy school culture for us to work in and for children to learn in. The School Family:

1. Optimizes brain development
2. Embeds resilience into the school culture
3. Helps heal the cycle leading from loss to violence
4. Fosters conflict resolution skills
5. Promotes the effectiveness of consequences
6. Models and teaches our highest values
7. Models shared power and democracy
8. Reignites the inherent joy of teaching and learning

> *Safety and connection with significant adults are the prerequisites for creating a sense of belonging.*

1. Optimizes Brain Development

Optimal brain development encourages the development of self-regulation and executive skills, fostering academic success. One of the core findings in brain research is that interpersonal relationships shape the function and structure of the brain. In my workshops I often say, "Connections on the outside create connections on the inside. These connections literally wire our brains for willingness and impulse control." It is critical for us to understand that human connections create neural connections that shape how we see life, handle stress and respond to life events. In simplistic terms, our earliest relationships determine whether we are more likely to grab a cookie or stick to the goal of losing weight.

Our earliest relationships with parents and caregivers shape five critical functions. The School Family culture of compassion helps optimize the development of all five:

Early relationships shape how we handle stress and how much stress is too much before we become overwhelmed or paralyzed. How is your internal state, your clacker? Overall, do you lose control or give up easily? How is your clacker right now? If needed, take three slow deep breaths before you keep reading.

Early relationships shape the way we perceive our world. Do you believe the world to be safe? Is your cup half full or half empty? How easy or hard is it for you to trust and rely on others?

Early relationships shape how we organize our memories into mental models to anticipate the future. The brain can be called an "anticipation machine." It constantly scans the environment, trying to predict what will happen next. Our early family relationships bias us toward such things as fright or delight, trust or distrust, and optimism or pessimism. Check your mental models: How much time do you think about what other people might say or feel (anticipating their reactions) in the hope of controlling the situation instead of being present? Do you carry around any of the following mental models?

- If you want something done, do it yourself
- The only person you can really trust is yourself
- Asking for help is a sign of weakness
- Big boys don't cry
- An obedient child is a sign of a good parent/teacher

Early relationships shape our capacity for interpersonal communication. Some people are able to pick up on the nonverbal facial cues of others and some miss this important part of communication. Some people seem to understand the impact of their actions on others and some seem ignorant of it. The ability to read others' emotions, see the world through others' eyes and empathize is developed through our early relationships. We can only see others as we were seen, soothe as we were soothed, and provide safety as it was offered, unless we consciously learn and practice a new way.

Early relationships shape our ability to focus and sustain attention. Emotional regulation and the development of attention are two sides to the same coin. We attend to what is important and our emotions determine what is important. If our emotions are regulated and stable, then so is our ability to aim and sustain our attention. If our emotions are all over the place, so is our attention.

Research is clear that relationships create the brain circuits responsible for the formation of meaning, the regulation of bodily states, the modulation of emotion, the ability to focus and sustain attention, the organization of memories, and the capacity for interpersonal communication. With traditional discipline models, we have been sacrificing all this in the name of trying to control children through external forces. We put their names on the board and offer rewards from the treasure box without ever addressing the core issues behind the behavior. It is time to reorganize our classrooms and schools in ways that reflect the most up-to-date brain information so our children have the best possible chance for lifelong success. It is time to address the whole child in whole classrooms taught by whole teachers in whole schools that are led by whole administrators. Instead of metaphorically saying, "If you leave your social and emotional self out of the classroom, I will give you a reward," or "If you bring your social and emotional self into the classroom, I will give you a consequence," the School Family says, "Bring your whole self into school, and we will all grow and learn together."

2. Embeds Resilience into the School Culture

Resilience is a person's ability to adapt to the moment, especially stressful moments. Among other things, a person with resilience can rise to a challenge, face adversity and cope with difficult situations in healthy ways. The development of resilience is closely linked to a quality John Seita and Larry Brendtro (2002) called "Family privilege," which encompasses the complex abilities listed above in the "Optimizes Brain Development" section. If a child's family provides the above abilities, then a School Family has the potential to strengthen them. If a child has been traumatized, lacked healthy early relationships or is otherwise missing family privilege, then a School Family has the potential to provide protective factors that rebuild these abilities and shift non-secure mental models toward security. In short, the School Family builds resilience in children who have experienced stress and trauma. It is the only model I know that can possibly offer every child an even start on the road to success by embedding protective factors such as resilience into the culture of the school.

Because of my family privilege, I felt safe enough, loved enough and capable enough to explore every corner of my physical and mental world. Family privilege afforded me the luxury of imagining I was Davy Crockett, a rock star, a princess and an inventor. I could make up any story, direct the play and change roles at any time. I didn't have to parent my parents or myself. I didn't have to worry about where my next meal would come from, whether my mother was coming back or who was going to keep me safe. I didn't have to stay on alert for violence or chaos. I was free to create with my toys, expand my mind with possibilities and imagine dragons in the clouds while I lie in the grass. Over time and with lots of practice, the benefits of family privilege enabled me to do things like set and achieve goals despite many obstacles, and reflect on my inner world in order to take responsibility for my behavior. Family privilege provided my brain, body and spirit the potential to develop in optimal ways. Don't get me wrong, my family has its share of dysfunction, but experiencing a loving bond, a felt sense of safety, a sense of belonging and optimal learning experiences gave me a secure enough base to afford me the opportunity to work hard to create the life of my imagination.

Many of us can't imagine what life would be like without family privilege. We assume that, like the air we breathe, it is available to almost everyone. Sadly, it is not. An increasing number of children are growing up in a world without stability, where fear and chaos replace the felt sense of safety provided by a connected family bond. A lack of family privilege robs children of explorative learning opportunities and derails the attachment bond, forming what Seita and Brendtro have shown to be a deficient or warped life blueprint.

In my *Creating the School Family* book, I tell the story of Mark, a second grade boy who tried to hang himself with his belt because recess was canceled. Mark and I spoke at length that day. He was homeless and staying at the local shelter. He revealed there were no safe areas to play at the shelter; even the children's playroom was rife with theft and beatings. School recess was the one place in the world where he felt safe enough to play and be a kid. I finally began to understand how Mark might feel recess was literally worth dying over.

There was no family privilege for Mark, no cloud dragons for him to explore in the sky, just real dragons that threatened his very existence, altered his brain to organize around fear instead of love, and derailed any blueprint for a successful life. The number of children lacking family privilege like Mark is growing in all demographics. Stressed adults lack the ability to form the bonds necessary for their children to develop optimally. Hurried lifestyles, poverty, poor quality child care, nannies, work pressures, divorce, addiction, disability, poverty, criminality and depression are interfering with parenting, putting family privilege at risk in all sectors of society. The combination of children on the edge and negative school climates is explosive, as we have seen from increasingly terrifying school violence headlines. Children who do not experience family privilege from some source lack the resilience to deal with basic stressors and are almost guaranteed to commit violence against themselves (self-sabotage, cutting, anorexia, suicide) or violence against others.

Schools can become an oasis for resilience or a battleground of resistance for children who are lacking family privilege. We know that the optimal learning state consists of high challenge and low stress. As we continue to raise our educational standards, we do create high challenge. However, when we put already stressed children and teachers in an environment of high challenge, we create additional stress, dysfunction, and a propensity for violence and academic failure. Watch how a teacher created a haven for one of her families, connecting the home family to the School Family.

3. Helps Heal the Cycle that Leads From Loss to Violence

Children are entering school more disorganized in their behavior than in years past. Greater numbers of children are experiencing loss from factors including divorce, relocation, absent parents due to death, addiction, incarceration or mental illness, lack of play, and exposure to media with increasingly mature themes. The relationship between loss and violence in schools is clear. If an attuned, caring adult does not appropriately respond to loss, that loss quickly morphs into anger. If anger is not appropriately acknowledged and met with self-regulation strategies, it turns into rage. Rage creates an insatiable desire for revenge. Revenge creates more loss and the cycle continues.

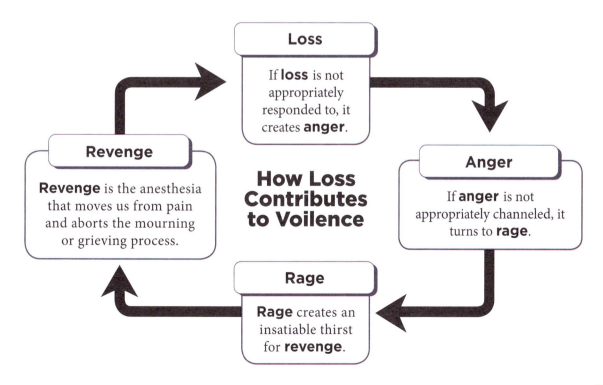

Watch how one school broke the cycle above.

Understanding this cycle empowers us to intervene and heal children trapped within it. The School Family culture is intentionally designed to meet the needs of those experiencing loss. It acknowledges loss through the classroom structures of Wishing Well and the We Care Center. It manages anger with The Safe Place Self-Regulation Center. It addresses rage through the Rage Program described in Chapter 8. Teachers are not trained counselors or psychologists; however, we can and must create a healthy culture that reduces the children's stressors in order to reach our academic goals.

4. Fosters Conflict Resolution Skills

In the School Family, the motivation to behave comes from the internal pleasure children experience when they help others, feel cared for and experience the confidence of being indispensable to the group. It also comes from the natural internal angst children feel when they treat others poorly or do not contribute their part to the whole.

If a child in a traditional (reward and punishment) classroom shoves another student in line, he might lose points, miss recess or lose a trip to the treasure box. In a School Family the child would experience the impact of his behavior on others. The teacher would coach the victim to say, "I don't like it when you shove me. Please walk slowly behind me in line." If the child has a relationship with the student he shoved, he may feel a twinge of angst for his hurtful actions. This hint of internal discomfort generates a willingness to do things differently and learn new skills. The teacher might coach the shover with, "You wanted him to walk faster. You may not shove. When you want him to go faster, say, *Please move up closer to the others. We're too far back in line.*"

We know from our own life experience that the motivation for our behavior comes from the nature of our relationships. When you and your partner are watching TV and everything's awesome, you get up to go to the bathroom, your partner says, "Can you bring me a snack," and you grab the chips without thinking twice. When your relationship is rocky, you think (or say), "You've got legs, get it yourself!" The pattern of helpful behavior when connected and unhelpful behavior when disconnected holds true for children. When a child feels connected to the School Family, conflicts become opportunities to learn missing social and emotional skills. Connected cultures become nearly bully-proof because the most potent single cause of bullying is a negative peer group climate (Brendtro, Ness, & Mitchell, 2001).

Read the following scenarios and see if you can feel the difference between conflict resolution in a competitive school culture versus a compassionate school culture.

Classroom A: Ms. Maynard

Ms. Maynard attended a two-day Conscious Discipline workshop. She found the information interesting but what really stood out was the topic of children solving conflicts with each other. This got her attention! After all, the constant tattling and bickering among some students was disrupting the learning of all the others. The skill was to address the victim of a situation first and coach that student to use her BIG Voice to teach others how she wanted to be treated. The basic phrase to say was, " I don't like it when you _____. Please _____." So a child who is pushed would face the aggressor and say, "I don't like it when you push. Please walk around me."

Ms. Maynard thought she would give it a try since her card-turning system wasn't working with a few children. She didn't have time for the School Family stuff and truly just wanted the conflicts to go away. On Monday, she gave it a go. Geoffrey hit Devon. She instructed Devon to say, "Geoffrey, I don't like it when you hit me. Please tap me on my arm when you want my attention." Devon rolled his eyes at Ms. Maynard and sarcastically gave it a try. Geoffrey barked rapidly in response, saying, "Yea, right! I would love to tap your arm! Tap, tap, tap," and punched Devon three times. Ms. Maynard turned both their cards to red and sent Geoffrey to the office with a referral as she proclaimed, "This Conscious Discipline stuff doesn't work! What a joke!"

Ms. Maynard was trying to plant conflict resolution in a classroom soil that was not conducive to growing willingness. Even the "right" words will often be ineffective unless we embed them in a compassionate School Family.

Classroom B: Mr. Kaufman

Mr. Kaufman attended the same two-day conference. After absorbing the whole of Conscious Discipline, he knew he needed to change the culture in his room. He was tired of children constantly vying for his attention both negative and positive. He hoped the children would be more respectful and caring about each other instead of forming and reforming cliques that excluded and distracted many of his students. It made sense that some of these issues would dwindle if he could create a sense of belonging, contribution and caring.

He spent about six weeks implementing a School Family. He started calling his classroom a School Family and the class created a class pledge that represented their values. Each child started doing a class job that they rotated every week. When children were in distress, they learned to be S.T.A.R., use the Safe Place and wish each other well instead of laughing. Most importantly, he changed how he saw conflict and was responding to it differently as a result of changing his job description to that of the Safekeeper. Mr. Kaufman slowly started noticing children instead of judging them and began doing connecting activities like greeting each child daily.

The change in the climate of the room was palpable. He could feel it, the children could feel it, and guests entering the room could feel it. Coworkers started commenting on his room. Encouraged by the growing sense of connection, he began teaching the children how to assertively use their BIG Voices. On this particular day, Paul pushed Kareem out of line. Mr. Kaufman approached Kareem, the victim in this event, and asked him to speak to Paul. Kareem took a deep breath and said. "I don't like it when you push me out of line. Please stay in your spot with your hands in your pockets." Paul hung his head at first, then looked up slowly and said, "Okay, I can do that. Sorry, buddy," and hopped back into his place in line. Mr. Kaufman thought, "This Conscious Discipline stuff is great!"

In Ms. Maynard's classroom, Geoffrey perceived Devon's BIG Voice as a threat. In Mr. Kaufman's class, Paul perceived Kareem's BIG Voice as a respectful limit. The class climate created this difference in perception. Climate impacts everything from academic achievement to social-emotional learning, from discipline effectiveness to absenteeism. When we coach children to resolve conflicts respectfully, we enhance and activate the higher centers of their brains. Their focus is placed internally on problem solving and learning new skills. However, this coaching will not succeed unless it is embedded in a culture of caring. A compassionate climate is more than a feel-good notion; it is an academic imperative that is at the heart of Conscious Discipline. Without first developing the safety and connection of a School Family, the child coached to say, "I don't like it when you shove me," might say it reluctantly or with attitude. The child who pushed might simply respond, "So, get a life." Without the safety, trust and connection of a School Family, conflict resolution and problem solving are impossible.

5. Promotes the Effectiveness of Consequences

The true consequence of an action is how we feel about the outcome. We often think the consequence of not doing schoolwork is failing. The real consequence is not about passing or failing, it is about how the child feels about passing or failing. Suspending a child who does not care produces no corrective results. Every teacher knows this. We find ourselves feeling powerless with both rewards and consequences when the child's response is a consistent, "I don't care." To care, children must feel they have been cared for. They must have enough family privilege for the caring system in their brains to develop.

When the caring system in the brain shuts down, it takes with it the prefrontal lobes and the ability to reflectively see the impact of an action on others. When children reach the state of "I don't care," they are immune to both the consequences of their choices and the rewards we use in attempts to motivate, bribe, teach or control them. The children we call "difficult" enter school with very little family privilege and the caring system offline. They always have their cards on red, lose recess and miss field trips. There is no "carrot on a stick" that will work with them. For these children who lack family privilege, the School Family is like a defibrillator, providing a shock that restores their heartbeats and jumpstarts their caring systems so they can learn from their mistakes instead of blame others and repeat unhealthy behavior patterns.

When we connect children via the School Family, we build their internal compasses by creating an environment that is safe enough and connected enough for them to be willing to learn from their missteps. The way a child feels about the result of his actions (the consequence) becomes the driving force for learning a better way to handle the situation next time. By developing a unified sense of community rather than a segregated system of "haves" and "have-nots," we help bring all children into the fold and use natural consequences rather than artificial ones as feedback for lasting behavioral change.

6. Models and Teaches Our Highest Values

The factory mindset of education, based on standardization and quality control, carries the unspoken belief that some child widgets will not and cannot succeed. When the notion of public school originally started, the beliefs of the time were that only certain children were educable. These children were wealthy white boys. As education began to include others it became two tiered, with some seen as capable of going to college and others, geared toward vocational school. Public schools began as an "us and them" industry and continues to grow in this basic categorization. We cannot persist in a system that values the education of some over others; we must adopt a new mindset that supports our modern values.

Conscious Discipline is based on unity. It is about valuing all children equally and valuing their individual strengths as important contributors to the School Family. It is about creating a healthy "we" from which each diversely gifted "I" can flourish and offer his gifts back to the community. The School Family is created on the foundational concept that all living things are interdependent. Every skill, power, structure and ritual supports the notion that we are all in this together. These two stories illustrate this point:

> I was visiting a self-contained classroom of children with exceptional needs in Miami, Florida. As with all School Families, each child had a meaningful job that contributes to the success of the classroom. One little girl with muscular dystrophy could barely support her body and had great difficulty speaking. At circle time, the children were doing stop and go movement activities. This little girl, harnessed tightly in her supportive chair, had a red stop sign in her lap. When the music stopped, she hoisted the sign high into the air, as if deadlifting 500 pounds, took a deep breath and eeked out the word "Stop." All the children came to a stop. Later, it took her about fifteen minutes to share with me how holding up the stop sign helped her School Family learn to control themselves so they could be helpful instead of hurtful to others. She understood how valuable she was to her School Family.

Being of service to others stimulates our executive state, fostering the development of our ability to set goals and keep them, get along with others, and solve problems. Just before entering this little girl's classroom, I was getting down on myself and feeling discouraged, thinking maybe Conscious Discipline was too hard for people to grasp and that my teaching of it was lacking. I watched this little girl lift that sign to help others and I was reminded we are all here for a reason. We all make a difference, including me.

> Romone took home many notes about his behavior at school. His mother had gotten used to being called into the school due to his behavior and would punish him at home in hopes it would help. In second grade, Romone had a teacher who used Conscious Discipline, and he joined the Shining Star School Family. His first note home that year read, "Romone was angry with his friend Darnell today and instead of pushing him, he took a deep breath (we call this being a S.T.A.R.), managed his anger, and asked Darnell to move. We celebrated him at school and were hoping you could join us in sharing Romone's success. Tomorrow he will be teaching others how to be a S.T.A.R. We hope you get a chance to drop in on our class sometime."

We can only live our highest values such as helpfulness, integrity, honesty and respect when our brain is in an integrated, executive state. In the School Family, members are offered the opportunity to live our highest values through:

- Being of service to one another
- Focusing their attention on daily acts of kindness
- Learning to resolve interpersonal conflicts effectively
- Experiencing being indispensable through daily jobs
- Authentically connecting face-to-face with friends
- Offering empathy on a daily basis
- Integrating music, movement and brain breaks into the daily schedule to foster optimal learning states

7. Models Shared Power and Democracy

We can create school cultures where children are motivated by being goal-oriented or stimulus-driven. A goal-oriented School Family moves control from external forces (reward and punishment) to internal resources relying on self-regulation and problem solving. Democracy means to self-govern. Without self-regulation, democracy cannot fulfill its potential. Autocracy is a government of a single person with unlimited power over others. It relies on outside forces to govern individual choices. The rights of an individual are delegated by those in power and earned for some but not others. Examples of autocratic countries include North Korea and China. Attending autocratic school systems to prepare youngsters to live in a democratic country encourages a population that has freedoms without the skills necessary to manage those freedoms responsibly. The School Family relies on self-governance and self-regulation, insuring the best opportunity for creating a safe culture where freedoms are infused with responsibility. The following pyramid shows how the School Family is governed.

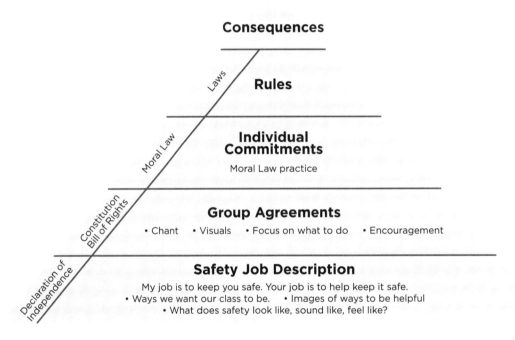

The foundational governing job description in the School Family is one of safety. You will hear the phrase "My job is to keep it safe; your job is to help keep it safe" repeatedly in this book. For years, safety has focused on the physical environment; now we turn our attention to social and emotional safety. This requires dialogue with children and with adults. What does safety look like, feel like and sound like? Growing up in my house, safety meant yelling without hitting. Growing up down the street meant problem-solving instead of yelling. Many children (and adults) grow up without any conscious notion of what safety looks like, sounds like or feels like. A felt sense and collective understanding of safety is your starting point.

The next step is to condense your understanding of safety into a set of School Family agreements. These agreements are guiding principles each member (including the teacher) commits to upholding with the rest of the School Family. These group agreements unify and encourage responsibility. Next on the pyramid is an individual daily commitment. Discovering what it feels like to make a commitment and be successful in keeping it is an essential prerequisite to following rules. It also allows us to practice living our own morals.

> *Agreements are promises we make to our School Family; commitments are promises we make to ourselves. Common School Family Agreements include keeping it safe, being helpful, doing your personal best, practicing active listening and breathing.*

The next tier of the pyramid is occupied by rules. Rules do not teach expected behavior; rules hold us accountable to that behavior. They are made when they are needed and are designed to be enforced. In the last few years, the average number of new laws (rules) created in the United States was approximately 40,000. Two decades ago, most of these laws were not perceived as necessary. In schools, we often start near the top of the pyramid and post our rules the first day of school. This approach requires working from the top down instead of the bottom up, creating a culture of bias and confusion as we seek to apply and enforce rules that have no foundation. Instead, the School Family begins with a firm foundation of safety, progresses through group agreements and individual commitments, and then creates rules as they are necessary. The very top of the pyramid is reserved for consequences.

Co-creating classroom and school governance in this fashion shifts cultures from a power-over system to one of shared power and responsibility, re-enacting our own journey toward democracy. When power is shared within a connected community, all stakeholders have both greater autonomy and greater responsibility. Tying free will to responsibility is essential for collaborative working environments and successful democracy. Freedom without responsibility creates chaos. Freedom with responsibility creates abundance.

> *Rules do not teach expected behavior; rules hold us accountable to that behavior.*

8. Reignites the Inherent Joy of Teaching and Learning

Optimal learning requires high challenge combined with low stress. We have successfully been increasing the challenge through high stakes testing, but we have not simultaneously lowered the stress. The School Family is scientifically and practically designed to reduce stress and create optimal learning states. One of the founding principles of Conscious Discipline is: "What you offer to others, you strengthen in yourself." **Getting** children to behave all day exhausts us with effort. **Giving** children the skills to behave feels rewarding.

Every classroom and every school has a culture that is integrally linked to the school's motivation system. A reward and punishment motivational system relies on externally applied, tangible consequences. The external consequence sets the behavioral expectation instead of teaching the responsibility inherent in shared power. Research conducted by Hoffman, Hutchinson and Reiss concludes that as a teacher's reliance on rewards and punishment increases, so does negativity in the school climate. Shifting to the safety, connection and problem-solving approach of Conscious Discipline reduces discipline referrals while simultaneously improving the school climate (Hoffman, Hutchinson & Reiss, 2009).

With Conscious Discipline, motivation comes from the connections we build with each other, the passion for the school mission and constant ongoing feedback called "noticing." Noticing is the attunement and feedback mechanism Conscious Discipline utilizes to encourage internal motivation. Noticing is a way of describing that encourages eye contact and promotes both conscious awareness and connection. Volumes of research show that effective feedback is accurate, specific, timely, nonjudgmental and offered in the context of goals. Noticing meets all of these criteria. It is an optimal form of feedback that serves as brain food while also nourishing relationships and motivational systems. Moving from judgment ("Good job!") to noticing ("You walked in, greeted your friends and began doing your School Family job just like this.") is foundational to creating safe classrooms and schools. Because of its importance, noticing will be covered in its many forms and applications throughout this book.

D.J. Batiste is a former gang leader who was repeatedly expelled from school (starting in Head Start) and caught in the juvenile justice system. He credits a Conscious Discipline teacher who noticed him as the turning point in his life. Watch a portal video where he articulates the motivational power of noticing as the center of his personal transformation from gang leader to graduate.

Once we move from factory to family, from control to connection and from judgment to noticing, our bodies relax, our fears dissolve, our joy for teaching rushes back and our love for our students returns. One teacher who came to the Conscious Discipline Summer Institute put it this way, "I was going to leave teaching. I had lost heart. I was not making a difference. Every day was a struggle. But now, I know I make a difference. I see the children caring for each other, contributing to everyone's success. I leave work inspired. I'm changing their lives and they're changing mine for the better, too. I'm going to teach forever!"

Welcome parents to the School Family

Creating Your School Family

We've already talked about the reciprocal nature of the powers and skills of Conscious Discipline and the School Family. The powers help us make the necessary perceptual shifts, the skills help us to upgrade to our skill set and the School Family creates a safe, connected culture where problem solving is possible. The more tangible aspects of the School Family are seen in the routines, rituals and classroom structures we explore at the end of each chapter. The structures, routines and rituals of the School Family, coupled with the powers and skills, will guide your journey. They also provide the opportunity to use the social-emotional components of your classroom to add depth in meeting common core standards. Discover ways to integrate Conscious Discipline and the common core on your portal.

> *Caring relationships create an optimal environment for learning, alter our physiological state and prime the brain for plasticity.*

Routines

Routines are how we teach expected behavior in classrooms and schools. If we were physically building a school, we would start with blueprints. Routines are like blueprints; they contribute to safety by telling others what is expected where and when, providing consistency and predictability. One basic routine is the hand-washing routine: 1. Squirt soap, 2. Rub hands, 3. Rinse with water, 4. Dry with a paper towel, 5. Wipe up any splashes, 6. Throw away paper towel. We visually post routines throughout the school and classroom. The hand-washing routine would be posted at the sink. The lining-up routine would be posted at the door. We also create class books about routines for children to read and to check out library-style to read with their parents. Children who have a difficult time with certain routines require individual routine books or social stories to help them through the day.

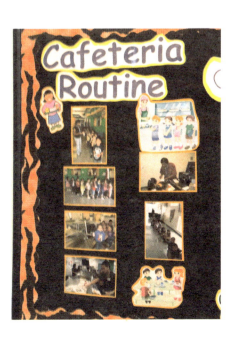

How many pictures in your classroom or school show children what to do in various situations? The more pictures we display to clearly demonstrate our expectations, the more compliance we will experience from children. Most chapters in this book will ask you to add to your existing routines and put them all in pictures.

Rituals

Rituals are an expression of unity. Just as they hold a family together, they also hold the School Family together. They are sacred spaces designated for togetherness and connection. Holiday rituals like gathering on Thanksgiving bond the family in gratitude. Birthday rituals like preparing a favorite meal honor and connect us. Athletic teams build rituals and research shows the teams who connect the best win the most. Street gangs also create rituals as they bond. Connecting rituals are essential because connection fosters willingness.

Rituals are sometimes hard for teachers who feel pushed for time in the constant race toward cognitive gains. It may be hard to release the "teaching" and begin allowing moments where the number one goal is connection, not learning, per se. The good news is that these rituals require very little time and often ask children to apply their academic learning in meaningful ways. They also soothe the lower centers of the brain, wiring children's brains for impulse control and willingness, and creating an optimal state for learning.

My mom used to say, "Night, night. Don't let the bed bugs bite." She always said it standing by my bedroom door just before she clicked the lights off. Fifty years later, she was wandering around one night as often happens with people with Alzheimer's. She wandered into my room. I sat straight up in bed, startled awake and thinking she was probably lost in an agitated state. She flicked on the lights and said, "Night, night, don't let the bed bugs bite." In the midst of 15 years living with this horrible disease, both she and I found each other for one more moment through this loving nightly ritual.

All cultures create rituals. There are many different ritual styles, some of which are no more reassuring than the, "Have a nice day," offered by a bored clerk at the mini mart. To be successful, your School Family rituals must be authentic expressions of togetherness and joy. The following are different ritual styles seen in homes, schools and classrooms. What types of rituals are promoted in your school? In your classroom? In your home? Take some time to really reflect.

Minimized Rituals: These rituals are not emphasized. Academic achievement is the goal. Little attention is placed on the whole child or social-emotional intelligence. Holidays and birthdays might be celebrated if time permits, work is complete and children have earned the break by demonstrating good behavior.

Interrupted Rituals: Interrupted rituals usually indicate some sort of crisis has taken precedence. This crisis could be the changing of teachers, state-mandated program changes, natural disasters, bomb threats, and human tragedy.

Rigid Rituals: The teacher creates and conducts rigid rituals the same way each year. Roles are highly prescribed. The emphasis is on doing the ritual correctly instead of connecting.

Imbalanced Rituals: Imbalanced rituals occur in classrooms that conduct only a small range of rituals. Instead of having good morning rituals, absent child rituals and the like, they only celebrate birthdays and holidays. These rituals usually represent one ethnic heritage.

Obligatory Rituals: Obligatory rituals exist because they "should." They lack true connection. The class sings the good morning song as a way to start the day, not as a way to connect. Rituals feel more like routines that mark the passage of time than meaningful events. A tired flight attendant robotically saying goodbye to 400 people exiting a 747 is an obligatory ritual.

Authentic Rituals: Authentic rituals are true rituals jointly created by the teacher and students. Authentic rituals are flexible. They capture and reflect the current needs of the group. They offer a sense of continuity and connectedness through time, bringing cohesiveness to the School Family. They emerge and dissolve with spontaneity and delight. They are a sacred space for putting the classroom values into action. They help establish relationships, mark life changes, heal wounds from hurtful experiences, voice the beliefs of the School Family and celebrate life itself. In the School Family, the goal is to create authentic rituals.

What Rituals Are Needed in Your School Family?

The beauty of using a healthy family as a model for creating your class culture is we all have some past references from which to draw. We can simply ask ourselves, "What would a healthy family do?" If a family member is sick, a common ritual is to send him a card that wishes him well. There are generally some structures to support the ritual (art supplies, card store, etc.) and it's someone's job to organize the task on behalf of the family. The same will be true in your School Family. Most class or school rituals will have tangible structures to support them and jobs distributed among the students to follow through with the task.

Not only are your School Family rituals the glue that builds connectedness, they also provide children practice in the social skills needed for life. Rituals occur day after day, in the same location, at the same time and for the same reason (connection). Patterning them in this way contributes to establish social trust. Without trust, children will not relax their defenses enough to be guided. Without guidance, there is no discipline, just various forms of coercion.

We will discuss several rituals within the chapters of this book, especially in the Encouragement chapter. If you work with infants and toddlers, you will conduct many of the rituals for the parents. For example if an infant is sick, the Wish Well card comes from the staff to the family, left in the child's cubby to be discovered by a tired parent upon the infant's return.

Here is a top ten list of suggested rituals for your classroom. As you implement Conscious Discipline in your School Family, you will find opportunities to create many more. *Creating the School Family* and Shubert's School provide additional detail for rituals.

Top Ten Suggested Rituals

1. Greeting / Goodbye Rituals
2. Safekeeper Ritual
3. School Family Agreement
4. Connecting Rituals
5. Kindness Rituals
6. Absent Child Ritual
7. Welcoming / Leaving Rituals
8. Wish Well Ritual
9. Testing Rituals
10. End-of-Year Rituals

Andrew and Ramy like to greet each other with the "Snake."

Greeting / Goodbye Rituals: The goal of these rituals is real connection, not just the process of saying, "Hello." In connection, you are hoping to achieve eye contact, touch and presence in a playful situation. This ritual affords you the opportunity to assess a child's inner state (survival, emotional, or executive) and upshift if necessary.

Select a location you will stand every morning to greet the children. You could have greeting choices from which they can choose. These choices can change and are limited only by your imagination. You can make up snake, skunk, superhero or seasonal greetings. Older children can create addition, subtraction and fraction greetings. The goal is to connect, touch, make eye contact and have fun.

At the close of the day, send each child off with a goodbye. One kindergarten teacher says to each child, "Tomorrow I will see your smile, crocodile," and then gives a hug. Another has a different saying for each week of school.

Greeting Choices

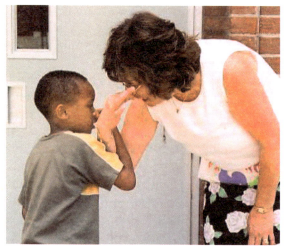
Skunk Greeting

Safekeeper Ritual: This ritual symbolically represents the focus on safety in the School Family. Children and adults are asked to consciously place a picture or other representation of themselves in a container to show their willingness and commitment to help keep the School Family safe. This is explained further in Composure, Chapter 4.

School Family Agreement Song or Chant: Each classroom can create a School Family song or chant. The song or chant represents the agreements for the classroom. Below is an agreement chant from a fourth-grade classroom.

"We are intelligent thinkers who persevere through difficult obstacles. We show compassion to people around us. We practice self-discipline in our work and actions. Together we can help each other make the world a better place."

Connecting Rituals: At specified times during the day, take time for connecting rituals. Connecting rituals are activities that ask children to consciously touch one another and make eye contact. They are often done with music and movement. The CDs *Kindness Counts*, *Brain Boogie Boosters* and *It Starts in the Heart* contain many songs that ask children to connect. In addition, my *I Love You Rituals* book and CDs provide connecting activities for children 0 to 8 years of age.

The Brain Smart Start routine in the morning and the closing routine at the end of the day provide two excellent times for connecting rituals. You can send rituals home for homework and use them in your reading buddy program. For infants and toddlers, connecting rituals are easily worked into diapering and toileting times. Each time a child goes to the diapering table or restroom, conduct a 1-minute I Love You Ritual. Integrating connecting rituals into your daily routine helps every child receive the brain-building connections required for optimal development and increased cooperation.

Kindness Rituals: There are many ways to document and celebrate acts of kindness. A Kindness Tree encourages children to place a heart on the tree to signify a kind act. A Kindness Recorder allows older students to write kindnesses in a notebook. We will explore kindness rituals further in the Encouragement, Chapter 6.

Absent Child Ritual: The School Family can brainstorm things to do for School Family members who return after an absence. Many classrooms use a Wish Well Board. Absent students are placed in the heart and wished well upon their return. The message to send is, "We noticed you were gone, we missed you and we are glad that you are back." Some classes make cards or poems. Others write songs. The following is an example of a song that could be used. It is sung to the tune of "Frere Jacques."

"We missed _____." (insert child's name)
"We missed _____." (insert child's name)
"Yes we did! Yes we did!"
"Glad that _____ is back." (insert child's name)
"Glad that _____ is back." (insert child's name)
"Now we're all together."
"Now we're all together."

Welcoming / Leaving Child Rituals: I frequently say teachers are always pregnant, they just don't know when the next child is coming. With the increased mobility of our society, children come and go frequently. Mark these transitions with rituals. A second grade classroom made T-shirts at the beginning of the year. Children decorated the shirts with their handprints, making extras in case a new child enrolls mid-year. When a new child arrives, they present him with a shirt during a welcoming ceremony. A first-grade class decided they would make a goodbye video for each child leaving the class. Similar to the process done at weddings, each child recorded a message on camera. The class then gave the recording to the leaving child.

Kindness Tree

Wish Well Board

Wish Well Ritual: The Wish Well Ritual asks children to wish others well when they are absent or struggling with a life issue from academics to death of a grandparent. We will explore wishing well further in the Composure, Chapter 4.

Testing Rituals: With increased emphasis on testing, testing rituals are needed to help ease students' anxieties and help them achieve an optimal brain state during tests. In one school, kindergartners wrote encouraging notes to older students and held a parade two days before the test. Enlisting music, movement, connection and encouragement are helpful components for rituals conducted just before test-taking time. View videos of several such rituals on your web portal.

End-of-Year Rituals: Ending the school year can be difficult and discipline issues can increase. Rituals help soothe this transition. One teacher had children create an "I will remember" book about the year. Another teacher asked children to write how each person in the class helped the School Family. The teacher collected and bound the writings into a personalized book for each child to take home.

Classroom Structures

The ultimate goal of the School Family is to provide a learning environment where all members (adults and children) spend more time in an executive state than not. We want children metaphorically asking, "What can I learn?" all day long instead of "Am I safe?" or "Am I loved?" Visual routines contribute to answering the question "Am I safe?" Rituals contribute to answering the question "Am I loved?" The classroom structures in Conscious Discipline contribute to answering the question, "What can I learn about getting along with others?"

Staying in an executive state so we can focus on what we want, see the best in others, offer empathy, solve conflict, maintain composure and utilize all our wonderful executive skills is a big challenge. The purpose of the classroom structures is to practice our social and emotional skills in the context of meaningful life events. Structures scaffold executive skill development, meet the self-regulatory and social emotional needs of class members, and provide practice living the values we are teaching. On a physical level, they also provide the supporting materials for routines, rituals and skills practice.

We know how to create effective structures. In designing our classrooms for learning, we seek to create spaces and provide materials that will enable students to be academically successful. If we are going to study insects, we plan for success with books, visuals, activities and materials. We must plan the same way for the social and emotional domains of learning. The difference is that social and emotional learning happens all year long and cannot always be preplanned. We cannot plan for a child's extended illness, the death of a family member, a divorce or a child's elation about learning to ride a bike. We must design our classroom environment so it can handle events when they arise as a natural part of life.

You might think, "That's not my job." Well, if you believe your job is teaching science, maybe not. But if you believe your job is to teach children, this definitely is your job. Classrooms harbor a constant flux of emotions that generate different internal states. Some states can facilitate learning. Others, such as anxiety and fear, can shut down the higher centers of the brain, making the achievement of academic goals impossible. If we are going to maximize learning, we must create environments where children can process their emotions and transform their inner states for optimal learning. They must be enveloped by a responsive school culture that acknowledges their inner lives as well as their external behaviors and accomplishments.

Vicky Hepler has been implementing Conscious Discipline brilliantly for more than a decade. In her 33rd year of teaching, Elijah joined her classroom midyear. Elijah was the angriest child Ms. Hepler had ever worked with. The day before he was to join her class, the principal came to her room to share the news of a new student, stating he had organized three staff members to support her if needed. Mrs. Hepler knew something was up. As her anxiety worked its way into her consciousness, she immediately began to calm herself. She committed to seeing the best in the new child and building a relationship with him. She read the book *Shubert's New Friend* to remind the children how to welcome a new student to the School Family.

The next day, Elijah arrived showing aggressive and explosive behaviors one moment and completely shutting down the next. The children sensed Elijah needed help. They had several classroom structures to help them conduct caring rituals. One child brought Elijah the angry Feeling Buddy to help him learn to calm down. Elijah threw it at her. The We Care Person brought him a teddy bear for comfort. Elijah threw it at him. Another child got the four breathing icons to help him take a deep breath. Elijah kicked them across the room and went on to overturn a table. Mrs. Hepler shared with the children that Elijah's last school did not have the rituals, routines and structures they do, so he did not know how to use the items they were sharing. "Let's all take deep breath and wish him well," she said.

Together, the School Family made it through those difficult first days. Mrs. Hepler says in reflection, "I can't imagine trying to deal with a child like Elijah without the buffer of the School Family." Elijah came to school without family privilege. He walked into a classroom where the power of love was stronger than the hurt he had experienced. The three pictures below show Elijah's transformation during the first 20 days in his School Family.

Day 1

Day 10

Day 20

What do the other children think about Elijah, who is still often disruptive and hurtful as he learns a better way? Jad said, "He's part of our School Family. We can still be friends even when he calls us names. He doesn't know yet. He's learning." Gavin shared, "He's our friend. He's doing much better and we will all help him." Hear more about Elijah's journey on the web portal.

If we are going to ask children to be kind and caring, then they must practice those skills daily. The structures of Conscious Discipline are designed to help us do just that. Elijah, who would have been perceived as a nightmare in most classrooms, gave his School Family the opportunity to practice compassion. His behavior asked everyone to use the structures Mrs. Hepler established in her classroom: The Kindness Tree helped everyone remember to focus on kind, helpful and caring behavior. The We Care Center offered empathy to children in need. The Time Machine and Class Meetings aided in conflict resolution. The Safe Place helped teach self-regulation. The Ways to be Helpful and Visual Routines helped them meet our expectations. Jobs helped them experience the benefits of contribution. The portal includes forms to organize and implement all of these wonderful routines, rituals and structures, plus more!

Ready... Set... Relationship!

The School Family is our key to building successful schools. It lowers the stress of all its members - children, teachers and administrators - allowing high challenge to be challenging instead of terrifying. It strengthens family privilege for those lucky enough to have experienced it, and provides family privilege and resilience for those who haven't. The School Family teaches and models respectful relationships based on helpfulness and contribution. It shows children how conflict can be used as a growth opportunity instead of a justification to inflict more pain.

The School Family models what a healthy family looks like, feels like and sounds like. Regardless of the amount of dysfunction previously experienced, every child (and adult) in the School Family will experience a blueprint for healthy communication and a healthy family structure.

Every teacher knows that disconnected children are dangerous. They disengage from learning and from others, creating daily distractions in the learning environment. As they become increasingly isolated, marginalized and void of connection, the likelihood of violence increases. It becomes possible to imagine these children saying, "I don't know why they're crying; I'm the one going to jail."

There is something in the bond children make with teachers, classmates and their school that changes a child's life trajectory. This "something" is hard to define and even harder to accurately measure. Whether we call it "school connectedness," "school climate," "school culture" or "School Family," it is powerful in the lives of children, second only to the home family in terms of its impact.

> *Positive, face-to-face, enthusiastic connection makes us smarter.*

Why We Create a School Family

School Family
The brain is a social organ

Fosters optimal learning states of high challenge / low stress

Optimizes brain development for academic success

Models and teaches our highest values and links home to school

Embeds resiliency into the school culture

Models shared power and democracy

Fosters conflict resolution, reduces aggression, increases social-emotional learning

Promotes the effectiveness of consequences

Watch the "Power of a School Family" video on your portal to learn how to help children following a trauma.

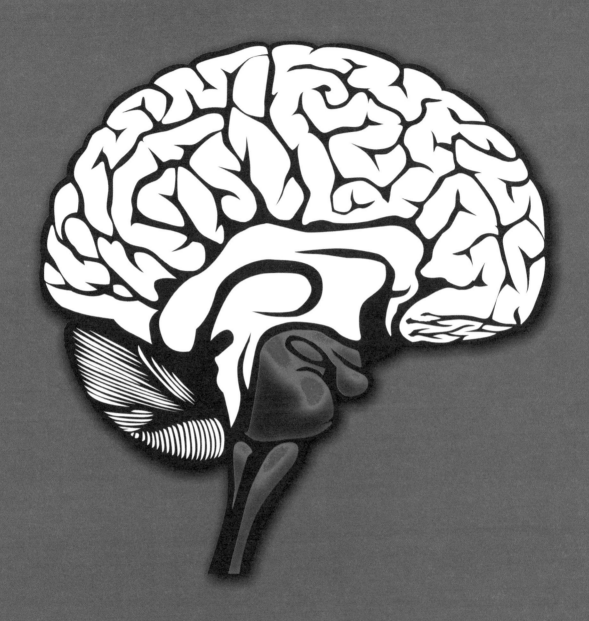

- Section 1 -
SAFETY

Survival State Skills

N = Noticing

A = Assertiveness (Adults)

R = Routines with Pictures

C = Composure

S = Safe Place and Safekeeper

Answering, "Yes!" to the question, "Am I safe?" is essential for optimal brain development, academic success and wellbeing. The Safety section is color-coded red, symbolized by the clacker, and represented by the brain stem and survival state.

The brain stem has two basic gears, safe and unsafe. When we feel safe, the higher centers of the brain can run the show. When we feel unsafe, all our energy is focused on fight or flight. Some children come from homes where the question, "Am I safe," is consistently answered, "Yes." With a little reassurance at school, these children connect, engage and actively participate in learning. Other children come to school from homes where this question is often answered, "No." These children come to school armored up, explosive, oppositional, physically aggressive or shut down. They defend against both connection and learning.

Every child must experience a felt sense of safety for optimal learning. The Skill of Composure allows us to see misbehavior as a call for help, while the Skill of Assertiveness allows us to vigilantly focus on the actions and outcomes we desire. These skills work together to lay the foundation for a felt sense of safety in our schools. In these chapters, we will learn the combined tools needed for safety, represented by the acronym N.A.R.C.S.

Combined Tools for Creating Safety

Noticing: Noticing involves verbally describing a child's nonverbal actions without judgment. It helps achieve the eye contact necessary to foster connection. The shift from judging to noticing is essential. With judgment no one is safe; with noticing all are safe.

Assertiveness: Assertiveness uses the voice of "no doubt" to communicate clearly and focus vigilantly on the behaviors we desire. Focusing on what we want generates encouragement and safety. Focusing on what we don't want generates discouragement and fear.

Routines in pictures: Predictability promotes a felt sense of safety, while inconsistency yields uncertainty. Clearly showing expected behaviors in pictures removes ambiguity, bias and uncertainty from the classroom.

Composure: Composure, the ability to self-regulate, is essential for safety. Without composure, no one feels safe.

Safekeeper and Safe Place: Adopt the new job descriptions, "My job is to keep it safe; your job is to help keep it safe," and establish a daily Safekeeper ritual. Create, teach and model use of the Safe Place Self-Regulation Center as a centerpoint in your classroom.

Chapter 4

COMPOSURE

Being the person you want others to become

Composure is self-regulation in action. It is the prerequisite skill adults need before disciplining children.

The Conscious Discipline journey begins with a focus on personal self-regulation. We have within us the capacity to be stressed out, and we also have the innate capacity to counter that stress. Take a moment to reflect on the power of our perceptions: Our level of upset dictates whether we will react with a preprogrammed retort or whether we will respond wisely. If we see one child hit another and perceive the situation as sheer meanness, we will respond in a punitive or attacking way toward the aggressive child. If we see the same situation and perceive two children who need help with their social skills, we will respond in a calming way that empowers us to teach them the necessary skills. One perception escalates the upset; the other perception fosters new learning. The Skill of Composure is the key that unlocks the Power of Perception. Composure determines our perception, and our perception dictates whether we punish and blame or teach new skills. Watch a video on the Power of Perception on the portal for a more in-depth understanding.

The Power of Perception reminds us composure is a choice we can make, regardless of how crazy the outside world appears to be. The icon for the Power of Perception is a star. In any situation, we can choose to be a S.T.A.R. This star represents <u>S</u>mile, <u>T</u>ake a deep breath <u>A</u>nd <u>R</u>elax.

The Power of Perception

The Power of Perception states that no one can make you angry without your permission. Happiness is a choice, not a fact. Healthy, secure relationships require us to control our upset and take back our power. "Look what you made me do." "Don't make me send you to time out." "You're driving me nuts." Have you said something similar? When we resort to these angry exclamations, we send the message that the child or situation is responsible for our upset. When we place someone or something in charge of our emotions, we put that person in charge of us. If we believe long lines make us crazy, then we have given our power away to a line. If we believe the children are making us scream at them, we have placed the children in charge of us. Placing others in charge of us leaves us feeling powerless and stressed. From a place of powerlessness, our emotional or survival state is activated, and we will blame or attack. It is time to take back our power and reduce the stress in our lives.

I often hear teachers say, "Look how you made her feel" or "How does that make you feel?" Imagine three children sitting in a circle, each pinching the next child in retaliation for getting pinched. The teacher says to child #1, "Look how you made child #2 feel." Then she says to child #2, "Look how you made child #3 feel." Then she says to child #3, "Look how you made child #1 feel." In this moment, she has taught each child that he is in charge of the inner state of the next child. She has put each child in charge of another, and unconsciously taught each child to be irresponsible for his own actions. Most of us received a similar message growing up. I would love to have a dollar for every time my mother said, "Becky, how would it make you feel if your brother did that to you?" or the opposite with my brother "making" me feel a certain way.

There are three major negative impacts of this kind of teaching:

1. If I am in charge of your inner state and you are in charge of mine, then we both can be rampantly irresponsible about managing ourselves. This results in the faulty belief that blame equals change, and we spend our lives looking for blame instead of composing ourselves and seeking solutions.
2. For me to manage my own inner state, I must control you. If you would give in to my tirades or the world would go my way, I could stay composed and happy. This results in the faulty belief that control equals love or helpfulness.
3. Others would be happier if I could just be better. If I could be smarter, more athletic, kinder, thinner or whatever, then the people I care for would magically be happier. This results in the faulty belief that I am not good enough after all my failed attempts at making others change or feel better.

> **Whomever you have placed in charge of your feelings, you have placed in charge of you.**

Whomever you have placed in charge of your feelings, you have placed in charge of you. Wouldn't you prefer to be in control of your own life? To do so, you must be prepared to manage your own upset, not blame it on others. Remember, it is your perception of an experience that creates your feelings about it, not the event itself. Pretend we've been dating a while and I bring you roses. As I arrive at the door, you might marvel at my thoughtfulness. With this perception, you are likely to experience joy at receiving the bouquet. What if I bring flowers again the next night? This time you might think, "What are these for?" With these kinds of thoughts, you would feel suspicious instead of happy. Did the flowers make you happy or suspicious? Did I make you happy or suspicious? Or did your thoughts about me and the flowers create your emotions? Our perception of events generates our emotions, not the events themselves.

Each of us carries an image or mental model of how we think the world should work. We are conscious of some aspects of this image and unconscious of others. We see the world not as it is, but through the lens of these judgments about what should be or what is desirable. This lens alters everything. When our children or our partners fail to meet our conscious or unconscious expectations, we become upset because the world didn't work as we thought it should. This activates an emotional internal state. It's the very same reason a toddler throws a fit when we take away the marker she's using to color the living room walls. To the toddler, coloring is what should happen. To you, drawing on walls is not the way things should be done. You both become upset, overcome by feeling powerless to run the world by your own plan. The upset is not caused by the other person or situation, it is triggered by it. Upset is an inside job.

Whining is a trigger for me. I can stay composed as a child uses profanity and even spits at me; however, a whiny tone can trigger me, especially if I have other stressors in my life. The trigger thoughts or events (in my case whining) activate the perception of threat or the false messages on our emotional state CD-Roms. I can remember my father's outrage and name calling of others he felt were weak in character, whiny or victim-like. His outrage is encoded on my personal CD-Rom. When I hear whining, the false messages flood me as wounds from my childhood become exposed. The good news is exposed wounds can be healed. Every time I am around whiny adults and children, I can heal that old wound by breathing, gaining composure and activating my prefrontal lobes to respond differently than my past preprogrammed CD-Rom dictates. This is my favorite part of Conscious Discipline! It allows me to heal myself by composing myself when triggered, changing the neural pathways in my brain, and ceasing to pass my guilt and triggers down to the next generation. Now that wows me!

> **Commitment:** I acknowledge that when I feel upset, it is because the world is not going my way or I feel threatened. I am willing to spend some time working on owning my upset. No one can make me feel a certain way. I no longer want to give my power away to others, and then blame them for taking it. I want more control in my life.
>
> Signature: _____ Date: _____

Oops!

When my granddaughter Maddie was just starting to talk, she would drop something or fall down and we would say, "Uh-oh," together. We said it so much that I thought she was going to call me "Uh-oh." As time passed, you could hear her say, "Uh-oh," or "Oops, try again," when she made a mistake. How I wish those words were in my head! When I make a mistake, I'm more likely to hear, "What were you thinking, Becky? You know better than this," from the critical voice in my head. This inner speech of mine, recorded on my private CD-Rom, can really get wicked with guilt, anger and disgust.

Negative self-talk like this bubbles up when we are acting in ways that don't match our internal image of what we should be doing or how the world should work. Change requires the willingness to make mistakes. We are less willing to risk new learning or to make behavioral changes when we listen to the inner tyrant who punishes us for our mistakes. Our negative self-talk locks us into the lower centers of our brains where we do what we've always done, promoting guilt instead of fostering change.

Changing our negative self-talk can only happen from an integrated executive state. When we are triggered into an emotional state by our mistakes, we can actively calm our way to a higher brain state and then let go of our need for perfection by saying, "Oops, try again," like Maddie. This frees us up to make meaningful changes in our lives.

Conscious Discipline requires us to make significant changes in our beliefs, perceptions and behaviors. It is impossible to make these changes without making mistakes. I remember when I first started to make my personal changes, I could never seem to remember the language. Often I would resort back to my favorite discipline skill, "Hey, hey, hey!" I was afraid to change. I told myself it was because I didn't want to look foolish in front of others, but truly I was afraid of how I would treat myself during the change process. The "Oops" technique emerged as a powerful ally. When I made an error in judgment, I would say to myself, "Oops, Becky! Try again!" It has taken many years to incorporate Oops into my daily inner speech, but every time I say, "Oops," instead of some form of "Stupid Becky," is a triumph for my composure and emotional wellbeing.

At the weeklong Conscious Discipline Institute that happens every summer in Orlando, Florida, we give out Oops Cards to practice being gentler to ourselves. When a person makes a mistake, someone hands him an Oops Card and says, "Oops, you made a mistake. You are beautiful to me." The goal of this intervention is to break the negative stressful private speech habit and create a new neural network of forgiveness. Find additional video examples of Oops in practice on the web portal.

> **Commitment:** I am willing to forgive perceived errors this month by saying to myself and others, "Oops, you made a mistake. You are beautiful to me." I want the freedom to make lasting changes in my behavior. This can only occur if I am willing to allow mistakes to be a simple Oops instead of a sin.
>
> Signature: _____ Date: _____

Anger, Trigger Thoughts and False Messages

Anger is a difficult emotion. The first step to learning to manage anger is to find out where it comes from and how it works. Stress and a trigger always precede an angry reaction. Stress is the gasoline and trigger thoughts or events are the match that ignites the explosion. A trigger is anything that activates the perception of threat or the false messages on our emotional CD-Roms. Remember, the false messages are wounds from our childhood that need healing. We can heal these wounds by breathing through them and consciously choosing different thoughts.

Blame and attack instinctively follow a feeling of powerlessness.

We began our discussion of the false messages preprogrammed on our CD-Rom with the Brain State Model (Chapter 2). Trigger thoughts and events are an extension of that discussion. Trigger thoughts distort the situation by making it seem bigger than it is, making children's behaviors seem deliberate, or pronouncing others as bad and needing punishment. An essential step in anger management is to learn the trigger thoughts and events most likely to trigger our upset. It is helpful to remember that the perceptual filters on our CD-Roms create the upset, not the event or person. Adapted from Schwartz and Gladding (2011), the process goes like this: An event triggers our CD-Roms. This activation starts a cascade of false messages, urges and desires. This flood of negative self-talk creates uncomfortable emotional sensations that change our body's biochemistry. Because these uncomfortable sensations feel so urgent, we react in automatic, habitual ways that generally aren't helpful. Instead of relying on internal resources, we often rely on external crutches (including addictions) to manage the uncomfortable sensation of distress. We yell, overeat, spank our children, pour a drink, exercise relentlessly, max out our credit cards, zone out on the web or television, or overwork ourselves in efforts to dull the discomfort of our emotions.

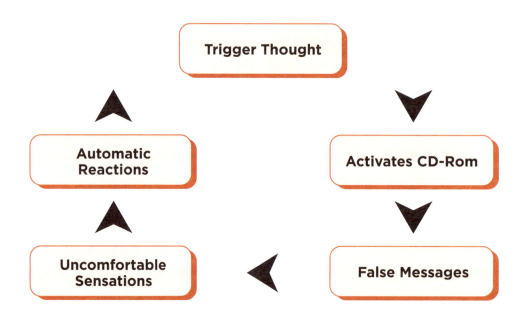

Ultimately, the triggering of our CD-Rom leaves us feeling helpless and powerless to deal with the current situation. When we feel powerless, we use blame as a weapon to try to make others suffer for what we believe they've done to us. Blame is a form of attack. It thwarts safety in our classrooms and our personal lives because we create danger any time we try to make someone else feel responsible for our upset. The perceptual lens of our CD-Rom also prevents us from seeing the underlying causes of behavior. As headlines tell of more children killing children, we also read about all the adults who missed the signs that the child was troubled. The signs are there, but our trigger thoughts blind us to them. Research by Matthew McKay, Patrick Fanning, Kim Paleg and Dana Landis (1996) group triggers thoughts into three main categories:

1. **Assumed Intent:** The teacher thinks the child is misbehaving deliberately to upset her, the classroom or another student.
2. **Magnification:** In the teacher's mind, the situation is much worse than it is.
3. **Labeling:** The teacher uses negative or derogatory words to describe the child or her behavior.

Activity for Determining Your Triggers

Read the following trigger thoughts. Mark the ones that sound familiar and contribute to your anger response. The list is adapted from McKay, Fanning, Paleg and Landis (1996). If your particular trigger thoughts are not listed, add them at the bottom of the list.

Assumed Intent
- ❏ You're just doing this to annoy me.
- ❏ You're deliberately defying me.
- ❏ You're driving me crazy.
- ❏ You're intentionally tuning me out.
- ❏ You're just doing this to get back at me, hurt me, embarrass me, spite me, etc.

Magnification
- ❏ I can't stand this one minute longer.
- ❏ You've gone too far this time.
- ❏ You never listen, pay attention, stay on task, etc.
- ❏ How dare you speak to me like that, look at me like that, etc.
- ❏ You turn everything into a power struggle, lousy time, nightmare, etc.

Labeling
- ❏ This is just plain manipulation.
- ❏ You're lazy, malicious, stubborn, disrespectful, ungrateful, willful, selfish, cruel, etc.
- ❏ You don't care about anyone but yourself.
- ❏ You're deliberately being mean, cruel, hurtful, a jerk, a smart mouth, etc.

Additional Triggers

- ❏ _____

- ❏ _____

> *You create danger anytime you try to make someone else feel responsible for your upset.*

As we stated earlier, trigger thoughts are the match that ignites the fuel of stress. When a stressed person experiences a trigger thought or event. . . Boom! She blows up in angry flames. Except when we are being physically threatened, the main function of anger is to alleviate stress. The stress response in the body emits chemicals such as adrenaline and cortisol. At high levels, these chemicals feel physically uncomfortable as the body becomes tense and rigid. Anger can momentarily block the awareness of these painful sensations. As stress increases, the body feels like it wants to blow. Angry outbursts act as a quick release valve for overstressed systems. Think back to a very stressful time in your life. Remember how edgy you felt. If you had noticed your body, it would have felt tight, uncomfortable and maybe even achy. Now think back to an angry outburst. You likely felt a sense of relief immediately after the blow up, before the guilt set in. A child's relationship with stress is the same.

The opposite of stress is composure. We can allow stress to accumulate, ignore the triggers and act out our anger on others, or we can manage our stress by using the composure skills, structures and routines in this chapter. Option one produces guilt, while option two is a guilt-free road to change. Which will you choose?

Teachers often say some children explode for no reason and seem to enjoy it. That is the release part of the equation. How was the child an hour later? Did she feel remorse (crying), go to sleep or demonstrate withdrawing behaviors, or did she seem unaffected? Children who appear unaffected are experiencing high levels of chronic stress that have overwhelmed their release valves.

Changing Trigger Thoughts to Calming Thoughts

The children and situations that push our buttons are offering us a gift. They allow us to release energy trapped in our bodies from old emotional wounds, freeing us to be all we can be and rewriting our CD-Roms before handing them to the next generation. Our most challenging children offer us the opportunity to heal!

We can change our trigger thoughts by breathing deeply and choosing one of two effective strategies: 1. We can use calming self-talk with belly breathing to override them. 2. We can limit our trigger thoughts with the Oops and Q.T.I.P. methods.

1. **Calming self-talk** sounds like, "I'm safe. Keep breathing. I can handle this." By saying, "I am safe," we send a message to our brain to turn off the stress alarm system. When we say, "Keep breathing," and actually pause to take three deep breaths, we assist our bodies in relaxing and short-circuit our habitual reactions. By saying, "I can handle this," we affirm that we are capable. Think of a situation you find stressful. Say to yourself slowly and intentionally, "I'm safe. Keep breathing (take three slow deep breaths). I can handle this." Can you feel any relief?

    This approach allows us to stay calm, heal our past wounds and access our executive skills. It also allows the child to be responsible for her actions. When we become upset, the child's focus shifts from her behavior to our reaction. We become the mean teacher. When we remain calm, it sends the message that the child has a problem to solve and our job is to help her come up with solutions (not badger her into feeling bad). Helping the child discover solutions enables her to experience success in solving her problems, thus building confidence, character and responsibility. Composure in the face of an outburst is a win-win of major proportions.

2. **Limiting our trigger thoughts** is another option. This requires us to understand that the negative chatter in our heads is false, and then refuse to listen to it. Everything awful or doubtful that our internal chatter says is simply playback of an old CD-Rom from childhood. We have already discussed Oops as one way to limit our trigger thoughts. The Q.T.I.P. method is another strategy to help us remember that negative chatter is just false, made-up junk. Q.T.I.P. is a simple reminder to Quit Taking It Personally. Our CD-Rom would have us believe that other people's actions are a statement about our self-worth. When we Q.T.I.P., we free ourselves to shift our attention, calm down and see the situation differently.

Commitment: I understand people or situations do not make me angry, but may produce anger by triggering my CD-Rom. My triggers stem from my sense of inadequacy and past wounds. By choosing, "I'm safe. Keep breathing. I can handle this," Oops and/or Q.T.I.P., I am able to heal and be proactive with children. I am ready to own my upset.

Signature: _____ Date: _____

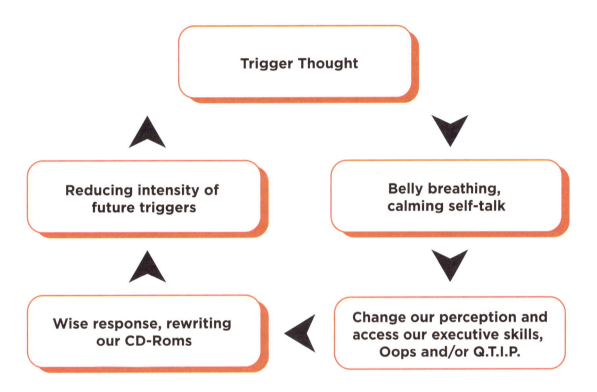

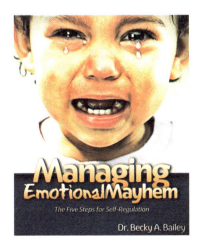

Managing Emotional Mayhem covers the topic of triggers and emotional management in detail.

Activity to Remove Your Buttons Children Push

 Think of a common upset and fill in the blanks accordingly. View a sample response to this activity on the web portal. This exercise is adapted from Reiss.

1. I seem to be upset because my trigger _____ (write in the child's name or the event) _____ _____ (write what has happened).

2. This triggers my CD-Rom chatter and feelings of _____ (use feeling words to describe the uncomfortable sensations in the body if possible).

3. My triggered CD-Rom thoughts that cause this feeling/sensation are _____ _____.

4. While upset, my inclination is to relieve my distress by automatically punishing the child by _____ or get the child to feel bad by _____ or to blame for _____.

5. I want to feel better. I want relief. I can say to myself, "I'm safe. Keep breathing. I can handle this." I accept and let go of my feelings _____ _____(write in the feelings from number 2 above), my thoughts that cause them_____ (write in trigger thoughts from number 3 above), and my need to be right and punish by _____ _____ (write answer from number 4).

6. I want to be responsible, happy and peaceful.

7. What I really want to happen is (use positive action words) _____ _____.

8. I am not really upset at this child or situation, but at my own thinking and ultimately at myself, for not knowing what to do and how to help.

9. I take responsibility, not blame, for all my actions, thoughts and feelings in regard to _____ _____ _____ (write child's name and/or situation).

10. I forgive myself and choose to connect with love instead of my upset. One loving thought I can think about the child is _____. One loving thought I can think about myself is_____.

11. Thank you _____ (child's name) for teaching me to listen to my true self instead of the false messages on my CD-Rom.

Hoffman, Hutchinson & Reiss (2009).

Children's Triggers and Temperament

Just as we must learn about our triggers, we must help children learn about their triggers as well. Historically in terms of discipline, disruptive behavior was attributed to problems within the child. Recently, some discipline programs and teachers have begun addressing the mismatch between the class environment and a child's skills, strengths or preferences. Mismatches have the potential to trigger children. For example, giving work assignments that are too difficult is a common mismatch that can trigger problematic behavior (Kern, Gallagher, Starosta, Hickman & George, 2006). Other class-wide triggers include a lack of predictability, a constant focus on behaviors that are not allowed, seating arrangement, class organization, pace of instruction, transitions, lack of choice, lack of maintaining student interest, etc.

Moving from within-child flaws to recognizing environmental triggers is a huge step in our understanding. Conscious Discipline advocates the next step in this journey, which is the dynamic interaction between individuals. It is imperative for teachers to notice if their response to a child's upset is helpful or hurtful. Will shouting to a child from across the room help the child settle down? Will composing yourself and speaking calmly help the child settle down? Noticing when we are triggering children into a more disorganized state is an essential step in Conscious Discipline. If the child is operating from an emotional state, asking, "Am I Loved?" and our response is to send him out of the room (abandonment), we have pushed him down into a survival state. Don't be surprised if he throws a chair on his way out the door. We must be able to identify our own state first, compose ourselves enough to access an executive state, and then identify the state the child is experiencing. Once we identify the child's state, we then can choose the skills that are likely to help the child move to an executive state. Once we have addressed the child's internal state, we are able to teach a new or missing life skill.

It is critical to remember that a child who is triggered into an emotional or survival state is like a vacuum that tries to pull us and the other children into the same state. We must consciously choose to upshift our state through composure or we will end up part of the problem instead of the solution.

In addition to environmental and learned triggers, we each have a certain temperament we can think of as the built-in wiring we are born with. Temperament is not reflected in occasional behavior; it's a pattern that's consistent over time. A child's temperament can be thought of as a constellation of nine characteristics. Each child will have each of the nine traits in different proportions. The nine traits are listed below. They are adapted from the work of Turecki and Tonner (1985). It is important to note that if a person lives in a survival, emotional or executive state for an extended period of time, it can turn from a state to a trait as life unfolds.

Activity Level: How much activity or restlessness does the child demonstrate? How much spontaneous movement is shown? A child with this trait at a difficult level would be very active, restless and fidgety. The child would rarely slow down and hate to be confined.

Quality of Mood: How would you describe the child's basic disposition? Positive and happy or negative and fussy? A child with this trait at the difficult level would be cranky or serious. The child would appear to get little pleasure from life.

Approach/Withdrawal: How does the child respond to new experiences? Does she approach them with enthusiasm or withdraw in fear? A child at a difficult level in this area would be shy and clingy. The child would stubbornly refuse to go forward into new situations.

Rhythmicity: How regular are the child's eating, sleeping and bowel habits? A child with this trait at the difficult level would get hungry and tired at unpredictable times, making regular mealtimes and bedtimes a source of conflict.

Adaptability: How does the child adapt to transition and change? A child with this trait at the difficult level would be anxious and resistant to changes in activity, routine, food or clothing. These children are inflexible and very particular.

Sensory Threshold: How does the child react to sensory stimuli such as noise, light, smells, tastes, pain, weather, touch, wet diapers? Does she get over stimulated easily? A child with a trait at the difficult level would be easily bothered by the way food smells, the way clothes feel, the brightness of lights or the loudness of noise.

Intensity of Reaction: How intense (loud) is the child's reaction to both positive and negative stimuli? A child with this trait at the difficult level would be loud and forceful with all emotions.

Distractibility: How distracted is the child, particularly when upset? Can she pay attention? A child with this trait at the difficult level has trouble concentrating and paying attention, daydreams instead of listening and tends to forget instructions.

Persistence: How long can the child remain focused on one thing? When happily engaged in an activity, does she stay with it for a long time? When unhappy, does she persist stubbornly with attempts to get her needs met?

 Children with difficult temperaments are easily triggered and have a difficult time composing themselves after an upset. Some are born with challenging temperaments. Others are born into stressful environments. Many parents who have more than one child can attest to the fact they interact differently with each child. A parent might experience constant power struggles with one child and few with the other child. We see a similar dynamic in the classroom where one teacher will find it difficult to interact with a certain child, but another teacher has few problems with him. Every child and adult creates a dance of interactions together. This dance represents the goodness of fit between the child's temperament and the adult's temperament (or CD-Rom). The "Attuned or Misattuned" video on the web portal explores this concept further. We, as adults, must look at our own triggers and examine how they fit with the triggers of the children in our care. We must learn to tame and reframe our triggers first if we hope to help children tame theirs.

Becoming Brain Smart

The Skill of Composure helps us balance our state of arousal and alarm system. It allows us to begin answering the question "Am I safe?" with a "Yes," turning off the fight-or-flight stress response. It also provides us with a steady flow of energy to support the optimal working of the brain.

Take a moment to ask yourself, "Is there a wolf chasing me?" Look around you. If the answer is "No," check your thoughts. Are you feeling anxious or worried? If the answer is "Yes," you are making up an imaginary wolf, disconnecting your brain from its ability to access your executive state to achieve goals or problem solve. Now take a moment to check on your clacker and arousal system. Are you alert and relaxed, stressed and can hardly remember what you are reading, or about to fall asleep? The system responsible for our arousal or clacker system is called the autonomic nervous system. It regulates everything that the brain and the body do, including all behavior and learning. It does this by managing the intake and output of energy, ideally by creating a nice steady beat for our clacker.

The autonomic nervous system is housed in the lower brain stem and has two basic subsystems. The sympathetic system mobilizes the body to respond to threat for fight or flight. The parasympathetic system fosters the relaxation response. If we imagine our bodies as cars, the sympathetic system would be the gas pedal and the parasympathetic system would be the brake.

In an optimal state, the sympathetic and parasympathetic systems are balanced: The learner is excited, interested and alert (sympathetic), yet relaxed and receptive (parasympathetic). This makes for a nice, balanced flow of energy and a steady clacker beat.

 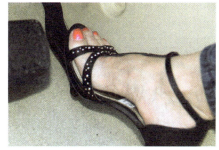

Parasympathetic - BRAKE   *Sympathetic - GAS*

An unbalanced autonomic system is one in which a child (or an adult) is unable to use his or her energy appropriately to manage a situation. As mentioned in Chapter 2, an over-aroused autonomic nervous system is like a clacker that goes too fast all day long. In these situations, the parasympathetic system's role as a brake can get over-aroused and becomes like another gas pedal. With two gas pedals and no brake, we call this "being stressed out." An under-aroused autonomic nervous system, on the other hand, is like a clacker that lethargically claps its hands every five minutes. Metaphorically, this would be like having two brake pedals and no gas pedal. We might call it "being burned out."

Using our car example, a balanced autonomic nervous system can easily drive through town, stopping when needed and obeying the speed limit signs. An over-aroused autonomic nervous system is like a car racing through town without any brakes. An under-aroused autonomic nervous system is like a car without a gas pedal, barely able to get out of the parking lot.

In an unbalanced autonomic nervous system, very little energy in the form of oxygen-rich blood and metabolized food makes its way to the higher centers of the brain. The prefrontal lobes shut down and the survival or emotional systems run the show. From these lower brain systems, the only "learning" that occurs will be about whether there is danger and how to avoid it. The brain sacrifices learning in favor of defending against new information and defending against connecting with others or following class rules. A healthy, balanced arousal and alarm system is essential for life.

Instead of learning math facts or English composition, the student with an unbalanced autonomic nervous system is concerned with how to protect himself by acting aggressively or hiding himself in withdrawal, TV, computer games, etc., so that others will not threaten him. His autonomic system overreacts, causing him to perceive threats where there are none. His repertoire of behaviors is fairly limited, consisting only of fight, flight or freeze. It does not matter how wonderful our curriculum is or what standards we expect them to achieve, it is impossible for him to be successful in these under or over-aroused states.

Many teachers and parents deal with children's aggressive or withdrawn behaviors without recognizing they are signs of poor clacker regulation. Pushing, defiance, name-calling and hostile acts are common in many classrooms and homes, as are children who are also continually bored, disengaged and inattentive. While temperament certainly plays a role in these behaviors, many of these states are acquired through conditioning. In other words, environmental factors have thrown their clackers out of whack, stressing them out.

How does a young child end up with a whacked-out clacker? Stress at young ages has the potential to wire children to be hypersensitive toward emotional and survival state reactions throughout life. The first three years of life are the most critical period in human neural development. At birth, the autonomic system is not fully developed, and it is our calming and soothing that balances it for the rest of their lives. During the stress of intense crying, the baby's clacker is thrown off balance. Young children cannot regulate their own clackers. Adults' calming presence, love and comfort regulate them. Without this calming presence, children grow up more prone to depression, anxiety disorders, alcohol addiction and a multitude of chronic diseases (Ludington-Hoe, McDonald & Satyshur, 2002; Caldji, Diorio, and Meaney, 2000). An abundance of research also indicates that children starting childcare early in life and attending for long hours show more aggression and noncompliant behaviors (Belsky, 2008; Cote, Borage, Geoffroy, Rutter & Tremblay, 2008; NICHD, 2003, 2005). Additionally, children under age five show rising levels of the stress hormone cortisol as the day progresses. It seems long hours in childcare can throw off a child's clacker. Without composed adults creating safe classrooms, we have no way to counteract this tendency.

During the early childhood years, the brain and body use experiences to "educate" the child's naive stress-response system. Exposure to a moderate amount of stressors during early childhood helps the child's autonomic nervous system learn to self-regulate. Too many stressors, however, are detrimental to the system, preventing higher order functions like the ability to delay gratification, overcome impulsiveness, feel remorse, establish closeness, demonstrate empathy for others, establish friendships and maintain composure from optimally developing.

Appropriate behavior in a school or family setting requires a clacker that is attuned to the demands of a predictable outside world. A balanced nervous system (clacker with a steady beat) responds appropriately and then recovers, whereas a hypersensitive nervous system may overreact and persist in a survival state. An unbalanced system may experience road rage when cut off in a traffic jam, carry that irritability home and later feel exhausted. A balanced system might feel upset in the same situation, but would quickly calm down so the body maintains its alertness for driving and conserves energy to respond to the next situation. A balanced autonomic nervous system responds appropriately. A hypersensitive or hyposensitive autonomic system overreacts or underreacts, and has trouble self-correcting.

Many of us need to retrain our own systems to self-correct before we can help children train theirs. Fortunately, the mechanics of retraining these systems are fairly simple through belly breathing and regulating our perceptions. (Unfortunately, the will and perseverance to do so are not always quite so easy to access.) Three deep belly breaths can shut off the stress response in the body and are integral to maintaining or regaining composure. Deepening and slowing the breath sends chemical messages throughout the body, especially to the autonomic nervous system. It quickens the parasympathetic system (brake), slows the rapid sympathetic expenditure of energy (gas) and allows us to begin balancing the two systems.

Think about the children who enter your classroom withdrawn or physically aggressive. They are asking, "Am I safe?" Our responses must promote a resounding "Yes!" if they and those around them are going to succeed in our schools. This "Yes!" is the result of a felt sense of safety that begins with the Skill of Composure.

The Skill of Composure

Let's review what we have learned about the brain. The neural circuits responsible for conscious self-control reside in the prefrontal lobe. When things are going well, the prefrontal lobe acts as control central, keeping our emotions and impulses in check. Life hums along smoothly. When stressed, the prefrontal lobe shuts down and transfers control to our more ancient brain systems, the limbic system and brain stem. With these lower centers engaged, we become slaves to our impulses, insecurities and anxieties. We lose it! We go from conscious to unconscious, from reflective thinking to reflexive action, and from responding wisely to reacting in preprogrammed knee-jerk ways. Certainly, it is not safe for us to go around with our primal impulses unchecked.

As we discussed in Becoming Brain Smart, composure is a reflection of a balanced nervous system in which our gas pedal (sympathetic nervous system) and our brake pedal (parasympathetic) are working together in harmony. A healthy way of putting on the brakes when life seems stressful or out of control is be a S.T.A.R. by Smiling, Taking a deep breath And Relaxing. Slowing down our clacker to a steady beat through deep belly breathing allows us to return to healthy social engagement and access an executive state so we can be consciously aware of our thoughts and feelings, and the thoughts and feelings of others, in order to consciously direct our behavior.

Becoming aware of our own thoughts and feelings is a major accomplishment. Most people don't have a clue what they are thinking. Ask them. Usually the answer is, "Nothing." Yet experts at the National Science Foundation estimate that each of us has more than 50,000 thoughts per day. Where are your thoughts right now? My mind wanders so much that sometimes while reading I realize I'm thinking about my to-do list. The irony is that I don't know what I've read and I haven't finished my tasks. In effect, my cluttered mind leaves me mindless.

As I began making the shift from being an unconscious adult relying on failed attempts at controlling others to a conscious adult who relies on self-regulation, I was discouraged by how often I would slip back into ranting and raving. I had always heard that to discipline children you must "be firm but fair, more positive than negative, treat children with respect, hold them responsible for their own behavior, be consistent and predictable, and model self-control." Yet I had never learned how to do all these fine things, especially during difficult times. How on earth is an adult supposed to remain calm when a child is screaming, "Shut up!" or taunting, "You can't make me!"?

We must retrain our minds, balance our clackers and take back our power! Exerting willpower over impulse and insecurity requires self-regulation. It becomes possible only when we learn to gain, regain and maintain composure. With composure, we integrate our brains in such a way that our prefrontal lobes can do their job of regulating our lower centers. Once we learn the Skill of Composure, then and only then, can we teach this vital skill to children.

Adults who have learned the Skill of Composure are capable of utilizing the prefrontal lobes (the CEO of the brain) to do the following:

- Focus on what they want the child to accomplish
- Utilize connection instead of control as the motivation to behave
- Celebrate the child's successes and choices
- See situations from the child's perspective as well as their own

- Teach the child how to communicate desires and frustrations in a socially-acceptable manner
- Hold the child accountable to those teachings

An out-of-control adult cannot do any of these things. Out-of-control adults focus on what they don't want to happen. ("Stop that this minute!") They see only from their own point of view. ("You are driving me crazy!") They punish or reward rather than teach. ("Move your card to red." "If you are good, we will have popcorn Friday.")

When we lose self-control, we lose our ability to discipline ourselves and our children. For this reason, self-control and the more comprehensive skill of self-regulation (the conscious awareness and management of our own thoughts, feelings and actions) must be our first priority as teachers. We can no longer have teachers who scream at children to be quiet. We can no longer attribute negative intent to children's behavior, yet expect them to respect each other. We can no longer bicker with faculty members while demanding children use problem-solving strategies. It's time to begin leading the way instead of simply demanding better ways from others. Composure is the first step.

Any composure program requires the following:

1. Identifying trigger thoughts and situations
2. Active calming through uploading and downloading calm
3. Reducing and managing stress

Collectively, Conscious Discipline refers to the three components above as the "Be a S.T.A.R." program. This program is the first component of Conscious Discipline you will implement. You will implement it with yourself first and then with your children, families and coworkers.

1. Identifying Trigger Thoughts and Situations

We've already spent quite a bit of time exploring trigger thoughts and events. We must change our perception of the trigger before we can hope to change our response to it. Every response we offer in our interactions with others will bring us closer to an executive state or move us closer to a survival state. We will either feel more connected with others (not triggered) or we will feel more separated (triggered) as a result. Becoming aware of our triggers is an essential first step, but it is only the first step. The second part is actively releasing our triggers and making permanent behavior changes.

2. Active Calming Through Uploading and Downloading Calm

Active calming is at the heart of composure and is a three-step process. Each step is in response to one of the three general brain states we are most likely to experience. From a survival state, the urge is to physically attack or withdraw. To manage this state, we S.T.A.R. by taking three deep belly breaths. From an emotional state, the urge is to verbally defend or attack through blame, name-calling or guilt-inducing lectures. To manage this state, we must actively overlay our CD-Rom chatter with the "I'm safe, keep breathing, I can handle this" mantra. From the executive state, we are able to access compassion by wishing well, Oops or Q.T.I.P, and utilizing our executive skills to discover win-win solutions.

We upload calm for ourselves first by conducting this active-calming process internally. Next, we download our calm state to the child. Then, and only then, are we ready to address the behavior, solve the problem and/or teach a new skill.

Uploading Calm for Ourselves: Active Calming

All conflict starts with upset. We cannot solve the problem if we are unable to manage the upset. Active calming allows us to begin to put a pause between the stimulus (triggers from misbehaving children) and our response. If we want a child to calm down and cooperate, we must become calm and cooperative. For a child to achieve an executive state, we must first achieve one ourselves. A child cannot be in a higher state than the adult. We must begin by uploading the internal state we want our children to achieve. Let's review the three steps for active calming; we must progress from one to the next, ultimately using all three:

- **In a survival state:** Be a S.T.A.R. by taking three deep belly breaths.
- **In an emotional state:** "I'm safe, keep breathing, I can handle this."
- **In an executive state:** Wish well, reframe as an Oops, activate the Q.T.I.P. perception and problem solve.

Survival State: Belly breathing, also known as diaphragmatic breathing or S.T.A.R. breathing, is one of our most important tools in regard to disciplining yourself and children, but it must begin with us. We instinctively hold our breath during acute stress. Ages ago, the survival systems of our brain developed this way so we could hear the tiniest of sounds and avoid being eaten by a tiger. Today, we see it regularly as parents of young children hold their breath to listen more closely whenever they sense something is amiss. Next time you start to feel out of control in the classroom, notice your breathing. The habitual reaction of holding your breath (or breathing shallowly from your chest) stems from the most primitive portion of your brain. It helps you survive; it does not help you think, reason or problem solve. Deep breathing, on the other hand, helps shut off the fight-or-flight survival response so we can respond consciously and learn new skills.

Conscious Discipline uses the acronym S.T.A.R. to remind us to **S**mile, **T**ake a deep breath **A**nd **R**elax. From this point forward, we will simply use "S.T.A.R." to signify the ability to take three deep belly breaths to balance our clackers. Here's how to do it:

Step 1: Smile! Attempting to smile in difficult situations can be extremely helpful even if it feels awkward. Moving the facial muscles into a smile can literally begin to change our internal state. The attempt to turn the corners of our mouth upward sets off a cascade of biochemical changes that helps up relax the body and shift from a negative to a more positive perception of life. The "S" in S.T.A.R. can also stand for "Stop." "Stop" may be helpful in situations that require impulse control, however, it is not as efficient in facilitating a change in inner state.

Step 2: Take a deep breath. Breathe in deeply through the nose. Nose breathing ensures your body's natural filtering, warming and moisturizing of the air in order to protect your lungs. As you inhale, move your belly out. This moves your diaphragm downward, gently massaging your internal organs.

Step 3: And. Pause briefly as you shift from inhaling to exhaling.

Step 4: Relax. Exhale slowly, moving your belly in. This moves your diaphragm up, squeezing the air out of your lungs. Control your exhale so it is longer than the inhale, consciously relaxing your shoulders and softening your facial muscles.

Emotional State: When we are triggered, we can overlay the chatter of our preprogrammed CD-Rom by consciously offering ourselves a calming mantra like, "I'm safe. Keep breathing. I can handle this." This mantra allows us to make a conscious shift in our attention from who did what to whom, who is right and who is wrong to a message of "enoughness." Remember, negative internal chatter tells us one of two things: "I am not good enough," or "You are not good enough." The biochemical result on the body is the same whether the voice puts our focus inward (condemning ourselves) or outward (condemning others).

Deep breathing and a reassuring internal voice equipped with sentiment like, "I'm safe, keep breathing, I can handle this," helps overlay the negative self-talk that tells us all sorts of untruths. The truth is we are all good enough; we are doing the best we can at any given moment. Reassuring self-talk helps us gain and maintain composure and deal with the situation in a helpful way, however, it must be combined with S.T.A.R. breathing to be effective. Saying, "Keep breathing," without actually breathing is just another form of mindless chatter.

Executive State: Think about something precious like an infant's smile, a peaceful sunrise or a darling puppy. Notice how these thoughts fill you up with love, gratitude and appreciation. This is the essence of wishing well. Wishing well is the process of generating a coherent heart, one that knows all is well in the world, and then sending that feeling outward with our intention. Wishing well is not a thought you offer someone but a field of energy you share. To wish well, focus your attention on your heart, imagine your heart opening and sending all the love in the universe through you and to those in need.

Wishing well serves three purposes: First, it centers us, setting our hearts and minds in alignment, which integrates our brain and activates our prefrontal lobes; second, it helps keep us from sliding back into the lower centers of the brain during conflict moments; finally, it radiates a coherent energy field of "all is well" that can upshift others from the lower centers to the higher centers of the brain (Heartmath.org). Wishing well harnesses that energy in support of maintaining our composure and helping others become composed, too. Wishing well holds the door open so everyone's problem-solving wisdom can rush in! It is essential to begin your Wish Well and Be a S.T.A.R. programs the very first week of school.

Downloading Calm to Others: The Mirror Neuron System

Emotions are contagious. Science has now proven what we already knew to be true: Grumpy people can download grumpiness to others, and peaceful folks can do the same. Mirror neurons in the brain play a key role in this process.

Mirror neurons are a special class of brain cells that fire when a person performs an action and when they observe another person. Most parents have been delighted and/or cringed when they watched their children imitating them in play. Stories abound of children spanking their dolls or screeching to them, "Don't you ever do that again!"

When my granddaughter was two years old, I added a round cardboard steering wheel to a shipping box to create a pretend car. Instantly, Maddie grabbed her purse and a small plastic cup, and headed for the car. Her mom, Julie, was laughing because she always takes a drink and her purse when they go for a drive. She said, "The only thing Maddie forgot was a cell phone." Maddie peeked out of the car and opened her purse to show us where she had put a pretend cell phone.

Mirror neurons in the brain are responsible for this ability. Our motor networks practice what we see being done, like Maddie in the above story. This is why "Do what I say, not what I do" is neurologically impossible. Our emotional networks mirror what we see others feeling and doing. Once we see an emotion on another person's face, we will begin to feel the way they are feeling. This is something we have all experienced. It only takes seconds to catch the same negative disposition as your coworkers as you begin complaining about the complaining.

We will either catch our children's upset or they will catch our calmness. Most of us are unconsciously catching others' upset. We see angry faces and our facial expression becomes angry as angry feelings emerge within us. We hear angry tones and our voice matches theirs, contributing to the anger in the situation and ultimately shutting down the CEO of our brain (and their brain). By using the skill of downloading, we can help reverse this situation. We can bring our calm to their upset. Instead of shutting down the prefrontal lobes, we can turn them on and access our brilliance in moments of conflicts. Watch videos of downloading on the portal to learn more.

5

My mother had emphysema and Alzheimer's. She was on oxygen due to 15 percent lung capacity, but the Alzheimer's left her unable to understand the oxygen tube in her nose and her shortness of breath. Her anxiety level about this was extremely high, creating a downward cycling spiral of terror. The more she could not breathe, the more anxious she became. The more anxious she became, the less she could breathe. The doctors prescribed boatloads of anti-anxiety medicines. The pills did not relieve her terror of gasping for that next breath.

What did help Mom was being a S.T.A.R. Since her ability to comprehend life was minimal, I relied on the mirror neuron system to help her breathe. I was hoping Mom would imitate me, not only in what I was doing but also in what I was feeling. I would get in front of her, achieve eye contact and breathe deeply. My belly would expand with each inhale. It would retract with each exhale. I breathed in through my nose and released the air slowly out of my mouth with tight lips to slow down my exhalation. Then I would relax my face and eyes and wish her well with all the love I could muster. Mom's mirror neuron system would kick in and she would begin to copy my actions and feel my calm state. The longer exhale balanced the carbon dioxide in her body and briefly, yet profoundly, turned off her stress response. Watching this happen with my mother made me a deep believer in our need to relearn how to breathe. We can help all children, including those with the most challenging behaviors, regain composure by utilizing deep belly breathing, wishing well and the mirror neuron system.

Noticing to Download: Noticing is a specific type of describing that invites connection through consciousness and eye contact. Downloading uses the mirror neuron system and requires we make eye contact with others. Children resist eye contact and touch when they are in a survival state. Use noticing to help them achieve eye contact so you can download calm.

Noticing is a valuable skill that requires us to see without judgment and can be used in a variety of contexts. In order to use noticing as an aid for downloading calm, we must describe and demonstrate what the child is doing. "Your face is going like this (demonstrate), your arms are going like this (demonstrate)." Demonstrating the child's body in this way creates a natural urge for the child to look at you. Noticing enables us to gently encourage eye contact without demanding compliance by saying, "Look at me," which can be perceived as a threat and further entrench a survival state. If a child continues to resist eye contact, take another deep breath and join with him in an attuned way.

Continue describing and demonstrating until he looks up. "Look at that! You've got the little truck, and you're going like this with it (demonstrate), and your finger just went boop (demonstrate)!"

The noticing to download formula is:
"Your _____ is going like this (demonstrate)."

 Noticing is a theme we will discuss in various contexts throughout the book. For now, learn more about noticing in a portal video and consider the following story:

Each morning, Mrs. Katz offers children a choice in greetings. For the upcoming President's Day holiday, the choices are a Lincoln, a Washington, a White House or a First Lady greeting. Most days, Aaron arrives in a survival state, refusing to make eye contact or be greeted. Today, Mrs. Katz tries downloading calm to Aaron. She takes a deep breath and notices, "Aaron, your arms are going like this and your head went like this." Aaron glances sideways to see what she's doing. Mrs. Katz instantly takes a slow, deep breath. Aaron's body automatically joins her, and he takes a breath, too. His body relaxes and Mrs. Katz asks which greeting he would like, pointing to the pictures representing the choices. Aaron gestures slightly toward Abe Lincoln. "You chose Abe!" Mrs. Katz says with delight. They position their bodies like the Lincoln monument in Washington D.C. and give a gentle fist bump.

Mrs. Katz demonstrated these steps for downloading calm:

1. Upload calm into your body.
2. Mirror and notice the child's body language. "Your feet/body/face are going like this…"
3. When the child makes eye contact, take a S.T.A.R. breath.
4. Offer the child choices or provide specific instructions.

Common mistakes when downloading calm:

🚫 We forget to upload before we can download. With challenging children, we unconsciously begin to guard against misbehavior before it occurs. We must enter the moment calm, assured and open to help the child be successful in complying.

🚫 We forget to physically demonstrate or mirror what the child is doing. If we say, "Your arms are going like this," we must move our arms like the child. We become a mirror for their actions.

🚫 We say, "Your hands covered your face," instead of, "Your hands went like this." "Your hands covered your face," does not give them a reason to look or activate the mirror neuron system. "Your hands went like this" encourages the child to make eye contact and activates the mirror neuron system.

🚫 We forget to take that deep, slow breath the instant the child makes eye contact.

🚫 We unconsciously download with the intent of making the child engage or comply instead of the intent of being helpful.

3. Reducing and Managing Stress

Place your left hand on your chest and your right hand on your belly. Breathe as you normally do. Which hand moves first? If your left hand moves first, you are shallow chest breathing. If your right hand moves first, you are belly breathing. A belly breath is a healthy, natural breath. A chest breath is a shallow, stifled breath.

Because of the constant pressure of stress in our lives, many of us do not breathe naturally. Physiology books tell us that the average rate of breathing while at rest is approximately 12 to 14 breaths a minute. Stop reading and count your breaths per minute. Many of us are breathing faster. We habitually hyperventilate, which means we take quick, shallow breaths from the top of our chests. This type of breathing sharply reduces the level of carbon dioxide in our blood. Contrary to popular belief, our bodies require certain levels of carbon dioxide in order to function properly (large concentrations, however, are toxic). The low levels of carbon dioxide created by shallow breathing cause our arteries to constrict, reducing the blood flow to the brain and body. As a result, our brain doesn't get the oxygen it requires to function optimally. The oxygen shortage switches on our fight-or-flight reflex, making us tense and irritable, reducing our ability to think clearly, locking out the prefrontal lobes, and putting us at the mercy of our negative internal chatter. All this happens before we even arrive at school, before Jason hits Parker for the 10th time, before Colby forgets his lunch, before Keisha cries for 30 minutes about missing her mom and before Cassandra forgets her homework again.

We have already explained S.T.A.R. breathing as the primary technique in the active calming process. Your S.T.A.R. program will expand as you teach children a variety of new composure strategies. S.T.A.R., Drain, Balloon and Pretzel are the four core composure techniques Conscious Discipline employs. The *I Can Calm* book teaches these techniques. Teach children to S.T.A.R. as described earlier in this chapter, and then continue with the three new skills described below. You can find more comprehensive instruction and video demonstrations by clicking on the Safe Place link in Shubert's School or by watching the video of children practicing the *I Can Calm* book on the web portal.

Draining: Extend both arms out in front of your body parallel to the floor. Have the fists closed palms facing down. Inhale squeezing and tightening your fists, arms and face. Pretend your arms are faucets on a sink. Your closed fists are acting as drains. To open the drain, exhale and relax your fingers by opening them and making a swishing noise (ssshhh). The noise represents water flowing out of a faucet. Close the drain by tightening your fist. Tighten them so that your arms, neck and face are constricted. Then, open the drain and release with the sound again.

Ballooning: Show children how you blow up a balloon, then demonstrate what happens when you hold the opening of the balloon and allow the air to escape. Explain this is what we can do with our lungs. Have the children inhale a number of times sucking in air and holding it as if to blow up their lungs like balloons. Then have the children purse their lips and allow the air to escape.

Pretzel: Sit or stand crossing the left ankle over the right ankle. Extend your arms out in front of you with your thumbs pointing down, and cross your left wrist over the right wrist. Interlace your fingers and draw your hands up toward your chest. Close your eyes and breathe. Press your tongue flat against the roof of your mouth when inhaling, and release it when exhaling. The pretzel shifts the electrical energy from the survival centers of the brain to the reasoning centers. Pressing your tongue against the roof of your mouth like this stimulates the limbic system to work with the frontal lobes. Dr. Dennison (1989) discovered that this posture releases emotional stress and can help with learning disabilities.

Did You Know?

- Breathing is our largest system for waste removal. 70 percent of the waste products produced in our body are removed via breathing. 30 percent is removed through the skin when we sweat, while only 10 percent remains for the kidneys and colon. This cleansing happens mostly on the exhale part of the breath. To be effective, the exhale must be longer than the inhale.
- The air we breathe in brings oxygen to every cell in the body. The brain requires 25-40 percent of our total oxygen supply to function properly. Without proper belly breathing, the brain can be short-changed in its oxygen supply by as much as 60 percent. An oxygen-starved brain is an educational disaster.
- If your diaphragm is not moving, your prefrontal lobes are not fully engaged. If your prefrontal lobes are not fully engaged, you will be reactive instead of responsive. Our choice is simple. We can be a responsive S.T.A.R. or a reactive maniac.

Composure Creates Safety in Your School Family

As you practice the aforementioned perceptual shifts and skills daily, the following routines, rituals and structures will create a felt sense of safety in your School Family.

Routine: Brain Smart Start

The Brain Smart Start is a routine that is scientifically based and designed to maintain optimal learning states during daily transitions. There are many transitions throughout the day that are often stressful for both children and teachers, but by far the most difficult one is the transition from home to school. The stress of getting up and out of the house is intense for many families. Even in homes with the best of routines, life happens. In many homes, children wake themselves up and dress younger siblings. They feed themselves, if food is available. When children arrive at school a lot has happened, in the home, on the bus, or in the halls. The same is true for teachers. The Brain Smart Start helps students and teachers make the shift required during the initial transition from home to school, as well as making the smaller shifts required of them throughout the day.

The Brain Smart Start is a routine that consists of four activities:
1. Activity to **Unite**
2. Activity to **Disengage Stress**
3. Activity to **Connect** the children to the teacher and each other
4. Activity to **Commit** oneself to learning

These four activities support our deepest values and are designed to create a biochemistry that balances and integrates brain function, mind and body.

> *Remember, the Brain Smart Start at the beginning of the day is only one of your many daily transitions. After each transition, conduct an abbreviated Brain Smart Start to improve attention and increase your teaching time.*

1. Activity to Unite

The Activity to Unite brings the scattered minds and bodies in the classroom into a more congruent whole. It gets everyone on the same page by singing the same song, reciting the same chant or moving in unison. Many schools unite with traditional activities like the Pledge of Allegiance. Creating or singing a School Family song or a song about your class agreements is another effective way to unite. Below are a School Family song and a rap third-grade students created to express their agreements to each other. Additional examples are on your portal.

"Our School Family" from *It Starts in the Heart*
This is our School Family
This is our School Family
This is our School Family
Wave to a friend (shake hands, pinky hug, etc.)

"Third Grade Agreements" Rap
This rap is about you. This rap is about me. This rap is about safety.
We may disagree. We may all agree. But we know the value of safety.
I'm ready to do my best, say, "So long to stress." (S.T.A.R.)
We are respectful. We are responsible. And we know the value of being helpful.
I've got your back. You've got mine. It's all fine.

2. Activity to Disengage Stress

When we experience stress, a cascade of more than 1,400 different biochemicals is released into the body (Sapolsky, 1998). These chemicals affect how we perceive, feel and behave. Most importantly, they have the power to shut down the prefrontal lobes, diverting our attention to survival instead of learning (Bailey, 2011). Introduce and practice the four major stress reducers mentioned previously (S.T.A.R., Drain, Pretzel, Balloon). Model and coach these skills during moments of upset, and practice them when children are calm so they are more likely to be able to access them when upset.

You can also use stretching, yoga and creative belly breathing techniques to help disengage stress. Stretching helps release tension from muscles and preoccupations from our minds. It improves circulation, strengthens breathing, relieves fatigue, releases nervousness, improves flexibility, promotes mental clarity and energizes the system. Creative breathing techniques can be made

up on the spot. Some classrooms use bunny breathing where children put two fingers up like bunny ears as they inhale and hop their fingers slowly away as they exhale. Others use superhero breathing and pretend to fly while inhaling and exhaling. Visit the web portal to review a video of additional belly breathing activities. The possibilities are endless.

The more stressed the child, the more assistance, prompting and practice he will need. Instruct children to lie on the floor with an object on their bellies, and watch the object go up and down as they breathe in and out. This simple form of biofeedback helps them be successful. Some very stressed children will resist belly breathing because it requires them to let their guard down. In this case, you or the class must breathe for the distressed child.

3. Activity to Connect

Once the body begins to relax and the stress response is turned off, connection with one another is possible. Cooperation follows connection. When children and teachers feel a sense of connection with each other and with the school, cooperation is more likely. Disconnected students are disruptive. Simply stated, starting your day with a connection activity will help it run more smoothly.

Disconnected students are disruptive because of a lack of impulse control, low frustration tolerance and decreased self-regulation skills. A connection activity (between children or with an adult) first thing in the morning stimulates the impulse control systems of the brain and generates a neurochemical bath that says, "Pay attention." Simply taking a moment to greet the person next you with a butterfly handshake is a connecting activity. (A butterfly handshake involves two students interlocking their thumbs with fingers extended, and wiggling their fingers like wings that flutter.) Activities to connect differ from activities to unite in that they require students to connect with each other face-to-face in a way that involves eye contact, touch, presence and playfulness. Morning Greetings and *I Love You Rituals* (Bailey, 1997) are excellent examples of activities to connect. Find examples of greeting and connection activities for all ages on the web portal.

You've Been Gone
I Love You Rituals, page 136 • *Songs for I Love You Rituals Volume 2*

You've been gone, *Chant classroom-wide.*
And you've been missed. *Chant classroom-wide.*
Where would you like your welcome back kiss? *A class representative uses a puppet or wand to deliver a "kiss" at the location the absent child indicates.*

Little Miss Muffet I Love You Ritual

I Love You Rituals, page 65 • *Songs for I Love You Rituals Volume 2*

Little Miss Muffet sat on her tuffet, *Clap your hands at "Muffet." Point toward your bottom at "tuffet." Child mirrors.*
Eating her oatmeal today. *Chew and make a face that says, "Yummy." Child mirrors.*
Along came a spider and sat down beside her, *Crawl a "spider" up the child's arm with your fingers, and "sit" the spider on the child's shoulder.*
And said, "Have a good day!" *Connect with a playful gesture like a nose beep, handshake, high five or wave.*

4. Activity to Commit

Commitments prime the brain for success and actively engage the prefrontal lobes. A commitment that is spoken out loud does many things, both psychologically and neurologically, that increase the likelihood of following through on the commitment. Making a commitment and following through builds self-worth and neurologically bathes the body in feel good chemicals that help us focus our attention.

Often, we toy with or dance around a commitment with phrases like, "I've been thinking about ___," "I need to get started on ___," and, "I should ___." The hidden message behind this language is, "If external issues, people and events allow, I could possibly move forward with my goal, provided something else doesn't happen." Phrases like, "I have to ___," imply someone else is running your life. Who really says you have to ___?

Commitments are powerful statements that declare, "I will do this regardless of external events." The phrase I encourage is, "I'm going to _____." Starting each day with an "I'm going to" commitment focuses the brain on a specific goal, activating the prefrontal lobes so the brain is ready for a day of learning.

Your Brain Smart Start commitment can be individual, like writing a personal commitment in a journal, or it can be a group commitment such as, "Today I will be helpful at least one time." Your commitment could also be in the form of a class chant such as, "Today I'm going to have listening ears, kind words, no put downs, the right to pass, and gentle touches, treating everyone as I would want to be treated." The web portal contains video examples of children making age-appropriate commitments.

To be successful, you must plan your Brain Smart Start for the beginning of the day and secondary Brain Smart Starts during transitions throughout the day. I speak all over the world, and I use Brain Smart Starts throughout every presentation. I strategically plan and incorporate these moments in order to help attendees shift their internal states to that of optimal learning and focus. I often hear, "I enjoyed your presentation. It really kept my attention going." The content I teach and my presentation style are engaging, but I know that without incorporating Brain Smart Starts after transitions and during times of low energy (like the 2 p.m. slump), attendees' ability to sustain attention will inevitably slip. The same is true in classrooms around the globe. As educators, we must be active participants in helping children maintain focus. The Brain Smart Start is a key player in this effort.

> **The Conscious Discipline Commitment to Remember Your Worth**
>
> **I** dedicate this time to becoming a more conscious, compassionate person.
> **WILL**ingly, I provide safety, support, and structure for the children in my care.
> **REMEMBER**ing that what I offer to others, I strengthen in myself. May I never forget
> **MY** worth depends on seeing the
> **WORTH** in others.

Activity to Discover How You Start the Day

In the space below, summarize how you begin your school day. After listing the activities, decide if you are using Brain Smart strategies. Do you have activities to unite, disengage stress, connect or affirm? If not, how might you begin to make changes? List one change you are willing to make.

Current beginning of the day: _____

_____

_____

_____

_____

Changes I could make in the near future: _____

_____

_____

_____

_____

One change I am willing to make right now: _____

_____

_____

_____

_____

These songs include music and movement activities that are helpful for your Brain Smart Start in the morning and other transitions. They provide the short, ideal brain breaks that are needed to turn off the stress response throughout the day.

Kindness Counts
"It's Brain Smart Time," "We All Count"

Brain Boogie Boosters
"Watch Me Listen," "Brain Breaks," "Greetings"

It Starts in the Heart
"My School Family," "Get Ready"

Songs for I Love You Rituals Volume 1
"Dancing Hands," "Twinkle, Twinkle," "Peter, Peter," "Humpty Dumpty," "Here's the Bunny"

Songs for I Love You Rituals Volume 2:
"Little Miss Muffet," "You've Been Gone," "I Like to be With You," "I'm a Helpful Person"

To purchase these music CDs, visit ConsciousDiscipline.com.

Ritual: Safekeeper Job Description and Ritual

Whether we are conscious of it or not, we often think it is our job to control children's behavior and demonstrate that control to our administrators. If we fail to control them, we are failures as teachers. It is time we consciously change this job description from one of force and coercion to one of self-regulation. The new job description is:

> *My job is to keep the classroom safe so children can learn.*
> *The children's job is to help keep the classroom safe.*

The Safekeeper job description is essential if we want all children to be successful, including typically developing children, children with difficult temperaments, children with special needs (ADHD, etc.) and children who have experienced stressors early in their lives. The Safekeeper job description helps change our intent from one of force to one of helping children be successful. Changing our intent changes how we speak to children.

Remember, we create danger every time we attempt to make others bad, wrong or responsible for our upset. To be a Safekeeper, we must take 100 percent responsibility for our own thoughts, feelings and actions. We must use composure ourselves, in order to discipline children from an executive state. A Safekeeper must choose to:

- Be a S.T.A.R. instead of losing it.
- Become aware of trigger thoughts and events.
- Wish children well and notice instead of judge.
- Use the language of safety instead of the language of fear.
- See conflict as an opportunity to teach.

Activity to Experience the Difference for Yourself

Do this activity to experience the difference between using language to create control and to create safety. Read both sentences and see if you can feel the difference. If you have a partner, one of you pretend to be the child and the other pretend to be the adult and share the differences between perspectives.

Language of Control	Language of Safety
Losing It You are driving me crazy. I've had it with you. Turn your card to red. One more outburst and you will leave my room.	**Active S.T.A.R. Calming** I am going to take a few deep breaths and calm myself down. Then I will speak to you.
Judging • I don't know how such a lovely girl can be so lazy. • J.J. is just mean. He bullies everyone in class. I have done everything except suspend him and nothing works!	**Noticing** • She is having a hard time getting started with her work. • J.J. doesn't know the words to use when he finds himself in a conflict.
Language of Fear • Walking feet, walking feet, walking feet! What did I just tell you? • Hold my hand. Do you want a car to hit you? • What is our rule about pushing in chairs?	**Language of Safety** • Walk in the classroom just like this (model) so everyone is safe. • Hold my hand so you are safe when we cross the street. • Push your chairs in so everyone is safe.

The Safekeeper ritual supports your role as Safekeeper in your classroom. Begin this ritual on the first day of school. You will need a Safekeeper box and a figure to represent each individual in your classroom. The figures might be as simple as popsicle sticks with names on them or photos of the children. The Safekeeper ritual itself can be done in many ways. The goal is for the students to consciously place their figures in the Safekeeper box while making a commitment to help keep the classroom a safe place to learn. (Many classrooms combine this process with attendance taking.) At the end of each day, remove the figures from the Safekeeper box and display them for the students to repeat the ritual the next morning.

Start the school year off by telling children your job description and teaching them how to do the Safekeeper ritual. Repeat over and over, "My job is to keep the classroom safe." Create a psychologically safe classroom by using composure to manage your own upset. Relate everything you do to safety. "Leaving materials on the floor is not safe. Someone could trip or the materials might get lost." Use conflict moments to repeat your job description. "Michael, pushing Jamey in hurtful. My job is to keep the classroom safe. What could you do now that would be helpful instead of hurtful?" View images and videos of the Safekeeper ritual in Shubert's School and on the web portal.

Structure: Safe Place Self-Regulation Learning Center

Once children practice composing themselves after transitions and minor stressors, the goal is to help them practice composing themselves in more difficult life situations. The Safe Place is a physical location in the classroom that serves as a self-regulation learning center. It is equipped with tools for calming and self-regulation, and supports the Skill of Composure by providing the opportunity for children to remove themselves from the group in order to become calm and maintain control when they are angry, frustrated, sad or scared.

Before placing a Safe Place in your classroom, you must examine some of your core beliefs about children. Read column A and column B and decide which beliefs best align with yours.

Column A	Column B
We must teach children how to compose themselves and give them the opportunity to practice.	Children should abide by rules and know how to compose themselves by now.
All children can learn this skill.	Some children are too young, old, lazy or manipulative to learn.
Children can remove themselves as needed and return to class successfully.	Children cannot be trusted to use (rather than abuse) the Safe Place.

We have a Safe Place. You go there when you are sad or angry. We calm down in the safe place.

If you found that the majority of your answers came from column B, you are not ready to implement this structure in your classroom.

Children must be willing to go to the Safe Place when upset. This willingness comes from the creation of a School Family. This book provides the necessary tools and perceptual shifts needed to create a School Family, while the *Creating the School Family* book provides additional depth on the subject. You will teach the children how to use the Safe Place within the connected School Family. No one would place microscopes in a science center without thoroughly teaching children how to use them; the same is true of the Safe Place. You will teach:

- When to go
- What to do when you get there
- How long to stay
- Who can help you

If school rules allow, I like to use a beanbag chair as the main structure in the Safe Place. When a child sits in the chair, it's as if the chair is embracing the child. Locate your Safe Place in an area that feels cozy but has a clear view of classroom activities. The Safe Place is not a substitute for or related to time out in anyway. It is a learning center where children are guided through the five steps to self-regulation. The five steps are (Bailey, 2011):

I Am

Step 1: I Am Upset: When a child is triggered, that is a signal for him to go to the Safe Place. The child can go on his own, with the help of the teacher or with a suggestion from a friend.

I Calm

Step 2: I Calm: The child picks one of the four core calming strategies: S.T.A.R., Drain, Balloon or Pretzel to help himself calm down. The teacher must post visual images of these strategies in the Safe Place and teach/practice them during every Brain Smart Start.

I Feel

Step 3: I Feel: The child identifies his current feeling state by pointing to a poster downloaded from ConsciousDiscipline.com/resources, selecting a Feeling Buddy from the *Feeling Buddy Self-Regulation Toolkit*, or selecting a feeling image from the *I Choose Self-Control Board*.

I Choose

Step 4: I Choose: The child chooses an activity from a predetermined set of choices contained in the Safe Place Case. Before opening your Safe Place for use, gather students' input about what would help them calm down and turn their thinking brains back on. Fill your Safe Place Case with the corresponding supplies. These supplies may include calming tools like lotion, drawing/writing supplies and inspirational books.

I Solve

Step 5: I Solve: Children can accomplish this step independently, but it will often require the teacher's assistance. Older children write down the problem and future solutions to discuss with the teacher. Young children will need specific, individual coaching. In general the solutions will fall into one of the following:

- Helping the child learn to ask for help.
- Helping the child learn how to resolve conflicts with friends. (Chapters 5, 10)
- Helping the child create visuals of routines or a visual social story for success. (Chapter 5)
- Helping the child learn additional strategies to manage situations outside of school that are impeding his learning (death in family, violence, divorce, etc.). (Chapter 8)

> Learn more about the five steps to self-regulation and how to implement a Safe Place in the *Feeling Buddies Self-Regulation Toolkit* and *Managing Emotional Mayhem*.

Post signage in your Safe Place that will help guide children's self-calming efforts. If you are an administrator, create Safe Places for the staff and children who show up in the office.

The best way to introduce the Safe Place and the stress reducing skills to your classroom is to read *Shubert is a S.T.A.R.*. Conscious Discipline provides many products that are helpful for implementing a Safe Place, as well as an extensive array of free videos and classroom examples available online in Shubert's School.

Friends and Family Board

The Friends and Family Board is a structure that supports both composure and encouragement. It includes photos of all the people who love, support and will be keeping students safe. The pictures range from students and their family members, to their teachers, cafeteria workers, bus drivers and principal. It helps students get to know one another, and links the home family and the School Family.

Select a display space for this yearlong project. If wall space is not available, use a photo album or scrapbook. Collect images of school personnel before school begins. Put them on your Friends and Family Board or in your Friends and Family Book. Then take pictures of the children and their families at an open house or collect photos over the first weeks of school. Add these photos to your board or book as well.

Constant involvement of your stakeholders is necessary in building your School Family. On parent nights, tell family members your job description: "My job is to keep your children safe at school so they can learn. Your job as a family is to help keep it safe." Then specifically discuss what families can do to help keep the School Family safe. This may include arrival and dismissal procedures, keeping sick children home, providing reading time at home with the child, structuring a time for homework, etc.

Next, discuss how you will keep the children safe while they are at school. Show them the Friends and Family Board you are creating so both the children and their families know who their Safekeepers are at school. Talk about how you will teach children how to be helpful and respectful to others, and share other key points about your School Family.

Composure Summary

Power:	Perception: No one can make you angry without your permission.
Becoming Brain Smart:	Composure gives you access to the higher centers of your brain.
Skill:	S.T.A.R.: "I'm safe. Keep breathing. I can handle this." Noticing and download: "Your face is going like this (demonstrate)."
School Family:	Brain Smart Start Routine, Safekeeper Ritual, Safe Place Self-Regulation Center, Friends and Family Board

Power of Perception Reflection

This month, remember perception is a choice not a fact. Ask yourself frequently, "Do I want to own my upset and maintain self-control, or do I want to give my power away and blame others for taking it?" The choice is yours and it never goes away. When you live a more composed life, you live your highest values and model what you want children to do.

- ❏ **Notice what false messages are on your CD-Rom when you feel triggered.** Use active calming to regulate them. As you vigilantly and repeatedly calm yourself you will be able to better tolerate the emotional sensations and change your knee-jerk reactions.

- ❏ **Listen to how often you blame others.** Notice how often you render yourself powerless by saying, "Don't make me." Replace these statements with "I'm going to." Instead of "Don't make me have to speak to you again," say, "I'm going to move you to another chair if you choose to continue talking."

- ❏ **Affirm to yourself, "When I put another person in charge of my feelings, I put them in charge of me."** Take back your power. Ask yourself frequently, "Where is my power?"

- ❏ **Watch the Power of Perception video** on the portal to deepen your reflection.

Brain Smart Teaching Moments

Children who are triggered become agitated before they lose control of themselves. This agitation is demonstrated by increases in certain behaviors and decreases in others. Their non-verbal indicators signal it is time for the child or class to do some or all of the components of a Brain Smart Start. You may disengage the stress by being a S.T.A.R., conduct a uniting brain break or do a connecting activity, ultimately recommitting to learning. You may also direct the child to the Safe Place. Look for these signs:

- **Darting eyes:** Children will look here and there with intensity, but with little focus.

- **Non-conversational language:** They respond with short answers. "Fine." "Nothing."

- **Busy hands and feet:** Students may drum their fingers, rub their thighs, open and close books, tug at clothes, kick the floor, swing their legs or tap their feet.

- **Moving in and out of groups:** Children may join a group, then pull away repeatedly.

- **Off and on task:** Children will start a task, do something else and then return to the task. You will usually see very little sustained attention.

- **Staring into space:** Watch for all forms of daydreaming.

- **Subdued language:** This is similar to the nonconversational language above, plus it is soft and weak. You may have to get close to hear what the child says.

- **Contained hands:** Children will take action to "contain" their hands. They put them in pockets, sit on them or put them in their armpits, appearing to sulk.

- **Withdrawal from activities:** They pull away from groups, lag behind when walking and choose to withdraw instead of engaging in activities or with people.

The above behaviors were conceptualized by Colvin (1993) and developed by Walker, Colvin and Ramsey (1995).

 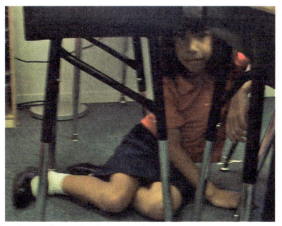

Children will find their own Safe Place if we don't provide one.

Skill Reflection: Common and Conscious

If possible, partner up with someone and say these two statements out loud. One statement is a common declaration that gives away our power, the other is an empowering way to discipline. After each statement share, "The difference between Common and Conscious for me was…"

Common	Conscious
Don't make me pull this car over.	I'm going to pull the car over while you fasten your seat belt so everyone will be safe.
See how you made her feel? She is crying. Give her back the toy.	See Sarah's face. It's saying, "I don't like it when you grab my toy. Please give it back."
You're making my life miserable!	I'm feeling very frustrated. I'm going to take a deep breath to calm down and then I will speak with you.

Model Safe Place Self-Regulation Learning Center

Watch Safe Place videos on your portal.

School Family Implementation Checklist

❏ **Start your Be a S.T.A.R. Program.**

❏ **Practice active calming** (S.T.A.R., "I'm safe. Keep breathing. I can handle this," wishing well).

❏ **Teach every child how and when to S.T.A.R., Drain, Balloon, Pretzel and Wish Well.**

❏ **When a child becomes upset, ask the entire class to help** by being a S.T.A.R. and wishing well.

❏ **Practice noticing** in order to actively download calm into children.

❏ **Use Oops and Q.T.I.P.** with yourself, colleagues and children.

❏ **Start each day with a Brain Smart Start** and utilize Brain Smart activities throughout the day, especially during transition times.

❏ **Discuss with children what safety looks like, sounds like and feels like.**

❏ **Teach children about the classroom job descriptions,** "My job is to keep the classroom safe. Your job is to help keep it safe," and create a daily Safekeeper ritual.

❏ **Create a Friends and Family Board/Book.**

❏ **Create a Safe Place** in your classroom and teach children how to successfully use it.

❏ **Visit Shubert's School and the book study portal online.**

❏ **Seek help from the Conscious Discipline community** by asking questions and sharing concerns on the Conscious Discipline Facebook page, and by visiting Pinterest to see images of what others have found successful.

❏ **Assess your implementation by using the rubrics on the portal.**

❏ **Review the implementation guide** to support your staff (administrators).

Ballooning in the Safe Place

Toddler Safe Place

Chapter 5

ASSERTIVENESS

Saying "no" and being heard: setting limits respectfully

Assertiveness is clear, vigilant communication that focuses children's attention on what we want them to do. It is essential for setting effective and respectful limits.

The mantra to remember as you practice assertiveness is, "What you focus on, you get more of." Right now take a slow, deep S.T.A.R. breath. As you breathe in say, "What I focus on." As you exhale say, "I get more of." Do this three times, letting the phrase and its meaning bathe your brain. Take a moment to reflect on your life. Where do you focus your attention? Do you dwell on what isn't done and how little time you have to do it, or do you focus on the many things you've accomplished? Do you focus on the strengths or shortcomings of your partner, your school, your children, yourself? Where you focus your attention determines your experience. The icon for the Power of Attention is a flashlight. Watch a video on the Power of Attention on the portal for a more in-depth understanding.

The Power of Attention

Attention is like the flashlight we use to light the sidewalk in the dark or the highlighter we use to mark important passages in a book. Our attention illuminates whatever it's focused on and all else fades into the background. Putting our attention on something places an inherent value on it. Helpfulness rises to the forefront and becomes valued when we place our attention on helpfulness. When we place our attention on annoyances, misbehavior, hurtfulness and problems, these also rise to the forefront and become valued. Where we place our attention consequently signals what we value and teaches children what to value. As you read each scene on the next page, notice how these two teachers utilize the Power of Attention while setting limits.

Teacher A sees two children off task and asks, "What are you two doing?" The children look at the teacher blankly. "What is our rule about visiting during work time? This is no way to act. Do you want me to turn your color card?" The teacher then walks away to address a question across the room.

Teacher B sees two children visiting with each other instead of working, walks over, calls the children by name, waits for eye contact and says, "Focus on your math. Start by completing problems two through four. I will watch you get started so I know you understand what it takes to be successful." As the children shift their focus from each other to their work, the teacher encourages them by saying, "There you go. You're doing it!"

Teacher A focused her attention on what was wrong or "not good enough." Teacher B focused on the action needed to solve the problem and followed up with encouragement. Do you want to focus on the problem or the solution? Both are options in each moment. The choice is yours!

If your attention is focused on the problem, it is not open to a solution.

We demonstrate what we value and teach children how to behave based on what we see in the world. Children quickly learn we will see them for either helpful or hurtful behavior. Most of us are accustomed to spending enormous energy focusing on what we don't want, training children to do the same. Learning instead to focus our attention on the outcome we desire brings enormous power and the opportunity to problem-solve. If our attention is focused on the problem, it is not open to a solution! Our mental picture of what we don't want is generally quite clear: "Don't hit!" "You're too loud!" "What is our rule about ___?" "Do you want a referral?" "Stop talking!" "Why are you still doing that?" "Don't run in the halls!" If our goal is to turn our attention to the behaviors we want, we must define our expectations for positive behaviors just as clearly. Focusing on what we want is a key technique for lifelong happiness because it literally wires our brain for success. Look around your school. How many visual images show children what to do?

Think about the last time you felt upset. Notice that even during minor upsets, you are focused on what you don't want to happen or what needs to stop immediately. When your mind is in a defensive state of upset (a survival or emotional state), it alerts you to danger and puts its energy into stopping the threat, not solving the problem. To focus on what you do want, you must be a calm model of self-control.

When I discuss the Power of Attention, teachers listen, laugh and nod their heads knowingly. When I finish explaining this power, a teacher will invariably ask, "How will this help me get my first-grade students to stop fighting?" I again guide the teacher toward the awareness of where his or her attention is by saying, "Think about what you do want the children to do." The usual response is, "I want them to stop hitting." Most of us have a deeply ingrained mental habit of focusing on outcomes we do not want, especially when we're upset. It takes conscious effort to shift and say, "I want children to learn how to verbally communicate in socially acceptable ways when frustrated." We must shift our focus to the positive action we want children to use in order to see the teaching that's necessary for us to scaffold their success.

It is vital to understand that when we are upset and triggered, we always focus on what we don't want. Think about the last time you felt upset and bring the scene fully to mind. As you recreate the moment, notice how you were focused on something you didn't want or something you wanted to stop. We cannot solve a problem while we remain focused on what we don't want; we must use our Power of Attention to focus on what we do want instead.

Retraining our minds with the Power of Attention is necessary to help ourselves and our children change. Many people try to change their behaviors without success. New Year's resolutions are great examples. Common resolutions are quitting smoking, eating less junk and spending less time at work. Usually, we keep these commitments for only a few weeks before backsliding. Why? One key reason for failing is we are trying to change behaviors by focusing on what we don't want (eat less junk) instead of what we do want (eat more vegetables).

Activity to Find Where You Focus Attention

Read the following scenarios and determine where the teacher's focus is directed.

Scene 1: "Michelle, why did you hit Jake? Would you like someone to hit you? Hitting hurts. Go turn your card to red. Then come back and be nice."

Teacher's overall focus: _____.

Scene 2: "Mark, what is our rule about fighting? You march yourself down to the principal's office. Fighting is not allowed in this school. Fighting is a serious offense."

Teacher's overall focus: _____.

Scene 3: "Cameron you wanted a marker. You didn't know the words to use to get it. You may not grab. When you want a marker say, *May I borrow your marker, please?* Say that now."

Teacher's overall focus: _____.

Scene 4: Think about the last discipline encounter you had with a child. Bring up a specific scene with dialogue. Write the dialogue in the space below:

_____

_____.

Your overall focus: _____.

In Scene 1, the teacher's focus was on hitting. In Scene 2, the focus was on fighting. In Scene 3, the focus was on communicating the skill, "May I borrow your marker, please?" Where was your focus in scene 4? Check the box that most accurately represents your focus.

❏ I was focused on the behavior I wanted to see.
   Encourage yourself! "I did it! I focused on the behavior I wanted to see!"

❏ I was focused on the problem and/or the behavior I didn't want.
   Say, "Oops!" and describe what you could do differently next time. (Give it your best shot; the upcoming section on "pivoting" will help if you're not sure.)

Commitment: When I am upset, I will take a deep breath and switch my focus from what I **don't** want to what I **do** want children to do. I will tell children what I want them to do and why. My "why" will be related to safety.

Signature _____ Date _____

Pivoting, "About Face!"

When we are upset, we are always focused on what we **don't** want instead of what we **do** want. The goal is not to eliminate life's frustrations, but to regain self-control so we can deal with them effectively. We must discipline ourselves first and our children second. Shifting our focus is essential to meeting this goal. Pivoting helps us shift our focus from what we don't want to what we do want. When we feel frenzied (triggered into an upset emotional state), it is helpful to pause, take a deep breath and say to ourselves, "I'm safe. Keep breathing. I can handle this," to access our executive state. Then ask, "Do I want more of this?" If the answer is "no," we can choose to pivot, shifting our minds from what we don't want to what we do want and then stating it assertively. (If the answer is a loud "I don't care," go ahead and lose it, but remember to forgive yourself later.)

Common Pivoting Opportunities

Triggered / Habitual Response	Assertive Statement
Don't touch!	Hold my hand so I can help you touch delicate objects safely.
You know better than that.	Say, "Excuse me," when you bump into others.
Stop. It's not nice to hit others.	When you want to get her attention, tap her on the shoulder gently like this and say her name.

Most of us know pivoting as a term for the physical movement of turning abruptly. We are more likely to remember experiences that are accompanied by motor activities, so making the physical motion of pivoting will help as we learn this new skill. The more we physically pivot during practice, the more likely we are to mentally and emotionally pivot during a real moment of upset.

Activity to Pivot

Role-play pivoting in the situations listed below. To add more power to your practice, stand up and physically make an about-face as you act out the scenarios.

Step 1: Walk two steps focusing on what you don't want in an upset tone.
Step 2: Rotate on the balls of your feet to turn yourself in the opposite direction as you consciously S.T.A.R. and affirm: "I'm safe. Keep breathing. I can handle this."
Step 3: Take two steps forward and transform your negative statements into a positive statement of what you want the child to do.

Situation 1: In the middle of telling Tom what you want him to do, he makes a face and says, "You're stupid and I don't have to listen to you." You snap back, "Don't you ever talk to me like that again!"

Situation 2: Two children are pushing and shoving in the back of the room. Eventually this form of bonding gets out of hand and one child hits the other. You arrive on the scene and yell, "Stop this nonsense. You know better than this!"

Situation 3: Recall the last time you lost it with a child. Breathe deeply, forgive yourself for losing it and then role-play the situation using your newfound pivoting skills.

Self-Check:

- Did you get upset and tell the child what not to do using the words in the situations above?
- Did you actively calm yourself by being a S.T.A.R. and affirming, "I'm safe. Keep breathing. I can handle this."?
- Did you check your willingness to pivot by asking, "Do I want more of this?"
- Did you pivot using the three steps above, painting a clear picture of what the child is to do?
- Did you focus on what you want the child to do? Use the Dead Person Assessment below as a guide if you're unsure.

> **Dead Person Assessment:** If a dead person can do it, you have **not** stated what to do, nor are you giving usable information. For example, "Can a dead person stop talking?" Yes. This means that you are still focusing on what you **don't** want. "Can a dead person sit quietly, cross his legs, put his hands in his lap and listen to the lesson?" Nope! This means you are focusing on what you **do** want.

Focusing on what you don't want creates more of what you don't want in your life. This month, pay attention to the many occasions when you tell yourself what **not** to do. Listen carefully to your private speech and how you speak to others. Then consciously redirect your attention by focusing on what **to** do and what you **do** want. Do this in every arena of your life (the food you will eat, the way you want children to act, the behavior you want from your spouse). Remember these universal principles: "What you focus on, you get more of," "When you are upset, you are always focused on what you don't want," and "If you are upset, you are resisting what is."

Becoming Brain Smart

Attention is a whole brain activity; when we intentionally direct our attention to something or someone, we are engaging circuits throughout the brain. Let's go back to the flashlight metaphor from the beginning of this chapter to help us understand how the whole brain works together. Pretend the goal is to take the flashlight (our attention) and focus it on our tent in the woods so we can find our way back from the lake. First, we must turn the flashlight on. To do this we need some arousal energy from our brain stem. We want just the right amount of clacker energy (review the clacker information in Chapter 2 if necessary). We don't want an AAA battery in a flashlight that requires a C battery or vice versa; our clacker needs a steady beat to supply just the right amount of energy. Second, we must be motivated to find that tent, remembering it is going to be a warm and cozy place to sleep with family members. We need the limbic system's functions of emotion, belonging and memory for this desire. Finally, we need our prefrontal lobes to hold that flashlight steady and maintain our focus on the tent. Without the steady aim of the prefrontal lobes, we might start waving the flashlight all around, looking at plants, animals and other distractions. We could lose sight of our goal and get lost in the woods.

Attention and Neuroplasticity

Where we place our attention literally alters the structure of our brains. Neuroplasticity is the word scientists use to describe the brain's ability to change its structure, circuits, chemical composition and function in response to changing needs. It allows us to wire and rewire our brains over and over again. We direct our brain's neuroplasticity whenever we focus our attention (Schwartz & Begley, 2002). This means that from a scientific perspective, neuroplasticity is at the heart of all learning.

In and of itself, neuroplasticity is neither good nor bad; it's just the process by which our brain adapts to changing environments. Coined "self-directed neuroplasticity" by Drs. Schwartz and Gladding, we have the power to mold our brains by consciously focusing our attention. Focused attention connects and stabilizes brain circuits so they wire together. Where we focus our attention tells bands of neurons to fire at the same time. Neurons that fire together, wire together. The Power of Attention is the key that determines whether neuroplasticity will be helpful or harmful. We create negative wiring when we focus our attention on the false messages on our CD-Rom. The more we focus our attention on these false messages, the stronger these pathways become. We become more reactive and hurtful. We also stress our immune, endocrine and cardiovascular systems. On the other hand, when we choose to focus our attention on seeing the positive, having faith that all is well and actively calming ourselves, we strengthen these pathways to become more peaceful, loving and healthy. Conscious Discipline helps us use neuroplasticity to rewire our brains in healthy ways so we can help children wire their brains in healthy ways, too.

Attention and Brain Chemistry

Focusing on what we don't want also pits our brain and body chemistry against our willpower, cutting down our chances for success. Dieting is a good example. Let's say you want to eat fewer sweets. You may tell yourself, "That's it, no more sweets for me. I'm not eating them." In saying these words, you are focusing on sweets. Your brain hears the word "sweet," and the brain regions responsible for your body chemistry adjust for an influx of sugar. Your blood sugar drops and your insulin levels change. Off to the candy aisle you go!

To successfully cut back on sweets, you must focus your attention on what you want. In this case your focus would be, "I love fruits and vegetables. I want more fruits and vegetables in my life." After vigilantly doing this for 21 days, your brain rewires itself and your body will be naturally drawn to the produce section in the grocery store. You have rewired your brain by consciously focusing on fruits and vegetables, preparing your prefrontal cortex for what it does best—selecting among a range of choices in the produce section and inhibiting impulses as you glide by the cookies and crackers. "I'll have veggies, please!"

All of this information about focus, neuroplasticity and habit formation boils down to this: We have the power to create the life we want. We can use the Power of Attention to focus on the false messages on our CD-Rom, or we can shift our focus to the mantra in the last chapter: "I'm safe. Keep breathing. I can handle this." We will strengthen whatever we choose to focus on, thereby creating a life of distress or calm. Now that is powerful!

Helping Children Develop Their Power of Attention

Remember, where we place our attention dictates our values. It also teaches children where to direct their attention and how to build their value system. When we focus our attention on what is wrong, missing or not going our way, we are unconsciously teaching children to focus on the same. We are using the brain's innate neuroplasticity to wire children for "not enoughness."

Today's children are growing up in a technology age where our media-saturated world is grabbing and holding their attention in some concerning ways. Dr. Diane Levin (2013) calls it culture clash. One culture is filled with the values, attitudes and behaviors many teachers and parents hope to instill, and the other is a culture of the messages children encounter through media. Media tends to focus its attention on violence, aggression, mean-spirited behavior, sex and appearances. Given the power of focused attention and neuroplasticity, more children are demonstrating play deficit disorders, problem-solving disorders and compassion deficit disorders (Levin, 2013). We have also seen an enormous amount of marketing geared toward children since the United States government deregulated marketing to children in 1984. Between the ages of 2 and 11, children see more than 25,000 advertisements just on television (Holt, Ippiloto, Desrochers & Kelley, 2007), creating an "I want it" cycle and promoting the notion that buying equals happiness. Children also see 4,000 food ads, 81 percent of which are for candy, fast food, sugary cereals or soft drinks (Kaiser Family Foundation, 2007), while simultaneously having their attention focused on slim, perfect bodies.

This culture clash has a profound impact on children. In addition, our persistence in focusing children's attention on what we don't want sets the scene for chronic failure. Watch a toddler when you say, "Don't touch the lamp." What does she do? She looks at you, looks at the lamp, points to it, touches it and then looks back at you. She was motivated to learn about the lamp by touching it. You helped her focus her attention on it further by saying, "Don't touch the lamp," but her immature prefrontal cortex couldn't associate "don't" with the rest of your statement. Her brain heard, "Touch the lamp," so she touched it and looked at you proudly as if to say, "I did it! I touched the lamp!" Imagine her confusion when you growl, "What did I tell you?" and push away her little hand. Instead of focusing on what you don't want, redirect the child with a positive command. When she spots the lamp, you could say, "You see a pretty lamp. Put your hand in mine and I will show you how to touch delicate objects so everything is safe."

Children younger than five or six years old have a hard time understanding negative verbs such as "do not." When you say, "Don't talk with your mouth full," you actually increase the chances your child will "disobey" and you'll get to watch him grind broccoli in living color. The child's brain comprehends the action (verb) and the thing (noun), but it doesn't comprehend the "not" (adverb). It would be more effective to say, "Chew with your lips closed like this." Descriptive language and demonstration focuses the child's attention on the actions we want. The noticing process accomplishes exactly this goal.

Noticing to Develop Children's Attention

Children (especially those with ADD, living in poverty, experiencing environmental stressors or younger than eight years old) need assistance developing executive skills like attention. Healthy attention is sustained and self-directed: It turns the flashlight on, keeps it on and aims it steadily toward a goal. Attention protects working memory in the brain and working memory drives cognition (Huang & Sekuler (2010), and Zanto, T. & Gazzaley, A. (2009)). Without memory, academic learning comes to a standstill.

We must scaffold children's attention by helping them aim their flashlights on the desired goals. As educators, we don't often think in terms of scaffolding a child's attention. We are usually focused on how to get a child's attention by catching it with theatrics, demanding it, rewarding it and manipulating it, but not supporting its development. We talked about noticing to download calm in the last chapter. Noticing also scaffolds and supports children's attention so it can develop optimally. It requires a clear, judgment-free description of what is happening and often includes physical modeling of the action. Noticing, "You folded the napkin in half and set it next to your plate," brings the child's awareness to his accomplishment. "Good job with the napkin," judges the action as satisfactory.

Noticing is the Power of Attention in action. It requires us to be the witness instead of the judge or juror. When we notice something, we bring it into our conscious awareness, activating both neuroplasticity and the prefrontal lobes. Noticing our thoughts and behaviors allows us to change them (or not). Noticing children directs their Power of Attention in the same way, creating self-awareness, activating neuroplasticity and the frontal lobes, and empowering change. On the other hand, judging a child's behavior as good or bad comes from an emotional state and is biased by our personal CD-Rom. It keeps us and our children locked into preprogrammed actions and reactions.

Activity to Feel the Difference Between Noticing and Judging

Find a partner to help you with the following exercise. Read the noticing statement and then read the judgment statement. Take turns giving and receiving the messages. At the end of the exercise, discuss how different each statement felt.

Noticing	Judging
Miley, you raised your hand just like this (demonstrate), so I knew you needed help.	Miley, I like the way you raised your hand.
Noah, you pushed your chair in just like this (demonstrate), so our classroom is safe.	Thank you for pushing in your chair.
Emma, you worked hard on question number two until you figured it out. That took persistence.	Good job Emma! Keep up the good work.
Zach, you got the paper towels and cleaned the water off the floor so everyone would be safe from slipping.	I wish everyone cleaned up like Zach does! What a good helper.

Noticing continually activates children's prefrontal lobes and strengthens their executive skills of sustained attention, empathy and problem-solving. However, it requires adults to consciously change our habits and rewire our brains to notice instead of judge. We might notice a child's facial expression. "See Taleese's face. Her face is saying, *I don't like it when you're so close; move over please.*" We might notice a child's body language. "Sean walked in with his shoulders slumped like this (demonstrate) and head down like this (demonstrate). He looks like he could use our help. Let's all take a deep breath and wish him well." We might notice children's behaviors. "Cooper raised his hand so I would know he needed help." We can notice children in many different ways and settings. Your portal includes additional noticing examples to help you on your journey.

Noticing helps scaffold children's Power of Attention by directing and sustaining their attention. Adults essentially hold their flashlights until children can hold and aim them on their own. Noticing is a powerful tool we will revisit in many contexts within this book. Its impact in the classroom is immediate, obvious and profound.

Years ago, I was observing a second-grade classroom doing a space program lesson that included NASA stickers. A little boy was struggling to get his stickers off the sheet. He stood up, looked around the room, picked a girl with long nails and went over to ask for help. I noticed this by saying, "You were having trouble getting your stickers off the sheet and looked carefully around the room to find someone you thought could be helpful. Then you walked over and asked for help. That allowed you to be successful." This was my only interaction with this child. Two weeks later, I was back at the school. He saw me in the hall, broke out of line and came up to me. I didn't recognize him at first. He said, "Don't you remember me? I'm the one who is successful at school!"

Activity to Notice Instead of Judge

Below are common judgments. Transform these into noticing opportunities that scaffold children's attention. Find sample answers and videos that demonstrate noticing on your portal.

- Good job on the quiz, Jose! _____
  _____

- Karen, do you know how to ask for a turn?_____
  _____

- Thank you for cleaning up the sink area. _____
  _____

- A common judgment I make: _____
  _____

- What I could say instead: _____
  _____

The Skill of Assertiveness

Assertiveness is the skill that emerges from the Power of Attention and teaches others how to treat us. It lets us set boundaries on what behaviors we consider appropriate, safe and permissible. It empowers us to say "no" to believing the false messages on our CD-Roms, "no" to behaviors that do not support our goals, and "no" to others. It enables us to say "no" to children and teach them acceptable ways to say "no" to others. It also enables us to say "yes" to interactions that support us and to teach children when "yes" is in order. Assertiveness allows us to express our needs, wants and desires constructively, without devaluing the other person's needs, wants and desires. In short, it is the medium through which we teach respect. Disrespect from children signals a lack of assertive adults in their lives. We must first master the Skill of Assertiveness ourselves, and then we can teach children how to assertively set limits with others.

Assertiveness is the medium through which we teach respect.

Assertiveness is vital to our success because it is one of few skills that are useful with all three brain states. Skills that are helpful with lower brain states are also generally helpful in higher brain states. However, skills specific for higher brain states are not generally effective in lower brain states. For example, offering two positive choices helps a child in an emotional state become more organized. Giving choices to a child experiencing a survival state, on the other hand, will increase his distress. (Think about a time when you were completely overwhelmed with stress. If someone asked if you'd like coffee or tea, you could easily collapse into "I don't know.") Assertiveness is one of the skills we can successfully use with all three states, like all the other N.A.R.C.S. skills.

Understanding the Three Voices

We teach others how to treat us in all of our relationships. Passivity invites aggression, aggression begets aggression and assertiveness dissipates aggression. People who seem doubtful or unsure invite other people to boss them around or "help" them even when they don't want or need help. People who speak aggressively teach others to be silent or aggressively defend their position. People who communicate assertively let other people know their limits while also respecting the needs of others.

> *Passivity invites aggression, aggression begets aggression and assertiveness dissipates aggression.*

Learning to distinguish between passive, aggressive and assertive voices is essential to being assertive. Once we are aware of the ways we communicate (both effective and ineffective), we can then consciously choose communication that is more likely to meet our goals.

Passivity

The goal of passivity is to please others. A passive person's speech and actions constantly say, "Approve of me. Agree with me. Love me." Passive people give their power to children as they manipulate them to behave. They relinquish this power by leaving decisions to others. "Where should we eat?" They ask permission. "Just let me hang up, honey, then Mommy will talk to you." By putting another person in charge, a passive person skirts responsibility if something goes awry.

Passive people seldom express direct desires for fear their desires may not be the "right" ones, instead dropping hints. "Wouldn't it be nice if we had faculty gatherings?" Sometimes they say what they don't want. "I don't want to be at work all day with people I don't know." They may ask questions instead of making statements. "Don't you think it is important for the faculty to bond?"

When passive adults surrender their power to children, they hope children will use that power to make the "right" choice (to act nice). If they don't, the adult is likely to feel powerless and frustrated, and this frustration often begets aggression. This passive-aggressive flip-flop produces guilt. Guilt promotes more passivity.

> **A passive teacher in action:** Mrs. Lee announces it is cleanup time. Her two-minute warning elicits a few whines, so she extends her warning to five minutes. She waits as long as possible to sing her cleanup song and help those who are having trouble. "Ella, it's time to clean up now, okay?" Ella busily puts the blocks on the shelf. "Cody, try to put all the same toys in the same bin, okay?" Alison asks for assistance and Mrs. Lee replies, "Let me finish here and I'll be over in a minute."
>
> Mrs. Lee walks around the room one last time to help the stragglers. "Markus, are you ready for circle time?" Markus continues to paint. Mrs. Lee, now a bit frustrated, asks, "What time is it, Markus? Where should you be? What should you be doing?" Markus ignores Mrs. Lee. She feels frustrated and powerless. Some of the children who had gone to the circle are starting to horse around. Mrs. Lee shouts, "Markus, stop right now! Don't make me send you to time out!" Markus continues painting. "I'm warning you. This is not very nice behavior. Why are you doing this?"

Mrs. Lee demonstrates almost all the behaviors of a passive teacher. At the beginning, she changes her time limit to accommodate the whining of a few children, putting her need to avoid conflict above the children's need for useful information and clearly stated expectations. She then repeatedly put the children in charge through comments like, "Ella, it's time to clean up, **okay**?" "Okay" implies the children have the choice to comply. She asks Cody to accomplish a nonspecific goal: "Try to clean up." She gives her power away without repercussion until Markus.

When Mrs. Lee gives Markus a choice about being ready for circle, he opts to continue painting. She makes statements that fail to provide usable information: "What time is it?" and "Where should you be?" These non-action questions confuse Markus and aggravate Mrs. Lee into threatening: "Don't **make me** send you to time out!" Mrs. Lee's "make me" language blames Markus for her passive choices and sends the message that Markus is in charge of her decision. Mrs. Lee unconsciously models irresponsibility, gives her power away and then finds it difficult to regain.

The following are characteristics of the passive person:

- A passive person asks the child to accomplish an intermediate but nonspecific task.
  Examples: Try to be nice. Try your best to clean up. Try to follow directions better.

- A passive person questions the child about his or her behavior. Questions don't give usable information.
  Examples: Where should you be? Why are you doing that?

- A passive person does not follow through on consequences and will adjust events to accommodate the child's emotions.
  Examples: Okay, once more but then it's time to stop. I'm warning you, just one more outburst!

- A passive person gives power away to the child, putting the child in charge.
  Examples: When you are ready, I will begin. Let me finish here, and I will help you.

- A passive person holds the child responsible for his anger and out-of-control behavior.
  Examples: You're making me send you to time out. Don't make me take that paper away!

- A passive person gives children choices when there are none.
  Examples: It's time to clean up, okay? Are you ready for rest time?

- A passive person may ignore a situation completely in hopes that the unacceptable behavior will magically disappear.

Passivity gives away our power. Once we have put others in charge, it is difficult to get our power back. This occurs in all relationships. At home we may find ourselves giving power to our partners by saying things like, "Honey, I'm feeling kind of grubby, so I'm thinking of taking a quick bath before bed, okay?" When we make this language a habit, we invite questions like, "Where are you going? What are you doing? Why didn't you talk to me before you did that?" We may find ourselves feeling angry, thinking, "Why do I have to tell him what I'm doing or ask his permission?" when we have actually encouraged this behavior. We teach others how to treat us.

Aggression

Aggressive communication aims to win by overpowering. "Winning" means getting the other person to do what we want. An aggressive teacher might not say she's won, but would say the technique worked.

An aggressive teacher often uses you/me statements like, "**You** always interrupt **me**." You/me statements focus on the other person, not the problem. If a teacher says, "You hurt me," a child feels attacked. If a teacher says, "I feel hurt," no attack is implied. Because you/me statements focus on the person, the recipient generally feels she must respond defensively. With adults, we call the resulting exchange an argument. With children, we call it talking back.

Aggressive people often speak for others and act as mind readers. They will describe the other person's viewpoint (often incorrectly). "You think you can get away with acting like that in my class. You'd better think again." Aggressive people also use the words "always" and "never" as forms of attack. "You never remember your lunch money." "You always put off big projects." With such extreme statements, we suggest the child is all good or all bad. By generalizing, we teach children to generalize about themselves and others. They may grow up saying things like, "I never do things well," or "All computer wizards are nerds."

An Aggressive Teacher in Action: Ms. Wall is having a rough day. She sees three children spraying each other at the water fountain and shouts, "What are you doing by that water fountain? How many times have I told you to stay in your seats? You never listen." Laura tries to explain to the teacher saying, "Ms. Wall, Karri has a cut on . . ." Ms. Wall interrupts, "You're just using Karri as an excuse to make a mess and get out of doing your work." "But, Ms. Wall," whines Tara. "Don't you talk back to me, young lady! Now get to work before I put your name on the board. You think you can do whatever you want, but you're wrong. I am in charge of this classroom and you are keeping other children from learning," Ms. Wall says. As the children drag themselves back to their seats, Ms. Wall begins to threaten them. "You don't have to act like that. You ought to be grateful I don't send you to the principal."

Ms. Wall demonstrated most of the characteristics of aggressive people:

- She spoke for others, often wrongly describing their viewpoints, instead of expressing her own thoughts and feelings. "You are just using Karri as an excuse to get out of work and make a mess in this classroom."
- She used the words "always" and "never." "You never listen."
- She viewed others as attacking her. "Don't you back talk me, young lady."
- She used punitive threats. "Now get back to work before I put your name on the board."
- She made "you" statements that focused on the other people, not the problem.

> **"You/me" accusations leave a child feeling attacked.**

Although Ms. Wall did not act in the following ways, aggressive people often do:

- Imposing consequences that are overly severe. "Detention for two weeks."
- Physically responding to a child out of anger such as shaking, squeezing the child's arm, jerking or hitting the child.

> **Any statement about the other person, rather than one's own feelings or thoughts, tends to have an attacking quality.**

Assertiveness

The goal of assertiveness is clear communication that paints a picture of what we want others to do. It has a voice tone of "no doubt" and comes from an intention of helping children be successful instead of making them behave. When we communicate assertively, we make straightforward statements about feelings, thoughts and wishes. It is assertive to say, "I want pizza today." It is not assertive to quiz others ("What would you like?"), think for them ("You probably want Chinese food like always!"), or try to control them ("Everyone loves pizza. Why don't you?"). To be assertive, we must concentrate on ourselves instead of focusing on what others might think, feel, say or do in response. We cannot set limits and take care of other people's feelings at the same time.

> **An Assertive Teacher in Action:** Grace seems to have trouble staying on task. During Open House, Mrs. Canipe observes Grace and her mother. Mom repeatedly attempts to get Grace's attention by saying, "Grace, please look at me. I am talking. Grace, are you listening to me? Grace, do you hear me? I am not going to speak to you again. Grace!" Mom then gets frustrated, grabs Grace's arm and lectures her on respect and listening. Mrs. Canipe approaches Grace differently. She walks over and gets down on eye level with her. She waits for Grace to notice her and make eye contact before beginning to speak. With a firm voice she says, "Grace, take your mother's hand. It is time to go home. I look forward to seeing you tomorrow at school." Mrs. Canipe waits for Grace to make any motion toward her mother and quickly says, "You did it! You looked for your Mom so you could find her hand."

> *Assertiveness clearly tells children what to do so they may successfully meet your expectations.*

Assertiveness requires we do the following:

- **Vigilantly give children usable information by telling them what to do** and by painting a picture of expected behaviors. Assertive: "Sit down and turn your head side-to-side to see if you and your friends have enough space." Nonassertive: "Don't sit too close to each other." "Sit nicely with your friends."

- **Notice children's behaviors** by using descriptive language that clearly communicates the desired goal without judgment. Assertive: "Miquel sat down, opened his science book to page 41 and is looking for his pencil." Nonassertive: "Good job, Miquel. I see you are almost ready."

- **Send the nonverbal message of "just do it"** with a tone of voice and body language. When used with a clear command, a nonverbal message of "no doubt" creates a felt sense of safety that allows many children to let down their guard and obey our commands.

- **Be conscious of the intent behind your communication.** The intent behind assertive communication is clarity. Your intent behind the words is more powerful than your actual choice of words. You are not being assertive if your intent is to avoid a conflict (passive) or to make/get children to obey (aggressive). When you shift your intent to a heartfelt desire for the child to be successful, your clarity will shine and disobedience will decline.

 If you aren't using all the components above, then you aren't being assertive! Watch a video on the portal of assertive directions in a third-grade classroom. Notice the lack of judgement and use of noticing.

Overview of the Three Voices

	Assertive	**Passive**	**Aggressive**
Intent:	Clarity and success	Avoids conflict through pleasing	Avoids conflict through dominating
Tone:	No doubt.	Asking permission?	Or else!
Power:	Within	Given away	Taken from others
Feelings:	Owned with direct expression	Projected with indirect expression	Projected with indirect expression
Information:	Usable, what to do	Unusable, confusing	Unusable, attacking

Activity to Recognize the Three Voices

With a partner, use a passive, an aggressive and an assertive voice to give the command, "Sit down and look at me." Give the command three times, using the voice as indicated. Record how each voice felt, sounded and looked on the chart below.

	Feels Like	Sounds Like	Looks Like
Passive:			
Aggressive:			
Assertive:			

Now, assess your current communication style. Note the percentage of time you speak to children with each communication style. Remember, to be assertive you must clearly tell children what you want, using a voice of no doubt. Can you tell how your voice changes when you are stressed?

Passive _____%   Aggressive _____%   Assertive _____%

Adult Assertiveness: Respectfully Increasing Compliance

In order to give assertive commands successfully, we must be clear on the difference between requests and commands. A command is about nonnegotiable compliance. "Put your notebook in your desk and line up for lunch." You cannot legally or morally leave the child in the room while you go to lunch. It is nonnegotiable; therefore, it is a command. When children choose to comply with a command, follow up with effective praise like, "You did it," or "Good for you" (Encouragement, Chapter 6). A request offers the child a choice by asking him to do something for us. "Would you please hand this pencil to Melissa for me?" When children choose to honor the relationship by being kind in response to a request, it is appropriate to teach manners with polite phrases like "please" and "thank you."

As children, most of us received commands worded as requests. "Keith, would you take out the trash?" actually meant, "Get up now and take the trash to the curb." Confusing commands and requests presents two problems. First, the child must figure it out. This can take days, months or years, and untold numbers of lectures and spankings. In that time, a lot of frustration, unnecessary anger and hurt feelings can develop. Second, people who grow up with this type of language eventually stop hearing choices. Life becomes one obligation after another. When an acquaintance asks us to dinner, our CD-Rom tells us we should go and plays the guilt track from those childhood lectures. Learning to give assertive commands eliminates such ambiguity.

Confusing commands and requests also confuses the child. Teachers will give a command, "Open your books to page 32," and follow with, "Thank you." Thank you says, "You opened your books for me." It robs the command of its assertive power. When we word our commands as requests or follow them with, "Thank you," we are saying, "Behave well for me; be successful for me; do things for me." Requests inject our relationship with the child into the situation. Children who have had painful relationships will automatically defy these requests in efforts to stay safe. If our goal is for children to choose compliance, we must take our relationship out of the situation by providing clear, assertive commands.

In addition to pivoting (discussed earlier in this chapter), the following skills will help children comply with our commands and follow our directions. Administrators must also utilize these assertiveness skills with employees.

1. Name, Verb, Paint all assertive commands
2. The voice of no doubt
3. Tell and Show for children who resist
4. Assertive commands for groups
5. Redirection
6. I-Messages

1. Name, Verb, Paint Assertive Commands

Mental models govern our behaviors. Most children have a mental model for how to use the restroom by the age of three. You have a mental model for how to drive from your house to the grocery store. Professional golfers rehearse a mental image of each shot before they hit the ball. Due to lack of mature inner speech, children use images for the mental models that govern their behavior. They must be able to visualize our commands in order to be successful in reproducing them. So, assertive communication with children seeks to help them create clear mental images by painting pictures of acceptable behaviors. Passive and aggressive communication fails to achieve this goal. The Name, Verb, Paint process helps us communicate assertively with the following steps:

Step 1, Name: Make eye contact. To establish eye contact, decrease the distance between your face and the child's until she notices you. For easily distracted or disengaged children, this distance may be as close as eight inches; for others, it could be three feet. If the child does not look up, notice her nonverbal cues and body language to obtain eye contact. "Your hands (head, arms, legs, etc.) are going like this (demonstrate)." Once you achieve eye contact, state the child's name.

> Some cultures instruct children not to make eye contact with adults in specific situations, usually when being reprimanded. Giving a command is not a reprimand; it's intent is for the child's success. Investigate further if you believe a lack of eye contact is cultural.

Step 2, Verb: Verbalize what you want to see. Begin the sentence with a verb and be as specific as possible. "Remove all papers and books, and put them in your desk."

Step 3, Paint: Paint a picture of the expected behavior using gestures and any visual cues possible to help the child be successful. Point to all the papers and books on the tables, then use your arms and hands to show where the child is to put the items as you say, "Remove all papers and books, and put them in your desk."

The more senses you can incorporate, the more effective your assertive commands will be. Examples of commands to go with each sense:

- **Visual**: Utilize eye contact and gestures
- **Auditory**: State the child's name and your expectations
- **Kinesthetic**: Move into proximity with the child
- **Tactile**: Touch the child, offering gentle guidance
- **Energetic**: With a loving, positive intent for clarity and success

Activity to Name, Verb, Paint

Which commands below create clear mental images? Rewrite the examples that don't. Remember, the image we create in children's heads becomes the blueprint for their behavior.

"STOP! No running. There is no running in the halls."

_____

_____

"Walking feet. Walking feet. Walking feet."

_____

_____

"What's our rule about running? What should you be doing right now?"

_____

_____

"Carol, walk in the hall just like this (demonstrate with your body), leaving plenty of space for your neighbor so everyone is safe, including you."

This clear and specific visual image wires the brain to successfully meet the expectation.

The more completely we paint a picture with our words and actions, the clearer a mental model we will instill in children's brains. Thus, Name, Verb, Paint significantly increases compliance.

2. The Voice of No Doubt

Your tone of voice is critical. It is estimated that 93 percent of all communication is nonverbal, including voice tone, intention and body language tone, intention and body language (Mehrabian, 1971). To find your assertive tone, do the following: Look around the room you're in. Look up and say, "That is the ceiling." Look down and say, "That is the floor." In the same tone of voice, say, "Sit down and look at me." You have just used an assertive tone! There is no doubt in your voice that the ceiling is above you, the floor is below you and your command is, "Sit down and look at me." Your "no doubt about it" voice ensures your nonverbal and your verbal communications match.

We've all heard a grumpy adult snap, "Yes, I love you. Now go out and play!" When our words say one thing and our underlying tone says another, it is called a mixed message. If our nonverbal cues are passive, our children may easily choose not to comply. If our nonverbal cues are aggressive, our children may resist in self-defense. A child who receives mixed messages does not know whether to believe the words he is hearing or what he is feeling based on the nonverbal message. Over time, this could lead him to distrust himself and lose contact with his internal guidance.

When our nonverbal and verbal communication match, we let children know we mean what we say and say what we mean. Before children decide whether to comply with a command, they will read our facial expressions, tone of voice and gestures. We increase the chances they will obey if we appear confident and in control, sound sure of ourselves, believe they can be successful, and use gestures to provide information.

3. Tell and Show for Children who Resist

Children who do not follow our assertive commands are communicating to us that they need additional support. If a child chooses not to comply with a command, we must change the structure to aid in the child's success. Ask, "What can I do to help this child meet my expectations and meet his own needs at the same time?" One helpful strategy for these situations is Tell and Show. It involves telling children what you want them to do, following up by showing them how to do it and then encouraging them along the way. The intentional message is, "Here is what is expected of you. I will assist you in performing it successfully."

Step 1: Give an assertive command. "Joshua, It is time to go to lunch. Put your pencil down and line up for lunch." If the child complies, say, "You did it," or "Good for you." If the child ignores you, continue to Step 2.

Step 2: Notice and download. When the world is not going our way, we are likely to slip into an emotional state. It's easy to feel frustrated or start shouting from a distance when children ignore us. We can choose to balance this tendency by beginning to breathe deeply as soon as we feel ignored. Take a deep breath, walk toward the child, and consciously notice his behaviors and body language until he makes eye contact. "Your head is down and your hand is going like this (mirror what the child is doing)." As soon as the child glances up to see what you are doing, be a S.T.A.R. to download calm into the child and proceed to Step 3.

Step 3: Say, "There you are! I'm going to show you how to get started." Say, "I am going to show you how to…" Guide the child gently to follow your command. "I am going to show you how to line up with the rest of the School Family." Then touch him gently on the back to physically guide him. If the child chooses to be cooperative, encourage him by saying, "That's it! You are doing it! You've got yourself ready to head to the door!" If he pulls away when you touch him, that would signal a survival state; proceed to Step 4.

Step 4: Notice and download, followed by two positive choices (Chapter 6). If the child's behavior indicates he is still in a survival state, notice his actions. "Your arm is going like this, your body is turned like this." Wait for eye contact, and take a couple of deep S.T.A.R. breaths to download calm and safety into the child. Next, offer two positive choices to help the child to achieve your goal. "Joshua, you have a choice. You can line up behind Malik or you can ask Malik if you can walk beside him in line. Which is better for you?" If Joshua cooperates, say, "There you go. You're doing it. You chose to ask your buddy." If Joshua is still resistant, go to Step 5.

Step 5: Repeat the choices in a consistent and calm state, regardless of what the child says or does. "Joshua, you have a choice: Behind Malik or next to Malik." Joshua might respond with an effort to trigger you into a power struggle. He may say, "You can't make me," or resort to profanity. Your job is to stay calm using all your Q.T.I.P. power. Calmly repeat, "Behind Malik or with Malik" up to four times. Then, if necessary, walk away. If you can remain calm and wish him well in tone, posture and intent, the child will often choose to comply. He may comply by walking with a stomp, rolling his eyes or muttering under his breath. Ignore these behaviors. These behaviors are just the child discharging excess adrenaline and cortisol. Once he complies, walk by Joshua in line and say, "It was tough, but you did it. Good for you, Joshua."

Like any skill, we can abuse Tell and Show. If our intention is for the child to be successful and capable, our actions will be guided accordingly. If our intention is to force the child to comply, we will communicate this also. If a child chronically ignores commands or refuses to comply, ask yourself if your expectations are appropriate and your intent loving. Do you have a connection with the child? Persistent resistance is often a sign to refocus our intent and/or rebuild a connection with the child. Remember, connection is the precursor to cooperation. Tell and Show takes practice, so allow yourself to Oops! as much as necessary.

4. Giving Assertive Commands to Groups

The process for giving assertive commands to groups is similar to the individual process we've focused on thus far, but it begins with a signal or unifying experience to get the group's attention. The signal will help them stop what they are doing and shift their attention to another activity (the new command). Many teachers and child caregivers use blinking the lights, a musical instrument such as a drum or triangle, or a specific transition chant or song. Teach the class both an auditory and visual signal. Give the auditory signal first then the visual one as shown in the following example:

> At the beginning of the year, Mrs. Pinder decides to use a drum as her auditory signal and children raising their hands as her visual signal. She frames her discussion of the drum with a Native American folklore story about the drum as a means for people of different languages to communicate. She states clearly that when the children hear the drum beat, they are to stop what they are doing, take a deep breath to help focus, look for the teacher, raise their hands to alert their friends and listen for the instructions that will follow.
>
> First, she provides the children discussion time. "Pretend you are drawing at your table and you hear the drum. What will you do?" "Pretend you are talking with your friends and you hear the drum. What will you do?" Next, she provides practice time. The children engage in activities that require actual talking and movement, and then they practice stopping, breathing, looking at her, raising their hands and listening for instruction. Each time they successfully stop what they are doing and shift their focus, Mrs. Pinder celebrates this accomplishment.

Sometimes children are so scattered that chaos seems eminent. At these times, a unifying activity is more effective than a signal. A unifying activity brings the whole class together doing the same thing. "Everybody do this, do this, do this. Everybody do this, do this now," is a unifying chant that's best used with a challenging or silly "do this" activity. A call and response activity is also unifying. If you are the Farias Tigers, the teacher might call out, "Farias Tigers!" and the class would chant back, "Helpful, ready and willing!" After the unifying activity, lead the class in being a S.T.A.R. and tell them what to do next.

This is the basic process for giving a command in a group setting:

Step 1: Utilize a signal and/or conduct a unifying chant or movement. Once you have the class's attention, lead them in being a S.T.A.R. (**S**mile, **T**ake a deep breath **A**nd **R**elax) or one of the other de-stressing activities such as Balloon, Drain, or Pretzel.

Step 2: Notice the children who stop. "Phillip, Reynaldo, Wayne, Ashley, each of you stopped, looked and are ready to listen. You heard the signal and are ready for what will happen next. Phillip you were talking to Reynaldo and you both turned like this (show actions)." Avoid statements that begin with "I like," such as "I like the way Maria stopped and looked up." When you insert "I" in the statement, you make it about you instead of the child.

Step 3: Verbally tell the children what you want them to do. As soon as you have the children's attention, begin telling them what you want them to do. Expecting children to wait (especially young ones) is a recipe for trouble.

Activity to Reflect on Your Current Group Commands

Reflect on the following:

1. Have you taught the class signal? Does it have an auditory, visual and kinesthetic (breathing) component? Did you practice it for 21 days to form a habit? _____

2. Have you framed the experience so children who hear the signal can help those who missed it to also be successful? (Raising hands to alert friends.) _____

3. Do you encourage children who follow the signal by noticing instead of judging their accomplishment? ("You stopped what you were doing, took a deep breath and looked for me.") Do you judge, fostering dependency? ("Good listening!") Do you manipulate through affection? ("I like the way ___ is listening.") _____

4. How are you going to modify your practices? I'm going to _____

    _____

    _____

    _____.

5. Redirection

Redirection shifts a child's attention from what she is currently doing to something safer or something that's preferable. It is a skill that has been around for ages and comes in many forms. Generally a redirection says, "You may not do X, but you can do Y," or, "You may not do X here, you can do X there or there." The most important part of redirection is to join your attention with the child first and then redirect. Below are the same situations handled two different ways, with the adult joining with the child and without the adult joining with the child. See if you can feel the difference.

Situation: Aster is visiting Grandma's house. He's trying to close a box of tea, diligently working on figuring out the latch.

Without joining: Mom says from across the room, "Aster, leave the box alone. Come in here and play with this toy I brought you. Aster, look at the toy! It has a switch! Look at the toy. It's really fun!"

With joining: Mom walks over to him, gets down on eye level and notices, "See this little edge of a tea bag hanging out. What could you do with it that might help the latch close?" Aster pushes the tea bag in, shuts the box, snaps the latch and looks right into his mom's eyes. She celebrates his success and then pulls out a toy she had brought for him to play with. "Come play with this toy in the living room." He takes it and sits down in the living room to explore the new item.

Situation: Amy is 18 months old. She just discovered the electrical outlet covers and is touching and pointing at them.

Without joining: The home care provider says, "No, no, Amy! That is not safe. You can play with your blocks or the stuffed bear. Leave it alone."

With joining: The home care provider walks over, points to the outlet and says, "You found the outlet covers and want to pull them off and play with them. That is not safe." She takes Amy by the hand and walks over to a pile of toys and says, "I am going to find something fun you can pull on and play with using those little fingers." She stays on the floor with Amy, giving her ample time to shift her attention.

Redirection requires face-to-face interaction, joint attention, clarification of the boundaries (exaggerated facial expressions that express "not safe"), and assistance in connecting with the new object. Be certain to use all four of these components when redirecting. Attention is a whole brain activity. When we redirect a child's attention, we are actually scaffolding their prefrontal lobe development. Helping children develop their prefrontal lobes is labor intensive for adults. We cannot facilitate prefrontal lobe development by hollering from across the room.

6. Use I-Messages

I-Messages tell children that we believe they have infringed upon us. Children are not born knowing the difference between respect and disrespect. We must teach them. When children attack us physically and verbally, we can dodge blows, say hurtful words, deliver negative consequences and send children to the office, or we can use the disruption to teach respectfulness and assertiveness by using an I-Message.

I-Messages originate from owning our feelings and claiming our power. We can only use I-Messages when we are in an executive state. So, the first step in delivering an I-Message is composure. If we believe the children are **making** us angry, we will be unsuccessful with I-Messages. We will use statements based on "you," that send a message of blame and imply the child is in charge of the adult. "You" statements inflict guilt. I-Messages set a limit and teach a new skill. There are several ways to deliver an I-Message. Pick the form that is most comfortable for you. The most important point to remember is to speak calmly but firmly from your heart.

Style 1: "I don't like it when you _____."
Follow with an assertive command and relate it to safety.

Style 2: "When you _____, I feel _____ because _____."
Follow with an assertive command.

> Mrs. Railey works with first graders. She instructs the children that it is time to put their journals away. One child completely ignores the command, so she walks toward him to secure his attention. The child makes a growling sound, balls up his fist and lightly punches her in the arm. She responds, "Why did you hit me? Do I hit you? We don't hit in this classroom." The child screams, "No," and begins to cry. As he cries, Mrs. Railey asks, "Why are you acting like this?" and calls the office for assistance in removing the child from class.

This teacher forfeited a teaching opportunity. The child's actions indicated he was in a survival state. Mrs. Railey asked him questions he could only respond to from an executive state. She also used an accusatory "you" and failed to offer usable information. The teacher would have been better able to teach a new skill by assertively setting a limit using an I-Message like, "Ouch (show exaggerated pain)! Hitting hurts. I don't like it when you hit me. When you want my attention, touch my arm like this (demonstrate) and wait for me to look at you. Do it now for practice." Or by saying, "Ouch! Hitting hurts. I don't like it when you hit me. When you feel angry say, *I feel angry! I want to finish writing.* Say it now for practice."

When we are treated with disrespect, we must respond assertively. If we respond aggressively, we are treating the child with disrespect while trying to teach respect. Below are examples of conscious I-Messages and unconscious reactions. Which communication style do you most often use?

Unconscious labeling: "You are rude to interrupt."
Conscious I-Message: "I don't like it when you interrupt. I can't remember what I was saying. Raise your hand and I will call on you. Do it now for practice."

Unconscious command: "Sit down, be quiet and stop running. Now!"
Conscious I-Message: "When you run through the house while I am trying to work, I feel distracted. I can't think. Walk quietly like this (demonstrate)." Wait for the child to comply and encourage by saying, "You're walking quietly. That is helpful."

Unconscious questioning: "Why did you do that? What's wrong with you?"
Conscious I-Message: "I don't like it when you talk in that tone of voice. When your tone matches mine, I will be happy to listen. Both you and what you say are important to me."

Unconscious sarcasm: "So you finally decided to join us for dinner. How nice."
Conscious I-Message: "Dinner time is important to our family. I miss you when you don't join us. Come when I call so we are all together."

Unconscious accusations: "You don't care about anybody but yourself. You should be ashamed."
Conscious I-Message: "I feel furious when you keep ignoring me. I'm going to go calm down and then I will speak with you."

Activity to Practice I-Messages

Speaking from your heart, respond to the following situations with an I-Message. Use a partner to role-play and/or fill in the blanks below.

1. You repeatedly ask the children to settle down. They continue joking around.

   _____

   _____

2. A child calls you stupid. _____

   _____

3. A child hits you. _____

   _____

Check in with yourself. Did you accomplish the following? If yes, say, "I did it!" If not, say, "Oops!" and try it again.

- ❑ "I" statements teach responsibility and reclaim our power. "You" statements send a message of blame, seek to inflict guilt and put the child in charge. Did you use "I" statements instead of "you" statements?

- ❑ Assertive communication requires the facial expression, body language and tone of voice of "no doubt." Were your face, tone and words calm and firm?

- ❑ What you focus on, you get more of. Did you end the statement by telling the child what to do in positive terms?

Additional Tips for Assertive Communication

Be clear and direct: Give children choices only when they exist. "Are you ready for a story?" implies the child has the choice. "It is story time. Sit quietly and listen," states what will happen next. Avoid asking questions. "Sit down and check to see if your friends have enough space," is assertive. "Who can show how to sit nicely?" is not.

Own and express your feelings: "I feel angry when you interrupt," is assertive. "Look what you made me do," and "Can't you be quiet while I'm talking?" are not.

Speak in concrete terms: Abstractions and judgments can be confusing. Teach children what it is to be good and nice without relying on labels. "Ask your friend if you can play by saying, *May I please play*," is assertive. Saying, "Be nice to your friends," is not.

Activity to Practice Communicating Assertively

Practice giving assertive commands in the following situations. Role-play with a partner and/or fill in the blanks provided using the skill suggested.

Name, Verb, Paint: Help a child who is dawdling at his table get in line.

_____

Tell and Show: Assist a child walking around the room to return to her seat.

_____

I-Message: Set a limit with a child who says, "Shut up!"

_____

Redirection: Help a child who is playing with a breakable item shift to a safe one.

_____

Recall a recent encounter when you failed to act assertively. Say, "Oops!" and write what you could say to use the Skill of Assertiveness next time.

_____

Commitment: This month I am willing to be conscious and vigilant in painting a picture of what I want children to do. I am willing to pivot and forgive myself with an Oops when I hear myself doing otherwise.

Signature:_____ Date:_____

Child Assertiveness: I-Messages for Verbal and Physical Aggression

Just as children infringe on the personal space and dignity of adults, they also intrude aggressively on each other. I-Messages are as essential for children as they are for adults. Accidental intrusions (unconsciously bumping into someone) and intentional intrusions (hitting to get something) are so common in schools that preschoolers are suspended at a rate that's 1300 percent higher than children in the K-12 years. In the average preschool classroom, there is one intrusive act every minute of every day! The good news is that we will have an opportunity to teach young children new social-emotional skills approximately every 60 seconds, and that their prefrontal lobes are developmentally primed and ready to learn these new skills at this age! The harsh reality is we, as adults, require new skills if we are to seize these moment-by-moment opportunities. The video "Are Children Safe in Preschool?" on your portal provides additional insights on this issue.

> Most classrooms have rules against physical and verbal aggression. The consequence of engaging in these activities is detention or a loss of privileges. As you will learn in Consequences (Chapter 10), these types of consequences are called "logical," and are made up by adults and given to children. Logical consequences motivate children to use skills they already possess; they do not teach new skills. That is why we see the same children losing privileges over and over again. They do not have the social, emotional, or language skills to successfully say, "I don't like it when you write on my paper; write on your own paper," so they push or name call. In Conscious Discipline, we use everyday interpersonal conflicts (not extreme fights) as teaching moments to help children internalize pro-social skills.

The first step in approaching a conflict is to harness our Power of Attention to focus on that which we value. If we value hurtful behavior and want to see more of it, we will go to the aggressor first and admonish him. If we value helpful behavior and want to see more problem-solving, we will go to the victim first and teach a helpful way to communicate. Children will quickly learn that certain behaviors are valued in their classrooms. Will you teach them to value hurtful behavior or helpful solutions? If you value helpfulness, the rule is "victim first." This applies to most situations. However, when we have an aggressive child who hurts multiple children in quick succession, we must attend to the aggressor first to provide safety in the classroom. It's a dramatic representation, but we might remember the victim first rule and its exception by using the following anecdotes:

> **Victim first:** Let's say we're chatting after a workshop when someone runs up, hits me in the head with a baseball bat and races out the door while I lie there bleeding. Would you help me or chase the person with the baseball bat? Hopefully, you would tend to my bleeding wound first and deal with the aggressor later. Remember this image when you're tempted to race after the aggressors in your classroom.
>
> **Exception:** Now let's say I'm speaking at an outdoor event, and there's a sniper shooting at all of us, one after another. Would you attend to the wounded or address the threat? In this case, you must deal with the sniper as soon as possible to help restore safety to the group.

Asking "Did you like it?" is a powerful phrase when you approach the victim first. This initial question accomplishes three things:

1. It activates the child's executive state in preparation for problem-solving.
2. It indicates the child's level of assertiveness.
3. It creates a powerful teaching moment for all involved.

1. It activates an executive state in preparation for problem-solving. "Did you like it?" has the power to activate the higher centers of the brain, calling on children to reflect. We often see this reflected on children's faces when they tattle on others. Watch carefully the next time children come to you to tattle. They may say, "She wrote on my paper." Watch their faces carefully as you respond, "Did you like it?" You will see their eyes move up and to the right as they reflect. Sometimes, children are too emotionally distraught for a question to be appropriate. In that case, you would help the children with composure first and assertiveness second.

2. It indicates the child's level of assertiveness. The child's response to "Did you like it?" provides important information for effective coaching. A loud, powerful, "No! I don't like it!" communicates that active calming would be helpful to bring the frustration down a notch before speaking to the other child. Coach this child in taking a few deep breaths and practice the words together to assure his tone is assertive instead of aggressive. A barely audible, "No," tells us that additional coaching is needed to help him achieve the voice of no doubt. Take some deep breaths, encourage him, and practice the exact words and tone until both his verbal and nonverbal cues are assertive.

3. It creates a powerful teaching moment in which all class members learn a new skill. The good news is we have many wonderful opportunities to teach new social, emotional and language skills. The bad news is that addressing every act of aggression individually is too much for one teacher to manage. Therefore, Conscious Discipline empowers every child in the classroom to be a social skills teacher. Assertiveness is the skill that teaches others how we want to be treated. When we teach a classroom of 22 children to say, "I don't like it when you grab my marker. If you want a turn say, *May I have a turn please,*" we then have 22 children teaching each other how to behave in the classroom, in the halls, on the bus and throughout their lives.

> "I don't like it" is a phrase utilized in both *Shubert's BIG Voice* and the *Conflict Resolution Time Machine. Shubert's BIG Voice* is an ideal way to teach assertiveness in the classroom. You can download free activity sheets for BIG Voice at ConsciousDiscipline.com/ resources. We will discuss the Time Machine as a conflict resolution tool at the end of this chapter and again in Consequences, Chapter 10.

"Did you like it?" is the key phrase in a larger problem-solving process. The following is the complete process to use when you see or hear one child infringing on another:

Step 1: Begin by calming yourself as you prepare to address the victim first. If you saw the event or its aftermath, notice what you see, wait for the victim's response, clarify as needed and then ask, "Did you like it?" If a child comes to you to report an issue (tattling), then simply ask, "Did you like it?"

> **Adult:** Your head is down and you are holding your ankle. Something happened?
> **Victim:** Mikael tripped me!
> **Adult:** Mikael stuck his foot out when you walked by. Did you like it?

> **Victim:** Parker just mooed at me and said, "Hey fatty, we're playing over here!"
> **Adult:** Did you like it?

Remember if the victim's response is weak or whiny, work to strengthen the assertive tone. If the response sounds aggressive, take some deep, calming breaths together. If needed, coach the victim in the next step by saying, "Match your voice to mine," until he is using an assertive tone.

Step 2: Next coach the victim to assertively say, "I don't like it when you ___(negative action)___," and quickly pivot the negative infraction to a positive action by helping the child come up with what he would like the aggressor to do instead. Give younger children the exact words to say and ask older children, "What do you want her to do instead of pushing?" Often the first response is, "I don't like it when you push me. Stop it." "Stop it," doesn't tell the aggressor what to do differently. We have not taught a new replacement skill to the aggressor, empowered the victim with assertive language or created a classroom of social skills teachers until we clearly state what we want. "Stop it," must become, "Let me know the line is moving by saying, *Look! The line is moving forward without us.*"

> **Adult:** Go tell Mikael, *"Tap me on the arm when you want my attention."*

> **Adult:** What do you want Parker to do instead of calling you names?
> **Victim:** Use my name!
> **Adult:** Tell Parker, "I don't like it when you call me names. Use my name, Janice, instead."
> **Victim:** I don't like it when you call me fat. Use my name instead."

Step 3: Finally, encourage the aggressor to complete the requested action or use the new skill. Willingness comes from connection and a sense of belonging. Children who feel connected are more likely to cooperate. Children who are marginalized are less likely to listen to their peers or us. It is essential to establish a School Family culture as our foundation for problem-solving. When the aggressor complies with the new action or language, notice this and celebrate!

> **Adult:** Let's practice together.
> (They practice the new shoulder-tapping skill.)
> **Adult:** You did it! Jayce, you taught your friend how to get your attention! And Mikael, you tapped his shoulder! That helps keep our classroom safe!

> **Adult:** Are you willing to call her by her name? Let's have a do-over!
> **Aggressor:** Hey, Janice, we're playing over here!
> **Adult:** You did it! Janice, you assertively told Parker that name-calling is not okay with you! And Parker, you committed to use Janice's name instead of hurtful words! That was helpful.

Tattling: When a child reports, "She hit me," teachers often respond in one of the following three ways (we'll discuss tattling as a teaching tool again in Chapter 10):

 "How did that make you feel" puts the aggressive child in charge of the inner state of the victim, and keeps all parties involved in their upset emotional states where they can argue over who had it first and who did what to whom. *"Did you like it?" sets children up to problem-solve rather than get more emotional.*

 "Use your words" asks children to come up with socially-acceptable words while they are in an upset emotional state or a survival state. If a child hits, the survival state response is to hit back. The emotional state response is to use the skills on their CD-Roms, which might be name-calling. *"Did you like it?" activates the executive state, allowing children to be coached.*

 Discern who is at fault and deliver the appropriate punishment. This response misses the teaching opportunity provided by the intrusion. Just as an incorrect answer on a math quiz shows us what math skills we need to teach, grabbing a pen instead of asking for it shows us what social skills to teach. Instead of fault-seeking, we need to use natural consequences. *The natural consequence of being hurtful to a friend is to learn how to be helpful.*

Assertiveness by Age

"I don't like it" is a powerful statement, but babies don't come out of the womb equipped with complete sentences. For nonverbal children, we do all the talking. We might say, "See her face. Her face is saying, *STOP!* She wants you to touch her like this." We would then take the toddler's hand, help him release the baby's hair and show him how to touch the hair gently. Below is a brief overview of the developmental progression of assertive language for coaching. The ages listed are a guideline; every child develops at a different pace. View children of all ages using their assertive voices on the portal.

Age	1st: Set up	2nd: Set limit	3rd: Tell what to do
Nonverbal children	See his face.	His face is saying, "Stop. I don't like it."	"Touch me like this." See his face. He likes that.
1 - 2 years	He doesn't like it when you __.	Say, "Stop," or hold up a hand in a "stop" motion.	He wants you to __.
2-3 years	Did you like it?	Say, "I don't like it."	She wants you to __.
3-4 years	Did you like it?	Say, "I don't like it when you push me."	She wants you to say, "Scoot over." Say it now.
5-12 years	Did you like it?	Tell __, "I don't like it when you __."	What do you want her to do next time to get __? Tell her, "Next time, please __."
12 and up	Is that alright with you?	If you don't like it, then you could say __.	

The process of coaching assertiveness, especially with younger children, relies heavily on noticing each child's behavior, interpreting that behavior for the other and giving both children the developmentally-appropriate words to use. The older the child, the more complex dialogue they can use. The younger the child, the more you will scaffold the process for them.

Ten-year-olds: Zara and Jackson are on the playground. Zara is carrying a ball over to play with a group of girls. Jackson jump-kicks the ball out of her grasp and across the field. Zara stands there staring at him. Go to the victim first and say, "Jackson kicked the ball out of your hands. Did you like it?" Zara looks at the ground and whines, "No. We were going to play with it." Breathe deeply with her and begin coaching, "Tell Jackson, *I feel frustrated when you horse around like that. We are playing with that ball. Give it back*. Say it now for practice." Zara squeaks out the words. Continue coaching her by saying, "Match your voice to mine," until she is using an assertive tone. Walk over with Zara and encourage her as she faces Jackson and says, "I feel frustrated when you horse around like that. Get your own ball. Give me my ball back." Jackson returns the ball and mumbles, "No hard feelings?" Zara says, "Nope." Now cement the interaction in their consciousness and celebrate their success through noticing, "Zara, you used an assertive voice to tell Jackson what you wanted. Jackson, you gave the ball back! Good for you both!"

Six-year-olds: Zara and Jackson are on the playground. Jackson snatches the ball out of Zara's hands. Zara starts screeching. Go to the victim first and say, "Zara your face is going like this!" When she makes eye contact, download calm and say, "You seem angry. Jackson took your ball and you didn't know what to do. Did you like it?" Zara yells, "No!" You continue, "Take a deep breath with me and then we'll talk with Jackson." Breathe deeply together and begin coaching, "Tell Jackson, *I don't like it when you take my ball. Give it back*. Say it now for practice." Practice with Zara until she is using a calm, assertive tone and then standby as she speaks with Jackson. Encourage Jackson to comply. Now cement it in their consciousness and celebrate their success through noticing, "Zara said, *I don't like it. Give it back*. And Jackson, you did it! You gave Zara the ball back. Good for you both!"

Two-year-olds: Zara and Jackson are on the playground. Jackson snatches the ball out of Zara's hands. Zara is poised to push him to get it back. Quickly go to the victim first and describe what happened, "Jackson took your ball." Then empower the victim with assertive words to use. "Tell Jackson, *Stop! My ball!*" Teach Jackson a socially-acceptable way to get his needs met by coaching him, "Jackson, you wanted a turn. When you want a turn, say, *Turn, please*." Then celebrate. "There you go, you did it! Zara said, *Stop! My ball*. And Jackson, you gave the ball back and said, *Turn, please*. Good for you both! I'm going to go get another ball so you can both play ball."

"You wanted" is a key phrase for teaching children with limited verbal skills to set assertive boundaries. "You wanted a turn with the crayon. When you want a turn, say, *Turn please!*" "You wanted Jojo's attention. When you want friends' attention, tap them on the arm, say their name and wait for them to look at you." We will discuss "You wanted" at length in Chapter 8, Positive Intent.

Nonverbal children: Use the phrase, "Look at her face," combined with, "I don't like it" to speak assertively on behalf of nonverbal children. "Look at her face" teaches the older child to read the younger child's nonverbal cues, while "I don't like it" teaches what the nonverbal cues mean. When a 5-year-old takes a 1-year-old's ball, say, "See her face. Her face is red, and her lips are quivering. She's saying, *I don't like it. I was playing with that ball. Give it back*." We must scaffold an assertive voice for nonverbal children until they can speak for themselves.

> While shopping at the mall, I heard some crying and looked up to see a mother pushing a double stroller with a 4-year-old in back and an infant in front. I watched the 4-year-old use the infant's head like a drum as the baby cried. To soothe the crying infant, the mother (who was unaware of the hitting) was pushing the stroller back and forth. I commented on her lovely children and asked if I could take a closer look. I bent down, looked at the 4-year-old, waited for him to make eye contact with me and said, "See your brother's face. He's crying. He is saying, *I don't like you to hit me. Please drum on your own tummy.*" The older boy had an awkward look on his face as he processed the information. I could almost hear him thinking, "So *that's* why he's crying."

Remember, in addition to specifically teaching assertiveness using "I don't like it," we are constantly teaching children to be passive, aggressive or assertive based on the ways we behave ourselves. We must train ourselves to use assertive communication first and foremost. The two core elements of assertive communication we want to focus on teaching and modeling for children of all ages are:

- **Telling others what to do in concrete terms.** Help children shift their focus from the intrusion or problem to the solution. Teach them to state their wants, needs and expectations clearly, simply and in a positive form (what to do instead of what not to do). Instead of, "Stop grabbing!" teach them to say, "Give me back the marker." State your wants and expectations to other adults this way as well.

- **Sending a nonverbal message of no doubt.** Teach children to use a verbal tone and nonverbal body language that says, "Just do it." If a child's nonverbal cues are too passive, other children may easily choose not to comply. If a child's nonverbal cues are too aggressive, other children will resist in self-defense. When nonverbal and verbal communications are assertive, others are more likely to comply. Facial expression, tone of voice and gestures that convey confidence increase the chances others will heed the child's words. Use the voice of no doubt whenever you speak with children and adults.

Blocks to Assertiveness

To be assertive, we must express our feelings, thoughts and wishes without diminishing those of other people. This sounds simple, but to clearly state our thoughts and desires, we must recognize them, own them and believe we have the right to have them. In short, we must value ourselves. We must shift our focus from what we assume others are thinking and feeling, to being conscious of our own mind's contents. Anyone can acquire assertiveness. It's not a personality trait some people have and others lack. Like passivity and aggression, assertiveness is learned behavior. To learn it, we must do the following:

- **Achieve self-awareness.** Do you tend to interact with your children passively, aggressively, with a passive-aggressive flip-flop or assertively?

- **Monitor your own thought patterns.** How do you talk to yourself? Do you address yourself passively, aggressively or assertively? Once you learn to speak to yourself more assertively, you will naturally use this skill with your children.

- **Teach and utilize assertiveness in all your relationships.** By becoming more assertive with yourself and other adults, you will model this skill for your children. When children in the classroom complain to you, "Emily pushed me," or "Nathan is looking at me," you will be ready to teach them the words needed to assertively state their limits.

Early in life, we internalize guidelines for social conduct — rules about what is good, polite behavior and what is rude, bad behavior. We learn to conceal and share certain kinds of feelings. We absorb these rules from parents and other role models. They are on our preprogrammed CD-Rom. It is difficult but important to remember that these rules are not cast in stone. We can change them if we consciously decide to do so.

Children cross boundaries with each other and us frequently. Our reactions to these conflicts act as models for children's development of interpersonal skills. If we yell in response to children's disobedience, we teach them to be rude to people who don't do their bidding. If we permissively allow children to ignore our limits, we teach them to infringe on others and let others infringe on them. Our style of limit-setting teaches children how to create and maintain boundaries in their future relationships. We often expect children to possess skills we have yet to develop. We simply cannot teach skills we do not possess!

> Assertiveness is a difficult journey for many, especially women and minorities who have spent generations in positions of powerlessness. People who have been historically disempowered in a culture can have a strong message written on their CD-Roms, falsely equating assertiveness with rudeness or harm. As a result, disempowered people tend to believe they must be passive or aggressive to be heard. Assertiveness, however, is the key to communication for **all** people.

Both the passive and aggressive voices are rooted in fear. An aggressive voice may come from a fear of not knowing how to respond if the misbehavior continues, a fear of losing control or a fear that bigger problems will arise. Children sense the fear behind our aggression, and it frightens them. On the other end of the spectrum, a passive voice is scary because it puts the child in charge of the adult. Children know they are not equipped to be in charge of adults. When young children hear either an aggressive or passive voice, they feel frightened and may turn it into a game to regain a sense of control. Toddlers do this with great panache.

Assertiveness begins with us and extends to our children.

Karen wanted her 2-year-old daughter Christina to get in the car seat so they could keep a doctor's appointment. Karen said, "Christina, get in your car seat. Over here honey, here is the car seat. Come get in." Christina paused for a moment to watch her mother. Karen got nervous about her dawdling. Karen's nervousness flared into anger and she shouted, "Don't start with me. Get over here now and get in your seat." Karen was angry because she was afraid they would be late. In response, Christina ran away, giggling as if they were playing tag. This game infuriated Karen who chased her daughter, shouting threats. Karen finally caught Christina, gave her a swat on the rear and forced her into the car seat.

Karen interpreted Christina's running as disrespect, but it was really a reaction to the fear in her voice. In cases like these, children turn tense situations into games adults do not want to play. Similar problems arise when parents or teachers use an aggressive or passive voice to send older children to the office. The child may run, refuse to go or go with an attitude (rolling eyes and other gestures). Again, they are turning the fearful situation into a game or power struggle so they can feel some control in the situation. To avoid problems, use an assertive voice, and keep fear out of your conflicts with children. Assertiveness begins with us and extends to our children.

> Still not convinced to develop your assertive voice? Consider this:
>
> - Assertiveness activates the adult's executive skills and puts us in touch with our wise internal advocate.
> - Assertiveness teaches respect to and for everyone.
> - Assertiveness paints a picture so children can be successful.
> - Assertiveness creates an opportunity to encourage at any moment.
> - Assertiveness allows you to set limits without guilt about your own behavior.
> - Assertiveness is essential for young children who turn fearful situations into a game or power struggle.
> - Assertiveness is the only voice children can hear from a survival state. It supports safety and builds trust.

Assertiveness Creates Safety Through Predictability and Consistency in Your School Family

As you practice the aforementioned perceptual shifts and skills daily, the following tools help create a felt sense of safety in your School Family. This is critical as we guide children to be successful in meeting school expectations.

Routine and Structure: Visual Routines, the Skeleton of Your School Family

Young children's brains use images (mental models) to govern behavior, making visual routines essential to children's success. Visual routines communicate our expectations to children through images. They are the ultimate form of assertive communication for young children. They illuminate the behaviors we expect of children, help them aim their flashlight on the given task, and scaffold their emerging executive skills of attention and time management. Knowing what to do, when to do it and how to do it is essential in building a School Family. Traditionally, rules have been used to provide order in classrooms. In Conscious Discipline, routines clearly delineate expected behaviors, and provide order, predictability and consistency. This structure fosters a felt sense of safety.

The brain is a pattern-seeking and pattern-making device. Our perceptual system is bombarded daily with billions of bits of information. Our brain allows that which is familiar (the pattern) to become background, so we can process new information (learning) in the foreground.

When children first enter school, everything is new. As predictable and consistent days pass, most children will be able to function without expending much conscious effort on where to put their homework or how to transition to lunch. This leaves the higher centers of the brain free to take in new information. Essentially, establishing consistent routines and rules allows the brain to feel safe enough to learn.

There is a difference between rules and routines. A rule has the goal of stopping misbehavior. They are enforced with consequences. A routine, on the other hand, is simply the way you expect something to be done. It is a taught procedure that brings order and predictability to the classroom. When we create predictable routines for everything from sharpening pencils to throwing away trash, it creates a felt sense of safety for children and helps them maintain and regain composure during times of stress. For routines to be effective, we must consciously take time to teach them. This is best done through the M.A.P. method.

M = **M**odel your procedures and expectations for the children
A = **A**dd visuals
P = **P**ractice, practice, practice

> We must post pictures of expected behaviors throughout schools, including the halls, classrooms, cafeteria and restrooms. Children encode these visuals into their prefrontal lobes and ultimately internalize them as mental models. Auditory reminders operate differently in the brain and do not create strong mental models.

If a child refuses to follow the taught routines, the teacher must assume that additional information or a different instructional style is needed. Watch on the portal how one teacher sees a child's need for more information when following a routine. Teaching a routine is no different than teaching long division. If a child fails to understand long division, we do not put his name on the board, remove recess time or have him turn a card from green to red. We simply try to figure out how to relay the information in a different way. The same must be held true for routines. The child might need more modeling, more concrete specific visuals or more practice. If, after all this, they are still unwilling to follow the routines of the day, then it is a relationship issue. Disconnected children are disruptive. We would then begin to work on repairing the relationship with the child and reconnecting the child with his School Family.

Chaos in the classroom or school thwarts safety and composure, and is an urgent call for visual routines. Transitions such as arrival, dismissal, going to the restroom, walking down the halls and eating in the cafeteria are common times of chaos. Providing visual images of what to do in these circumstances is like giving students a mini-rehearsal of our expectations and procedures. It allows students to practice a routine over and over again at any given time.

Take a moment right now to think about where you have chaos in your day. This indicates a place where you need to create a routine and break it down visually. The visual could be a single picture or visual routine book that applies to a difficulty one child is experiencing, or a series of pictures representing each step in a process for the whole class.

Routines add predictability and consistency to the classroom. They are the skeleton that supports the School Family, just as our skeleton supports our body. Use the following brain-compatible practices to strengthen your routines:

1. **Write down all the routines** for the day so you can be clear about what you expect your children to do and know. Ask yourself the following questions as a guide:

   - What do I expect children to do upon arriving to my program? (arrival routines)
   - What role do children play in management task routines? (attendance, lunch count, permission slips, cleaning up routines, etc.)
   - What do I expect from children during transition times? (transition routines)
   - What do I expect children to do when lining up? (lining up routines)
   - What do I expect children to do during snack and lunch? (eating routines)
   - What are my hygiene expectations of the children? (toilet use, hand washing, nose blowing, etc.)
   - What do I expect children to do for program dismissal? (dismissal routines)

2. **Systematically and assertively teach** the routines to your children. Begin by writing down the steps to all your routines. This will help you become aware of the amount of sequencing you are asking children to learn and retain. Next, decide which routines you will teach first and what strategies you will use to teach them. Utilize the M.A.P. process and remember that making up rules cannot replace teaching routines.

3. **Create individual and group class-made routine books** for trouble spots. For younger children, take photos of the expected steps in the routine and bind them together in book format. Older children can be responsible for making the books themselves using photos or illustrations and sentence strips. If an individual child is having difficulty, make a personalized routine book featuring photos of him successfully completing each step of the routine. Encourage him to read it just before the troubling transition or event at school, and send the book home for him to read with his family.

4. **Learn more about visual routines** in Chapter 6 of the School Family book and see them in action in Shubert's School on our website.

I stand in a straight line at a level 0 voice.

I wait patiently for my turn.

Structure: Daily Schedules

Daily schedules are essential for young children. They are the manner by which young children tell time and learn to regulate their internal clocks. A daily schedule is a representation of the main things that will happen during your day. It teaches children to predict what will happen next and helps them feel empowered to tackle the next task.

Putting your daily schedule in pictures creates a sense of safety. When a child feels safe, her brain can focus its energies on learning, growth and connection rather than uncertainty, fear and protection. Because children's brains use images to govern their behavior (as we just discussed in Visual Routines), we must post our daily schedule in both pictures and words.

The goal of a daily schedule is not to show every activity that occurs, but to post key events and events that change on a daily basis. Your daily schedule will include a series of photos of these events with a brief description printed below the image. Photos of your students conducting the activities are ideal, but you can also reuse generic photos year after year. Simply apply self-adhesive Velcro to the back of the images and place them in chronological order. Change the schedule as needed on a daily or weekly basis.

> **Daily schedules are essential for creating a sense of safety and predictability both at home and in school.**

Join with children each morning to talk through your daily schedule so they know what to expect throughout the day. When a child asks, "What's next?" "When do I do Karate?" or "How long 'til lunch?" go to the daily schedule together and locate the appropriate scheduling item. Eventually children will start accessing the daily schedule to answer these questions for themselves. A child who has continued difficulty with transitions or other aspects of the daily schedule may require an individual schedule posted at his desk.

The following images of home and school schedules for different ages will help you get started. Many products can also help you in this endeavor, including the *Daily Routine Cards* and the *Make-n-Take CD-Rom* available through Conscious Discipline.

School Schedule

Home Schedule

Structure: Conflict Resolution Time Machine

The purpose of the Time Machine is to provide a way for children to change hurtful interactions with peers into helpful exchanges. Assertive language is essential to the success of the Time Machine. The following is a brief demonstration of the assertive communication utilized in the Time Machine. We will discuss the Time Machine in depth as a problem-solving consequence in Chapter 10. For a demonstration of the Time Machine in action, visit Shubert's School.

> While working independently on a math assignment, a fourth-grade teacher overhears Lasandra say to Marcus, "Shut up!" The teacher approaches Marcus (going to the victim first) and says, "Marcus, Lasandra just told you to shut up. Are you willing to go back in time for a do-over, helping your School Family learn another way to treat each other?" Marcus answers, "Yes."
>
> The teacher then turns her attention to Lasandra and says, "Lasandra, are you willing to learn another way of communicating with your friends and help our School Family learn a better way?" She agrees. Both students and the teacher walk over to the Time Machine. The mat has footprints representing each step in the conflict resolution process. They start by being a S.T.A.R. and move to the next step where they wish each other well. Next they say, "1, 2, 3, let's do it."
>
> Marcus uses the sentence stems on the mat to say, "I don't like it when you tell me to shut up. Quit it!" Since Marcus did not give Lasandra a positive action to take, the teacher steps in to coach, "Marcus, what do you want Lasandra to say if you are talking and she can't hear the lesson?" Marcus gets an "Aha!" look on his face and says, "Next time, say, *Please be quiet. I can't hear the lesson.*" Lasandra looks down to the mat for guidance and says, "Okay, I can do that." In the final step on the mat, both children give each other knuckle bumps to express the problem is solved and there are no hard feelings. Both students return to their seats and continue their math project. The rest of the class watched the interaction, learning valuable communication skills.

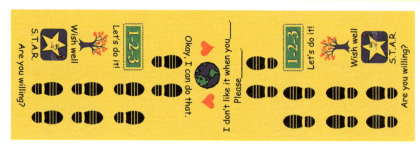

Conflict Resolution Time Machine

Conflicts, disobedience and disrespect happen in every classroom. Seeking a magic bullet to keep them out creates a climate of control and domination, modeling bullying behaviors. Creating a School Family allows small interpersonal conflicts to occur so we can see and scaffold the development of missing social-emotional skills. A healthy conflict cycle begins with connection, moves through disconnection and ends with repairing the connection. This cycle strengthens connection and trust. After a conflict, it is important to repair the relationship. The *Conflict Resolution Time Machine* builds this into the problem-solving process. A brief connecting ritual symbolizes, "We have solved our problem, we've let go of hard feelings and we are moving forward as a compassionate School Family," and is essential to the connect-break-repair cycle of healthy relationships.

Assertiveness Summary

Power:	Attention: What you focus on, you get more of
Becoming Brain Smart:	Attention directs neuroplasticity and all learning
Skill:	Paint for assertive commands, "I'm going to," Tell and Show, "I don't like it," redirection
School Family:	M.A.P. Visual Routines, Visual Daily Schedule, Time Machine, Routine Books

Power of Attention Reflection

We see what we expect to see and what we want to see. If we choose to see the negative instead of the positive, the question is, "Why?" This month vigilantly practice the following to focus on the behaviors you want to see more of:

❏ **Consciously pay attention to your focus:** Are you focusing on the action and behaviors you want to see or the ones you don't want? Say to yourself often, "What I focus on, I value and teach others to value."

❏ **Pivot when you are upset:** Say to yourself, "I'm safe. Keep breathing. I can handle this." Then honestly ask yourself, "Do I want more of this behavior?" If the answer is, "No," breathe deeply (be a S.T.A.R.: **S**mile, **T**ake a deep breath **A**nd **R**elax). Then, paint a picture of what you want children to do and why. Relate the "why" to the language of safety.

❏ **Breathe deeply and affirm the following principles three times a day:** 1. What I focus on, I get more of. I'm going to focus on behaviors I want to see. 2. When I'm upset, I always focus on what I don't want. I can choose to pivot instead. 3. I am upset because I'm resisting what is. I can take three deep breaths and say, "The moment is as it is."

❏ **Listen to the language around the school:** Can you hear passive, aggressive and assertive voices? Breathe and wish well to those struggling with assertiveness. Listen to your language. When you hear your passive or aggressive voice, be a S.T.A.R., Oops! and restate the same command in an assertive voice.

❏ **Watch the Power of Attention video** on the portal to deepen your reflection.

Brain Smart Teaching Moments

Every conflict and every expectation about children's behavior is a teaching moment for assertiveness. Key teaching moments include:

- **When giving a command:** Use your assertive voice to Name, Verb, Paint a picture of what you want to see happen. Follow up with encouragement (Chapter 6).

- **When a child has attacked your dignity, belongings or personal space:** Use I-Messages. "I don't like it when you wave your hand in my face. Raise your hand over your head like this (demonstrate)."

- **When a child does not comply:** If a child does not follow an assertive command, it creates a new teaching moment. This allows us to model composure during times of distress and hold tight to the value of respect by vigilantly using the Tell and Show process.

- **When there is disorganization or chaos in the room:** Clear visual routines are necessary for the entire class; put them in class books and post them in logical places throughout the classroom. Individual children who are struggling with specific routines benefit from personalized books and postings.

- **When children are disrespectful and aggressive with each other:** Use this opportunity to teach children how to use their assertive voices and become social skills teachers in your classroom.

Skill Reflection: Common and Conscious

If possible, partner up with someone and say the following two statements out loud. See if you can feel the difference. After each statement share, "The difference between Common and Conscious for me was…"

Common	Conscious
Don't make me send you to the principal's office.	I don't like it when you speak to me using hurtful words. Take a breath, and use a calm tone and respectful words so I can help you.
Let me finish this up and then I'll come help you.	I'm going to finish up and then I will help you.
I can't turn the page until you are all in your seats.	Sit down in your space with your bottom on your circle so everyone can see the book.
You do this in public just to embarrass me!	I'm feeling very frustrated. I'm going to take a deep breath to calm down and then I will speak with you.

It's time to form a circle for our class meeting, okay?	Close your book, push in your chair and walk over to your place in the circle. Turn your head to see that your friends have enough space just like this (demonstrate).
How nice of you to join us (with sarcasm)!	When you show up late, I feel disappointed and frustrated because our time together is important to me.

School Family Implementation Checklist

❏ **Name, Verb, Paint when giving assertive commands.** Paint a picture of the behaviors you want.

❏ **Tell and Show when children start to become defiant or noncompliant.** Say, "I'm going to show you what to do, how to get started, what is expected," etc.

❏ **Actively calm yourself and give an I-Message when a child acts disrespectfully.** Make sure each I–Message ends with what you want the child to do.

❏ **Redirect young children** with face-to-face contact, joint attention, clarification of boundaries and assistance in connecting with the new object/activity to nurture prefrontal lobe development.

❏ **Use modeling and "I don't like it"** to teach children to be assertive with each other.

❏ **M.A.P. all school-wide routines** including arrival, dismissal, walking in the halls and the cafeteria. Post visuals throughout the school.

❏ **M.A.P. classroom procedures.** Notice any classroom transitions that still create chaos. Go back and re-M.A.P. the procedures for these transitions.

❏ **Post your daily schedule visually.**

❏ **Create class-made books** so children can read the daily schedule and routines. Place them in the class library and have children check out the routine books to read at home.

❏ **Create individual routine books** for children who have difficulty seeing the patterns in the school day.

❏ **Review additional helpful resources on the portal and visit Shubert's School,** focusing on visual routines and the Time Machine.

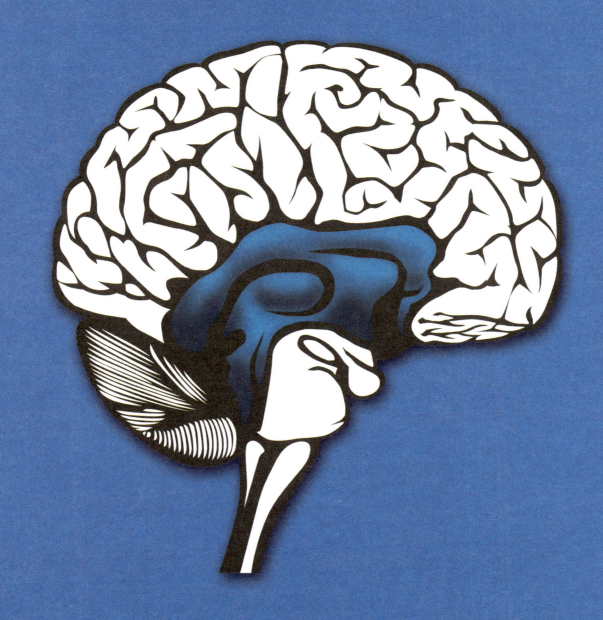

- Section 2 -
CONNECTION

Emotional State Skills

R = Rituals
E = Encouragement
J = Jobs
E = Empathy
C = Choices
T = The School Family

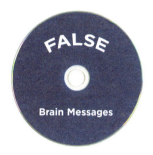

Answering, "Yes!" to the question, "Am I loved?" is essential for optimal brain development, academic success, wellbeing and the willingness to cooperate. The connection section is color-coded blue, symbolized by a CD-Rom, and represented by the limbic system and emotional state.

The emotional state plays a foundational role in how we form relationships, memories and emotions. We etch perceptual filters onto our CD-Roms. If our CD-Roms judge something as bad, the flow of energy goes down to the brain stem and our bodies mobilize for fight or flight. If our CD-Roms judge something as good, the energy flows up to the prefrontal lobes and we can access wise responses. Relationships are the gatekeeper of all learning; our CD-Rom filters must perceive safe, loving relationships for energy to flow up to the prefrontal lobes for learning.

Some children come from homes where, "Am I safe," and, "Am I loved," are answered, "Yes." These children feel secure in giving and receiving love, and engage in learning. Some children come from homes where these questions are vaguely answered, "Sometimes." These children experience insecure bonds, and act out through neediness, attention-seeking, aggression, blaming, exclusion and defending against connection.

Regardless of how they enter school, children must experience healthy connections and a sense of belonging for optimal learning. The Skills of Encouragement, Choices and Empathy teach us how to create a connected, compassionate culture where all children can learn. Within these chapters, the combined tools of R.E.J.E.C.T. foster the secure relationships required for this endeavor.

Combined Tools for Creating Connection

Rituals: Rituals provide valuable opportunities to connect. Implementing caring classroom rituals cultivates compassion. Compassion motivates altruistic behavior.

Encouragement: Encouragement is accepting children for who they are. It's based on noticing and connecting, and teaches what classroom values like "helpful" look like, sound like and feel like.

Jobs: Being of service to others activates the higher centers of the brain. With a job for every student, each child contributes daily to the success of the classroom.

Empathy: Empathy teaches emotional regulation and integrates the brain so children can take personal responsibility for their actions.

Choices: Internally motivated choices foster cooperation, enhance decision-making and help children focus their attention.

The School Family: Calling your class a "School Family" and using a healthy family model as the blueprint for its organization meets all children's connection needs.

Chapter 6

ENCOURAGEMENT

Building the School Family

Encouraging children to help others creates a sense of belonging in which the intrinsic desire to be of service outshines attention-seeking behaviors.

Let's pretend for a moment that all of humanity is one entity with many cells working together, similar to our bodies. Imagine each person you encounter represents a cell whose unique, healthy functioning is essential to your wellbeing. Would you choose to bathe your cells in the stress chemicals produced by judgment, criticism and condemnation, or would you prefer to bathe them in the feel-good, brain-building chemicals of joy and connection?

The Power of Unity operates from the notion that the above "pretend" scenario is essentially true: we are each unique, yet intricately and inextricably connected to one another. Our drive for connection is hardwired into our DNA. Some of our thoughts and actions strengthen this wiring, while others poison it.

The Power of Unity reminds us we are interconnected; we are all in this together. In Conscious Discipline, we express this belief by creating a School Family, as described in Chapter 3. All of the powers and skills of Conscious Discipline are embedded in the School Family, however, the Power of Unity and the Skill of Encouragement are so intertwined with the School Family that they are nearly inseparable. The Power of Unity, as expressed through the School Family, creates a compassionate culture that is scientifically and practically designed to correct the life paths of disconnected, hurtful children while simultaneously encouraging all children to contribute to the health of the whole. The icon for the Power of Unity is a globe. Watch a video about the Power of Unity on the portal for a more in-depth understanding.

The Power of Unity

Have you ever wondered how wireless communication works? Recently, I called a friend in Africa on my cell phone. Shortly following that, I called my neighbor. Both calls made a wireless connection with the other person almost instantly. That seems like a miracle to me! Wireless technology works because of electromagnetic waves that pass through the air at the speed of light. We can't see these waves, but they carry energy and information. Evidently, the empty space between us is not so empty!

Research indicates humans also communicate wirelessly. Most of us know this from our life's experiences as we sense someone is looking at us as, know the phone is going to ring right before it happens, or sense our loved ones' distress. It seems we, too, can communicate energetically through the sea of electromagnetic waves in which we live. The electromagnetic waves humans emit can be measured through devices like the electrocardiogram (EKG) and the electroencephalogram (EEG). The amount of electromagnetic energy emitted by our brains can run a 10-watt light bulb (McCraty, Tiller, Atkinson, 1996). Everything we see and don't see around us is vibrating at one frequency or another, and so are we. We all live in the same ocean of energy and information, and so we are quite literally "all in this together."

It is a basic physiological fact that our heart and brain exchange information that governs how we think, act and feel. Research at the Institute of HeartMath.org shows that heart-brain interactions also occur between individuals. The findings show that at a conversational distance, the electromagnetic signal generated by one person's heart can influence the other person's brain rhythms (McCraty, Deyhle & Childre, 2012). Most of us have experienced this by being around a person we instantly enjoyed or with whom something felt slightly off. Both of these interactions changed our internal states and biased our perception of the other person. We also feel this energy when walking into schools. Some feel happy and welcoming, while others feel tense and negative. This is due to resonance, a term referring to the act of frequencies of energy lining up and beating in unison. When an extremely high energy meets a lower energy, the energies must harmonize by reaching some form of equilibrium. The stronger vibration almost always wins. If one child in a classroom is experiencing rage and the rest of the classroom is being a S.T.A.R. (**S**mile, **T**ake a deep breath **A**nd **R**elax) and wishing well, the raging child will calm. Of course, the reverse is also true: If a raging child is in a classroom with the teacher yelling, "Calm down," and the rest of the class feels the threat, they all will eventually end up in a survival state. That is the Power of Unity.

Activity for Wishing Well
Try this experiment: Take a deep S.T.A.R. breath and wish well from deep in your heart the next time you encounter a grumpy, complaining person. Don't say a word; just notice if any changes occur through wishing well in that "empty" space.

Accepting the fact that we are all in this together leads us directly to a compassionate worldview. It is amazing to look at all the world's religions and discover they each call upon some version of the Golden Rule: to treat others the way you want to be treated. This concept is an ethical code that has guided much of humanity's morality. Christianity states, "Do unto others as you would have them do unto you." In the Talmud, Rabbi Hillel is believed to have said, "What is hateful to yourself, do not do to your fellow man. That is the whole Torah; the rest is just commentary." Islam states, "None of you (truly) believes until he wishes for his brother what he wishes for himself." All religions point us to an idea of oneness and compassion that basically says, "We are all in this together. When one is harmed, all are harmed. When one is helped, all are healed." The School Family is built upon a foundational belief in our connection to each other. It goes beyond creating a positive school climate or a cooperative learning community, to creating a compassionate school culture based on the principles of unity. Thus, the Golden Rule is the law of the land in the School Family.

> **Commitment:**
> I am willing to acknowledge that on some level we are all interconnected to each other. This oneness cannot be seen, but is sensed and felt on a deeper level. I am willing to embrace everyone as part of my extended family, treating each person as I wish to be treated.
>
> Signature _____ Date _____

Uniqueness Unifies, Specialness Divides

We are all unique expressions of a common energy. Our true nature is both unity and uniqueness. Our interconnectedness does not erase our individuality; it accentuates it. No two people are alike and each person has the opportunity to contribute her unique talents to the success of the whole. The body, as I described it earlier, is a good metaphor for the simultaneousness of integration and uniqueness. All cells in the body are interrelated. Yet each cell performs specific, unique functions to support the whole. Without each and every cell contributing its unique function, the whole organism suffers. (Imagine how poorly our bodies would function if the liver said, "I refuse to work with the lungs; they're stubborn and incompetent!") We are all cells in the body of humanity and we can no longer operate under the notion that we're separate. As such, our job is to discover our unique gifts and offer them to the whole.

Traditionally, we have utilized specialness as a way to build self-esteem. We asked children to be special helpers and write, "I am special because _____." Unfortunately, programs that seek to help children feel special teach them to focus on being better than or less than others. Getting ahead through competition becomes more important than getting along with others. This "getting" relies on external forces to deliver a sense of worthiness. (Adults operating under the same mindset seek fulfillment through external means like getting a new car, getting children to behave or getting others' approval.)

Programs based on the Power of Unity operate differently. They teach children to focus on giving. Giving relies on our internal resources to bring about a sense of worthiness. Giving is transformative in that it requires us to be the change we want to see instead of getting others to do things differently. We break the cycle of "Do what I say, not what I do" and become models for the behaviors we seek. To access the Power of Unity, we must relinquish the need to be special (which comes from judging behavior as good or bad) in favor of embracing our innate uniqueness and need to be of service. We ask children to write, "I am unique because _____ and it helps my School Family by _____."

As discussed in the School Family chapter, most schools have competitive, individualistic school climates. Children who are good (special) are rewarded, often sacrificing our intrinsic desire for connection with a drive to be better than others. This competitive striving systematically categorizes people as good and bad, haves and have-nots, or winners and losers. In order for one person to be special (better than), someone else must be less than. This creates a persistent state of stress as children live in constant fear of becoming the lesser person. Many will simply give up or seek to find their specialness outside the norm through negative attention rather than connection.

> *Essentially, specialness happens in one of two ways: By seeking to be the best, have the best or do the best, or by seeking to be the worst, be oppositional or be shut down.*

Specialness is the antithesis of unity, based on comparisons instead of contributions. Separating people into the two categories of good and bad provides children with two conceptual buckets they will fill with prejudicial views of humanity. Some may come to believe that good people are Caucasian, while bad people are people of color. Others may come to see good people as thin, while heavy-set people are bad. These buckets become the lens they use to separate each other into "us" and "them," forgetting that our true nature is the unity of "we." Institutions that seek to embrace diversity, yet utilize systems relying on specialness (including rewards and punishments), will not obtain their most valued goals. Diversity can only be accepted on a foundation of unity.

I remember attending my first World Organization for Early Childhood Education (OMEP) Conference. It was held in Poland. I was young, the cold war was raging and Poland was a communist country. Growing up, I was taught communism was a serious threat. Arriving in Warsaw, I saw men with guns, which further solidified my fears. I was literally sick to my stomach. My mind held all Polish people as the bad guys, and I was the good guy. It took less than a day for me to interact with enough people to see our commonality. My Polish neighbors were people just like me who wanted to raise their children to be healthy, have loving relationships and earn a decent living. I remember my anger at the United States for the propaganda I had received and even more angry with myself for believing that people are their governments. My commitment to myself at that young age was to see all people as an extension of myself, to see past their beliefs, see past their behaviors and see the unity underlying us all. It was a profound trip that changed the course of my life.

If we see behavior through the lens of good and bad, we create two categories of people and two value systems for their treatment. Children judged to be good deserve to be treated with respect, deserve to be a part of the group, deserve to feel worthy and are often seen as innocent victims of circumstance when they misbehave. Children judged to be bad deserve whatever it takes to put them in line, deserve to be excluded from the group, deserve to feel unworthy and are seen as flawed when they misbehave.

Instead of systematically judging good and bad, Conscious Discipline offers a healthier perception by focusing on safety. Perceiving behavior as safe or unsafe sets us up to see misbehavior as a call for help rather than disrespect. Safe behavior implies an inner state of peace or appreciation. Unsafe behavior indicates some form of distress. If a child's inner state is one of peace, his behavior is most likely helpful and he is willing to look for solutions. If a child's inner state is one of upset, his behavior is most likely hurtful. He is calling for help. The following chart summarizes these two views of behaviors.

Stressful Way to Perceive Behavior		Healthy Way to Perceive Behavior	
Good	Bad	Safe	Unsafe (dangerous)
Deserving	Undeserving	Calm	Distressed
Should feel good	Should feel bad	Helpful	Hurtful
Innocent	Guilty	Solutions	Calling for help

> **Safe behavior implies an inner state of peace or appreciation. Unsafe behavior indicates some form of distress.**

Traditional systems based on rewards, punishments and specialness teach children that positive attention is better than connection and negative attention is better than no attention at all. It takes away from our essential message of belonging: "We are all in this together, and each person's unique talents are essential." Focusing on specialness instead of seeing children as unique, essential contributors is counterproductive to creating a felt sense of belonging. If we recall the highlighter and flashlight example from the Power of Attention, our focus illuminates the aspects of life we deem valuable. One teacher might say, "Good job, Beth. You got a 100 percent on your spelling test. Three more of these and you will earn a pencil with your name on it." Another teacher might say, "You did it, Beth. You worked hard on your spelling and look what you accomplished! You can now help others with spelling difficulties." Both responses comment on the child's success, but they do it in different ways. The first response fosters specialness and values the accumulation of material goods. The second one supports unity, connection and service to others. We have the fundamental choice to teach children to value their own personal specialness or we can teach them to value contributing their unique talents for the betterment of all. The choice is ours.

> Children need to be of service. Whom and how they serve must be developmentally appropriate in order to be meaningful. A child's understanding of the world expands with age. Kindergarteners best understand being of service to their families and class members. By fourth grade, they can also relate to the benefits of community service. Developmentally, asking kindergarteners to participate in a food drive is not as effective a form of service as having them carry groceries into their own homes. Younger students can be cheerleaders for older students who take part in state and national tests. Older children can do community projects like adopting "grandparents" at a nursing home or helping the homeless. These efforts may be tied to curriculum areas, adding meaning to academics.

How We See Defines What We See

Our unity yields some profound truths that impact the way we define our world, each other and ourselves.

True connection flows from one worthy person to another in the form of giving. Each of us has tried to answer the question, "Who am I?" We have assigned ourselves numerous traits and roles based on our expectations and judgments, yet we can only truly discover who we are through our interactions with others. The way we perceive and interact with each other answers, "Who am I?" in one of two ways: "I am worthy," or "I am unworthy." The way we answer this fundamental question colors how we interact with the world.

> **The way we answer the fundamental question, "Who am I?" colors how we interact with the world.**

We do not earn self-worth through accomplishments and getting. We reaffirm or deny our worthiness every day in interactions with other people. When we see others as lacking, we feel inadequate ourselves. In this state of inadequacy, we experience ourselves as isolated and separate. We feel lonely, and we project our fears and insecurities onto others. We spend our lives trying to get our needs met. Life becomes about getting instead of giving.

Seeing the best in others creates worthiness within us and defines others as worthy. From this state of worthiness and equality, we can experience our true connection with others. Life becomes about giving instead of getting. A teacher who sees through the eyes of unity might say to a fidgety, disruptive child, "Looking at all those problems can be overwhelming. What help do you need to get focused?" She encourages a sense of worthiness in the child and herself. We cannot create an encouraging School Family unless we change our perceptions and children's perceptions of misbehavior and conflict.

We place value on and give meaning to situations based on our mental models. As we've already discussed, our perceptions saturate our world with meaning. Because of this, teachers have an awesome responsibility to be conscious of the meaning they attribute to life events. Our internal state dictates the meaning we will attribute, so we must vigilantly commit to the Skill of Composure in order to stay in the higher centers of our brains. The way we perceive others, events and situations trains our students to see these things in the same way. It also defines each child as worthy or unworthy.

Whatever we offer others (love, judgment, criticism, compassion), we strengthen within ourselves. We exist, not in empty space, but in a sea of information and energy that is transferred from one to another. In the material world, when we give something (a toaster) to someone else, we no longer possess it. The other person has the toaster and we do not. The same does not apply in the realm of thoughts and emotions. We can't get rid of negative, positive or guilty thoughts by giving them to someone else. Unlike toasters, thoughts never leave their source. The judgments, criticisms, complaints, encouragement, joy and love we think we are giving to others are really gifts to ourselves.

The situations below seek to clarify these concepts:

> Teacher A sees a child off task and comments, "What should you be doing? You better get busy. You will never finish if you continue to waste time." This teacher did not err in what she said; her mistake was her perception. In seeing the child off task, the teacher judged the child to be acting poorly. She discourages herself first by seeing what was not good enough, then discourages the child as she speaks from that perception. Both teacher and child are left feeling disconnected, discouraged and inadequate. In addition, the teacher has trained the other children in the class to view this child in the same negative light.

Teacher B sees a child who needs help focusing. She walks over and offers assistance: "You have a choice. You can start working on your math by yourself, or you can raise your hand and I will find someone to help you. Which is better for you?" Seeing the child's behavior as a call for help, the teacher feels encouraged to act on his behalf and extends this encouragement to him. In addition, she trains other children in the class to see misbehavior as a call for assistance rather than labeling the child bad. These children will begin to see misbehavior as a call for help, providing them with the opportunity to respond in helpful ways. As they contribute to others' welfare, they build their own self-worth.

Activity to Connect How We See to What We See

Our perception can be encouraging or discouraging, depending on where we put our attention. Reflect on the questions below. First, record how you would view them from a relaxed, alert executive state. Then record how you would view them when stressed, operating from an upset emotional state. What values do you communicate from each state? Can you see a relationship between how you see others and how you feel about yourself? Which state is encouraging? Conducive to seeing worthiness?

	Executive State	Emotional State	Reflection
How do I view a parent screaming at a child in the store?			
How do I view politics and the evening news?			
How do I view homeless people asking for handouts?			
How do I view my coworkers, children and significant others when they make mistakes?			

The "Call for Help" Perceptual Frame

Teachers play a significant role in how children perceive each other and misbehavior. We have a choice. We can teach children to see others who act inappropriately as bad and deserving rejection, or we can teach children that these behaviors are a call for help. The choice to teach condemnation or compassion is ours.

Conscious Discipline asks us to use compassionate eyes to see **all** misbehavior as a plea that says, "Help me handle this in a successful way." Take a deep breath and then think about the following common occurrences:

- A child bumps into another on his way to the bathroom.
- A child pushes another aside while selecting her crayons.
- A child calls his friend a big, fat snob.

Which of these children need help learning a new skill and which are troublemakers?

Conscious Discipline teaches that all of these children are missing important skills. The first child may need help in focusing attention, becoming aware of his body's cues and/or managing spatial relationships. The second child may need help with impulse control and the social skill of asking for a turn. The third child may need help learning to manage and express powerful emotions (like frustration) constructively.

At any given moment, children feel safe and are extending love to others through helpful behaviors, or they feel threatened and are calling for help by acting in ways that are hurtful to themselves or others. We can judge and punish children for behaviors like the ones in the examples above, or we can see the call for help and teach new skills. The way in which we choose to perceive misbehavior dictates both how we will resolve the situation and how the rest of the class will perceive the misbehaving child. One perception creates a discouraging culture and a need to be "good enough" in order to belong. The other creates an encouraging culture with a felt sense of belonging. Seeing the call for help is not about letting children get away with poor behavior; it is about teaching children what we expect them to do and holding them accountable to those teachings.

A two-step process guides our path when we choose to respond to a child's call for help. This process teaches new skills to the misbehaving child, to the children she has impacted and to bystanders who are observing. Step one involves approaching the children who were impacted and teaching them to set an assertive limit. Step two teaches the misbehaving child a helpful way to get her needs met.

Below are two situations where teachers respond to a child's call for help. One teacher responds by unconsciously labeling the child as bad. The other sees the child's call for help. Which perception would you rather model for yourself and the children in your care?

Situation 1: Jeb Needs Help Focusing or Jeb is Being Disruptive

Jeb is sitting at a table with four other children. The class is independently working on journal writing. Jeb is not focused on his writing. Instead, he is talking and fidgeting. The other children look distracted and annoyed.

The Two-step Call for Help Teaching Process
Step 1: Empower the students to respond to Jeb
The teacher walks over to the table. She speaks first to the children who seem distraught with Jeb's behavior by saying, "Is Jeb's talking and fidgeting bothering you?" If the response is affirmative, the teacher then coaches the students to assertively communicate with Jeb. She might say, "Tap Jeb on the shoulder, wait for him to look at you and say, *I can't focus on my work when you are talking. Please be quiet.*"

Step 2: Using a Call for Help perceptual frame
The teacher then turns to Jeb. She might say, "Jeb, it seems you are having trouble focusing on your journal. What could you do to help yourself stay focused?" The teacher could also elicit assistance from the children by saying, "Jeb seems to be having trouble staying focused on his journal. What could we do to help him?"

Labeling the Child Bad, a One-step Process
Step 1: Deliver the prescribed consequence to Jeb
The teacher sees the disruption and walks over to the table. She speaks firmly and directly to Jeb. "Jeb, what should you be doing? It is time for journal writing. You are bothering the other students at your table. Go move your sign to yellow."

Situation 2: Eileen Needs Help Managing a Difficult Morning or Eileen is Being Rude

Eileen enters the classroom with a grumpy look on her face. Her body is tense. She ignores the greeter and bumps into several children, knocking them out of the way. The children scream for the teacher.

The Two-step Call for Help Teaching Process
Step 1: Empower the students to respond to Eileen
The teacher responds to the situation by going to the children who were bumped and notices, "Eileen bumped into you as she walked by. Did you like it?" Several children shake their heads. "Then tell Eileen, *Please watch where you are going. It hurt when you bumped me.*"

Step 2: Using a Call for Help perceptual frame
The teacher then turns to Eileen and notices, "Eileen, you seem grumpy and tense this morning. Something seems to be frustrating you. What could you do that would help you handle this moment?" The teacher could also elicit assistance from the children in the classroom by saying, "Eileen seems to have had some frustrations getting to school this morning. What could we do to help her calm herself?" (Remember to say, "Help her feel better," instead of, "Make her feel better.")

Labeling the Child Bad, a One-step Process
Step 1: Deliver the prescribed consequence to Eileen
The teacher hears the children's cries and goes directly to Eileen. She looks at her disapprovingly and says, "Eileen, it is not nice to push your friends. Pay attention to where you're going. How would you feel if they bumped into you like that? Take a slip from the box. If you get two more slips, you will not have recess today."

Activity for Seeing Misbehavior as a Call for Help

Role-play a Call for Help perceptual frame in the following scenarios. Use a partner (if possible) and record your responses.

1. Michael is walking very slowly in line. He is holding up others who are getting impatient and angry.

   Step 1: Empower the other children to solve the problem by saying _____

   _____

   _____

   _____

   Step 2: Respond to the call for help by saying _____

   _____

   _____

   _____

2. Several children are working on a collaborative project. Mariah is constantly grabbing items from others.

   Step 1: Empower the victimized children to respond assertively by _____

   _____

   _____

   _____

   Step 2: Respond to the call for help by saying _____

   _____

   _____

   _____

> *The way we perceive a child's behavior and the way we respond to that behavior will create a safe, encouraging School Family climate or a fearful classroom that discourages everyone.*

Becoming Brain Smart

"The Golden Rule is genetically embedded deep in our neurobiology (Cozolino, 2013). Relationships are the cradle of all learning. Brains grow best when they are face-to-face, mind-to-mind and heart-to-heart with caring others." Our brains are wired to connect, attune with, resonate with and learn from each other. For this reason, a child must be able to answer the questions "Am I safe?" and "Am I loved?" in the affirmative in order to develop skills like goal achievement, self-regulation and getting along with others. Without these skills, education reform is no more than rearranging the deck chairs on the Titanic. At birth, a human is essentially helpless. Biology creates an innate need for connection to ensure the baby survives. Our basic need to connect with others jumpstarts a 24-year process of prefrontal lobe development.

At birth, the prefrontal lobes are particularly undeveloped and require social nurturing and attuned relationships to develop into the goal-achieving, problem-solving, empathetic powerhouse it is capable of becoming. Being excluded from a group is painful and derails the functioning of the brain, significantly dampening academic achievement. Yet the majority of common discipline practices are designed to exclude.

> *Did you know? Social and emotional pain is mediated by the same neural systems that regulate physical pain.*

Wiring the Brain Top-Down for Impulse Control and Willingness

When we examine all the fascinating research about the brain, one gem emerges: Nurturing, attuned connections with others builds neural connections within the brain that literally wire it for willingness and impulse control. Our attachment with our babies and our connection with our students integrates the brain. The survival state communicates with the emotional state, which communicates with the executive state. These systems must work in an integrated fashion for optimal success, with the higher systems regulating the lower systems. We call this top-down brain integration.

Imagine we live in Orlando, Florida and want to drive to Miami, Florida. It would be helpful to have a road. It would be extremely helpful if that road was a major highway. Without such roads, we would be trudging through swamps amid spiders, snakes and alligators! We might find ourselves giving up on the journey or living in such terror that every shadow looks like a wolf (or in this case an alligator). This is what can happen to children who lack nurturing relationships. The neural pathways (roads) from the lowers centers of the brain (brain stem and limbic system) to the higher centers of the brain (prefrontal lobes) are unpaved, making them difficult to travel. This causes children to get stuck in unregulated, stressful states where they may react explosively or rigidly try to control everything. We pave our neural pathways through face–to-face interactions that involve eye contact, touch and presence in a playful situation.

Most everyone has played a social game with a baby (patty-cake, peekaboo) or has giggled with glee roughhousing with preschoolers. One of my favorite games with my granddaughter is adapted from Baby Doll Circle Time: "All around the room I look. Where is Maddie? I look up high, I look down low. BOO! Maddie was hiding." I call these types of social games are "I Love

You Rituals." They're face-to-face, high intensity, relational moments that involve eye contact, touch and presence in a playful situation. These moments produce joy juice, a combination of positive brain chemicals including dopamine, oxytocin and opioids. This brain chemistry creates joyful feelings that literally wire the brain for impulse control and willingness. Using our highway metaphor, it paves a road through the swamp from Miami to Orlando! Joy juice enhances the regulatory functions of the prefrontal lobe to a degree scientists say is similar to the positive effects of a dose of Ritalin (Panksepp & Burgdorf, 2003). Joy juice also promotes resiliency in the face of stress and creates a "Yes I can!" life attitude (Sunderland, 2006).

> *Joy juice is a combination of positive brain chemicals including dopamine, oxytocin and opioids. This brain chemistry creates joyful feelings that literally wire the brain for impulse control and willingness.*

Our social brains are wired to benefit from connecting activities like I Love You Rituals. They're not just for infants and preschoolers. Loving moments of connection that involve eye contact, touch and presence in a playful situation are essential at all ages. Watch the "I Love You Rituals - Your Guide For Meaningful Connections" video on your portal. Children who have trouble with eye contact, touch, being present, engaging and being appropriately playful are our most challenging children. They have not formed the roads from our highway metaphor needed for regulation. No reward or punishment can make a child behave appropriately without this integrated wiring; it's like asking a child without arms to throw a ball. It is essential that our school cultures include connection-intensive activities daily so both children and adults get regular doses of brain-enriching joy juice. Remember, these activities require face-to-face interactions that involve eye contact, touch, presence and a playful situation. All of us could use a little help managing our thoughts, emotions and behaviors, being more willing to work with others, keeping our attention system online, and handling stress more effectively. Connection-intensive activities provide the top-down brain integration necessary for all this and more.

Neuroscientist Dr. Candace Pert (1999) says each of us has a drugstore within us, with the finest drugs at the cheapest cost. Some of the hormones and neurochemicals that surge through our bodies feel great and some feel awful. Too much relational stress in childhood robs many of us of steady access to the feel-good chemicals. Connection, belonging and being of service to others stimulate the brain's reward pathway to release joy juice. Without these beneficial chemicals, many children will trade inner joy for a quick high from external drugs.

Connection vs. Attention

Connection floods our systems with beneficial joy juice. Unfortunately, connection is often confused with attention. I would love to have a dime for every time I have heard a teacher or parent say, "Ignore him, he just wants attention."

"Ignore him, he just wants attention," never made sense to me. All behavior is a form of communication. If a child is communicating to us, why would we ignore the communication and think a problem is going to improve? I am also very clear that getting too much attention is no more helpful than ignoring attention-seeking behaviors. Look at celebrities; they receive enormous amounts of attention and many of their lives are a mess. The solution can only come when we meet the underlying need for connection.

Attention is a call for help. It is an effort to draw others' attention to a missing skill, thing or quality. Calling for attention is something we do when we fall overboard on a ship: We make as much noise as possible in hopes that we are seen, our need is realized and someone tosses us a lifeline! Calling for attention says, "Something within me is missing," and the missing need is often related to connection and the beneficial joy juice that comes with it.

Connection is a form of responsive attunement. It is a gift we give when we relinquish our self-centered view of the world in order to participate fully with another person. When we connect, we let go of our judgments about how others should be, release our biases of how things should go, stop listening to the false messages chattering in our heads and become present. In these moments of connection, all is well.

Children require authentic connection (with eye contact, touch, presence and playfulness as previously discussed) for growth and development. Children who seek attention are defending against connection. They learned early in life that the vulnerability of connection generates pain and loss. So, they traded in connection with its feel-good, brain-building joy juice and settled for whatever bits of positive or negative attention they could get. Many educators have compounded this problem by trading the joy juice of connection for the "stuff" of tangible rewards.

We've already discussed how connection fast tracks our access to joy juice. Being of service to others has a similar effect. Research demonstrates the following:

- Being of service to others changes our brain chemistry, activating our prefrontal lobes and integrating the brain for optimal learning.
- Helping others triggers the reward centers in the brain. MRI studies show that cooperative and kind acts arouse the brain's reward centers and flood the brain with happiness-inducing dopamine (Emory University Health Sciences Center, 2002).
- Being of service to others helps regulate the clacker of our autonomic nervous system and turns off the fight-or-flight response in the body.
- People who offer compassion to others experience increased oxytocin levels. Oxytocin promotes long-term bonds, caring and commitments to others, and gives us a feeling of trust and connection (Keltner, Marsh, & Smith, 2010).

Rubin is a young boy attending public school at Alkali Creek Elementary in Billings, Montana. His story demonstrates the power of being of service. Rubin has a very difficult time regulating himself, especially during loosely-structured times like the beginning of school. His school had been implementing Conscious Discipline for years and knew he needed additional assistance regulating himself. Their answer was to give Rubin more opportunities to be helpful to others. On Monday, Rubin was the office helper, on Tuesday he helped the librarian and so on. Rubin said the following in a recorded interview, "I like helping because it shows I care and it helps me not be mean to others." Watch Rubin share his wisdom in a video on the portal.

The adults' job in Conscious Discipline is to keep the classroom safe and the children's job is to help keep it safe. Essentially, the children's job is to be helpful. When children contribute to others by being helpful, the brain's natural joy juice serves as a powerful replacement for the "stuff" of external rewards. Any system that relies on controlling others through punishment and reward removes the social problem solving that is crucial for prefrontal lobe development. Each person in a group (whether it be a school, family or society), requires social connection and encouragement to know how important her unique contribution is to the whole system. We need to offer each other comfort, support, ideas, feedback and encouragement to help build our own and each other's prefrontal lobes and self-worth.

> *In Conscious Discipline the children's job is "To help keep the classroom safe." When children contribute to others by being helpful, the brain's natural joy juice serves as a powerful replacement for external rewards.*

Relationships shape the function and structure of our brain. The prefrontal lobes develop in reciprocal and attuned interactions with others. The days in school where we demand six hours of looking at your own paper, eyes forward, with no talking and minding your own business have got to give way—not to distract from education but to enhance it. We must teach children to seek help from each other, offer help to each other, and create relationships based on trust, caring and mutual respect.

The Skill of Encouragement

Encouragement is about noticing, connecting and accepting children. Most of us have heard young children say, "Look at me!" a million times or so. Children want and need to be seen. Our focused attention (as described in the last chapter) is a powerful force, and the way we express that focused attention can be encouraging or discouraging. Children's growth can be stymied when we repeatedly judge them by saying, "Good job," "Good girl," or "You're the best." Children will be tickled when we respond, "Yes, I see you." Children's brain development will be optimized when we notice by saying, "Wow! You are balancing on one foot and your arms are like this (demonstrate arm position for the child)." If our goal is to meet the developmental needs of children in optimal ways, all we really need to do is describe the efforts and accomplishments we see through noticing.

Noticing, as discussed earlier, is essentially the act of reflecting the child's actions back to him without judgment. It is essential to encouragement.

> *When we judge too often, the excited 4-year-old child who shouts, "Look at me!" grows into an anxious 8-year-old who asks, "Is this okay?"*

Noticing for Encouragement

Encouragement is about accepting children for who they are. When we judge children, we tell them who we think they should be by putting a label on them and their behavior. Judgment demonstrates **conditional** love—love that makes demands. Acceptance demonstrates **unconditional** love—love that makes no demands. Judging makes it about us, while noticing makes it about the children. Judgment comes from our emotional state and stimulates the emotional state of children. Noticing comes from our executive state and stimulates the executive state of children. Noticing tends to connect us with others while judgment disconnects us.

> *Judgment demonstrates conditional love—love that makes demands. Acceptance demonstrates unconditional love—love that makes no demands. Judging makes it about us, while noticing makes it about the children.*

We will get more of the behaviors on which we focus (Power of Attention, Chapter 5). Our focus also determines what we strengthen within ourselves and others. When we focus on children being good, we teach them to please others and seek specialness (to be better than others) in order to feel worthy. When we focus on children being bad, we teach them to rebel and seek specialness through negative attention or being less than. When we notice their strengths, we teach them about their abilities. When we notice their choice to comply with an assertive command, we increase compliance. When we encourage their contributions to others, we teach them the importance of sharing their strengths. We can use noticing to encourage children in a variety of situations. For now we will focus on noticing to encourage compliance after giving an assertive command, to highlight kind and helpful acts, and to encourage children's unique gifts.

Noticing to Encourage Compliance After an Assertive Command

It is essential to use noticing for children who choose to comply with our commands. As we recall from Chapter 5, a request is optional and can be appropriately acknowledged with a "thanks." However, if we use "thank you" with an assertive command, it sends the message that compliance is about our approval instead of their accomplishment. The same is true when we respond to a child's compliance to a nonnegotiable command with "Good job." Good job is about our evaluation of the child's initiative, while "You did it" or "Good for you" is all about the child's autonomy. To encourage compliance and praise effectively, use noticing.

> **The formula for noticing compliance with an assertive command:**
> You did it!
> You _____(describe in detail without judgment).
>
> "You did it! You put on your backpack and stood by the front door."
>
> **Optional ending:** Tag with "Good for you!" "Way to go!"

Noticing compliance focuses on the behavior we want to see and brings children's awareness to all they have accomplished. Choosing to comply with an assertive command is a major achievement! Encourage children using the formula for noticing compliance, even after repeating the command five times. A child's decision to cooperate is always worth encouraging, even if it sometimes takes longer than we think it should. Use phrases like "You did it," "Good for you," and "Way to go," rather than "Good job," or "Thank you."

Noticing to Encourage Kindness and Helpfulness

"My job is to keep the classroom safe. Your job is to help keep it safe," is the Safekeeper's mantra. Children's main job in the classroom is to be helpful. We must notice their helpful acts in order for them to be successful at this job. Notice helpful acts privately to each child and publicly to the class. During the first six weeks of school, notice at least 10 kind and helpful acts per day.

The formula for noticing helpful and kind acts:
You ____ so ____. That was ____.

"Jonas, you saw that Becca needed some paper so you offered her some of yours. That was helpful."

Step 1: Start the sentence with the child's name or the pronoun "you." This is an important step in breaking the judgment habit. Judging statements generally start with the words "good" or "great." Start with a name, "You," "You did it," or "Look at you," to help break the judgment habit. "Kevin, you..." "You did it! You..."

Step 2: Describe what the child did in detail. Pretend you are a video camera. Before you speak, ask yourself, "Can a video camera record what I am about to say?" If not, then you are still judging. You might be about to say, "Thank you, Kevin, for being so kind." A camera cannot record that! Rephrase the statement. "Kevin, you found Mia's blanket and gave it to her..."

Step 3: Relate the child's behavior to how it helped someone else or the entire class. Stating the behavior's impact on others demonstrates that we are all in this together while teaching the value of connection and helpfulness. "So ____," accomplishes this goal. "Kevin, you found Mia's blanket and gave it to her so she could cuddle it in the Safe Place."

Step 4: End the description with a tag. Tags can help us wean ourselves off of judgments and toward acceptance. At first, it may feel odd to describe without judging "Good job" or "Thank you." Start using the tag "That was helpful." Then broaden the tags to describe attributes or values. Eventually, drop the tags entirely and just notice. Below is a list of tags and suggested uses.

Tags that describe attributes—use regularly:

- That took determination.
- That was gutsy.
- You sure are organized.

Tags that describe values—use lavishly:

- That was helpful.
- That was thoughtful.
- That was kind, caring, loving, etc.

You may ask, "Can't I ever tell children they did a wonderful job?" Of course you can, but don't overuse this kind of general praise. Such comments are like antibiotics—when overused they can cause long-term problems.

Activity to Encourage Kindness, Helpfulness and Compliance Through Noticing

 Notice the following acts of kindness, helpfulness, and compliance. Say your answers out loud using the formula "You _____ so _____. That was helpful." Review sample answers on your portal.

Situation 1: Kyle and Kimberly worked on a science project. Kimberly got frustrated with reading. Kyle helped her with some of the more difficult words.

Situation 2: Arlie followed through when you said, "Pick your books up off the floor and put them on the shelf with the spine facing out like this."

Situation 3: Maynard was upset and could not find her carpet square to sit on for story time. Marcia waved to her and said, "You can sit with me."

Situation 4: Ms. Jackson said, "Leila, put down the colored pencils, push in your chair and line up behind Jacob with your hands at your sides," four times before Leila finally stood up, understanding all four commands at once.

Situation 5: After working on some math problems, Alex cleaned up his table space and organized his materials.

> I have been giving workshops for decades now, most of which include speaker evaluations. At first, I was surprised by how my focus on two or three negative evaluations could negate thousands of positive ones. As I pondered this, I thought about how I was praised and admonished as a child. Look at the formula above again. If used, it tells the child that her efforts in life contribute to the welfare of others and that contribution has a name (helpful, kind, thoughtful, etc.). Now reflect on your upbringing and how you praise your children. When I did something deemed bad, my parents used a version of the above formula to describe exactly what I had done wrong ("Becky, you have whined and complained every inch of this family trip"), how it impacted others ("ruining the vacation for all of us"), and providing a tag delineating my faults ("you are spoiled"). At the same time, when I did something deemed good, I generally received a simple, "Good job, Becky." My failures were focused on in detail and made the world a bad place for everyone. My successes were all about me and were glossed over. No wonder those few negative evaluations seemed so important; I didn't want to let the whole world down! No wonder those thousands of successful evaluations were easy to dismiss; I didn't want to be conceited!

We can do this differently for the next generation of children. We can let children know that their kindness, helpfulness and thoughtfulness impacts those around them for the betterment of our planet. How satisfying to know that "Who I am naturally is a gift to others!"

Noticing to Encourage Children's Unique Strengths

To feel adequate, children must feel useful and know their contributions count. As mentioned in the Brain Smart section of this chapter (Page 173), being of service stimulates the development of the prefrontal lobes and supports the emerging executive skills. Help children feel useful by identifying their talents and suggesting ways they might use them to contribute to the classroom. In order to highlight children's unique gifts, we will use another variation of noticing.

The formula for noticing children's unique strengths:
You ____(describe their unique talent).
Would you be willing to ____(share how that talent is beneficial in a wider sense)?

Below are examples of specific ways to encourage children's unique gifts in the classroom. Note how these phrases ask for internal willingness instead of external obedience.

"Malcolm, you sound out words when you don't recognize them when reading. This skill is helpful for reading. Would you be willing to share how you do this with Tyree?"

"Melissa, you take time to plan how you're going to keep your work together. That's called an organizational skill. Would you be willing to show Ashley how you organized your planner and see if she needs help with hers?"

Putting It All Together

Compare noticing compliance, noticing kind and helpful acts, and noticing children's unique strengths:

The formula for noticing compliance with an assertive command:
You did it!
You ____(describe in detail without judgment).
Optional ending: Tag with "Good for you" or "Way to go!"

The formula for noticing helpful and kind acts:
You ____(describe in detail without judgment)
so ____(relate to how it helped others).
That was ____(helpful, etc.).

The formula for noticing children's unique strengths:
You ____(describe their unique talent).
Would you be willing to ____(share how that talent is beneficial in a wider sense)?

Watch videos of teachers encouraging students on your portal.

Other Ways to Acknowledge Children's Unique Contributions

There are many ways to acknowledge children's individual talents and unique contributions to the School Family. Below are additional ideas that are vital to encouragement.

Have children represent their strengths and assets. Asking children to write or draw about their strengths and assets builds self-awareness, self-confidence, helpfulness and unity. Remember to avoid activities that say, "I am special because ___." Special implies better than/less than categorization. Instead, use sentence stems to encourage children to think about their strengths in terms of helping others. "One thing I do in school that seems easy for me is ___ and I can share it with others by ___." "I enjoy doing ___ in school and it helps my School Family by ___."

Structure the environment so children's gifts are made public. At class meetings and during whole group instruction, notice when children have shared their strengths and gifts with each other.

- "Today during reading, Malcolm, who sounds out words he does not recognize when he is reading, helped Ashley with a word. That was kind of Malcolm."

- "On the playground, Ashley, who has the ability to double jump rope, showed two of her friends how they could be successful. That was very helpful."

- "In the cafeteria, two girls were calling another student names. Maya saw this and said, *See her face? Name-calling is hurtful. Be kind or walk away. That was supportive.*"

Create a "Ways to be Helpful" bulletin board, class book and/or directory on the class computer where children list their areas of expertise to be of service to others. Include pictures of the children helping one another, pointing out each one's contributions to the success of the School Family and completing the statement "I help my School Family by ____." It is essential that each person's skill be related to helping others. To optimize brain development, it's not about being better than; it's about being of service!

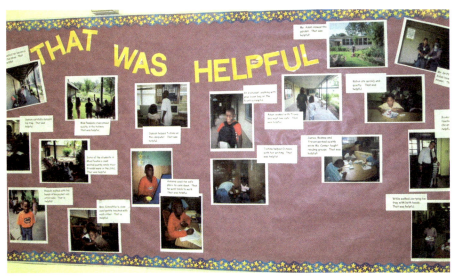

Ways to be Helpful Board

Activity to Encourage Children's Strengths Through Noticing

Notice the following children's strengths. How would you share these publicly with the School Family or privately with the individual child? Locate sample answers and images of Ways to be Helpful boards/books on your portal.

Caroline: Oh, how she loves to spell. She meticulously copies all the words off the word wall into her personal spelling dictionary. She is able to spell or look up almost any word she needs. Carl struggles with spelling.

To Caroline you say: "_____
_____."

If Caroline chooses to help Carl, you could highlight this by saying to the School Family:

"_____
_____."

Chance: Chance would rather do math than do almost anything. His work is neat and accurate. He understands the math concepts and can explain them to others. Carlos struggles with math.

To Chance you say: "_____
_____."

If Chance chooses to help Carlos, you could highlight this by saying to the School Family:

"_____
_____."

Counterproductive Praise

We've spent quite a few pages focused on offering encouragement through noticing compliance, kind and helpful acts, and children's unique strengths instead of offering traditional praise. Most of us were brought up thinking that praising children would foster enhanced self-worth. However, three decades of research have shown that this is not always true. Traditional praise is about overlaying children's sense of self with judgments about who we think they should be. Encouragement is about accepting children for who they are. Research indicates the following kinds of praise can inhibit a child's self-esteem:

With too much general praise, a child may feel pressure to live up to unrealistic standards. Perhaps you grew up hearing, "She is my perfect little angel." "He is always so helpful." Hearing this again and again left you with two options: You could try to live up to the perfect image adults had bestowed upon you, or you could act out, hoping they would see the real you.

> *Traditional praise is about overlaying children's sense of self with judgments about who we think they should be. Encouragement is about accepting children for who they are.*

Praise that relies on value judgments teaches children that being good equals pleasing others, and being bad equals displeasing others. Praise based on judgment has side effects, mainly: 1. Children can become judgment junkies. They will ask, "Is this good? Did I do this right?" with anxiety. 2. It trains children to focus on what others think of them as opposed to listening to their own inner wisdom.

Praise that focuses on catching them being good teaches children to seek approval. When we praise children in attempts to make them behave well, we will fail because our intention is to get, not give. We might say, "I like the way Jeb is sitting quietly," in hopes of future good behavior or influencing others to straighten up. This sends the message, "I like you when you please me." Children may conclude, "I am worthy when I please others and not good enough when others are displeased." When we teach children that something outside of themselves is the source of their joy, we prepare them not for contribution to society (giving) but for addictive behaviors (getting). Encouragement is different. It says, "You have gifts that support us all and they reflect your innate worth."

> *Trying to pump people up from the outside doesn't build self-esteem on the inside, it plants the seed of addiction.*

Praising children only for successful, completed tasks teaches them that effort doesn't matter, only accomplishments matter. Many adults give children commands, only offering praise when those commands are carried out. Imagine how boring a football game would be if the fans sat in silence until their team made a touchdown. Football fans don't act that way—they scream throughout the game to encourage the players. If we treat our children like we treat our favorite athletes, we will create a serious home-court advantage! Children need to learn that the process counts as much as the product. Focus on children's efforts and the small steps they take, not just on the touchdown. "That's it. You are doing it. Way to go, you're almost there. You did it!"

> *When we praise only finished jobs that are done well, we teach children to devalue effort.*

Praise that relies on external rewards works against our natural brain chemistry and devalues relationships. Phase out praise that relies on external rewards. We've replaced human connections like noticing, acknowledging and appreciating children with material rewards. Material rewards either become meaningless over time or teach children their value depends on the things they acquire. They also sacrifice access to the brain's natural joy juice, and shift our focus from establishing and honoring relationships to valuing material goods. Phase out reward programs and replace external motivation with the internal joy of being a contributing member of a School Family.

Activity for Self-Encouragement

Are you willing to offer encouragement through noticing instead of rewarding or praising? If so, offer encouragement to yourself first and it will soon become natural to offer it to children. Think of something helpful you did today and use the core formula to encourage yourself. Mine is, "Becky, you took time to write a book so others might find something of value within it to improve their lives. That was helpful." Now it's your turn:

You _____

so _____ .

That was _____ .

Encouraging Children Who Have Made Poor Choices

We all make inappropriate choices. The last thing we need is a lecture. Focus on encouraging children to solve their own problems. Some examples include:

- "You almost did it. You were so close. Try again. You just need some practice."
- "I'm confident you will think up another way of handling this."
- "You'll figure out a way to be helpful. I know you. Inside, you don't like to be hurtful."
- "That's a rough spot you are in, but I know you can work it out. Let me know if you need help."
- "Oops! We all make mistakes. What could you do now that would be helpful?"
- "You can do it."

The Skill of Encouragement is at the core of the compassionate school climate we call the School Family. Children and adults need to feel a sense of belonging and self-worth. The Power of Unity teaches us that what we offer to others, we experience within ourselves. Essentially, this means giving and receiving are one. During a drought in Florida, we had severe fires. Firefighters from all over the country came to help put them out. As the fires came closer to my home, the smoke became intense. I decided to volunteer at a nearby shelter to help those who were forced to evacuate their homes. While at the shelter, I felt I was truly helping others. The feeling of being blessed poured over me. I knew I was worthy, valuable and loved. Many of us have had comparable experiences. Similarly, children need the opportunity to be significant contributors to the School Family.

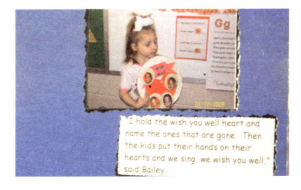

"I hold the wish you well heart and name the ones that are gone. Then the kids put their hands on their hearts and we sing, we wish you well," said Bailey.

"I squirt soap in everyone's hands," said Eric.

Encouragement Builds Connection in the School Family

As we practice the perceptual shifts and skills from this chapter, the following routines, rituals and structures help us create a strong sense of belonging and a felt sense of connection in our School Family. The top 10 School Family rituals discussed in Chapter 3 are also essential in this effort.

The first six weeks of school is a time to really focus on routines and rituals. Routines will provide safety, while rituals will provide connection. The sooner children can answer the two fundamental questions "Am I safe?" (routines) and "Am I loved?" (rituals) in the affirmative, the sooner we can focus on achieving our academic goals.

Ritual: "I See" Song

The I See Song is a ritual for noticing. In the I See Song, the teacher connects with and demonstrates valuing each child as an individual by noticing (not judging) her.

Conduct the song during circle time. Within the framework of the song, notice two things each child is doing by saying, "His __(name the body part) is going like this," and then demonstrating the posture or movement. Be certain to say, "Going like this," and demonstrate (rather than describing the action verbally) in order to help achieve eye contact. After singing the verse, share a moment of delighted connection through eye contact and then continue to the next child.

It is extremely important **not** to mention physical attributes, clothing, jewelry, etc. during this ritual. The goal is to achieve a moment of connection and to train ourselves and children to see others for who they really are, not for what they might wear or possess. Place your focus squarely on the essence of the child as demonstrated below:

I See Song
Sing to the tune of "Frère Jacques"
"Hello Marcy." *Children echo.*
"I see Marcy." *Children echo.*
Now, look to see what Marcy is doing. Are her hands folded in her lap? Then sing:
"Her hands are going like this." *Demonstrate by folding your hands in your lap.*
Children echo and fold their hands.
What else is Marcy is doing? She moved her foot! Sing:
 "Her foot is going like this." *Demonstrate by moving your foot.*
Children echo and move their feet.

 Watch videos of young children, including those with hearing impairments, using the I See Song on your portal.

Ritual: Connecting Rituals

Connecting rituals were discussed in Chapter 3, the School Family. Hopefully you've watched the videos on the portal and have begun implementing them. Connecting rituals provide excellent brain breaks for your classroom. With infants and toddlers, connection comes from the adult through one-on-one attunement. By preschool, children begin partnering with peers. At any age, it's essential we find ways to embed caring touches and face-to-face connection in our schools. When we touch one another, it releases a hormone called nerve growth factor that is essential to neural function and learning. The following are suggestions and resources for connecting rituals. Watch examples of the items below on your portal.

> **Remember, connection involves eye contact, touch and presence in a playful situation!**

I Love You Rituals

We explored these as part of your Brain Smart Start in Chapter 4. These activities do four things: 1. Increase a child's attention, impulse control and willingness to cooperate, 2. Increase a child's learning potential through caring touch, 3. Promote literacy and social skills, and 4. Enhance attachment and bonding. Conduct connecting rituals in whole groups or with partners.

Peter, Peter (*I Love You Rituals*, page 62)
Peter, Peter, pumpkin eater.
Pump your arms and shake your hips.
Had a friend he (she) loved to greet.
Reach out and shake your partner's hand.
Treated her with kind respect.
Put your left arm on the right shoulder of your partner.
And in the morning hugged his (her) neck.
Move into a gentle hug.

Twinkle, Twinkle (*I Love You Rituals*, page 63)
Twinkle, twinkle, little star.
Hold arms up and wiggle your fingers together.
What a wonderful friend you are!
Place arms on each other's shoulders.
With bright eyes and nice round cheeks,
Point to your eyes and to your cheeks.
A talented person from head to feet.
Touch partner's head and feet.
Twinkle, twinkle, little star.
Hold arms up and wiggle your fingers together.
What a wonderful friend you are!
Give a gentle hug, high five or thumbs up.

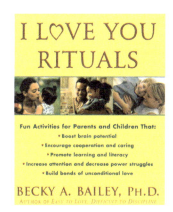

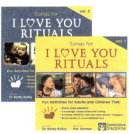

I Love You Rituals

Extend the above nursery rhymes into literacy lessons. Take pictures of children doing the activities to create class-made books. Send these books home for the children to read to their parents and conduct the activities with them. Add I Love You Rituals to older students' reading buddy programs with younger children.

Music and Movement

The music CDs offered by Conscious Discipline are designed to connect children to each other (Chapter 4). Older children enjoy using popular music. Simply cut an appropriate song down to about two minutes and have children create partner motions that foster eye contact, touch, presence and playful situation.

Brain Breaks

Partner up for quick activities that help children refocus and hit the refresh button on their brains. Again, eye contact, touch, presence and playful situation are needed to reap the brain-boosting benefits of connection. The ideas below will help you get started. Find additional brain breaks on your portal.

Handshakes: Have children create handshakes. Older children can repeat the handshake with the left hand and with both hands simultaneously, or conduct a cumulative handshake. In a cumulative handshake, each person conducts the existing handshake and then adds something new. For example, Person A does a knuckle bump, Person B does a knuckle bump and adds a high five, etc.

Quickmath (based on an activity by Jean Blaydes Madigan): Face a partner and put your hands behind your back. On the count of three, each person holds out a different number of fingers. Add the numbers together and say the answer. Celebrate success in a way that focuses on eye contact and caring touch.

Slap Letter (by Scott Miller): Face your partner with hands forward and face up. The one with the largest hand goes first and is Person A. Person A takes her right hand and crosses over to slap Person B's right hand lightly, saying the letter A. Then Person B takes her left hand and crosses over and slaps Person A's left hand lightly, saying the letter B. Next comes C and D. Repeat this process all the way through the alphabet. Older children can say the alphabet backward or forward, saying only every other letter.

Structure: Ways To Be Helpful Board or Book

The Ways To Be Helpful Board or Book accomplishes two main goals: 1. It provides visual images that concretely illustrate expected behaviors in order to scaffold children's attention and encourage helpfulness. 2. It honors the ways children are helpful to each other.

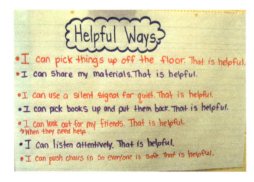

Announce the School Family job descriptions (as discussed in the Composure chapter) on the first day of school: "My job is to keep you safe. Your job is to help keep the classroom safe." Work with students to discern what is helpful in keeping the classroom safe and teach them how to accomplish their helpful job.

Lead discussions about what it looks like, feels like and sounds like to be helpful. Have children draw and/or write about the many forms of helpfulness in a class book. Help children be specific in this process. Children may suggest being nice, sharing, taking turns and being respectful. Guide them with specific scenarios and examples so they know the exact language and actions to use to accomplish these goals.

Children's brains encode information in pictures rather than with words. Showing helpful acts visually provides information in a form their brains can readily use, so they are better able to integrate the helpful act into their regular behavior. These visual depictions scaffold children's creation of positive mental models for progressing through the school day.

Begin the year with a classroom bulletin board that shows ways to be helpful using a combination of art, photographs and words. If "lending supplies to a friend in need" is a way to be helpful in your class, photograph one child lending another a pencil. If "taking turns" is a way to be helpful, include a photograph of children taking turns. Share what you are doing with parents. Have children make Ways To Be Helpful books for home and school, and send them home to be read. Ask parents to take Ways To Be Helpful photographs and post them on the refrigerator at home.

Structure: Kindness Tree and Kindness Recorder

The Kindness Tree and Kindness Recorder are commonly used forms of the kindness rituals described in Chapter 3. They honor kind and helpful acts, help adults and children shift from focusing on what is wrong to what is going well (what you focus on you get more of), and help highlight the many ways we serve one another. Be conscious of your intention when using the Kindness Tree and Kindness Recorder; they are ways to notice innate goodness, not catch children being good.

School-wide Kindness Tree

The **Kindness Tree** takes on many forms (not all of them are trees), depending on the age of the children. It is easily integrated with math, language arts, social studies and science. You will need various props and may combine the Kindness Trees with a Kindness Recorder, depending on the age of the students. Some examples of Kindness Trees include:

Watch video examples on the portal.

- A felt tree with Velcro heart-shaped leaves encourages students to place a leaf on the tree to honor each kind, caring or helpful act they experience in the classroom. At the end of the day, the teacher leads students in counting the number of kind acts, sharing several and celebrating the group's helpfulness.
- A designated space for written notes encourages students to write out acts of kindness and place them in the space for all to see. A Kindness Recorder might read several of the notes at a kindness celebration at the end of the day.
- Sticky notes, pens and a centrally located bulletin board encourage faculty and staff to notice the kindness of coworkers.

> *Be creative and use symbols that are important to your classroom. For example, a Native American school put feathers on an eagle to symbolize kind acts.*

The **Kindness Recorder** is appropriate for older classrooms and is a wonderful literacy-building tool. This structure requires a notebook, pen or pencil, and the Kindness Recorder School Family job. This person is responsible for recording kind acts he sees and those that are reported to him by classmates throughout the day. At the close of the day, the Kindness Recorder reads several kind acts to the class, reinforcing the belief that we are all in this together.

Older classrooms may choose to use both a Kindness Tree and a Kindness Recorder. In this case, the students would write notes to put on the tree and the Kindness Recorder would read the acts of kindness off of the tree at the end of the day (instead of out of the notebook). One middle school teacher posts magnetic hands by the door. As children change classes, they slap up high fives for kindnesses witnessed during their class period.

> *All classroom structures can also be used with staff or faculty. Start noticing and recording acts of kindness in staff meetings, and watch the same systems appear in the classrooms. See examples of this on your portal.*

Structure: Job Board

Being of service activates the optimal learning state of relaxed alertness, which leads to greater academic gains. As each child contributes to the wellbeing of the School Family by completing a job, he experiences the brain benefits of being of service. It is essential that children understand their jobs are meaningful to the functioning of the classroom. If a job is not perceived as meaningful, teach it with more understanding or remove it from the job list. Props often increase interest in the jobs.

In a Conscious Discipline classroom, each child in the classroom will hold a job. If you have 28 children, you will have 28 jobs. The Job Board helps manage the jobs. The *School Family Job Board* from Conscious Discipline provides extensive instructions, job cards and a Job Board to help you establish this essential classroom structure. Alternately, you could create your own Job Board by gluing library card pockets on a poster board. On each pocket, put a picture of the job and write the job's title. Have each child glue a photo of herself on a popsicle stick. Place a stick in each of the pocket holders to designate who is responsible for each job. Rotate the sticks weekly as children change jobs. You will teach children how to do each job at the beginning of the year. The best way to do this is to teach each job as the need for it arises.

Teaching jobs takes time and lesson planning, but it is time well spent. Integrate the teaching of these jobs into your language arts program. After the initial lessons, each child teaches the next child who will serve in that position.

Do the following to discern what jobs your class needs:

- Make a list of all the class management tasks you do. Decide which jobs can be turned over to children.
- Involve the children. Ask for their assistance in coming up with the jobs, writing job descriptions and creating the Job Board.
- Think in terms of jobs that can provide the social and emotional support children need and enjoy.

Below are a handful of class jobs that support the Power of Unity and the School Family:

Morning Message Writer: This person's job is to write (or draw a picture of) a welcoming and encouraging idea for children to see as they enter the classroom in the morning.

Greeter: This job involves greeting children as they enter the classroom. The greeters give handshakes, pinky hugs or thumb touches to students as they enter class. The class may create additional greetings, for example:

- **Butterfly:** Lock right hand thumbs and wiggle fingers as you fly up and down.
- **Fireworks fist bump:** Fist bump, followed by making motions and sounds to represent fireworks.
- **Multiplication:** On the count of three, both children hold out a number of fingers. The child being greeted multiplies the two numbers together. If correct, high five each other. If incorrect, the greeter says, "Oops," they work together on the correct answer and then give a high five.

Encourager: This person's job is to notice children who are feeling discouraged with schoolwork, home life or friends, and to offer encouragement. The encouragement can be a poem, a note saying, "Hang in there," a pat on the back or a class heart that says, "We care about you and want you to succeed." Older children can write and design encouragements as part of their language arts program. Younger children can draw pictures or hand out prefabricated hearts.

Absent Child Committee: This job can belong to a person or a committee. The job is to do something for an absent child that communicates the message, "We noticed you were gone. We are glad you are back." They might make a welcome back card, song or poem, or use the I Love You Ritual "You've Been Gone" shared in Chapter 4. Video of Absent Child Rituals can be found in Shubert's Classroom by clicking on the Wish Well Board.

New Child Buddy: This person's job is to be the buddy of a new child who enters the school and classroom. Ask the children, "How would it feel to enter a new classroom not knowing anything about the school?" From this discussion, develop a list of duties the buddy would be involved with. The following are example duties:

- Sit next to the new child and introduce him to others.
- Give the new child a tour introducing the office staff, media specialist, etc.
- Walk in line with the new child and play with him at recess.
- Sit together at lunch, showing the new child the necessary rules and procedures.
- Help the child learn the daily routine, secure necessary supplies and understand how we treat each other in the School Family.

S.T.A.R. Person: This person's job is to lead the class in active calming activities. This could be done as part of the Brain Smart Start of the daily routine discussed in the Composure chapter. At the specified time, the S.T.A.R. Person holds up a star-tipped wand or uses some other star prop to signal the class to **S**mile, **T**ake a deep breath **A**nd **R**elax. This person may also lead the class in draining, ballooning or the pretzel. Throughout the day, the S.T.A.R. Person may also help calm students who appear tense or frustrated. The S.T.A.R. Person might walk over to the upset child, use the star prop and say, "Breathe with me. You can do it."

Wish Well Leader: This student's job is to lead the wish well activities that are created by the class or the teacher. Wishing well is something the class might do when a fellow classmate is sick, upset or going through a difficult time. The Wish Well Leader can help the class sing the lyrics below to the tune of "The Farmer in the Dell."

We Wish You Well
We wish you well!
We wish you well!
All through the day today,
We wish you well!

The Wish Well Leader could also help students write down wish wells and place them on the Wish Well Board during designated times in the day. For additional information, read Chapter 11 in *Creating the School Family* and visit Shubert's Classroom online. Videos on your portal also show how to use jobs with very young children, older children, and children with special needs or mental health issues.

Structure: Friends and Family Board

As mentioned in Chapter 4, the Friends and Family Board (and/or book) is a structure that supports both composure and encouragement. It displays photos of family, loved ones and all the people who are committed to keeping children safe at school (principal, cafeteria workers, school secretary, speech and language therapist, etc.). It symbolizes the Power of Unity, the fundamental principle that we are all in this together.

Friends and Family Board

Friends and Family Book

Encouragement Summary

Power:	**Unity:** We are all in this together.
Becoming Brain Smart:	Encouragement, connection and belonging prime the brain for academic achievement.
Skill:	Notice instead of judge as the basis for encouragement, "You did it! You ___ so____. That was helpful."
School Family:	The "I See" Song, Connecting Rituals, Ways to Be Helpful, Kindness Tree or Recorder, Job Board, Friends and Family Board/Book

Power of Unity Reflection

We can choose to see a world of separation and judgment, or a world of interconnection and hope. The Power of Unity inspires us to co-create a School Family filled with intrinsic motivation, contribution, helpfulness and the limitless expression of each person's unique gifts for the betterment of the whole. We can do it! We can build the connected, compassionate classrooms of our dreams! The following will help in our success:

❏ **Treat others as we wish to be treated.**

❏ **Become consciously aware of our tendency to judge instead of notice**.

❏ **Observe how willing or resistant we are to see a call for help** instead of misbehavior. Use the two-step call for help formula instead of judging or labeling.

❏ **Help children be of service.** Replace activities that focus on specialness with ones that focus on unity, helpfulness and contribution: "I am unique because _____ and it contributes to my School Family by _____." "Are you willing to help your classmate by _____?"

❏ **Watch the Power of Encouragement video** on the portal to deepen your reflection.

Brain Smart Teaching Moments

Use acts of helpfulness as the core of your character-building curriculum. Notice the following acts in the classroom frequently:

- Helpfulness
- Kindness
- Taking turns
- Caring
- Thoughtfulness
- Courtesy
- Cooperation
- Concern

Every assertive command is a teaching moment. We can make the moment about us by saying, "Thank you" or "Good job," or we can honor the child's willingness and effort by saying, "You did it!" "Good for you!" or "Way to go!" Notice children's strengths and encourage them to be of service by offering their unique gifts to others.

Skill Reflection: Common and Conscious

If possible, partner up with someone and say the two statements out loud. See if you can feel the difference. After each statement share, "The difference between Common and Conscious for me was…"

Common	Conscious
"Thank you, Erica."	"Erica, you carefully matched the toy with the label and put it in the bin so everyone can find it. That was helpful."
"Good job, Roberto."	"Roberto, you did it! You finished all your homework. Good for you!"
"That was a great slide!"	"You did it! You came down the slide feet first and landed right in my arms."
"You are so good at math."	"You finished all your math problems and checked your work carefully. Would you be willing to help Kareem so he can be successful, too?"

School Family Implementation Checklist

❏ **Encourage through noticing**, "You did it! You ___." At least three times a day, catch yourself before you issue a judgment (Good job) and encourage instead.

❏ **Shift to "You did it!" "Way to go!" or "Good for you!"** (instead of "Thank you" or "Good job!") after compliance.

❏ **Consciously notice helpful acts daily** using the formula "You ___ so___. That was helpful."

❏ **Encourage children who make poor choices.** "You almost did it. Try again. You can do it!"

❏ **Implement a job for every student** and organize it with a job board.

❏ **Create a Ways to be Helpful bulletin board, book or directory.** Plaster your school with images of what you want children to do, demonstrating the values you hold dear.

❏ **Create a Kindness Tree and/or Kindness Recorder** to honor helpfulness, not "catch children being good."

❏ **Set aside time for connecting rituals** and use student jobs to organize, plan and run them.

❏ **Add more music, movement and brain breaks into the day.**

❏ **Visit Shubert's School and the portal** to gain additional insight, with a particular focus on implementing a Kindness Tree, Jobs, Ways to Be Helpful and Connecting Rituals.

You Did it! You cleaned the paint supplies, so they could be reused. That was Helpful!

Chapter 7
CHOICES
Building self-esteem and willpower

Internally motivated choices bathe the brain in helpful chemicals that foster an optimistic "I can" attitude, increase compliance, enhance decision-making and focus attention.

Life is filled with choices. One of the most fundamental choices is whether to actively change ourselves or spend our energy trying to make others change. Often, we believe it's our job to make others act a certain way. The Power of Free Will says, "The only person you can **make** change is yourself," the implications of which are life-changing.

Think about your significant relationships. How much time have you spent thinking, feeling or acting from the perspective, "If only he/she would ___, then I could _____"? Focusing our attention on changing others puts us in a **get** mode instead of a **give** mode, ultimately discouraging ourselves and others, and setting us up for failure and loss of composure. The icon for the Power of Free Will is a direction sign. Watch a video about the Power of Free Will on the portal for a more in-depth understanding.

The Power of Free Will

The Power of Free Will means I am in charge of me and I'm the only person who can make myself change. It also means you are in charge of you and you are the only person who can make yourself change. Free will requires us to honor our will and the will of others, including the children in our care.

Free will has been and continues to be one of the hardest powers for me to embrace. I keep making two mistakes. First, I continue to believe outside events are forcing me to choose certain things in my life. My speech reveals this. "I have to exercise." "I should call Michael." "Don't make me ask you about this again." These are choices, not externally imposed situations. I could just as easily have said, "I am going to exercise," "I will call Michael," or "I'm going to follow up with you if I don't hear back within a week." Second, I believe I can make others choose to act in ways I desire. These mistakes are two sides of the same coin: If I believe others can make me act a certain way, it is reasonable to assume I can make others act in a certain way. Both these beliefs are false; yet both are widely held, causing great trouble in relationships and profoundly shaping how we handle discipline.

> **Believing outside forces control our behavior and believing we can control others' behavior are two sides of the same coin. Every person is in charge of his own behavior.**

Who is in Charge of You?

Free will is about claiming responsibility for our choices and behavior. Notice how often you use the words "have to," "should" and "make me." Every time we use these phrases, we declare ourselves victims of the world around us, put someone else in charge of running our lives, give away our Power of Free Will and leave ourselves powerless to change. Practice changing "should" into "could," and changing "have to" and "make me" into "I'm going to," and see if you can feel the difference.

"Make me" language allows us to avoid responsibility and accountability for our actions because it essentially says, "Someone or something external forced me to choose this or act this way." This robs us of both the joy of our successes and of the ability to learn from our mistakes. We must not operate as victims, but live from an empowered state. Changing "should," "have to" and "make me," transfers the responsibility for our life choices from others to us. We put ourselves in charge and model personal responsibility for children. As we stop blaming others, so do the children in our care.

> **Power comes from choice, not force.**

When we hear that voice in our heads saying, "I have to get that paperwork in by Friday," change it to, "I'm going to get the paperwork in on Friday." When we hear that voice saying, "The children are driving me crazy," change it to, "I am choosing to go crazy over the noise in this classroom. I am safe. Keep breathing. I can choose differently." In saying this, we maintain our self-control and send the message that we are in charge of our choices and the child is in charge of his. We model responsibility and empowerment. Power comes from choice, not force.

When we give our power away to children, many of them try not to abuse their reign. When we say, "Don't make me have to speak to you again," these children straighten up and immediately try to regain our love and approval. They have learned that their power comes from pleasing others, not from choosing for themselves. Other children respond differently. When we say, "You're making me angry," these children seem to experiment with this information. It's as if they're thinking, "If this makes her angry, what would it take to make her cry?" They have learned that their power comes from controlling others, not from their own choices.

> *Giving our power away to children sets them up to be pleasers or controllers. It also sets us up to blame.*

When we give up our Power of Free Will to children, we never know which type of personality will respond. Once we give our power away, we must seek to get it back (often through power struggles) or resign to living as a victim to life's experiences. When we use the language of responsibility and choice, we reclaim our power and provide a healthy model for both people-pleasing and control-seeking children to learn new skills from.

Activity to Shift From Powerless to Powerful

Practice changing your powerless language to the language of responsibility and choice. If possible, partner up with a friend and take turns reading the statements below out loud. Begin by saying a statement from the Language of Powerlessness. Pause and then read the corresponding statement from the Language of Responsibility and Choice. Did you feel a difference between the two? Discuss. Then have your partner repeat the process with the next statement.

Language of Powerlessness	Language of Responsibility and Choice
I should contribute to that potluck on Friday.	I could contribute to that potluck on Friday.
Don't make me pull this car over!	I'm going to pull the car over until the seatbelts are on and everyone is safe.
I have to get a haircut.	I could get a haircut.
I made my husband go to the show.	It took a little persuasion, but he decided to go with me.

Commit to listening to your own language and the language of others for one week. When you find yourself using "make me," "should," "have to" or other powerless language, make the choice to change it!

Who Are We Really in Charge Of?

The belief that adults can change others or make children behave is as common as the air we breathe. Parents are judged on how well they make their children behave. Teachers are evaluated on how well they control their classrooms. Administrators measure school disruptions as a reflection of the school's performance and their own success. Schools hold parent conferences so parents will make their children behave better. "Look what you made me do." "Look how you made her feel." Over and over again we sacrifice our Power of Free Will and rob children of theirs. This approach creates enormous stress for all parties involved because making others change is ultimately impossible. We can certainly attempt to threaten or manipulate others into submission; however, they are ultimately responsible for choosing whether or not to comply. Most of us have met children who do not respond to threats, removal, loss of privileges or other forms of control. No matter how much pressure we put on children to behave, it is still their choice to submit their will to us.

> **No matter how much pressure we put on children to behave, it is ultimately their choice to submit their will to us.**

Instead of expecting others to change, we must discipline ourselves first by changing our beliefs. Changing our beliefs starts a cascade of events: It changes our thoughts, which changes our feelings, which changes our behavior so new practices may emerge. Parent-teacher conferences become opportunities to create a cooperative plan to help children be more successful. Instead of tracking infractions, principals cover classes so teachers can work one-on-one with difficult children. Teachers say, "See her face, she looks sad," instead of, "Look how you made her feel." These might seem like slight modifications, but they are reflections of quantum shifts in beliefs.

> **Keep children in charge of their own feelings by saying, "See her face, she looks sad," instead of, "Look how you made her feel."**

Changing and managing ourselves is called self-regulation and is the basis for democracy (self-governance). Attempting to control others is the basis for autocracy (a single person with unlimited power). When we try to make others do things, we prime ourselves to rely on force. Our strong-arm tactics teach children it's legitimate to use force to influence others. By removing their choices, we replace their internal willpower with external forcefulness that models a power-over relationship dynamic. This is the same relationship imbalance seen in bullying among children and domestic violence among adults. Attempting to use force to make children behave strips children of their willpower and self-worth. When we say, "The only person you can make change is yourself," we are also saying that it's the other person's choice to submit his will to us. Whether someone chooses to submit his will depends on a number of factors, most importantly, the health of the relationship. Connection fosters cooperation.

> I've had trouble making it to the gym with my workout partner. To say, "She is making me go to the gym" gives my power away, leaving me feeling powerless. "She is helping me" supports my connection to others and feels loving. "I am choosing" empowers me. Each approach has a different meaning, belief and biochemistry.

Moving from Entitlement to Empowerment

Few of us grew up in families that embraced the concept, "The only person you can make change is you." In most homes, adults were entitled to obedience simply because they were adults. Because of this mindset, the language we grew up hearing was rarely the language of choice, responsibility and free will. The language we heard implied we were responsible for others' feelings and actions. Perhaps the most classic of these is the "make me" punishment threat: "Don't make me come in there." "Don't make me spank you." After years of hearing that we made our parents behave a certain way, we began to feel a lingering sense of inadequacy. If we controlled our parents, why couldn't we make them happy? Why couldn't we be good enough to make everything better? We couldn't do these things because we were never really in charge. Our well-meaning parents simply gave us the false impression that we were responsible for them and for others. As we grew up, this false message became etched onto our internal CD-Roms. Now that we are the adults, we must ask ourselves if we want to rewrite our CD-Roms or unconsciously hand them down to the next generation.

Activity for Empowerment

We often use phrases stemming from a CD-Rom message that says children should obey us because we are adults, not because of our actions. This models entitlement instead of empowerment. These phrases also send the false message that the children control the adults, their peers or the classroom. Use the language of responsibility and choice to rewrite each phrase in the space below.

1. When you are quiet, I can begin.

    I'm going to_____

2. Let me finish reading the story and I will help you.

    I'm going to _____

3. Don't make me have to speak to you again.

    (Assertive command)_____

4. You're driving me crazy.

    I'm going to _____

5. Look how you made your friend feel.

    Look at her face_____

6. You are ruining the story for everyone!

    (Assertive command)_____

Now, list two common phrases you use to give your power away. Rewrite them from a position of entitlement (they owe me their obedience) to empowerment (I am responsible for my thoughts, feelings and actions).

Old, entitled phrase: _____

New, empowered phrase: _____

Old, entitled phrase: _____

New, empowered phrase: _____

The Blame Game

If we believe we can make others change and we fail to perform this duty, we begin to feel inadequate. We fight these feelings of powerlessness by starting a blame game whereby teachers blame parents, parents blame school systems and everyone, when exhausted, blames the children. In actuality, the blame game begins and ends with each of us.

We make choices every moment of every day, yet we often move through the day on automatic pilot, forgetting we are the ones in charge of our decisions. Life seems to happen to us because we lack the awareness that we choose our perceptions and thoughts. We come home from work moaning, "Boy, did I have a bad day." The big question is, who decided how the day went? Did the day choose our thoughts about it? "Traffic was horrible." Was it horrible or were there simply a lot of cars on the road? Traffic is not inherently horrible, but we can choose to perceive it as such.

> *Change "don't make me" into "I'm going to" to reclaim your power.*

Giving our power away results in upset. Upset is usually followed by blame. Blame removes the possibility of finding solutions because we are focused on what we don't want. What we focus on, we get more of. The cycle continues. At any moment we can seek to administer blame or look for solutions. The choice is ours.

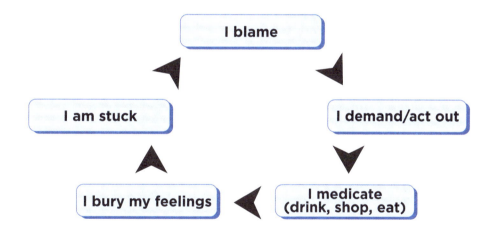

Reframing Blame

"He made me do it! It wasn't my fault! He pushed first!" These are common phrases uttered by children who have internalized the notion that offering blame instead of solutions is the best approach to life's upsets. Children tend to blame others in direct proportion to the amount and severity of the punishment they receive. This is because the adults' response to conflict has thrown the children into emotional states where blame and attack are automatic. They are afraid to own their choices and take responsibility for them. Children who are chronically in trouble and live on a diet of regular punishments at home and school are more reluctant to own their role in misbehavior. It is also more likely that they will lie out of fear.

The fear of punishment must be minimal for children to begin taking responsibility for all of their choices and making wise decisions. The focus must be on solutions and problem-solving. The "Who Is the Boss of You" skill below will help children who tend to blame others for their actions reclaim their power.

Child statement: "Lexi made me do it!"
Adult response: "So Lexi is the boss of you?"
Child replies: "No."
Adult response: "What could you do differently if you were your own boss?"

Child statement: "Lexi made me do it"
Adult response: "So Lexi is the boss of you?"
Child replies: "Yes!"
Adult response: "How sad! That must be hard for you with Lexi bossing you all the time."

Activity to Reframe Blame Behavior

Role-play the following blame situations. Reframe the blame in your response:

1. Child says, "Brynn made me late to class."
2. Child says, "It wasn't my fault. Jose pushed me first."

Ask a New Question

We must change the question we ask ourselves if we intend to shift from making children behave to relying on the Power of Free Will. Generally teachers ask, "How can I get the children to stay on task?" Asking, "How can I get ____?" is the same as asking, "How can I make ____?" These questions ask our brains to come up with every feared, forced, coercive or manipulative strategy we have ever learned. If we ask a new question, we will get new answers. By asking ourselves, "How can I help the children successfully ____?" we ask our brains to come up with a different set of answers. These new answers will be more creative, will ask us to reflect on each child's needs and will result in developmentally-appropriate discipline strategies.

> A family living in a small town in the rural Midwest was out shopping. Each child had a list of things to find to contribute to the family. The older child, Dillon, had the task of finding a certain type of dog food. The small store was out of that kind of food and Dillon did not take it well. He began to throw a fit. Mom heard her inner speech say, "In front of everyone?! How can I get him to shut up?" She immediately took a deep, calming breath and asked a new question: "How can I help Dillon be successful at regulating his disappointment?" She took more deep breaths and said, "That was disappointing. You were hoping to get the food for Max. I wonder, if you fed Max cat food, would he say, Meow-bark?" That lightness was all it took to help Dillon recover.

I have done a fair number of television and magazine interviews. The questions are always a form of "How do I get my child to do X?" (X could be to finish homework, sleep through the night or stop hitting.) I find it very challenging in a two-minute sound bite to say, "You've asked the wrong question. Change the question and then answer it." It's time to ask a different question! It's time to harness the Power of Free Will.

Becoming Brain Smart

Neuroscientific research about free will is controversial at best. The debate is basically over whether we have free will or free won't (Klemm, 2010). Some studies have shown that a decision appears to manifest in the unconscious brain a half second before the conscious brain makes the decision (Kühn & Brass, 2009). According to some research, we are not the chooser, but we do possess veto power once we become conscious of a choice. Either way, we still decide to have the cookie or not.

Three decades of self-determination research, however, clearly shows that we improve our goal achievement (Deci & Ryan, 2008) and self-regulation (Muraven, 2008) when we make a choice that is self-driven, motivated from within and lacking in coercion. This research makes perfect sense to me based on my life experiences. I quit smoking over 35 years ago. I was an athlete. My friends, coaches and family nagged me to stop. I resisted these efforts, digging myself deeper into believing, "It's my life and no one will tell me what to do." Walking down the street in Atlanta one day, I decided it was time to quit. That was my last cigarette. When we choose to do something of our own volition, the chance of achieving our goal is much greater than when we are nagged or manipulated.

Making a choice based on our needs, values and aspirations feels good. It activates the reward center in the brain and releases a pharmacy of feel-good chemicals like dopamine. This is why it is essential to have children personally choose (or not) the classroom's commitments. It is also why this book provides opportunities to make personal commitments in each chapter. Making a choice to please others, meet others' expectations or avoid punishment has the reverse effect, and is the fast road to depression and other forms of psychological distress. We usually see this as burnout in adults, and as laziness, apathy or a discipline problem in children.

Choices made from internal desires enhance self-regulation; choices motivated by external control do not (Legault & Inzlicht, 2013). Therefore, reward and punishment-based classrooms cannot and do not teach self-regulation. On the other hand, the compassionate School Family creates a democratic environment that enhances self-regulation, promotes free will and encourages children to make prosocial choices that are rewarded by the body's internal feel good brain chemicals. Offering choice provides many benefits. The top five are:

1. Fosters general well-being
2. Increases prosocial behavior and responsibility
3. Improves academic achievement
4. Raises teacher morale and enhances all classroom relationships
5. Advances self-regulation and intrinsic motivation (Legault & Inzlicht, 2013)

Decision Fatigue

As much as we gain from feeling in control of our lives through choices, there is also a downside. It is called decision fatigue. The decision fatigue concept was first identified by the research of Dr. Roy Baumeister (Baumeister & Tierney, 2011). In one research study, participants were shown a table loaded with products. They were told they would get to keep one of the products at the end of the experiment. One group went through a series of choices, each time between two items. (A pen or a candle? A black shirt or red shirt?) The other group spent the same amount of time contemplating all the same products without having to make any choices. Everyone was then given a test of self-control. The group offered too many repetitive choices did significantly worse.

The results of this study and others like it indicate that decision-making affects our willpower and operates like a muscle: We can strengthen our willpower by making decisions and we can fatigue it through overuse. When we overuse choices, our prefrontal lobes slip offline and we are left operating from a state of unrestrained impulsiveness.

> Decision fatigue affects everyone. There is no magic number of choices that will work for all, but this general formula is helpful: If a child can handle and understand a one-step command, he should be able to manage two choices. If a child is able to follow a two-step command, he can process three or four choices.

Two prime examples of decision fatigue that many of us have experienced: 1. Our children do well at school all day then come home and act like wild animals. The wild behavior is the decision fatigue of school taking a toll on their self-regulation. 2. We "shop 'til we drop" and end up with more purchases than intended. The decision fatigue of over-saturating ourselves with shopping choices causes our willpower to drop, too.

Now, what does all this have to do with schools? The implications are as follows:

- Brain breaks are needed approximately every 20 minutes throughout the day. Children need to move, sing and play in short bouts to avoid decision fatigue. View several videos of brain breaks on your portal.
- Children need to make choices that are developmentally appropriate.
- Schools must be built democratically, using shared power as the decision-making tool.
- Giving our power away to children puts them in charge of us, fosters chronic decision fatigue and impulsiveness, and reduces children's ability to develop self-regulation.
- The choices offered to children today are overwhelming. We must break the choices down by offering two positive choices to help avoid decision fatigue (more on this shortly).

The sense of powerlessness that comes from feeling we lack choices produces stress, shuts down the prefrontal lobes and leaves us at the mercy of our impulses and insecurities. In this state, motivation and morale are low, and learning efficiency is poor. Choices, on the other hand, trigger the release of the brain's optimal thinking chemicals, fostering a confident "I can" attitude.

> **Commitment:** I understand that when I choose to believe others are making me behave certain ways, I give my power away, stress my body, and set myself up to blame and punish others for my actions. I am willing to take responsibility for my choices instead.
>
> Signature: _____ Date: _____

In our Class We have Choices.

We Choose to be helpful.

The Skill of Choices

It is developmentally necessary for children to experiment with limits in order to establish a sense of self (what is "me" and "not me") and discover what behaviors are appropriate. Children, still developing their own sense of autonomy, often need to assert themselves when they hear an adult command. We can help children fulfill our expectations while still encouraging their autonomy by offering two positive choices instead of giving an assertive command. Two positive choices allow children to comply with our wishes while honoring their Power of Free Will. By offering two positive choices, we help children do the following:

- Focus their attention on the tasks we deem important
- Comply with our wishes
- Learn decision-making skills
- Feel empowered, thereby reducing power struggles
- Redirect their behavior and learn impulse control
- Establish and maintain self-control

Ms. Barry is working with Mara to help her control her impulses and follow through with cleaning up after center time. She goes to where Mara is playing, kneels down close by and waits for her to make eye contact. Then Ms. Barry gives an assertive command. "Put your toys in the bin. You can tell where each toy belongs by looking at the pictures on the bins." Ms. Barry consciously points to the bins and the pictures as she speaks. She knows nonverbal gestures will help Mara attend to her words. Ms. Barry also waits for Mara to begin putting the toys away so she can encourage her choice to comply. Once Mara seems focused and on task, Ms. Barry leaves to assist other children.

Several minutes later, Ms. Barry checks on Mara. The child has emptied the toy bin and is sitting in it, taking off her clothes. With a deep breath, Ms. Barry silently reaffirms what she wants Mara to do and then verbally offers her two positive choices. "Mara, you have a choice. You may climb out of the bin and put on your shirt, or you may climb out and put on your shoes. What do you choose?" Mara begins climbing out and says, "Shoes." Ms. Barry notices her choice by saying in an upbeat voice, "You chose to put on your shoes, good for you!" Mara's choice empowered her to take action. She channeled her will and curbed her impulses to continue playing when she committed herself to putting on her shoes.

Ms. Barry offered Mara two positive choices. Most of us were not raised this way, so thinking in this manner may seem awkward at first. We are accustomed to giving a positive choice and a negative choice. We heard our parents say, "You can eat what is offered or starve." "You can go to sleep now or never have another sleepover." These are false choices. They have coercion as their intent. When we offer a false choice, we set children up to believe that when they think, feel or choose differently than us, they are bad, wrong or disrespectful (instead of simply making a choice). This has devastating effects later in life as some people try to coerce their partners into thinking, feeling and acting the same as them, and others try to make choices that will please their partners. Offering two positive choices teaches the autonomy and personal responsibility that help end this unhappy cycle in the future, while also encouraging children to choose compliance in the moment.

Two Positive Choices

Two positive choices reinforce the child's Power of Free Will while providing acceptable parameters for behavior. The following steps will help you deliver two positive choices:

Step 1: **Breathe deeply and make a conscious decision to focus on what you want the child to do.** In the earlier situation, Ms. Barry wanted the child to get out of the bin and put on her clothes. With a focus squarely on the behavior we want to see (rather than the undesired behavior) we are ready to offer two choices to achieve that goal.

Step 2: **Tell the child, "You have a choice!" in an upbeat tone.** Our positive attitude will lighten the situation, especially if the child seems resistant. It will also help the child perceive the options as choices. For older children we might say, "Seems to me you have a couple of options."

Step 3: **Clearly state two choices that will achieve the goal.** Say, "You may _____ or you may _____." For older children we might say, "Feel free to _____ or _____."

Step 4: **Complete the process by asking the child for a commitment.** We might say, "What is your choice?" For older children we might say, "What would be better for you?" If the child hesitates, repeat the options with calm enthusiasm.

Step 5: **Notice the child's choice.** Do this by saying, "You chose _____!" in an encouraging voice with loving intent. This imparts the child with crucial awareness about his choice. Many people make choices unconsciously and end up feeling controlled by life. Children who are aware of their choices possess greater self-control, and feel less controlled and victimized by external events and people.

Delivering Two Positive Choices

 Think in terms of what you want children to do, the behaviors you want to see and what the goal looks like.

 Think in terms of the problem or what you don't want.

 Offer true, positive choices by voicing two options that are acceptable to you.

 Offer false, coercive choices by voicing a positive option and a negative option.

 "You have a choice! You can begin working on the next assignment by yourself or you can sit quietly until the bell rings. Which is better for you?"

 "You can sit there and be quiet or you can lose five minutes of free time."

When to Use Two Positive Choices

Offering two positive choices helps children upshift from an emotional state to an executive state. It is an essential tool for helping children direct their attention when they're having trouble focusing, helping them recover from situations where they feel powerless and calming down after an emotional state episode. Providing two choices offers some degree of power while asking children to activate their prefrontal lobes for decision-making and focused attention. The emotional state develops rapidly from 15 months to around five years old, so the skill of two positive choices can feel like a miracle for toddlers and preschoolers.

Two positive choices are not helpful for a child in the overwhelmed state of survival. We know this from our own lives. When we are stressed out and overwhelmed, the choice between coffee or tea can push us over the edge, barking, "I don't care. Just give me something." Children (as well as adults) in a survival state require assertive commands to be successful.

Two positive choices are also not the most helpful approach for children operating from an executive state. These children have access to their creativity and wisdom, and may find two positive choices confining. Instead, encourage these children to think through and create their own options by using open-ended questions. "What would help you get started?" would be a more effective approach for a child operating from an executive state.

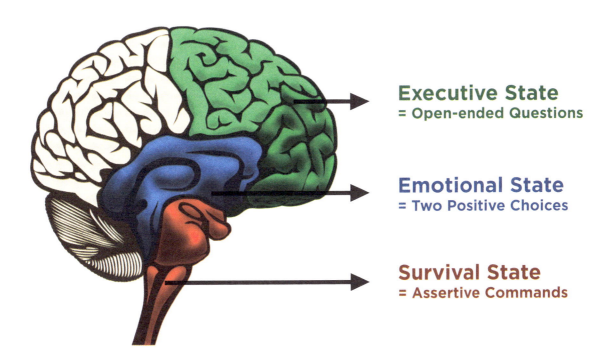

Executive State
= Open-ended Questions

Emotional State
= Two Positive Choices

Survival State
= Assertive Commands

Noticing with Two Positive Choices

After a child makes a choice, even if it took a few moments or some repetition on you part, notice the choice he picked. Noticing aims our energy toward that which we value. As we aim our energy, we also direct the child's attention to his accomplishment. Once we've noticed the child's choice, follow up with some form of encouragement (you did it, good for you, way to go). For example:

Teacher: You have a choice. You may work on problems one and two, or you may work on problems three and four. What is better for you?

Child: Three and four.

Teacher: You chose to move down a little on your paper and start with problems three and four (point to the page). Good for you!

 ## Activity to Create Two Positive Choices

Think of what you want the child to do and then offer two choices that will allow him to achieve that goal. Write your responses below. Role-play if possible, expressing the choices in an upbeat manner. Before you begin watch videos of choices on your portal.

Scene: Playing with food

Three-year-old Nathan is pounding his fist on his pizza during lunchtime. (Remember, "Stop pounding!" is not a positive action.)

_____

_____

Scene: Listening

Eight-year-old Meredith is playing with an eraser cover instead of listening to you.

_____

_____

Scene: Finishing work

Ten-year-old Cameron is sketching airplanes on his notepad instead of completing his math.

_____

_____

Now, assess your answers:

1. Did you take a deep breath and then focus on what you wanted the children to do? Could you feel your mind wanting to focus on the errors instead of the solutions?
2. Did you offer two positive solutions that gave the child the opportunity to get back on track?
3. Did you use the general format?: "You have a choice! You may _____ or _____. Which is better for you?"
4. Did you remember to notice and encourage the child when she made a conscious choice to control her impulses and comply with your structure by saying, "You chose _____. Good for you!" (or "Way to go!")

Children Who Have Trouble with Choices

Children who have trouble making choices generally fall into these categories:

1. Those who refuse to choose
2. Those who resist the structure given (given a choice of A or B, they pick C)
3. Those who change their minds (given a choice of A or B, they pick A, then switch to B, back to A, etc.)
4. Those who developmentally do not understand the concept of choice (developmental delays)

1. Helping Children Who Refuse to Choose

A teacher gave CeCe the choice to put her backpack on the shelf or hang it on the hook. CeCe stared at her teacher and then burst into tears. For CeCe, the decision was overwhelming. Children who find decision-making very difficult have tremendous anxiety brewing within them. They are often in a chronic state of decision fatigue due to life stressors. Their difficulty with decisions is a way of saying, "My world is overwhelming." The anxiety may have its roots in major life events, developmental disabilities, or everyday aggravations like fighting with friends, teasing from classmates, disappointing their parents or disappointing themselves.

Depending on their temperament, some children become overwhelmed easily. Others seem to roll with life like a surfer on a wave. Don't fight the child's temperament. Instead, learn how to best respond to it. To assist children who have trouble making choices, do the following:

Point out the many choices the child is making throughout the day. When she decides to color with crayons, say, "CeCe, you chose to draw today." The child may look at you as if to say, "Duh." That's great! It means the child is aware of her own actions. Slow, discouraged or at-risk learners generally have inappropriate self-convincer strategies (Jensen, 1997). Simply put, they often don't know what they know. It is our job to raise their consciousness by announcing and noticing their choices.

Offer the child small choices that involve closeness with you. For example, say, "Marvin, you have a choice. You may hold my left hand or right hand to walk in the building. Which do you pick? You chose my right hand! Holding hands with you feels warm and fuzzy." Making choices demands autonomy. At certain times, autonomy is scary for some children. To ease the child towards independence, use closeness with you as a starting point.

Model acceptance of mistakes with the Think Aloud process. Children who refuse to choose may fear disappointing others or being wrong. Model the fact that everyone slips up. Thinking aloud and modeling Oops is helpful for these children. Saying our inner thoughts out loud allows children to see how we handle making a mistake, problem solve or offer forgiveness to self and others.

A teacher says, "Where is my stapler? You children know better than to take things off my desk. Who took it? Speak up! It's important to respect other people's property." Carmen responds, "But teacher, Mrs. McElwain borrowed your stapler yesterday." The teacher realizes she's made a mistake by attacking the class. She also realizes this is a perfect time to think aloud. "Well, I made a big mistake. I was mad about the missing

> stapler. I thought you were being disrespectful by not asking me first. Actually, I was the one who was disrespectful. I blamed you and tried to make you feel as rotten as I felt. Oops! I am going to take a deep breath and forgive myself for my mistakes. Next time I feel upset, I'm going to breathe deeply, collect more information instead of blaming and treat you with respect."

By thinking aloud, this teacher modeled the constructive handling of a mistake and making a commitment to change her behavior. Many children learn that no matter what you do, an apology will eliminate the problem. Children must learn that while it is important to express regrets about misdeeds, it is more important to change misguided behavior.

> **Teach children how to change their behavior (instead of simply saying "sorry") by thinking aloud when your own behavior would benefit from a do-over.**

2. Helping Children Who Resist the Given Structure

Some children will use the structured choices you offer as an opportunity for a power struggle. Before we learn how to handle resistance, it is helpful to understand why control matters so greatly and what prompts some children to oppose structure.

Developmental Opposition

All young children go through a process researchers call individuation and separation. This process transforms a helpless, dependent infant into a person with a unique, autonomous identity. During this journey towards selfhood, the child starts to define himself as "not Mom" or "not Dad." Any assertive stance from an adult prompts the child to react with the opposite behavior. Children in the oppositional years often show their resistance by ignoring structured choices. They are simply testing to figure out who they are (where they end and we begin) and discovering their uniqueness, not trying to see what they can get away with or make us angry. To help a child who resists structured choices for developmental reasons, do the following:

Realize that if we allow ourselves to be dragged into a power struggle, we have become part of the problem not the solution. To avoid this trap, take a deep S.T.A.R. breath, become conscious of our thoughts and focus on what we want the child to do. If we slip into focusing on what we don't want (stop crying, stop talking, don't hit) we will be probably end up in a power struggle.

Once we are in control of ourselves, we must recognize the child will or will not choose to operate within our framework. Coercion is the problem, not the answer. Consciously choose to rely on the Power of Free Will. We all have a choice of how to behave. We can control our own actions, but not the child's.

Use the Parroting technique. This involves repeating the options in a calm, assertive voice. Think about how children persist when asking for something they want. "I want a cookie." We respond, "Not now, it's time for dinner." They persist, "I want a cookie." We continue to attempt reason with the unreasonable. They vigilantly wear us down through repetition. Parroting is the same strategy, but with the adult in the repetitive position:

Adult: "Joseph, it is time to put away these toys. You have a choice. You can begin by picking up small blocks or large ones. What is your choice?"
Child: "No!"
Adult: "Joseph, it is time to clean up. You have a choice — Small blocks or large ones. What is your choice?"
Child: "You can't make me. I hate you."
Adult: "Small blocks or large ones. What is your choice?"

As we continue to calmly repeat the choices, the child will most likely choose (sometimes begrudgingly). The most important point is that we remain composed. If we lose our peace of mind even a tiny bit, we will enter into a power struggle. The child will often escalate, with each round getting more intense with the goal of goading us into to a power struggle. Choose not to play, using Q.T.I.P. (**Q**uit **T**aking **I**t **P**ersonally) and active calming to help children learn that power comes from choice, not force.

When the child chooses to cooperate, celebrate his choice. Recognize how much willpower and energy he harnessed to transform his negative response into a positive one. Have you ever been so upset that your negative thoughts inflated to the point of outrage? Think about how much strength it took to stop that landslide of blame, anger and self-righteousness in order to become cooperative again. From the depths of your heart, encourage the child and celebrate his victory. Your words will be perfect if your intention is to celebrate his achievement of choosing cooperation over opposition. Any leftover huffs and puffs he may mutter are just the bleeding off of the adrenaline that was rushing through his body during the conflict. Breathe and wish him well.

Learned Opposition

The second type of child who resists choices has learned resistance is a way to get needs met. Children learn resistance in three basic ways: 1. From parenting that fails to meet the child's needs. 2. Through permissive parenting. 3. Through serious family troubles and trauma.

The first way a child learns to resist structured choices begins in infancy and pertains to the way a baby's needs were met or not met. When a baby has a need (hunger, warmth, comfort) he enters an aroused state. When an adult fulfills the baby's need, it produces a relaxed state. A baby will remain in an aroused state if the parent does not respond to the baby's call. A baby will also remain in an overly-aroused state if a parent responds, but cannot soothe him due to colic, premature birth or other problems. From the infant's perspective, his needs are not being met. These children expend a lot of energy trying to steer the world their way because they believe this is their best chance for survival. As he grows, he may become controlling and resist imposed structure. Such children do not resist structure to test the boundaries of their power, they do so in order to feel safe. They have a low tolerance for frustration.

Permissive parents either cave in to the child when he becomes upset or try to dance around an issue to avoid upsetting him. These actions teach a youngster to fight limits and misbehave to get his way. They also teach children that adults don't mean what they say.

The last way a child learns to oppose structured choices is through the experience of serious family trauma (a depressed parent, divorce, death, a drug-abusing parent, etc.). Such troubles create enormous stress, leaving the child feeling overwhelmed and unable to make choices. This child may attempt to control a life that seems out of control.

To help children who have learned to oppose structure, diligently practice all the techniques of Conscious Discipline. Although an oppositional child will challenge your patience, you must maintain self-control to help him and refrain from entering power struggles. Children who are willful and controlling are not likely to respond to the old fear-based approach to discipline.

Regardless of the discipline style we use, power struggles will occur. Power struggles always require two willing participants. When we refuse to engage in a power struggle, the child is left trying to play tug-of-war with himself. If we do engage in a power struggle, these steps enable both adult and child to heal afterward:

Step 1: **Forgive yourself. Forgiveness takes place in three steps, the Three R's of Forgiveness.** 1. Recognize and accept your feelings. Tell yourself, "I feel angry and anxious and that's okay." 2. Reframe the experience. Forget about finding a good guy and a villain. Admit that given both your states of mind, you did your best and so did the child. 3. Request help. Calmly ask your child to work with you in co-creating new patterns of behavior.

Step 2: **Help the child feel some sense of personal power.** Do this by giving her the chance to participate often in activities she enjoys and at which she can succeed. Most importantly, make sure the child has plenty of opportunities to be of service to others and notice the child's helpful acts to the School Family.

Step 3: **Spend time with the child to develop a trusting relationship.** This is done through face-to-face interactions that are playful, such as the I Love You Rituals (Pages 172-173) we've previously discussed. To see many of these rituals in action, visit Shubert's School on our website.

Step 4: **Help the child learn how to handle frustration and engage in healthy problem-solving.** Handling frustration requires learning to be a S.T.A.R. (Smile, Take a breath And Relax). One child drew a picture with a big star and as many little stars as would fit around it. He handed the picture to the teacher and said, "I drew this for you because sometimes it takes a lot of practice being a S.T.A.R. before you actually figure it out." She had worked faithfully with him all year and, indeed, he got it.

Some oppositional children may have neurological imbalances, attention deficits or sensory integration issues. Chronic issues require evaluation. Misbehavior is a call for help; sometimes the call is for mental health services, social services or medical services.

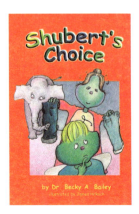 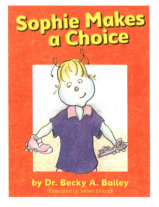

Shubert and Sophie books help teachers and children make two positive choices.

3. Helping Children Who Change Their Minds

Morgan's teacher offered her the choice of milk or juice for a snack. She selected milk. When the teacher served the milk, Morgan pushed it away and said, "No. Juice." The teacher then passed her some juice and Morgan said, "I want milk." The teacher was ready to dump both drinks on her head.

Children like Morgan are signaling they are stressed. They may, at an indecisive moment, be feeling down on themselves or their world for many reasons. Through indecisiveness, Morgan is trying to control her environment. Children who pick "C" after being given a choice between "A" and "B," are launching a direct, aggressive confrontation. Children like Morgan, on the other hand, use passive-aggressive methods rather than direct means to control others.

Helping these children begins with a diagnosis. Is this a developmental issue or a learned behavior? Is indecisiveness a new behavior for this child or is it chronic?

When an inability to choose appears from nowhere and occurs infrequently, the child may be overwhelmed by stress. Children who are stressed often regress developmentally (they revert to behaviors you would expect from a younger child). When children regress, they need assertive commands rather than choices. The teacher could say, "Morgan, you are having trouble choosing for yourself this morning. Here is the milk. Drink it if you like." Commands teach children what to do. Choices teach children how to make decisions and keep commitments. Teaching decision-making to a six-month-old infant would be silly. The same is true for a highly-stressed, older child who has regressed.

If the problem is chronic, there is a good chance it is a learned behavior. The child gets more attention by changing her mind than she does for being cooperative. This is a side effect of living in a hurry-up world. When children are indecisive, we often pause to accommodate their choosing and re-choosing. Whether our pause is patient or frustrated, it can still occupy several minutes of our time rather than the 30 seconds a compliant child might receive. As this pattern repeats itself, some children learn to use indecisiveness as a way to get attention. The child is really calling for connection.

First, make time to connect with children who chronically change their minds. Activities like I Love You Rituals (Bailey, 1997) and Baby Doll Circle Time (Bailey & Montero-Cefalo, 2012) are excellent connecting tools. (Videos of both these types of activities are found in Shubert's School online.) Then, be certain to slow down and make eye contact when offering two positive choices with these children. When a child like Morgan chooses milk, give it to her and celebrate her choice, "You chose the milk!" If she then requests the juice, say in a quiet but firm voice, "You chose the milk. Here is your milk. You may drink it or you may leave it." Often the child will sulk or fuss. Use empathy (Chapter 7) to help her process the upset. Be firm and consistent, and the child will ultimately learn that changing her mind no longer earns extra attention.

The *Baby Doll Circle Time* curriculum (Bailey & Montero-Cefalo, 2012) helps childcare centers provide the one-on-one connections that help children develop healthy blueprints for attachment, self-regulation, relationship and sense of self.

4. Helping Children Who Do Not Understand Choice (Developmental Delays)

Children with special needs may require structured assistance in understanding the concept of choices. They may need physical adaptations in the environment like communication boards to make their choices. To assist in this process, the adult can point out the choices they make and structure controlled choices for them. To structure a controlled choice, observe the children playing to see what toys they prefer. Present the child with a favorite toy and a different type of toy. Generally, the child will select his or her favorite toy by eye gaze, pointing, touching or verbalizing. As the child makes the selection, reinforce the choice. "You made a choice! You chose the block. Here it is for you to play with." You can also do this exercise with pictures of toys instead of the toys themselves.

> Cindy is preverbal. She loves horses. She would spend the entire day with the plastic horses if the teacher would let her! Mr. Worrel uses this information to assist Cindy in understanding the concept of choice. He puts a fire truck and a horse in front of Cindy and says, "Cindy, you have a choice. You can play with the fire truck or the horse. What is your choice?" Cindy reaches for the horse with a loud squeal. "The horse! You did it!" says Mr. Worrell to bring Cindy's awareness to her choice using simple language and an encouraging, loving intent.

 Often children with developmental delays require extensive visual input and information to understand their choices. Watch a portal video of a young child with autism successfully navigating choices with this kind of assistance.

Choices Build Connection in Your School Family

As you practice the aforementioned perceptual shifts and skills daily, the following structure will help you create a strong sense of belonging and a felt sense of connection in your School Family.

Structure: Visual Rules with Two Positive Choices

Rules are important in any classroom and we create them. A child cannot harness her Power of Free Will to choose to comply with the rules if they are not specific, clearly communicated and based on useable information. As mentioned in Chapter 2, teachers often confuse rules, agreements and routines. Remember, rules are created to be enforced.

You may enjoy your lunch without talking.

You may talk quietly with your friends during lunch.

You may not talk loudly or yell while at lunch.

In early childhood and elementary school, it is helpful to post two pictures of what children can do and one picture of unacceptable behavior for each rule you create. For example, you would make pictures that illustrate the following: "You may raise your hand to speak," "You may wait for a turn to speak," and, "You may not speak at the same time as someone else." You can take photos of students to create these picture rules or utilize *Shubert's Picture Rule Cards* available from Loving Guidance. When a child finds himself being hurtful (breaking the rule), the first consequence is to guide him to the two images of what he could do to be helpful and ask him to make a helpful choice.

The following is typical in a traditional classroom:

1. Rules are written and posted on the wall and are often confused with agreements.
2. Rules are posted beside the consequence for rule infractions.
3. Consequences are written in a 1, 2, 3 format, listing what happens on the first offense, second offense, etc. The consequence of the first offense is often a warning.

The following is typical in a Conscious Discipline classroom:

1. Rules are displayed in written and visual format, showing two choices of how to be helpful and one visual of hurtful behavior.
2. The visual rules are posted throughout the classroom where the rule is needed. For example, if lining up becomes a problem beyond the ability of your routines to manage, the visual rule would be posted at the door.
3. The consequence of the first offense, instead of a warning, is to choose again and be helpful in the School Family. (Further information about consequences is provided in Chapter 10.)

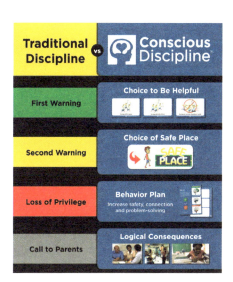

For example, Lina is talking while others are talking. The teacher points to the visual rule on the wall that shows what to do while others are talking. She says, "Lina, you may not talk while others are talking. Look up here at your choices about what is helpful in our School Family and make another choice." The teacher points to the pictures and reads, "You may raise your hand or wait for a turn to speak. Which is better for you?" When a child loses sight of what to do, our job is to bring their cognitive resources back to that point of focus with clear, assertive communication. If the child chooses not to change her behavior or resists obeying the rule, she then has the choice of going to the Safe Place to calm down. Once she returns, her two helpful choices are still available. The chart above shows the difference between a traditional classroom with warnings and loss of privileges and a Conscious Discipline classroom. The entire chart with additional consequences will be discussed in further detail in Chapter 10. For now begin shifting from using warnings to choices as your first consequence.

Using visual rules that depict two positive and one negative choice, and then providing the opportunity to choose again as the first consequence (instead of warnings) does the following:

- Treats misbehavior as an opportunity to learn as opposed to seeing it as a negative experience that demands the guilty party be punished.
- Provides the teacher with a quick visual reference for offering two positive choices without having to come up with them on the spot.
- Transforms misbehavior into a choice to learn and practice prosocial skills.
- Empowers teachers to focus on what we want and models this behavior for children.
- Teaches children to create positive mental images of their own goals and expectations.
- Encourages children to turn poor choices into wise decisions.
- Sends the powerful message, "You are inherently worthy, you made a poor choice this time and you have the power to choose differently."
- Vigilantly keeps children focused on what to do and how to help keep the classroom safe.

> Take a photo of what compliance looks like and tape it to the desks of children who struggle with individual rules so they have visual references for what to do to be successful. Children cannot choose to follow a rule unless they are completely clear on it. Watch a portal video of a teacher helping a struggling child with a desktop photo choice.

I often hear teachers say, "That was a good choice," "Remember to make good choices," or "Stop, think and make a good choice." Unfortunately, a good choice in one situation may be a poor choice in another. The frontal lobes of the brain allow us to adapt to changing environments. As the frontal lobes mature and our brains become more integrated, we are able to change our behavior based on the current context. We learn to behave a certain way in church, another way in school and yet another way on the playground. We become conscious of how to respond wisely in each situation. Ultimately, we want our children to make wise choices based on the context of the moment instead of using preprogrammed good and bad choices.

Most children learn that a good choice involves being polite, getting along with others and treating their friends with respect. What happens when that child is faced with a peer pressure situation in which she must go against her good choice programming in order to make a wise decision by saying, "No," to friends who are planning something dangerous? In this context, she may need to be forceful and rude to refuse in a way the group can hear. In Conscious Discipline, we teach children to make wise, adaptive decisions based on the present moment instead of focusing on preprogrammed good choices.

Becoming aware of our choices as adults and passing this awareness on to children is a powerful gift. Once we accept that we are constantly making choices, we can take charge of our actions and our lives. We realize our power lies within us, not in our attempts to control or manipulate others. When we take back our power by taking responsibility for our thoughts, feelings and actions, we activate our prefrontal lobes and are able to see life differently.

We have learned to call on the Skill of Composure so we can remain calm enough to override our impulsive reactions. The Skill of Assertiveness helps us focus on what we want and give clear directives. Focusing our attention toward a goal sets us up to use the Skill of Encouragement. No matter how much we utilize these first three skills, we will run into roadblocks of unwillingness and power struggles. To handle these roadblocks, we can use the Skill of Choices to increase the likelihood of compliance. Even with these wonderful skills in our toolbelts, upset will occur! The next chapter focuses on the Skill of Empathy to help us handle children's fussing and fits when the world does not go as expected.

Choices Summary

Power:	**Free Will:** The only person you can make change is yourself.
Becoming Brain Smart:	Choices motivate from within, improve goal-achievement and facilitate self-regulation.
Skill:	Two positive choices, reframing blame, Parroting technique, Who is the boss of you?
School Family:	Visual Rules

Power of Free Will Reflection

Many of us have spent a large portion of our lives seeking to change others. The Power of Free Will states, "The only person you can make change is yourself." We can continue attempting to make others act a certain way or we can claim our Power of Free Will by accepting that change can only happen within us. This month vigilantly embrace free will with these steps:

❏ **Become conscious of how often we attempt to control others and how often we think others are making us do things.**

❏ **Convert "make me" language into the language of choice.** Instead of saying, "Don't make me stop this car," say, "I am going to stop the car until you have your seat belt on and everyone is safe."

❏ **Catch ourselves thinking, "How can I make the child _____?" or "How can I get the child to _____?"** Change the question to, "How can I help the child successfully _____?"

❏ **Change "should" to "could," and then make a choice.** When we begin to think, "I should run to the dry cleaner," own the choice and say, "I could run to the dry cleaner," instead. Then decide whether to do it or not. There is no should or ought to, only choices. Start choosing!

❏ **Practice allowing others to have their own thoughts and feelings.** Resist the urge to try to make others happy.

❏ **For one day, give up the attitude, "I don't know and I don't care."** This attitude allows us to give up our power by avoiding choices. We must act as if we do know and do care. If a friend asks where to go for lunch, state your preferences clearly. "I'd like Chinese food."

❏ **Watch the Power of Free Will video** on the portal to deepen your reflection.

Brain Smart Teaching Moments

Assertive commands are essential for children operating from the survival state. Two positive choices provide a way for us to be assertive while empowering children. They are best utilized with those who are in the emotional state. A child in an executive state does best with open-ended questions like, "What would help you get started?" Use the lists below as a guide:

These children experiencing a survival state often benefit from assertive commands:

- Children who chronically change their minds
- Children who are overly stressed
- Children who are easily overwhelmed

These children experiencing an emotional state often benefit from two positive choices:

- Children who do not follow the directions the first time
- Children who have difficulty focusing and staying on task
- Children who are somewhat defiant and like to boss others around
- Children who have trouble making choices
- Children who seem to feel powerless
- Children who appear stressed from life experiences

Children operating from an integrated, executive state often benefit from open-ended questions.

Skill Reflection: Common and Conscious

If possible, partner up to say the two statements out loud. See if you can feel the difference. After each statement share, "The difference between Common and Conscious for me was…"

Common	Conscious
Look how you made her feel.	See her face? Her face is saying, "I don't like it when you push me. Please walk around me."
You can finish your math or miss recess!	You have a choice. You can finish problem four first or problem five. Which is better for you?
Don't make me have to walk back and separate you two from talking.	I'm going to separate you two so each of you can focus better on your work. You will have time to visit at recess.
How can I get my children to listen during large group time?	How can I help my School Family listen successfully during large group time?
I have to stop after work to pick up some things at the grocery store.	I could stop after work and pick up some things at the grocery store.
Kenisha are you making good choices?	Kenisha, take a deep breath and look at the other children. What would be a wise choice for being successful as part of our School Family?

School Family Implementation Checklist

- ❏ **Post picture visual rules as needed and where needed**, using the formula of two positive choices and one "no" choice.

- ❏ **Verbally offer two positive choices to children** when they are in an emotional state to facilitate compliance.

- ❏ **Use the Parroting technique** for oppositional children.

- ❏ **Reframe blame** by saying, "So _____ is the boss of you! What could you do that was helpful if you were the boss of you?"

- ❏ **Create individualized plans** for children who have trouble making choices.

- ❏ **Use the website**, including Shubert's School and the portal, with a focus on Picture Rule Cards/Visual Rules.

Visual rule example with younger children

| *We can scoop the mulch into the dump trucks.* | *We can build mulch mountains.* | *We may not throw the mulch at each other.* |

Visual rule example with older children

| *You may sit and read by yourself.* | *You may sit and read with a friend.* | *You may not stand in the hall.* |

Chapter 8
EMPATHY
Teaching children to manage their emotions

Empathy teaches emotional regulation, integrating the brain so children can take personal responsibility for their actions.

Remember the Beatles song, "Let It Be." Sing a few bars of the chorus. Can you feel your body relax? Similar to the idea of letting it be, the Power of Acceptance states, "The moment is as it is." As you reflect on this, think of how often you believe things should have gone differently. You may fight against what is happening by saying, "What should you be doing?" or "I can't believe you're acting like this!" You may negate and deny what is happening by saying, "We don't run in the halls!" or "That's not the way we treat each other in this school!"

When we accept the moment instead of fighting it, we put ourselves in a position to offer empathy to ourselves and others, and to see from multiple points of view. Acceptance and empathy are the prerequisites for change and transformation. Without them, we stagnate in old patterns and encounter the same problems year after year.

Let's begin our exploration of the Power of Acceptance by pausing for a short meditation: Take a deep breath. As you inhale, say to yourself, "This moment is as it is." As you exhale, relax and say, "Demanding the world go my way creates struggle, not change." Now sit quietly for several moments and let it be. The icon for the Power of Acceptance is Shubert holding his feeling buddies. Watch a portal video about the Power of Acceptance for a deeper understanding of this powerful concept.

The Power of Acceptance

Acceptance is the active, nonjudgmental embracing of experience in the here and now. It is mindfulness in action, and improves the wellbeing of adults and children (Burke, 2010 and Teper, R., Segal, Z., & Inzlicht, M., 2013). I often think of acceptance as the neutral gear in a car with manual transmission. If we want to shift from first gear to second gear, we must pass through neutral to be successful. If we try to avoid neutral, we will grind the gears. I don't know about you, but I have spent a great deal of my life grinding the gears!

Resistance facilitates conflict and firmly entrenches old behavior patterns in the brain. When we passionately struggle saying, "This shouldn't be" or "This should be," we program the brain to be resistant and reactive. What we resist persists; we solidify old CD-Rom beliefs and behaviors so we are ready to be triggered again. Anger and disappointment binds us to our judgments instead of to each other. We refuse to question our judgments (what needs to be, should be or shouldn't have been) and attack anything that contradicts them. Our judgments also generate a fear of mistakes, making learning and change impossible.

> As mentioned throughout the book, lack of acceptance of our internal states often leads to addiction as we attempt to negate and medicate our emotions through food, shopping, alcohol, work, cleaning, exercise, etc. Our false hope is that something outside of us will change what we are feeling inside. Distractions may relieve the immediate discomfort of emotional distress, but they do nothing to heal us and ultimately sabotage our highest goals.

The Power of Acceptance, on the other hand, provides a frame of mind that promotes change by quietly observing the moment without the need to change or fix it. As our own neutral gear, acceptance involves fully embracing the moment rather than ignoring, distracting, escaping or denying what's happening in it. It is the key to offering attuned empathy to others and ourselves. Letting the moment be (without it being good or bad) allows us to consider how each person might perceive a situation differently and frees us of damaging judgments and expectations. Truth becomes relative and compassion becomes real. We tend to confuse acceptance with resignation or agreement, but we can accept the moment and still have a preference for a different way.

Resisting the Moment is the Prerequisite for Attack

Recently I was visiting preschools for my granddaughter. We visited three different schools one morning. I began resisting from the moment I entered the schools. "Preschools should be much better than this" was my trigger judgment. I couldn't believe the lack of play and lack of understanding of child development in these early childhood programs. It threw me into such an uncontrollable state that I couldn't even speak to the directors. I was afraid my lack of acceptance would slip from my inner speech into my outer speech. My inner voice ranted, "I've worked long and hard, dedicating my life to improving education, yet my own grandchild can't find a quality program! All my effort has been wasted! This is unbelievable!" As soon as we left the centers, the words in my head started spewing out of my mouth. I was not accepting the moment; I had gotten stuck in the world not going my way. Can you see how personal this was for me? My Q.T.I.P. power was non-existent!

Our unwillingness to accept the moment paves the way for attacking others and ourselves. I use the term "fussing and fits" to describe the emotional outbursts that often come when the world does not go our way. A toddler scribbling on the walls cries when we take away the crayon. A 4-year-old who wants a cracker yells, "I hate you," ignoring the fact that we have none. A 9-year-old slams doors when we deny her request to sleep at a friend's house. A 30-year-old teacher gets aggravated when children forget to raise their hands. A 61-year-old grandparent throws a fit over subpar preschool programs.

Resisting the moment creates upset, keeps us in an emotional state, fosters attacking behaviors and prevents us from offering empathy. People need empathy — not our judgments — to grow and thrive. Yet we often negate the moment rather than embrace it! The preschool ordeal wasn't my first adult fit, nor was it my last. Over the years, I have become aware of how many fits adults have. I estimate we are throwing fits more than 80 percent of the time. Adult fits range from mild complaints (right prefrontal lobe executive state) to moderate verbal attacks through criticism, name-calling and judgment (emotional state) to severe attacks involving physical harm (survival state).

Emotions can be tough. We all need to learn how to handle them constructively. We have ample opportunities to learn to do this ourselves and to teach our children. Every time a child shows us the world is not going his way by whining, stomping his feet, screaming, name calling or otherwise attacking himself or others, we receive an opportunity to teach. We must accept the moment as it is: Yes, little Todd just called you a stupid idiot. Yes, progress reports are due and six students are failing. Yes, the sink is clogged again. Yes, you feel angry and hurt. From the position of "Yes, this is happening," we access the Skill of Empathy and teach children to manage emotional upset constructively.

> *Resisting the moment creates upset. Upset keeps us in the lower centers of the brain, preventing us from seeing the world from anyone else's point of view and inhibiting any chance of conflict resolution.*

Emotional Messages, Regulation and Acceptance

We all experience moments when we act out our emotions instead of manage them. Later, we often feel guilt over our outbursts and inadequacy for our inability to control our emotions. Emotions are like weather patterns. Some days are stormy, some are cloudy with a chance of rain and some have abundant sunshine. We can no more control our emotions than we can the weather. We can, however, be consciously aware of probable weather conditions and respond wisely by carrying an umbrella on rainy days or wearing sunglasses on sunny ones. The same is true for our emotions: We can learn to become aware of them and respond wisely. Conscious acceptance is necessary for this to occur.

For many of us, emotions got a bad rap as we were growing up. Often, our well-meaning parents unconsciously ignored, dismissed or punished our emotions. They said things like, "It's not that bad," "Don't worry about it," "Quit fussing, it's no big deal," or "Don't think about it, do something else to get your mind off it." Parents also rescued us from the consequences of our choices, hoping to save us from experiencing difficult emotions. They would bring forgotten lunch money to school when we forgot it, help with projects we procrastinated starting or buy a new ice cream cone when we dropped ours. Sometimes they would save us from experiencing the tough feelings that came with our poor choices, only to berate us: "How on earth could you forget again? Do you even bother to think?" "If you had started last week like I said to, this wouldn't have happened." "I told you you'd drop your ice cream if you kept moving around, but you kept right on doing it." Their responses to our disappointing choices demanded us to focus on their anger instead of our remorse. As a result, our adult perceptions of emotions are often skewed, and our ability to handle tough emotions—our own or others'—is weak or lacking.

> Adults often confuse thoughts with feelings. If we ask a friend, "How do you feel?" and she responds, "I feel like nothing is going my way," she has expressed a thought, not a feeling. Just for practice, how do you feel right now? Did you answer with a feeling word such as anxious, excited, sad or frustrated? If not, it was probably a thought. Replacing feelings with thoughts distances us from our emotions. Distance prevents us from managing them effectively.

Most of us allow ourselves to experience positive feelings of joy, happiness and excitement, and we run from feelings labeled negative like sadness, anger and fear. We believe if we allow ourselves to feel these feelings, they will never go away, we will become irrational and our emotions will overtake us. We fear feeling. The irony is that the more we resist our feelings, the more diligently they persist. If we let our feelings bubble up, feel them and accept them as part of us, they will dissipate.

Emotions aren't bad guys; they serve vital purposes in our lives. They are our internal guidance system, our moral navigators and our core system for discerning right from wrong. They tell us when life is off track and nudge us to return to a path of love. We do not need to control them; we need to become acutely aware of them, manage them, listen to their message for returning to our highest values and then learn how to express them more appropriately. Emotions provide a bridge between problem and solution.

Feelings are the bridge between problems and solutions.

In general, women tend to get on top of the bridge and camp out, asking friends to join in as they stay stuck in retelling the story and talking about their feelings. Hanging out on the bridge holds tight to suffering and prevents them from getting over to the land of solutions. Men, on the other hand, tend to avoid the bridge altogether. They catapult right over it in order to take action. A woman might come home and proclaim, "My job is getting harder and harder. These kids are so out-of-control! I don't know how much longer I can stand this!" Her husband's response is, "Get a new job." He vaults over the feelings of frustration and fear, and goes straight for a solution. Skipping the emotional component robs us of the important messages our feelings are sending, and often results in ineffective or incomplete solutions.

Each emotion starts off as bodily sensations such as butterflies in our stomach or tightness in our throat. These sensations appear unconsciously in our face, body and tone of voice (this is why we use noticing). They hijack our perceptions and we become the emotion. This is apparent in our language. I often hear myself say, "I am frustrated!" Of course, I'm not frustrated; I am Becky who feels frustrated. When an emotion takes over our identity like this, we will act it out instead of regulate it. If we instead allow our emotions to bubble up through conscious acceptance (without judgment), we can claim, name and tame them. First, we can claim them by becoming aware of them as feelings. Then, we can give the feelings a name. Finally, we can tame them by linking them to life events and learning to manage them enough to take our wisest next step. We can coach children through this natural process or inhibit it with our judgments. Thus, conscious acceptance is essential for emotional regulation. A video on the portal shows the impact of claim, name and tame on a family learning to regulate severe anxiety.

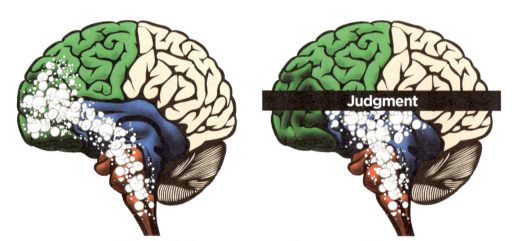

Judgment blocks awareness to what we are feeling

Alexandra is a third grade student who has a program on her CD-Rom that prompts her to blurt out, "Shut up, stupid!" when someone says something she doesn't like. Alexandra's teacher is quick to punish her emotional outbursts. She says things like, "Alexandra, it's hateful and rude to call names. That is not how we treat each other in this classroom. You will miss recess today." The teacher's judgmental response inhibits Alexandra's ability to identify her feeling and therefore regulate it. Without any new skills, Alexandra just works harder at not being caught. She learns to hold her anger until the teacher isn't looking. Some children tattle and complain about her attacks, but Alexandra denies her actions. The teacher's judgment inhibited Alexandra from learning how to regulate frustration and express it in healthy ways. Instead, she learns to deny her own feelings and lie to avoid punishment.

Regulating emotions includes both acceptance and the teaching of new strategies (Fruzetti, Lowry, Mosco, & Shenk 2003) Once we can regulate our emotions, we automatically change states to become more integrated. From an integrated executive state we can see the problem from all sides, allowing us the opportunity to choose to reframe the problem and obtain viable solutions. Conscious Discipline teaches the following five steps to self-regulation (Bailey, 2011) as a more detailed process for the claim, name and tame description discussed previously. Once we learn to how to regulate our emotions, we can teach this skill to others.

ⓘ Am

Step 1: I Am
I am triggered and I become my emotions.

ⓘ Calm

Step 2: I Calm
Breathe and notice the internal state, letting emotions bubble up.

ⓘ Feel

Step 3: I Feel
Identify and name the feeling, shifting from "I am angry" to "I feel angry."

ⓘ Choose

Step 4: I Choose
Relax, change states and reframe the problem.

ⓘ Solve

Step 5: I Solve
Win-win solutions are abundant.

> *Managing Emotional Mayhem (Bailey, 2011) delves into the world of emotions and self-regulation so adults and children can learn to better manage tough feelings. The **Feeling Buddies Self-Regulation Toolkit** provides extensive resources and props for teaching the five steps of self-regulation to children.*

I Choose Self Control Board

Feeling Buddies

With a teacher who is adept at the self-regulation process, Alexandra's story would end differently: When Alexandra blurts out, "Shut up, stupid!" Anger wells up within the teacher, but she realizes she is triggered, accepts the anger as it bubbles up, and uses the Skill of Composure to calm down and turn off the automatic CD-Rom playing in her head. From an executive state, she can see Alexandra is calling for help and respond, "You seem angry. You wanted her to talk to you respectfully."

With this empathetic understanding, Alexandra is able to provide additional information like, "She always touches my hair and calls me curly." The teacher can then help Alexandra learn to be more assertive by validating, "No wonder you were feeing angry. You didn't know the words to use to teach her how to treat you. Do you like it when she touches your hair and calls you curly?" When Alexandra shakes her head, the teacher prompts helpful new words by saying, "Tell her, *I don't like it when you touch my hair and call me curly. When you want my attention call my name.*"

We must start consciously accepting and befriending our feelings so we can regulate them. We all talk to ourselves in our heads; it is time to talk to ourselves in a way that is helpful for emotional regulation. Then we can teach this same helpful regulatory language to our children. We must accept our feelings before we can empathize with children and help them accept theirs. Begin using the following self-talk when an emotion bubbles up to consciousness: "You seem ____(add a feeling word). You wanted ____(state what you wanted)," or "You were hoping ____(state your hopes)." In dealing with my grandchild's preschool, mine would go like this: "Becky, you seem disappointed? You were hoping our country was full of developmentally-appropriate preschools so you could help pick the perfect one for Maddie."

> At any given time, we are asking for information or understanding. A person in an emotional state is asking for understanding in the form of empathy. A person in an executive state is asking for information. Our job is to attune with children, discerning when to offer empathy and when to offer information. A mismatch between empathy and information can damage the relationships, also damaging the willingness to change and the ability to regulate impulses.

If we don't identify our feelings, we will act them out. Children tend to act out feelings aggressively (hitting, tantrums, name calling), passively (shutting down, whining, feeling ill) or passive aggressively (manipulation, guilt). In addition, adults tend to act out feelings by being critical and making judgments. Every time we negate what is happening, we are negating what we are feeling. Until we accept the moment as it is, allowing us to feel our feelings, we will not allow children to feel theirs.

Until we feel our feelings, we will not allow children to feel theirs.

Margaret, a mother of three, was returning to teaching after staying home with her children for years. She felt scared about her new job and her abilities. Margaret tried to stay busy to avoid feeling her feelings, but she simply could not escape a deep sense of inadequacy. She tried to silence her self-doubt by outwardly being positive and convincing her children they were splendid, saying things like, "Mardell, you are such a good little girl." She attempted to control her children's feelings instead of managing her own. She dismissed their upset by saying, "You're all right," or "There's no need to be upset." She wouldn't let her own anxiety surface, so unconsciously, she wouldn't allow it in her children either. We cannot help children manage their emotions while denying our own. As adults, we can consciously choose to be egocentric or empathetic. What we choose is what we will teach children.

It is impossible for us to teach children skills we have not mastered ourselves; therefore, we must learn to feel our feelings and express them in constructive ways. The skills we learn to help children with their emotional regulation are the same skills we can apply to ourselves. It's a win-win, indeed!

Commitment: This month I will focus on feeling my feelings instead of judging them. This can only occur when I practice the Power of Acceptance. Each time I think a moment, event, thought or feeling isn't as it should be, I will consciously shift my focus to letting it be.

Signature: _____ Date: _____

Becoming Brain Smart

We have spoken throughout this book about the importance of creating secure attachment with children. The way children build attachment with significant adults creates their blueprints for establishing close relationships for the rest of their lives. However, not every interaction with young children is an attachment interaction. The attachment system is activated under distress and works like this: A child experiences distress. The emotional upset activates the attachment system that says, "Seek comfort from your attachment figure." Ideally, the attachment figure provides attuned empathy and comfort that relieves the child's distress and offers a felt sense of safety. This relief turns off the attachment system and turns on the exploration/learning system so the child can return to learning or playing. If this cycle is completed in a healthy way over and over again, the child begins to learn emotional regulation and tolerate a wide range of distress sensations. Disconnected children, on the other hand, spend the day with their attachment system on, negatively impacting learning.

Attachment system on = Learning systems off
Attachment system off = Learning systems on

Distress tolerance is the amount of distress we can endure and still remain calm enough to attend to the present moment. Everyone has a different range or set point of distress tolerance for emotions, and we all cope better on some days than others. We all know at least one friend or family member who has a narrow range of distress tolerance. These individuals fly off the handle at the slightest provocation or live in a constant state of worry. We also have friends who stay calm in chaotic situations. A child and his attachment figures co-establish distress set points for each different emotion early in life. We can help children establish healthy set points through regular, attuned responses to their distress. The following chart shows the cycle.

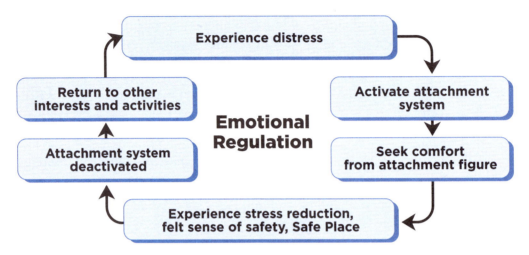

All too often, a child exhibits emotional upset and the adult does not respond in an empathetic, attuned manner that offers relief. The child's distressed attachment system stays on if we do not deactivate it through attuned empathy. Arousal continues, the child's clacker speeds up, and the child spends his day seeking or defending against connection rather than learning. Emotional regulation and the ability to sustain attention go hand in hand. Whenever the attachment system is on, the prefrontal lobe is off. Learning and paying attention become a challenge with a clacker that pounds away loudly (Wesselmann, Schweitzer & Armstrong, 2014, and Siegel, 2010).

We have all felt the anxiety of having our attachment system on for extended periods of time. Think of the times you've argued with your significant other. Once the anger subsides, there is an urge to reconnect. That urge is your attachment system telling you to seek comfort. If your partner is ready to reconnect, the distress (anxiety) is soothed and you are off to a productive day. If your partner is not ready to reconnect, your attachment system stays activated and the rest of the day is very difficult.

The ultimate goal is to help children develop tolerance to a wide range of emotional distress. Our ability to meet this goal, of course, is dependent on the way we respond to children's distress. If we offer mature empathy, the child is seen, soothed and feels safe. We help him learn to regulate his emotions, create a secure attachment mental model, and improve his ability to attend and learn.

Empathy and Brain Integration

Optimal brain development requires integration. There are far more neural fibers going from the limbic system to the prefrontal lobes than fibers going from the prefrontal lobes to the limbic system. What does this mean? It means that emotions are powerful integrators. Emotions chart the course for moment-to-moment choices as well as long-term goals. Unless we learn how to manage our emotions, they can lead us into destructive patterns. Joseph

LeDoux (1996) states, "When fear becomes anxiety, desire gives way to greed, or annoyance turns to anger, anger to hatred, friendship to envy, love to obsession or pleasure to addiction, our emotions start working against us." Mental health requires good emotional hygiene. Empathy is the source of this emotional hygiene. Most emotions occur without our conscious awareness. Empathy provides the mirror for children to become aware of their feelings and, in turn, aware of themselves. The more empathy a child receives, the more whole he becomes and the more his brain integrates. Essentially, empathy wires the brain for personal responsibility and lifelong success by allowing us to move from a survival state to an emotional state and then integrate with an executive state.

In this chapter, we generally refer to empathy as a conscious, intentional process adults conduct with children; however, empathy is also a set of processes in the brain that integrate networks involving the body, emotions, thoughts and behaviors. There are several types and stages of empathy: motor empathy, emotional empathy, cognitive empathy and mature empathy.

When we watch an ice skater perform or a child jump off a diving board, our brain registers these movements in the same neurons we would use if we were ice-skating or jumping. These so-called mirror neurons fire within the brain, lending us an appreciation of another person's activities. This **motor empathy** is the foundation of one of our basic survival skills: the ability to mentally imagine the actions of another. For the most part, motor empathy is unconscious; it constantly happens just below the surface of conscious awareness. The same neurology allows both motor empathy and synchrony. Military organizations emphasize exercises like marching and chanting in unison for many reasons, one of which is that it unites. Research indicates that walking, singing or moving in synchrony increases cooperation. The central tempo of 60-80 beats per minute is a primal rhythm that unites everyone in the memory of the maternal heartbeat in the womb. Eighty beats per minute enhances the parasympathetic nervous system (the brakes) and balances the clacker, turning off the fight or flight response (Behrends, Müller & Dziobek, 2012). In Conscious Discipline, we capitalize on motor empathy with the uniting activities of music and movement in the Brain Smart Start. Conscious Discipline also seeks to move motor empathy from an unconscious activity to a conscious activity through noticing. "Your arm is going like this (demonstrate) and your face is going like this (demonstrate)."

Emotional empathy is also a mostly unconscious activity. It allows us to feel what another person is feeling. Examples of emotional empathy include crying at the sad parts of a movie, laughing with others, feeling an aversion to a food when we see someone make a face after eating it and understanding a child's pain when she scrapes her knee. Emotional empathy is a basic survival skill, the roots of which originate in the limbic system. Mirror neurons allow us to see an expression on another person's face and immediately sense what that person is feeling. The goal in Conscious Discipline is to move this from a mostly unconscious activity to a conscious activity through noticing and then labeling the feeling. "You seem angry."

Cognitive empathy requires the prefrontal lobes. Cognitive empathy, sometimes referred to as Theory of Mind, requires imagination (imagining what the other must be experiencing, wanting or hoping for) and language skills. We say to ourselves, "That child is having a hard time. If I were in that situation, I would be having a hard time, too." Cognitive empathy is conscious, but without nonjudgmental acceptance, it can still result in the false empathy examples we will discuss shortly. The goal in Conscious Discipline is to remove our judgment filters so the child truly feels seen. "You were hoping to get another day to finish your project. It's hard to feel so overwhelmed."

Cognitive empathy requires the adult be in an executive state of relaxed alertness. If our prefrontal lobes, which can imagine the child' perspective, are disconnected from the rest of our brains' empathy structures, we may judge the situation as if it were happening in our own lives. We will relate the child's pain to our personal history or give advice. We might feel the child's pain emotionally and use our frontal lobes to judge it. We may try to rescue the child or gush with sympathy, unconsciously believing we couldn't handle that sort of situation ourselves.

Mature empathy is the integration of motor, emotional and cognitive empathy. It is based on our conscious, loving decision to be present with another during moments of discomfort and pain. It is based on our clear understanding that we are not responsible for another person's feelings, thoughts or behaviors; however, we can comprehend what he might be experiencing and make a conscious decision to be present, loving and accepting of the moment.

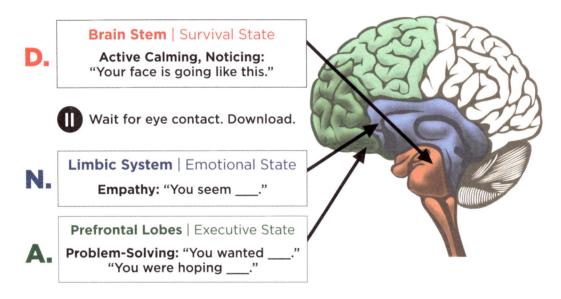

The Skill of Empathy

The Skill of Empathy links discipline correction with connection by addressing children's upset states first and behavioral changes second. It helps adults and children know their relationship can stay strong even when limits are set and conflict ensues. Empathy demonstrates that the relationship can bend instead of break during conflict and intense emotion (Tronick, 2007). It also empowers children to own their feelings and become responsible for regulating them. Out-of-control, upset children need empathy to become organized and access the higher centers of the brain.

Unfortunately, few of us consistently offer or receive the attuned empathy that provides relief and fosters integration. Instead, most of us experience empathy styles that can be described as ignoring, saving, punishing or dismissing. Before we can successfully practice the Skill of Empathy with the children in our care, we must become aware of the type of empathy we commonly received from our attachment figures and the kind of empathy we tend to offer to others. Conduct the following assessment and then read about the styles of empathy researchers have identified over the years.

Assessment: Empathy Style Pretest

Write how you would respond to the following situation. Write down the exact words you would use.

Situation: Calvin arrives at school late and enters the classroom. You tell him to go to the office and check in. This sets Calvin off. He stomps his feet and shouts, "I'm not going to the damn office and you can't make me!" You become triggered and react from your CD-Rom. Write the words you would automatically say in the space below.

Your likely CD-Rom reaction:

Our words are an indicator of our unconscious empathy styles. Researchers have identified four immature styles, described below. The fifth style, Coaching, is the mature style of empathy advocated by Conscious Discipline. Which seems closest to your CD-Rom empathy style?

Empathy style #1: Ignoring. Adults in this category ignore emotions and focus only on behaviors. They fail to use emotional moments to connect with children, and fail to teach them to manage or express their feelings constructively.

"Calvin you know the rules at school. If you come in late you must check in at the office. It's how we know who is here and who is absent." Some of the other children are watching Calvin and the teacher. The teacher instructs them to pay attention to what they should be doing. She returns to Calving and says, "You also know better than to use foul language in the classroom. You know all these rules. Now go to the office and check in. Hand this note to the principal. She is going to talk to you about your language at school."

This teacher typifies a teacher who ignores feelings and trains other children to ignore feelings. Calvin's upset was not relevant to her agenda. Using the emotional regulation chart on page 226, reflect: When we ignore children's emotional selves, what happens to emotional regulation, the child's clacker and learning?

Empathy style #2: Saving. Some adults notice children's feelings, but approach with the goal of saving them from distress. Their goal is to "happy up" children by fixing whatever problem they are experiencing.

"Oh Calvin, you seem so upset this morning. Something must have happened at home or on the bus. It's okay. You're at school now. There's no need for that kind of language. You know our School Family is here for you. I will call the office and tell them you are here. They have to know so we can keep you safe."

The teacher's efforts to save Calvin from his discomfort forfeit an opportunity to teach responsibility and help Calvin manage his anger. Often, adults who are driven to fix a situation or save children from difficult feelings do so because they are uncomfortable with managing their own feelings. They have no idea how to help children manage theirs. How does insulating children from emotional upset impact their ability to learn effective emotional regulation?

Empathy style #3: Punishing. These adults criticize children's feelings. They may forbid displays of anger and punish irritability. Emotions, especially negative ones, are seen as disrespectful.

"Calvin how dare you enter my room using foul language and disrespecting me! You will go to the office and you will go now. If you don't think I can make you walk to the office, just watch me call your mother! I am not your baby sitter; I am your teacher. Now march down to that office, check in and give this referral to the principal for your outburst."

Punitive approaches almost always model the exact behavior they try to eliminate. Notice how the teacher's and Calvin's behaviors are similar. Look back at the chart: What impact will offering punitive responses to children have on their future ability to cope with difficult emotions and the child's metaphoric clacker? What impact will this have on Calvin's distress tolerance?

> **Before we can empathize, we must stop equating disobedience with disrespect.**

Empathy style #4: Dismissing. These adults brush aside children's upset by minimizing their feelings or attempting to push quickly through them. The goal is to stop the upset, not to manage the feeling. The general sentiment is, "It's no big deal," no matter how upset the child feels.

"Calvin, be careful with what you say next. Your card could end up on red before the day even begins! Whatever's gotten you into such a state is over now and not worth the fuss. Cursing solves nothing. Now pull yourself together and go check in at the office."

The teacher did nothing to help Calvin process his emotions. She dismisses his upset by telling him it's not a big deal and tries to control him with her card system. None of her actions help him feel, accept and transform his emotions into healthy skills. What impact does dismissing emotions have on the development of emotional regulation, attention and future relationships?

Empathy style #5: Coaching. Some teachers understand that misbehavior often represents an intense feeling without an appropriate outlet. These teachers utilize moments of upset as opportunities to teach emotional regulation through empathetic coaching using the D.N.A. process we will discuss at length later in this chapter.

As soon as Calvin becomes oppositional, the teacher takes a few deep breaths to calm herself. She says to herself, "I'm safe. Keep breathing. I can handle this." After opening her heart and wishing well, she reminds herself that Calvin is calling for help.

"Calvin, your feet went like this. Your arms went like this. And your face is going like this (demonstrate). As soon as Calvin turns to look at her, she pauses to take a deep S.T.A.R. breath and downloads calm into Calvin. He automatically breathes with her and his body begins to relax slightly. The teacher says, "You seem angry this morning. Something tough must have happened on the way to school."

Calvin's face softens and tears emerge. "My Dad is leaving us. They had a big fight. The police came."

"No wonder you said what you did," the teacher responds. "Your big emotions got ahold of you." She touches Calvin as he begins to sob. "This morning was scary. I will keep you safe right now. Breathe with me, Calvin."

It is important to note that the teacher will discuss the inappropriate language and behavior with Calvin when he is calm. "You wanted me to know you were feeling big emotions, so you used hurtful language and showed me with your body how angry you were feeling. Next time you have big emotions say, *I have big emotions and I need help*. Say that now for practice." She will also see that he adheres to the school's policy, with support as needed. You can walk to the office by yourself or walk with Jake, the We Care person for this week. What is better for you?

> **When children are upset, our task is to act like a mirror, reflecting back their inner state so they can regulate it enough to adjust their outer behavior.**

Activity: Empathy Style Post-Test

Watch the Managing Emotional Mayhem videos on your portal to delve deeper into common empathy styles. Reflect on whether your pretest answers were attuned (coaching) or misattuned (ignoring, saving, punishing or dismissing). Now reflect on the style of empathy your key attachment figures offered during your childhood.

1. What level of empathy do/did your mother, father and significant others operate from (ignore, save, punish, dismiss or coach)?

2. How did they offer empathy to you?

    When I felt sad, they offered _____ empathy.

    When I felt angry, they offered _____ empathy.

    When I felt disappointed, they offered _____ empathy.

    When I felt _____, they offered _____ empathy.

    When I felt _____, they offered _____ empathy.

3. What level(s) do you operate from with children at school, your own children, friends and your significant others?

4. Discuss with a partner why empathy is often more difficult with loved ones than strangers.

Common Practices Instead of Empathy

The first four empathy styles explained above result from attempting empathy without first using the Power of Acceptance to acknowledge the moment without judgment or the need to change it. Ignoring, saving, punishing and dismissing are all immature empathy styles. We've devised many responses that promote immature empathy. See if any sound familiar:

Sharing similar experiences from our own lives: Michael approaches the teacher and shares, "Last night we had to put our dog, Murphy, to sleep." The teacher responds, "I know how awful you must feel. Two years ago we had to put our dog, Bo, to sleep. It's really, really sad."

When we do this, our intention is to save others by easing their upset through talking about our own experiences. Talking about ourselves distracts others from their feelings and stops the emotional bubbling up process that is essential for well-being. We do this because when a person shares a story with us, it triggers a resonance in our brain that recalls similar experiences. It takes conscious effort to override this natural physiological reaction, set aside our need to talk about our experiences and truly listen to the other person.

Giving "fix-it" advice: Carlos was upset. He had lost his lunch money on the bus. As he explains the situation to his teacher, she begins immediately solving his problem and offering him advice. In doing so, she misses Carlos' main concern. His upset is not about lunch, but about his grandmother's response to his carelessness.

When we attempt to solve someone else's problems, we often send the subtle message, "Stop bothering me and do something about it." Adults who tend to deal with their own feelings by staying busy and distracting themselves often offer advice that sends the message, "Do something constructive and the feelings will go away; it works for me." Either way, we have taken it upon ourselves to fix the situation for the child rather than offering empathy so he can discover his own solutions. With young children, responding to distress with advice trains them to believe it's other people's job to keep them happy.

Offering humor to lighten the situation: Courtney has lost her homework. She is very upset and cannot seem to retrace her steps or recall its location. As she explains her upset to the teacher, the teacher's response is, "I guess you need to Velcro it to your body."

Some adults dismiss other people's distress through humor and making light of a situation. A jokester offers distraction instead of emotional engagement. These adults often possess a lot of nervous energy and use humor as a defense against boredom, connection and emotional situations they feel unsure about handling.

Reassuring: Melissa is doing a cooperative group project. She is meticulous about her work and thinks the other group members aren't trying very hard. She comes to the teacher upset about the poor work the others are producing. The teacher's response is, "Everything will be fine, just you wait and see."

Reassuring others is a subtle way of dismissing them. The underlying message is, "There is no need to feel this way." Many failed attempts at empathy take the form of telling children not to feel the way they do. This usually stems from the adult's own uneasiness with emotions. In essence, the adult is saying, "Don't upset me with your upset." Most people are concerned about future events and share this worry with us. If we could control the future, reassurance would be appropriate. We cannot control the future, so listening to the concern and offering conscious empathy is necessary.

Gushing with sympathy: Vanessa has just returned from school after her family was involved in a car wreck. Her mother and younger brother are still in the hospital. Vanessa begins to share her experience with the class when Mrs. McClean says, "Oh, how awful! You poor child and your family! How devastating! You must be worried about your mom and your brother!"

Mrs. McClean's exaggerated concern for Vanessa and her family is not related to Vanessa's experience. In fact, Mrs. McClean barely hears Vanessa because she's so busy sending the message, "You poor helpless thing!" She has caught Vanessa's feelings instead of listening to them. Some adults believe that gushing with sympathy is the same as empathy. They do this to show others they care and have good manners.

Activity to Change Empathy Styles

Use the examples of immature empathy above to help you become conscious of your own empathy style. Decide if you have fallen into the trap of trying to offer empathy without first accepting the moment. Write the type of false empathy you tend to offer in the blanks below (ordered from most common to least common). Then, read the statement to the right of each and circle the response you choose.

1. _____ I will forgive myself and change.   Yes   No

2. _____ I will forgive myself and change.   Yes   No

3. _____ I will forgive myself and change.   Yes   No

4. _____ I will forgive myself and change.   Yes   No

5. _____ I will forgive myself and change.   Yes   No

Commitment: I am willing to become conscious of the false and unconscious ways I tend to offer empathy. I will vigilantly work to see from other people's perspectives instead of judging, fixing or catching their upset. In short, I will accept the moment as it is, without judging "This is good" or "This is bad."

Signature: _____ Date: _____

Conscious Empathy and Play

The desire to be understood is a powerful human motivator. It is one of our basic survival needs. Violence (every war and every argument) has its roots in a lack of empathy. Without empathy, we seek to destroy one another. With empathy, we create oneness where attack is impossible. In *The Lost Art of Listening*, Dr. Nichols (1996) states, "The yearning to be listened to and understood is a yearning to escape our separateness and bridge the space that divides us. We reach out and try to overcome that separateness by revealing what's on our minds and in our hearts, hoping for understanding." Empathy transforms relationships. It reminds us of our interdependence and strengthens our sense of self. When others understand and empathize with us, we feel connected, clarify our thoughts, uncover our feelings and understand ourselves better. The integrative process of empathy helps us feel whole.

Conscious mature empathy has two components, an emotional component and a cognitive one (Findlay, Girardi & Coplan, 2006). Both components depend on play for healthy development.

The **emotional** component of empathy asks us to understand what another person feels in order to help him become conscious of himself. It serves to co-regulate emotions. Adults and young children co-regulate and enhance positive emotions through playfulness. They co-regulate and reduce negative emotions through empathy. Both empathy and playfulness are essential for emotional wellbeing. Face-to-face social play with activities like rough housing and I Love You Rituals are key to self-regulation. Children with emotional regulation and attention issues require additional face-to-face play with significant adults.

> *Face-to-face playfulness regulates positive emotions and empathy regulates negative emotions.*

The **cognitive** component of empathy asks us to possess insight into someone else's thoughts and actions in order to help her gain insight and clarity for herself. It is an act of imagination; we must imagine what it would be like to walk in another person's shoes. Cognitive empathy helps children see how their perceptions, emotions and actions interrelate.

Our empathy builds a foundation for children's sound emotional development. It is the motivation for prosocial behavior (de Waal, 2008). Imaginative play also supports children's emotional development. Reducing or limiting imaginative play in young children stunts their development of empathy. We can give ourselves and children no greater gift than an attuned, empathetic environment with many opportunities for imaginative play. We realize how vital empathy is when we see what becomes of people who never develop it. Heinous criminals—rapists, child molesters and perpetrators of family violence—lack empathy. People can only willfully hurt others when they lack empathy.

> *How you respond to your child's upset teaches her how to respond to the upset of others.*

Developmental Levels of Cognitive Empathy: Theory of Mind

Many of us believe we must join in others' upset to truly care. When a friend calls to share how she's been unfairly treated, we think we are supposed to agree and join in her misery. Conscious empathy requires judgment-free acceptance rather than joining in misery. Empathy is developed in predictable increments, beginning in infancy (Zahn-Waxler & Radke-Yarrow, 1990). Trauma and consistently being offered immature empathy can derail this process, resulting in false beliefs like equating "joining in" with empathy. Using the stages of empathetic development below, can you see how our perception of empathy has become skewed? Which stage of empathy are you most commonly practicing?

Stage 1: Empathic distress (0 to 12 months): Being born with the innate ability for empathy, infants react to nearby distress as if it is their own. When one baby in the center begins to cry, the others join in! Watch the children in your classroom. Do they seem to cry when others do? Notice yourself. Do you tend to take on the feelings of others as your own?

Stage 2: Egocentric empathy (1 to 6 years): Once babies cognitively differentiate themselves from others, they may exhibit concern for others' distress. As young toddlers begin to realize that others' misery is not their own, their task becomes what to do about it. Toddlers may use inappropriate means of comforting because they see the world primarily from their own perspective. Caroline (3 years old) approaches a screaming baby (1 year old) and offers him some cookies. The infant attempts to escape. Caroline follows him, shoving cookies in his face and patting his back. The baby grows increasingly frantic. Caroline demonstrates an understanding of his distress and seeks to comfort him in ways that have been used with her (food and touching), completely unaware that her behavior is causing more distress.

The type of empathy children use speaks volumes about the empathy offered by their primary caregivers. Do you and the children in your care offer comfort through hugs, food, words of comfort, poking fun or distraction? How many times have you found yourself offering advice despite a friend's continued cry to be heard?

Stage 3: Reciprocal empathy (6 to 9 years): A child's growing cognitive maturity allows for a more reciprocal empathy to evolve. Empathetic efforts are still centered close to home and school, but children of this age are able to discern if the empathy they offer is helpful to the recipient. Think about yourself and the children in your care. Are you able to see a situation from the others' perspectives? Do you adapt your responses based on whether they appear helpful?

Stage 4: Global empathy (9 to 11 years): As the child moves toward adolescence, another cognitive shift in perspective occurs. The preadolescent is able to react to the global distress of categories of people, becoming concerned about oppression, poverty and illness. Before this time, empathy was limited to the specific, immediate distresses within their own lives. Projects such as world hunger, the rainforest and homelessness become meaningful, and are important channels for their developing empathetic energy.

Stage 5: Conscious empathy (11 years and up): Conscious empathy is mature empathy. It is based on acceptance and a conscious form of love. Love always does the following five things:

1. Increases security (reduces the fear of loss)
2. Goes from the worthy to the worthy (to give love you must feel lovable)
3. Acknowledges free will (people choose their perceptions, thoughts, feelings and actions)
4. Holds an image of others as "good enough"
5. Relies on faith that all is well instead of worry

Conscious empathy involves listening while holding a mental image of the upset person as capable of handling the emotions and situation at hand. It resists seeing those in distress as victims and refuses to judge the situation as negative (even if the other person is heavily invested in that perception). If you are able to hold an accepting space for others so they may process their emotions, you practice conscious empathy.

> Maximize children's growth by providing age-appropriate activities that match the developmental stages of empathy. For example, encouraging a group of 6-year-olds to work on a global empathy project like saving the rainforest is counter-productive to their development. Instead, focus their efforts closer to home with activities in your classroom and immediate community. When they are developmentally ready for global empathy, the rainforest project will naturally garner their interest and flourish.

Applying Conscious Empathy with D.N.A.

To offer children empathy, we must be willing to let them experience distress. If our distress tolerance zone is narrow, we will be unconsciously triggered by children's upset, rendering us unable to empathize with them and narrowing their distress tolerance. Conscious Discipline's D.N.A. process helps us bolster distress tolerance and master this difficult skill. It will help us move toward offering conscious empathy and coaching children from the lower centers to the higher centers of their brains in order to solve problems effectively. As we scaffold this process during times of upset, we provide children with an outside voice that will ultimately contribute to a healthy self-regulatory inner voice.

> *Empathizing does not change the limits on behavior;*
> *it helps children to become better able to accept them.*

Let's begin our description of the D.N.A. process by reviewing emotional upset and the brain using a three-story building metaphor. The basement represents the survival state. The ground floor represents the emotional state. The top floor represents the executive state where the CEO has her office. Any conflict is resolved on the top floor in the CEO's office.

All conflict begins with upset, so we must manage our upset before we can truly resolve the conflict. With intense emotions (ones we physically act out) we would enter our building's elevator on the basement floor and head up to the top. With slightly less intense emotions (ones we verbally act out) we would enter the elevator on the ground floor and go up. With a small, non-emotional complaint, we might already be on the top floor but we must still walk down to the CEO's office. On the walk down the hall, we must flip our complaint from what we don't want to what we do want. The goal is to arrive at the CEO's office ready and willing to solve the problem instead of ranting, raving or complaining. Each floor offers a different form of empathy, each one moving us up a floor. The basement has a D button for **D**escribe. The ground level has an N button for **N**ame. The top floor is labeled A for **A**cknowledge.

Describe

Describe what we are seeing in terms of emotional signals (face and body cues) and physical actions using motor empathy. The goal is to verbally capture the moment without judgment and to achieve eye contact. We do this through noticing, as discussed in previous chapters. We might say, "Your arm is going like this (demonstrate), your face is going like this (demonstrate).

> Recall from page 103 that mirroring back or demonstrating the child's movements and expressions will usually bring the child's gaze to us so we can download calm.

When the child looks at us, we can begin the regulation process by taking a deep breath to download calm and cut the intensity of the moment. This pause gives the child's system time to begin dissipating the emotional intensity and slowing the perceived urgency of the survival state. Describing through noticing is essential to help move the child to the ground floor emotional state where sustained connection is possible.

> **Describing through noticing to achieve eye contact +**
> **Downloading calm = Likely to move up a floor**

Name

Name the feeling the child is communicating. "You seem angry." Use a questioning tone of voice and your best educated guess. (This gives the child the opportunity to correct you if your guess is off.) Naming is a quick walk across the feeling bridge and a brief stop on the ground floor of our building metaphor. We must quickly link Naming to Acknowledging. If we pause too long, we invite the child to get off on the ground floor emotional state. The ground floor invites stagnation as children are likely to get into the story of who did what to whom, who had it first and the various reasons they hate each other. The example below is between a teacher and two girls who got off the elevator and stuck around on the ground floor.

Teacher: You seem frustrated. (Pause.)
Allie: Yeah. I hate her. She is always calling me names.
Beya: I hate you, too. You called me a name first!
Allie: That's a lie. Liar!
Beya: You always lie. No wonder no one likes you and everybody hates you and I hate you!

Even the smallest pause after "you seem frustrated" leaves both girls in an emotional state, wandering in circles on the ground floor (much like the women stuck on the bridge talking about their feelings as described earlier). Naming the feeling elevates us from "I am angry" to "I feel angry," mobilizing the regulation process full steam ahead toward the executive state, so we must move quickly to the next floor.

Acknowledge

The last step of the empathetic process is acknowledging the child's desire with positive intent while validating the experience. This is part of the cognitive component of empathy. Two phrases that are very helpful are, "You wanted _____" and "You were hoping _____." These statements help us acknowledge the child's most heartfelt wishes and facilitate problem solving. Make these statements as tentative guesses to be confirmed or denied (just like naming the feeling). Say, "You seem angry. You wanted her to call you by your given name," without a pause.

When we don't have a clue about what the child wanted, we can ask for assistance. "You seem angry. Something happened?" Then proceed toward problem solving using the additional information. "Oh, you were hoping _____."

Sometimes we may wish to validate children's experience beyond "You wanted" and "You were hoping." At these times, our heartfelt responses must come from listening closely and reflecting back the essence of what was said. Our reflections offer tangible evidence that we have listened and understood children's perspectives without judging them. A child might say, "You can't make me take a shower. It's my body!" You could reflect back, "You seem frustrated. You want me to know you are responsible for taking care of your own body." Active listening is hard to teach because it comes through our presence. The following are some examples to help you on your journey.

- "You seem frustrated. It's hard to stop doing something you love and start something else. Keep breathing. You can do this."
- "You seem scared. That was frightening. No wonder you wanted to run. I will keep you safe. Breathe with me. I am here to help you."
- "You seem sad. Losing someone you love is hard. We will get through this together. You are not alone."

Now let's take another look at the example with the two girls who were name calling:

Teacher: You both seem frustrated. You wanted to solve a problem, but didn't know what to do.
Allie: She called me stupid.
Beya: She said my hair looked like a bunny's butt.
Teacher: No wonder you both seem angry. Neither one of you knew how to share your frustrations in a respectful way.
Teacher to Allie: Did you like it when she called you stupid?
Allie: No.
Teacher to Beya: Did you like it when she compared your hair to a bunny?
Beya: No.
Teacher to both: It seems you both need help using your BIG Voice to teach others how you want to be treated.
Teacher to Allie: Tell Beya, "I don't like it when you call me names. When you want to talk to me, use my name."
Teacher to Beya: Tell Allie, "I don't like it when you make fun of my hair. When you talk to me about my hair, either compliment it or say nothing."

Complete the process with the girls demonstrating their willingness to use the new skill and repairing the relationship through a reconnection ritual like a high five or a pinkie hug.

Naming + Acknowledging = More likely to move up to the top floor

Remember, it is vital to quickly follow **Naming** with **Acknowledging**. Moving rapidly facilitates problem-solving, while pausing stalls the process in an emotional, conflicted state. Do not get off the elevator on the emotionally-charged ground floor! For another example of applying the D.N.A. process in real life, watch the portal video of noticing and empathy in action.

Acknowledging children's desires helps them shift from what they don't want to what they do want. It echoes the pivoting process discussed in the Assertiveness chapter (Chapter 5) and utilizes positive intent, which we will discuss in the next chapter. When we, children, parents and coworkers are complaining (focusing on what we don't want), we are wandering around on the top floor without access to the CEO's office. The problem-solving power of the CEO's office is only available to us when we focus on what we want by pivoting.

Acknowledging + Pivoting = Readiness to problem-solve

Child Says	Teacher Acknowledges
No one likes me.	You were hoping to have friends who care.
He took my pencil.	You wanted the pencil back.
I don't care about math.	You were hoping we would continue with science.
Everyone bothers me.	You wanted to be left alone.

> **What if I Guess Wrong?** Children will correct us when we guess wrong. If we say, "You were hoping to have friends to play with," the child might respond, "No, I wanted Olivia to help me with my picture." Pick up the conversation from there by saying, "Oh, so you wanted some help from Olivia."

Activity to Practice Elevator Empathy

Using the elevator metaphor, practice deciding which floor you would enter the elevator on (basement survival state, ground floor emotional state or top floor executive state), and which skills you will begin with (D, N or A) in the following situations:

Situation	Floor	Skill
1. Child says, "Shut up!"		
2. Child is hiding his face.		
3. Child says, "Why math again?"		
4. Child says, "Math is stupid!"		
5. Child throws her backpack.		

Check the portal for possible answers.

Common Mistakes During the D.N.A. process

Questioning instead of noticing and sounding all-knowing instead of offering gentle reflections are two common mistakes when conducting the D.N.A. process.

The purpose of questioning is to elicit information. The purpose of noticing is to increase the child's self-awareness. If we are asking questions, we are not **D**escribing, **N**aming or **A**cknowledging. Questions ask children to think about feelings, not feel and regulate them. Avoid saying things like, "Are you angry?" and "Why are you angry?"

Sounding all-knowing also thwarts empathy. Our reflections of children's feelings and motives ought to be tentative and correctable. We want to leave plenty of space for the child to respond and correct us as needed. Tentative inquiries like, "You seem angry?" are helpful. Avoid saying things like, "You must be feeling sad," and "I know you are angry."

When we empathize, we symbolically say, "I see you, feel you and hear you." This builds or repairs bonds as children feel seen, safe and soothed. The D.N.A. process enables us to deal with children's emotional states first so we can teach, coach or deliver a consequence on the metaphorical top floor in the CEO's office. Our awareness of children's states is key to the D.N.A. process and to encouraging emotional regulation. If our minds are preoccupied with what supplies we'll need for the science lesson, how we don't have time to deal with upset or

what we will cook for dinner when we get home, we are going to miss the facial and body signals that point us toward helping children self-regulate. Describing and demonstrating a child's face during upset helps us attune with children and stay in the present moment, thus accessing the higher centers of our brains to offer empathy and guidance. It also helps the distressed child and all School Family members who are watching the interaction become consciously aware of nonverbal cues, and the emotions and desires these cues indicate.

Empathy as an Aid for Owning Our Feelings

The Composure chapter reminds us, "Whomever we believe to be in charge of our feelings, we have placed in charge of us," so we can reclaim our power. Empathy is the skill we use to help children reclaim their power, enforcing the belief that they are in charge of their feelings, and they have the power and the responsibility to regulate them. Imagine a beach ball with the words **feelings**, **power** and **responsibility** written on it.

Whoever is holding the ball is responsible for the feelings, and has the power and responsibility to regulate them. If I believe my brother has made me mad, then he is holding my beach ball. He has the power and responsibility to manage my upset. If he doesn't change in some way, then I could be upset for decades! For personal wellbeing and healthy relationships, we must each hold our own beach balls. Attempting to make others responsible for our internal states gives our power away leaving us a victim to life. Watch a video demonstration of the beach ball concept on your portal.

When children are born, our internal state regulates their internal state. Survival demands we hold their beach balls, regulate their states for them and respond to their needs in an attuned manner. As infants grow into toddlers, their world expands from needs (survival) to wants (pleasure). They want to play all day and not take naps. As we begin to put limits on their behavior, upset ensues and tantrums may follow. The adult who once relieved the infant's distress is now the source of distress as she enforces healthy limits. The intensity of the toddler's emotions overtakes him because the emotions are big and his repertoire of skills is small. The adult's job at this age is to gently hand the beach ball of feelings, power and responsibility back to the child, empowering him to learn to regulate his emotions. Adults now serve as co-regulators and coaches.

It is essential that we gently return the beach ball to children using the D.N.A. process. However, a screaming child doesn't always receive this handoff with grace. The Composure chapter (Chapter 4) and the Safe Place become exceedingly helpful during these times. It is a child's job to project his upset onto us by throwing the beach ball to us saying, "It's your fault I feel mad!" It's our job to gently hand him back his power with the Skill of Empathy, scaffolding his emotional regulation and building a template for him to utilize conscious empathy with others. The gentle handing back of the beach ball through the D.N.A. process is our co-regulation duty. Once the child is holding his own beach ball, he is ready for problem solving or assistance with complying. Supplementing empathy with the Skill of Choices (Chapter 7) will increase compliance. Supplementing empathy with the Skill of Consequences (Chapter 10) will increase learning from mistakes. See if you can detect how the powers and skills of Conscious Discipline work together in the following example:

Adult command after two-minute warning: Emilia, it's time to put away your book and return to your seat.
Emilia: No! I'm not finished! Just leave me alone! I'm not hurting anyone.
Adult: You seem disappointed. You were hoping to finish and it's hard to stop. You can do it. Breathe with me. You have a choice. You can mark your page with a sticky note or your bookmark. What is best for you?
Emilia: All right (rolling her eyes). Bookmark.
Adult: Good for you, Emilia. It can be hard to switch gears; take a couple of deep breaths on the way to your seat.

Emilia tossed her beach ball to the teacher, essentially saying, "If you let me do what I want, I can remain calm and all will be well." Instead of taking responsibility for Emilia's feelings, the teacher gently gives the ball back by using empathy, choices, encouragement and composure. Did you notice the teacher was able to discern that Emilia was in an emotional state (ground floor in our building metaphor), and offered her empathy beginning with <u>N</u>aming and moving quickly to <u>A</u>cknowledging?

> Just like toddlers, adults aren't always ready or willing to hold our own beach balls. Sometimes we need time and additional skills. The Safe Place serves this purpose for children. The Safe Place for adults is an internal space called acceptance.

Activity to Practice Handing Back the Beach Ball

 Watch the portal videos about the D.N.A. process and compliance, and then apply this new knowledge in the activity below:

Adult command: Open your books to page 32. (Everyone complies except Santiago.)

Adult: Lauren, would you be willing to help Santiago get started on page 32?

Santiago: Shut up! Everyone just leave me alone.

Adult: You seem _____.

You were hoping _____

_____.

You have a choice. You may _____ or _____.

Which is better for you? (Santiago complies with the second choice.)

Adult: Good for you! You _____.

Healing Anger Through Empathy

Sometimes when I am doing a workshop, I will have participants write down the Seven Basic Skills of Discipline on seven separate cards. I read scenarios and the teachers hold up the skill card that is most effective in beginning the interaction with the child. During this exercise, I give an example of a child who falls and skins her knee, and participants raise empathy cards. I give a situation where a child is mad at a friend and I see empathy cards. I give a scenario that ends with a child calling the teacher stupid and a sea of consequences cards swells. Empathy is just as essential for the child who calls us stupid as it is for the child who skins her knee. Resisting the urge to attack those who attack us is a huge task, yet to teach children self-control, we must learn and model the skills ourselves. Diligently practice empathy through the D.N.A. process with angry children to help them learn to calm, self-regulate and heal.

Tantrums and Frustration Fits

Tantrums and frustration fits are both expressions of anger. Let's start by differentiating between survival state tantrums and emotional state frustration fits. A tantrum is a specific, extreme behavior. It is an uncontrollable burst of anger that usually arises from a child's thwarted efforts to control a situation. It is often followed by sadness or crying. A tantrum says, "I have tried desperately to make the world go my way. Now, I'm so frazzled I can't stand it. I feel terrified, helpless and powerless." A child throwing a tantrum is unable to speak coherently, has a facial expression of extreme distress or pain, and cries tears.

The whiny frustration fits that result from a child's inability to get what she wants are not tantrums. Frustration fits are children's attempts to express upset and make adults give in to their demands. During frustration fits, children are upset, yet are able to state their demands (often through whining) and lack real tears.

Tantrums are often associated with young children and occur mostly between the ages of 1- and 4-years-old. Frustration fits can last a lifetime. The difference between the two and how we handle each is critical. Using our building metaphor, tantrums happen in the survival-level basement and require downloading composure from the adult to the child. Frustration fits happen on the emotional-level ground floor and require a little empathy to make it to the executive-level top floor.

Tantrums happen because essential pathways between a child's higher brain and lower brain haven't developed yet, or the pathways are offline due to lack of sleep, hunger or stress. A tantrum occurs when something activates the alarm system in the lower centers of brain, knocking the child's arousal system (the clacker) severely out of balance. Stress chemicals surge through the child's body. It is a truly distressful time where the intensity of the emotion greatly outweighs the system's capacity.

Frustration Fit

Tantrum

Uncomforted distress, such as the distress a child experiences during a tantrum, can leave her with toxic levels of stress hormones. Repeatedly ignoring or getting angry with children who have tantrum can inhibit their brain development. Rejection, abandonment and shame create more rage, increasing the odds of more tantrums. We must consciously soothe their distress through downloading composure and the reassurance, "You are safe," to help them develop vital stress-regulating systems and reduce the frequency of future tantrums.

> Remember, only by staying in control of ourselves can we help an out-of-control child. As the flight attendants say, "Put your own oxygen mask on first. Then put the mask on the child." Shift focus from stopping tantrums to helping children move through them.

When we help children move through tantrums, we teach them better ways to cope with and affect their world. Tantrums occur in two modes: out-of-control with no physical threat to themselves or others, and out-of-control with threats to themselves or others. When no threat is involved, composure, empathy and time can restore the tantruming child to an organized state. When threat is involved, we must safely restrain the child, download calm and reassure, "You're safe. I will keep you safe."

Melissa, age six, hates when anyone gets in her very large personal space. One morning during opening circle, Cassandra sits on Melissa's carpet square. Melissa throws herself on the floor kicking and screaming. Mrs. Brookes calls the office for help and immediately starts taking several deep breaths. She tells herself, "This moment is as it is. Relax and solve the problem." She starts describing what she sees. "Melissa, your arms are going like this (demonstrates)." Melissa continues flailing her arms and hollering. "Your face is scrunched up." Mrs. Brookes makes a face like Melissa's. Melissa looks up briefly and makes eye contact. Mrs. Brookes continues to actively calm herself, downloading calm to Melissa. "Your whole body is telling me you feel angry." Melissa glares at Cassandra and shakes a fist at her.

Mrs. Brookes facilitates this communication by saying, "Cassandra, Melissa shook her fist to tell you she felt angry when you sat on her carpet square." Mrs. Brookes continues, "You seem so very angry, Melissa. You wanted Cassandra to move off your square." Melissa starts to relax and cry. Mrs. Brookes guides her to the Safe Place where she can calm herself further. Later, Mrs. Brookes does a mini Time Machine (Chapter 10) with Melissa and Cassandra, replaying the scene with new helpful skills: "Melissa, you wanted Cassandra to move off your square. When you want someone to move, say, *Move, please*. Practice that now." Melissa is able to say, "Move, please." Cassandra moves and all three celebrate!

In this story, Mrs. Brookes used the Skill of Composure to keep herself calm enough to use the Skill of Empathy to help Melissa through her tantrum. She offers compassion to Melissa and teaches the rest of the class how to offer compassion to those who are out-of-control. She also knows Melissa well enough to realize she needs to call the office to get some support for the rest of the class so she can remain present with Melissa rather than splitting her attention.

Later that day, another child accidentally sits on Melissa's carpet square. Melissa starts screaming and throws her body on the floor. Mrs. Brookes calls the office for help again and begins describing, "Your arms are swinging and your heels are kicking the floor." As Mrs. Brookes demonstrates, Melissa kicks her. Mrs. Brookes yelps in pain and grabs her shin. Melissa swings her fist at her.

Mrs. Brookes takes several deep breaths and restrains Melissa, making sure her arms are tucked tightly into her own chest. Mrs. Brookes states, "I will keep you safe. I will not let you hurt yourself or anyone else." After this statement of the limits, Mrs. Brookes breathes deeply, downloading calm. She only offers empathy once Melissa's body begins to relax, signaling that her clacker is slowing down. She starts with describing, "Your arms are pushing against my body, your feet are moving just like this (demonstrating the movements as much as possible while keeping the child safe). Your whole body is saying you feel angry. It's scary to be out of control. I will keep you safe. I will not let you hurt yourself or anyone else."

Melissa yells, "Let me go. I'll be good. Just let me go." Mrs. Brookes says, "You seem more in control and want me to let you go. I will let you go when your body begins to relax and you are breathing deeply like me." At first Melissa struggles harder, but within seconds she begins to breathe and her body relaxes. She begins to sob. Mrs. Brookes holds her, rocks her and says, "It's okay to cry. That was scary. I will keep you safe." Mrs. Brookes gently takes Melissa to the Safe Place where she will continue the calming process independently.

Mrs. Brookes followed the following steps for offering composure, safety and empathy during a tantrum:

1. See the behavior as a call for help so we can remain present with the child.
2. Consciously compose ourselves with active calming, downloading calm to the child.
3. Offer empathy through the D.N.A. process after the child's body begins to relax.
4. Restrain the child, if necessary for safety reasons, using the following language:
   "I will keep you safe. I will not let you hurt yourself or anyone else."
   "I will let you go when your body is relaxed and you are breathing like me."
   "You're safe. Breathe with me."

Frustration fits require the adult to offer empathy to help the child take personal responsibility for her upset and choices for redirection. Since the child is using the frustration fit as strategy to get something she wants or to get us to change our minds, we must offer empathy and choices. If this is not effective, we must disengage from the pleading, threats and backtalk by walking away, giving the child the time and space to choose differently.

> In a toddler classroom, Camden is having fun at the water table. His mom comes to pick him up. He sees his mom and starts screaming, "No, No, No!" He stomps his feet and falls to the floor saying, "Me play, me play." Mrs. O'Neil intervenes by saying, "Your arms are going like this (demonstrates). Your face is going like this (demonstrates)." Once Camden looks at her, she takes a deep breath to download a little calm into Camden's body. His response is, "No!" She continues, "You seem frustrated. You saw Mommy and knew it was time to stop playing and get ready to go home. You wanted to play longer. That is so hard." She picks up Camden and says, "You have a choice. You can say, Bye-bye water table, or you can say, Hello to mommy who loves your nose (as she touches his nose with a boink sound)." Camden says, "Mommy."

Beyond Tantrums: Rage

Anger demands children calm down. Rage demands children move first and calm down second because rage is a higher intensity than anger. To help children manage rage, we must teach them to consciously recognize it in its initial onset (before it gets a firm foothold). We must actively help children recognize the warning signals for rage just as we would help a child with epilepsy learn the warning signals for a seizure. Children often describe the onset of a rage as "the yucky feeling." Providing a place where children can run, jump or ride a stationary bike as soon as they detect the yucky feeling will help them discharge the bodily arousal. Do the following to help children manage rage:

Step 1: **Set up support services** within your school to help you carry out your rage plan and educate all parties involved about the procedures (including parents).
- How will you call for additional adult help?
- Who will you call?
- Have the adult who comes watch your class while you help the student.
- Teach the rest of the class to start S.T.A.R. breathing and wishing well as soon as their School Family member is in distress.

Step 2: **Help children become aware** of their rage triggers in the environment and build rage awareness about their bodies. When children are in a relaxed, alert executive state, help them discern where they first feel rage. Print a blank Feeling Buddy from the portal and instruct children to color where the yucky feeling starts in their bodies. Do all their muscles feel tight, do their faces get hot, etc.? Use this information to teach children to recognize when rage is coming on and then teach them ways to discharge the yucky feeling.

Step 3: **Spend time with the child to develop a trusting relationship.** This is done through face-to-face interactions that are playful, like the I Love You Rituals (Bailey, 1997). To see many of these rituals in action go to the Conscious Discipline website and visit Shubert's School.

Step 4: Create a rage book like the example on your portal by taking a picture of the child before the rage, showing the destruction that resulted from the rage and demonstrating healthy alternatives for when the yucky feeling arises. The alternatives will include three steps:

1. Move the large muscles in the legs (run, climb, bike, etc.) to discharge the bodily arousal. Show specific procedures for where the child is to go, what the child is to do and who will help.

2. Go the Safe Place and conduct the five steps for self-regulation to return to an integrated executive state. Learn more about the five steps in *Managing Emotional Mayhem* (Bailey, 2011) and the *Feeling Buddies Self-Regulation Toolkit*.

3. Add the Feeling Buddies to your curriculum and/or have the school counselor provide small group practice with the Buddies.

As with all the skills in Conscious Discipline, our intent is critical to the use of empathy. If our intent is to make children stop feeling a certain way, we will try to use empathy to manipulate and our tone of voice will betray our motives. I once heard a frustrated teacher say harshly, "I know it's hard to stop what you are doing. Now put your journal away!" Her attempt at empathy was aimed at making the child obey, not helping the child become organized and aware of herself. Often in workshops, a teacher will say, "I tried empathy and it didn't work!" My question is, "What do you mean work?" The answer is usually that the child did not happily obey. Empathy is bigger than obedience. It wires children's brains to process disappointment, frustration and anger without acting out these emotions in a hurtful manner. Like any skill, it must be offered long before it is internalized. If we labeled "cup" for an infant three times, would you expect the child to learn the word? No. The same is true for empathy. Emotional regulation requires adult scaffolding and lots of practice. The children who need empathy the most are the ones who are out-of-control the most often.

There are no magic words or skills that will teach children emotional regulation on the first or fiftieth try. Emotional regulation is a process that develops slowly over years and decades. To facilitate development, we must first consciously change our response to children's upset. All conflict starts with upset. If we cannot manage upset, we cannot solve problems. Our empathy empowers children to take ownership of their inner states. Ownership is critical to learning and change. Remember, the goal is to help the child hold her own beach ball!

Empathy Creates Connection in the School Family

As we practice the aforementioned perceptual shifts and skills daily, the following structure will support connection in the School Family.

Classroom Structure: We Care Center

Every social-emotional skill requires structured opportunities for meaningful practice. The We Care Center provides children with a symbolic way of expressing empathy. The symbolic form will vary depending on the age and literacy of the children. Teach children how to use the We Care Center and its significance, just as we would teach the color purple or multiplication tables. Tie this center into language arts and core standards.

We Care Center

I use or we Kar
bos to hlp my frenjos

Kindergarten: Mrs. Lee's kindergarten class decided the We Care Center would be a tote bag filled with ways for children to offer empathy to each other. Mrs. Lee wrote the following quote on the bag: "In our School Family, we care about each other." One day, Mrs. Lee was reading a book during center time. All of a sudden, Kasy began to cry. Kareem, who was the We Care Person for that week, picked up the We Care Bag and walked over to Kasy. He said, "Would this help?" In the We Care Bag was a stuffed animal, several Band-Aids, a bottle of lotion and a small baby blanket for Kasy to choose from. Without a word, she reached in, pulled out the stuffed bear and held it. Her body began to relax.

Fifth Grade: In Mr. Carter's fifth grade class, Michelle had been suspended from school for a series of infractions. Several class members went to the classroom We Care Center, which consisted of fancy stationary, pens and envelopes. They wrote Michelle letters to keep in touch with her and wish her well while she was away. Each of the letters said she was missed in the School Family and that the class was looking forward to her return. Mr. Carter structured the letter writing to combine it with practicing common core requirements.

The goal of the We Care Center is to utilize empathy as a way of classroom life so children learn to read and understand nonverbal cues of distress in themselves and others, and then respond in loving ways. We Care Centers are helpful for students, and also for staff and faculty. One school using Conscious Discipline decided to change the school clinic into a We Care Station. In another school, a fourth grade class wrote lyrics for a reassuring rap for a frightened School Family member who was having his tonsils removed. Some second graders created a class collage to support a child's sadness over the loss of her Golden Retriever. Others implement online We Care Centers using free greeting card software. The possibilities are as limitless as the creativity and love the children seek to share.

Explore the videos in Shubert's School and read Chapter 14 in *Creating the School Family* for additional We Care implementation ideas.

So far, we've learned to create safety by calling on the Skills of **Composure** and **Assertiveness**. Composure allows us to remain calm enough to choose to be assertive. Assertiveness asks us to vigilantly focus on what we want children to do. We've learned to foster connection and belonging through the Skills of **Encouragement**, **Choices** and **Empathy**. Focusing on what we want allows us to use the Skill of Encouragement, creating supportive, caring classrooms where each person helps others be successful. Focusing on step-by-step success helps all parties stay in an optimal learning state. The Skill of Choices helps increase the likelihood of compliance, while still staying focused on our educational expectations. When upset occurs, the Skill of Empathy helps us handle the fussing and fits resulting from ineffective choices in regard to limits, agreements and rules.

Our skills so far have allowed us to create a School Family that answers the following questions, "Am I safe?" and "Am I loved?" in the affirmative. They organize the brain so children are ready and willing to solve problems. This brings us to Section 3, Problem Solving. Take ample time to reflect and hone the Skill of Empathy in preparation for the problem-solving section that is to come.

Empathy Summary

Power:	**Acceptance:** The moment is as it is.
Becoming Brain Smart:	Empathy integrates the brain for personal responsibility and self-control.
Skill:	D.N.A. process for emotional regulation, rage book and program
School Family:	We Care Center

Power of Acceptance Reflection

Focus on letting it be and being conscious of all the "shoulds" we place on ourselves and others. We must accept thoughts, feelings, actions, others, ourselves and situations as they are in order to make the wisest possible choice in the moment. Negating the moment negates everyone in it. Start implementing the Power of Acceptance with the following steps:

❏ **Notice how often we want things to be different** by paying attention to thoughts like, "They/I should _____," "They/I need to _____," "Why don't they/I _____," "We don't _____ in our classroom."

❏ **Practice linking our frustrations in life with a lack of acceptance** in that moment; upset stems from resistance.

❏ **Notice if we are confusing thoughts with feelings.** Practice saying, "I feel ____," followed by a feeling word (disappointed, angry, happy, etc.).

❏ **Practice being present** and listening to upset colleagues, significant others and friends. Resist the tendency to judge anyone as a victim.

❏ **Become conscious of empathy styles** and how we distract ourselves from our feelings (shopping, cleaning, drinking, working, eating, etc.).

❏ **Watch the Power of Acceptance video** on the portal to deepen your reflection.

Brain Smart Teaching Moments

Watch how children express feelings and offer empathy. Watch for verbal, nonverbal (facial expressions, body language) and physical (actions such as crossing arms, hitting, stomping feet) expressions of sadness, disappointment, anger, frustration, happiness, joy, anxiety and fear. The following list helps us focus on the emotional aspects of the classroom:

Disappointment and Sadness

Verbal Expressions:	Nonverbal Expressions:	Physical Expressions:
• "It's not fair." • "I wish we could __." • "This sucks." • "Bummer." • "I don't care."	• Downcast eyes • Steamed shrimp posture • Droopy eyes and face • Slow movements • Shuffling feet	• Withdrawing • Reluctance to engage • Crying • Pouting • Whining • Complaining

Frustration and Anger

Verbal Expressions:	Nonverbal Expressions:	Physical Expressions:
• "This is stupid." • "I hate you." • "I hate __." • Cursing • Name calling • "You can't make me." • "You said we could __."	• Furrowing eyebrows • Tight face • Folding arms • Tense muscles • Clenching fists • Reddening face	• Screaming and shouting • Throwing items • Stomping • Physically attacking (hitting, kicking, biting, etc.)

Anxiety and Fear

Verbal Expressions:	Nonverbal Expressions:	Physical Expressions:
• "Do we have to?" • Excuses and blame • "I don't know." • "I don't want to." • "I can't."	• Wide eyes • Shallow breathing • Darting eyes • Lack of eye contact	• Fidgeting and hyperactivity • Busy hands, sitting on hands • Nail biting • Rubbing arms, legs, etc. • Withdrawal and hiding • Non-conversational language ("Fine." "Okay.") • Physical complaints (headache, stomachache)

Skill Reflection: Common and Conscious

If possible, partner up to say the two statements out loud. See if you can feel the difference. After each statement share, "The difference between Common and Conscious for me was…"

Common	Conscious
Why are you feeling that way?	You seem disappointed. You were hoping to go out to dinner.
There is no need to act like that.	You seem anxious. You wanted more time before the test.
It is not that big of a deal, let it go.	You seem frustrated. It's hard when others ignore your advice.

School Family Implementation Checklist

❏ **Feel your feelings instead of judging them**, talking about them or distracting from them.

❏ **Acknowledge your feelings** using the following inner speech: "I seem _____. I wanted _____." (Or "I was hoping _____.")

❏ **Think, "The moment is as it is, relax (breathe) and solve the problem,"** when the world is not going as we'd like.

❏ **Offer empathy to upset children using the D.N.A. process daily.** "Your eyes are going like this. Your mouth is going like this. (pause and download with eye contact) You seem _____. You wanted _____. Or You were hoping _____."

❏ **Differentiate a distress tantrum from a frustration fit** and handle each accordingly.

❏ **Start a rage program,** if needed.

❏ **Continue noticing what brain state a child is operating from** (survival, emotional, executive) in order to start the interaction with the most effective skill.

❏ **Create a We Care Center** in the classroom and/or school.

❏ **Review additional helpful web resources**, including Shubert's School and the web portal.

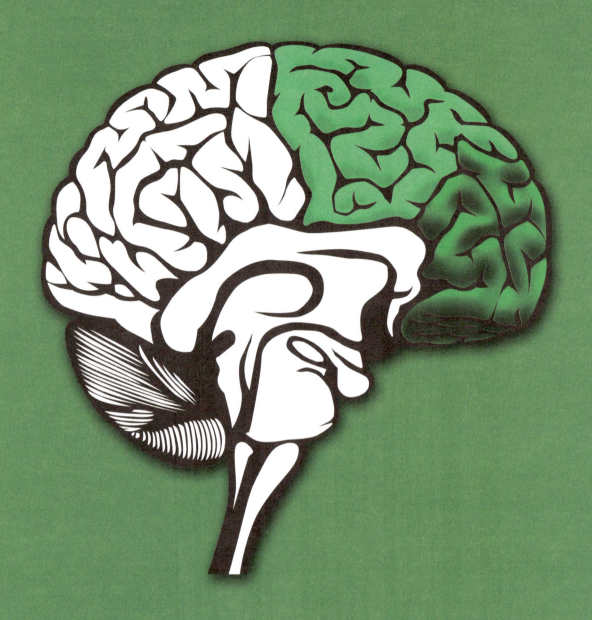

- Section 3 -

PROBLEM SOLVING

Executive State Skills

S = Solutions
P = Positive Intent
A = Academic Integration
C = Consequences
E = Executive Skills

Answering, "Yes!" to, "Am I safe," and, "Am I loved," integrates the brain. Integration provides access to the higher brain centers so children can ask, "What can I learn?" The Problem Solving section is color-coded green, symbolized by heart-shaped glasses, and represented by the prefrontal lobes and an executive state.

The prefrontal lobes conduct the regulatory functions that override the impulses and insecurities of the limbic system and brain stem. These regulatory functions allow us to see from another person's point of view and pause before acting, giving us time to choose helpful responses over hurtful reactions. This pause is where we self-regulate, focus our attention, reflect on our thoughts, feelings and actions, access moral reasoning, and set and achieve goals.

The executive state requires relaxed alertness fostered by positive emotions. It is achieved in climates of high challenge and low stress. High stakes testing, without a school culture that meets children's safety and connection needs, is toxic to our long-term educational goals. Children must answer, "Am I safe," and "Am I loved," in the affirmative before asking the executive state question, "What can I learn?" Most discipline problems in schools are regulatory deficits. Reward and punishment stifle instead of scaffold children's development of self-regulation. The Skills of Positive Intent and Consequences teach us the combined tools (S.P.A.C.E.) needed to scaffold prefrontal lobe development and self-regulatory functions.

Combined Tools for Problem-Solving

Solutions: Problem-solving is impossible without a vigilant focus on solutions instead of blame.

Positive Intent: We must see children differently, especially our most challenging children, before they can act differently. Offering positive intent to children fosters integration, and the willingness to reflect on and change behavior.

Academic Integration: As we embrace the School Family concepts and skills, integration between classroom management, discipline, social-emotional learning and the academic curriculum becomes seamless.

Consequences: Effective consequences teach children to examine their behavior, reflect on its impact and make changes until reaching their goals. Ineffective consequences are applied again and again without behavioral changes.

Executive Skills: Adults must lend their executive skills to scaffold children's development. Once we see misbehavior as a call for help, we can begin the integrative process of coaching children for academic and social-emotional success.

Chapter 9

POSITIVE INTENT

Creating teaching moments with oppositional and aggressive children

We must see children differently in order for them to behave differently.

We have a choice to see the best or worst in each other. The Power of Love asks us to see the best. It allows us to see the light within every person at any time. Seeing the spark of beauty in each person does not excuse behavior or eliminate consequences; it allows us to hold hope for the hopeless, safety for the fearful and encouragement for the discouraged. The Power of Love is faith in action—faith, not as a religious affiliation, but as a belief that's not based on observable proof.

Take a deep breath. As you inhale, say to yourself, "I am willing to see…" As you exhale, say to yourself, "…the best in others." It is easy to see the best in others when they act as we think they should. It is much harder to choose this perception when we think they've made poor choices. When children are misbehaving, they often trigger our upset, throwing us into the lower centers of the brain. From a survival state, we perceive conflict as a threat to our authority, our ability to teach, our safety, etc. From this perception, we see conflict as bad and those who create it as deserving of punishment. From an emotional state, we perceive conflict as irritating, the offending person as trying to make our lives hard and conflict as something to stop. Only when we access an integrated executive state can we access all our executive skills, including the ability to see from another's point of view. From this more global perspective, we then have a choice. We can see an intense call for help or intolerable disobedience. We can teach new skills or punish. We can choose at any time, to tap into the Power of Love, an extremely potent and largely neglected resource. We can discern the communication embedded in the child's behavior. The icon for the Power of Love is heart-shaped glasses. Watch a video on the Power of Love on the portal for a more in-depth understanding.

State Dictates Perception
Perception Dictates Intent / Intent Dictates Action

Executive State	Conflict is a call for help and a teaching opportunity. It must be **solved** with new skills.
Emotional State	Conflict is irritating and upsetting. It must be **stopped.**
Survival State	Conflict is threatening and bad. It must be **punished.**

The Power of Love

The Power of Love fosters the development of compassion. Compassion is a way of viewing the world through the eyes of interdependence and interconnection. "What you offer to others you strengthen within yourself," is the overriding principle Conscious Discipline is founded on. One of the myths we have grown to embrace is that we can attack others (verbally or physically) without harm to ourselves. Recently, a friend of mine said, "I will never forgive my nephew." She decided to hold on to her anger with the misguided illusion that it would somehow change her nephew or hold him accountable for his actions. We cannot harbor negative thoughts toward others without also negatively impacting ourselves. Choosing to see the best in others defines both them and us in the highest possible way. It encourages ownership of thoughts, feelings and actions, and fosters the willingness to change and learn new skills as needed. We can only live the positive, empowered life of our dreams when we choose to use the Power of Love to see the best in others.

The Power of Love requires us to harness all of the tools we have learned up to this moment. Managing our triggers and remaining calm enough to see the best in others is an extremely difficult task, especially for those of us working with challenging children! On the most basic level, we must become masters of composure, able to override our triggers. Then we must suspend our judgments about others' intentions and be willing to see those who act in hurtful ways as people calling for help.

Think back to a time in your life when you lashed out at loved ones. Was your deepest desire at that moment to make things worse, have them feel less than whole or simply to get personal relief from your own intense emotional distress? Now reflect on the aftermath of your actions. Immediately, you may have felt a sense of righteous relief, but guilt or shame tends to erase all sense of satisfaction over time. Children who act out experience the same volley of emotions. Our job is to remain calm enough to see the best and help them learn new skills. Our skills are only as effective as our ability to manage our triggers.

Judging Others' Intentions

Pretend a friend commits to call on Friday to discuss a very important issue with you. Friday rolls around and she doesn't call. You call her house, but there is no answer. You start contemplating why she didn't respond. You wonder if she is upset with you. Did something happen?

Most of us are unaware of how much time we spend trying to figure out others' motives, essentially what they are "really up to." We consciously and unconsciously take in every subtle cue available from words, facial expressions, gestures and body posture to create theories about why people act as they do. We test our theories by asking calculated questions. We play back conversations like court transcripts in our heads. We check new information against previous conversations and evidence we've heard from other sources. Once we have a relatively complete theory, we draw in friends to discuss our assumptions. These conversations could last hours or days, involving more and more people. Finally, after all this investigative work, we decide we have the answer. Whether we are right or not, we will treat the person as if we know her motivation. Rather than accepting the moment as it is, we spend enormous amounts of time and energy trying to determine others' motivations in efforts to plan a response that protects us from possible attack, humiliation, appearing ungrateful, etc.

Most of us believe we can assess others' intentions accurately. In fact, research involving infants and toddlers proves that we do innately possess this ability. As we age, however, our CD-Roms provide automatic filters through which we interpret events. Our adult judgments are based on these filters created from our past, not the present moment or the person's actual intentions. The Power of Love encourages us to see past our CD-Rom filters and the falseness of our judgments, come to the present moment, and choose to see the best in others. It is only through faith in the goodness of others that we can create the life of kindness we desire.

Children (and adults) will attempt to meet their needs through whatever skills they've been taught. A college student of mine named Ginger had a grade school teacher who taught the class to put their heads down on their desks when they were bad. This practice remained dormant in her unconscious until one day in high school she and her friends were talking during the teacher's lecture. The teacher stopped the lesson to chastise the girls for being inconsiderate. Ginger immediately put her head down as bad feelings cycled through her body. The teacher shouted, "Well, Miss Ginger, if you don't find my words interesting or worth staying awake for, you can march yourself down to the principal's office. I don't tolerate students who are disrespectful." In Ginger's mind, putting her head down was a way to show respect and regret for her actions. The teacher, however, judged Ginger's head-down position as a sign of disrespect.

Years ago a boy and his dog, a black Labrador, got lost in Florida's Ocala National Forest. Fortunately, both were found the next day. Reporters announced that the dog had stayed with the boy to keep him warm. I wondered, "Who interviewed that dog?" Soon after, sales of Labrador puppies in Florida soared as parents bought dogs to protect their children. If we are going to attribute intentions to others, why not attribute noble ones? If an entire state can see the best in a dog's actions, let's do the same for each other, ourselves and students like Ginger!

Many children learn inappropriate ways of expressing emotion and getting their needs met, either through direct teaching of strategies (like Ginger's experience) or through modeling of negative behavior from adults. Screaming when angry, hitting when frustrated, manipulating when wanting something, and lying or appeasing others to avoid conflict are all common strategies. We can judge the motives behind these actions as disrespectful or hateful and label the children "bad," or we can suspend our negative judgments and use the Power of Love to see all these behaviors as calls for help.

On the other hand, when a child makes a decision we like, most of us accept that he has earned our positive regard. We often express this through praise, the underlying message of which is, "When you do what I want, you earn my love." This links love with approval, making love conditional on behavior. Many adults have internalized this kind of thinking, seeking approval and struggling to please others. We act appropriately not because we love others, but because we fear they won't love us.

Adults who link love with approval consequently withhold love from children when they make mistakes or behave hurtfully. Children who repeatedly make poor choices generally feel poorly about themselves. They often are the ones who did not experience enough family privilege to develop trust and the perception that the world is safe. Withholding love and positive regard from these children reinforces the negative beliefs they hold about themselves and the world. The Power of Love sees a call for help and a seed of potential behind these defensively guarded children who are hurtful to themselves and others. We must be willing to see these children differently so they can see themselves differently.

> I've noticed I make terrible choices when I'm feeling unsure, undeserving or not good enough. I'm often short-tempered and critical towards others and myself during these times. I may also overwork and find other ways to indulge my feelings of failure. At these times I need compassion, not lectures that provoke more guilt within me. The same idea applies to children who are acting out.

While visiting an inner city middle school, I was looking for the office to sign in as a visitor. It was a large school and I was lost. I turned a corner. Standing in front of me was a six-foot tall student spray-painting obscenities on the wall outside of the gym. We spotted each other and froze. I must admit my first reaction was one of complete shock. I contemplated running and I am sure he pondered the same. However, I calmed myself down, consciously relaxed my body and harnessed the Power of Love to see the best in him. "You wanted to let everyone know you've had a bad day and a very hard life, based on what you're writing." He stood there just staring at me. I continued, "Who in this school do you think cares about you?" He mumbled, "No one." I said, "Well, that is a problem. Given your answer, what you are doing makes complete sense to me." He started to lower his spray can and his shoulders relaxed slightly. I asked, "Is there anyone in the school that some of the kids trust." He responded, "Coach Carnes, I guess." "Well then," I said, "That's who we need to go see."

Believe it or not, he led me to Coach Carnes. The three of us then began a discussion about helping this young man be successful at school and planning how he would clean the gym wall.

I started the interaction by breathing so I could consciously choose to see the best in him before opening my mouth and saying, "You wanted to let everyone know you have had a bad day." How do you think the outcome would have changed if I had reacted from an emotional state ("What do you think you are doing by destroying school property?") or survival state (running toward or away from him) instead of self-calming enough to access the Power of Love?

Finding fault in others means we are more invested in blame and punishment than we are in change, or that we are too triggered to problem solve. Refusing to see the call for help labels the core of the child as bad and sets us up to punish instead of teach. The child then has two options: To accept the fact that he is indeed a bad child or try to defend his self-worth by engaging in a power struggle.

When we set aside punitive approaches and see difficult behavior as a call for help, we free ourselves to set limits and teach new skills in a healthy manner. Sometimes we mistakenly believe acting from the Power of Love means we will be permissive. Was I permissive in my approach with the boy spraying graffiti? No! The Power of Love allows us to reflect a compassionate motive to the child who is struggling, helping him claim ownership and clarity for his actions. My loving intent helped the boy reflect on the root of his anger. He worked with the coach on a plan that included attending a different study hall to help him be more successful and connected at the school, and he was held accountable for the spray-painting by cleaning it up during in-school suspension. Personal responsibility can only be cultivated, not coerced or forced, and is required before a child can choose to change his behavior or learn new skills. The Power of Love has the ability to turn even the most difficult children around, transforming aggressive or withdrawn children into cooperative members of the School Family.

> DJ Batiste was a powerful gang leader when his teacher planted a seed of potential within him through positive intent. He is now employed, in college and part of the Conscious Discipline team, traveling the country to inspire teachers and troubled youth to see their inner potential. Watch another video about DJ's transformation.

Negative intent sees a child as unworthy. From this perception, a child has a choice to accept the belief that he is unworthy or fight to maintain his self-worth. Children who defend their worth will engage in a power struggle in efforts to make the other person the unworthy one. This struggle is always a lose-lose proposition, as both parties will attack and defend in efforts to maintain their worth.

There is another way: positive intent sees every child as a seed of potential. From this perception, the child has the choice to accept his inherent worth or fight against it. A child who has experienced years of negative intent may, at first, fight against the notion that he is worthy, loveable and capable. Patient and consistent use of positive intent is required to help these troubled seeds grow and bloom.

> **Commitment:** I am willing to use the Power of Love to see the best in at least two challenging children this year. I understand that by seeing others compassionately, I do not let them off the hook; I simply invite the possibility of self-reflection, solutions and change instead of punishment and blame.
>
> Signature: _____ Date: _____

The Power of Love sees a call for help and a seed of potential in children who are being hurtful toward themselves and others.

Becoming Brain Smart

Within the limbic system, the amygdala constantly scans our surroundings for potential danger, serves as the gatekeeper for the flow of energy in the brain, and tags and stores negative emotional events in our memory for future reference. As the gatekeeper, the amygdala can send the flow of energy and information up to the executive state, organizing the child. The amygdala can also send the flow of energy and information down to the survival state, creating a more disorganized, misbehaving child. The quality of our relationships will either help calm the amygdala, resulting in healthy threat perception and a sense of safety, or exacerbate it, sensitizing us to fear, threat and distrust.

Healthy relationships release oxytocin in the brain to calm the amygdala, allowing greater access to our executive state and the Power of Love (love as a conscious choice to see the best, not as a romantic feeling). It allows us to trust others and ensures we feel safe in their presence. It can only be accessed in the present moment or as Eckhart Tolle calls it, "the now moment" (Tolle, 2004). Love requires our presence; presence requires us to suspend our judgments and forecasts of other's intentions.

> Oxytocin is a hormone in the brain involved in bonding. It affects generosity, increases empathy and develops trust between people (Kosfeld, Heinrichs, Zak, Fischbacher, & Fehr, 2005 and Zak, Stanton, & Ahmadi, 2007)

Unhealthy relationships, on the other hand, cause cortisol in the brain to hype up the amygdala and distrusting others becomes the preferred stance. Unhealthy relationships create strong, distorted CD-Rom filters that skew our views of others. Without access to the Power of Love, we are constantly looking for what is wrong and believing others are disrespecting us or being hurtful. We take others' behavior personally, overlooking the fact that we are making this meaning up and can change our perception at any time. With an overactive amygdala and CD-Rom filter, we remain guarded and ready to defend, attack, manipulate and coerce. This leaves our body in a constant state of stress and our brain in the lower centers. We erroneously believe if we can predict the next moment, we can control it, make the world go our way and keep ourselves safe. There can be no safety in a mind preoccupied with the past and projecting into the future. Safety can only be found in the present moment.

Attachment with caregivers during the first three years of life and the quality of our significant relationships as we grow determine whether the amygdala is hyped up or on healthy alert. Our relationship history helps determine how we see others' intentions. When we look through a lens of distrust, we see conniving, manipulative people who will take advantage of us if we let our guard down. When we look through the lens of love and trust, we are willing to offer positive intent, see others as doing the best they can with the skills they have and perceive the call for help behind every difficult behavior. Our relationship history shapes the set points on our CD-Rom but does not define them. Each of us is free to utilize the Power of Love to see differently at any time; some of us simply require more diligence and practice than others. Check in with yourself: Are you resistant to seeing the best in colleagues and the children in your care? Check to see if your early relationship history could be a factor.

We stress ourselves when we see the world in negative, judgmental terms. As our negative emotions become involved, the brain launches a biochemical response that prepares the body to act through the release of cortisol. Cortisol is meant to be a quick fix to help our bodies fight or flee; it is not meant to be triggered for periods of prolonged stress. Excess cortisol kills brain cells, damages the hippocampus in the brain, reduces the capacity to store information and may be responsible for many degenerative diseases. Holding onto judgment, bitterness, control, fear and anger inhibits change and learning, and causes real damage to the body and brain. The Power of Love helps us train our minds to see the best instead. It is essential we do this to improve our physical health and the health of our relationships, and to help children wire their brains in healthy ways.

Accurately assessing the intentions of others is impossible; we make up their motivations based on our amygdala's set points and the filters on our CD-Rom. When we make up negative motives, we are guarded and operate out of the lower centers of the brain. When we make up positive motives, we are calm and can access the prefrontal lobes, executive skills and transformative Power of Love. Our internal CD-Roms may predispose us to making it up positively or negatively, but ultimately we are responsible for the choice to act on that impulse or override it. Wishing well, mentioned in Chapter 4 as part of the active calming process, is also a way to call on the Power of Love at any time. We have a choice in every moment to close our hearts through judgment or open our hearts and wish well. As our hearts open and close, so do the higher centers of the brain.

Integrating the Left and Right Hemispheres

The brain is divided into two hemispheres, the left and the right. Each hemisphere processes different types of information in very different ways. The Power of Love and the Skill of Positive Intent help integrate the left and right prefrontal lobes so we can achieve long-term goals. Before we learn how and why this integration is important, we must first understand how the hemispheres of the brain process information.

Right and Left Prefrontal Cortex

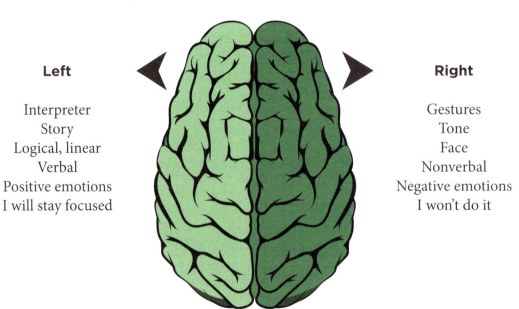

Left	Right
Interpreter	Gestures
Story	Tone
Logical, linear	Face
Verbal	Nonverbal
Positive emotions	Negative emotions
I will stay focused	I won't do it

The left hemisphere is specialized to control well-established patterns under ordinary and familiar circumstances. It handles positive emotions and processes verbal, conscious, rational and serial linear information. When things are familiar, orderly and predictable, the left hemisphere allows us to approach life easily, stay focused and stick to our plans (Cozolino, 2013). This makes complete sense to me, as I feel much more at ease with information, people and situations I already know. I engage more and feel more attentive in these situations.

The right hemisphere is the primary seat of emotional arousal and processes new information. It handles negative emotions and withdrawal from situations. It is also very adept at using nonverbal communication to gather information. All nonverbal, unconscious, holistic and emotional information processing takes place in the right hemisphere. It is the seat of impulse control because of its dense connections to the limbic system and the brain stem (Cozolino, 2013). This also makes sense to me because in new situations I feel a little more hesitant and am more conscious of nonverbal information from facial expressions, tone of voice and body language. I've also experienced times when too much negative emotional energy has overloaded my right prefrontal lobe and I've watched myself behave stupidly on impulse rather than with wisdom.

The chart below shows the two informational processing systems:

Left Hemisphere	Right Hemisphere
Familiar	Novel
Verbal information	Nonverbal information
Logical information	Emotional information
Conscious	Unconscious
Linear information	Holistic, big picture
Literal	Contextual
Words	Images
Letter of the law	Spirit of the law

Self-regulation starts in the right hemisphere

The right hemisphere is more densely connected to the lower centers of the brain (limbic system and brain stem). This allows us to get "gut feelings," and receive and interpret emotional information. It is also the right hemisphere that can get triggered by big emotions, prompting children to say, "I hate you! Leave me alone." Most of us attempt to discipline from a left-brain stance, but the right brain (with its strong connections to the limbic system and brain stem) is the seat of impulse control. This is why adults must verbally notice children's nonverbal behaviors and put behavioral standards in visual images. We must integrate the right and the left hemisphere in order to help children discipline themselves. Notice in the following graphic how the energy from the lower centers of the brain flows up to the right hemisphere.

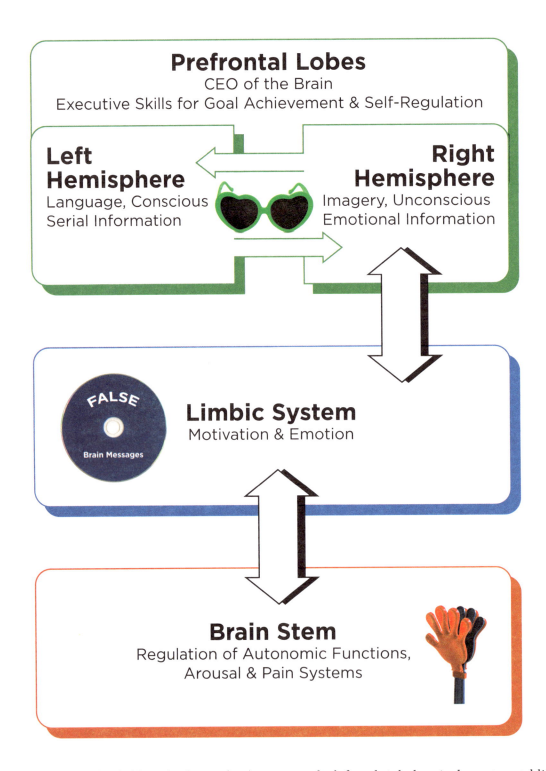

The goal is to help children (and ourselves) integrate the left and right hemispheres to establish and maintain healthy relationships and optimal learning states. If we lean too far to the right, we will be flooded with big emotions and lose control often. If we lean too far to the left, we will be rigid in our need to control everyone and everything, unwilling to cooperate or negotiate. Integration is the key!

The collective discipline practices, school curriculum and culture of the western world values left-hemisphere brain processing. This unbalanced brain integration impedes the wellbeing and educational success of our children. Success requires we:

1. **Model our personal right hemisphere self-regulatory skills for children.** Research on self-regulation indicates that the way parents (adults) treat each other is even more powerful for a child's development of self-regulation than the way the parents (adults) treat the child (Volling, Blandon & Kolak, 2006). We must model the skills we wish to see in all our interactions, not just with children. Although this book is written for educators, it provides skills that enhance all relationships. Practice these skills with your significant others, coworkers and your own children.

2. **Incorporate more personal storytelling.** Encourage children to share personal stories about upsetting experiences. Storytelling integrates the left and right hemispheres. To tell a story that makes sense, the left hemisphere must put things in order using words and logic. The right hemisphere contributes emotions and personal memories. Often adults avoid talking about upsetting events. We think talking about the event will reinforce the pain or make things worse, or we believe it's the counselor or parent's job. Incorporating the sharing of stories that evoke big emotions into our literacy programs encourages profound brain integration. Watch a portal video of a sixth grade teacher using personal storytelling in her classroom.

3. **Value play and the arts.** Create learning opportunities and environments that promote right-hemisphere information processing by bringing the arts and play to the forefront of the curriculum. Three types of play are essential for the development of self-regulation: rough-and-tumble play, dramatic play and interactive face-to-face social play (I Love You Rituals, Baby Doll Circle Time).

4. **Practice and incorporate the Skill of Positive Intent to reach all children, especially the most difficult.** Difficult children lack integration. The Skill of Positive Intent integrates the left prefrontal lobe with the right prefrontal lobe. This fosters a focus on long-term goals instead of short-term relief. The left prefrontal lobe says, "I will stay focused on my goals." The right prefrontal lobe says, "I will not be distracted by impulsive behavior." Integrating the two through positive intent and other means allows us to stay focused on long-term goals (helping us to stay on a diet instead of eating a cookie). Kelly McGonigal (2012), in her book *The Willpower Instinct*, divides the prefrontal lobe into three areas as pictured below:

I Will, I Won't, I Want

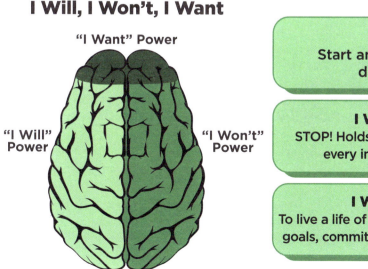

"I Want" Power

"I Will" Power

"I Won't" Power

I Will (left)
Start and stick to boring, difficult tasks.

I Won't (right)
STOP! Holds us back from following every impulse and craving.

I Want (center)
To live a life of purpose remembering our goals, commitments and highest values.

In the last decade, education has increased focus on testing, standards and core subjects. Prescriptive linear teaching practices, less recess, less arts and formalizing kindergarten have become the norm in the current era of accountability. We are systematically reducing our offering of right hemisphere-enriching activities in order to focus more time on left-hemisphere acquisition of core subjects and accountability. While our efforts may make children's progress more measurable, they inhibit the development of executive skills, goal achievement, morality and self-regulation that make true progress possible.

It is critical for educators to understand that we cannot and will not meet our educational vision for children unless we integrate the right hemisphere with the left. When we focus so heavily on left hemisphere practices, we teach children to know right from wrong, but not how to do right from wrong. Knowing we should be respectful and then behaving respectfully requires brain integration. A portal video explaining this information can help increase your understanding of these concepts.

The Skill of Positive Intent

Positive intent starts in the heart and can open our minds. It upshifts the brain from the lower centers to the higher centers and frames situations in a way that all parties in a conflict can problem-solve together. It also provides a way of integrating the left and right hemispheres so we can access our wise advocate and brilliance to produce win-win results.

> *Positive intent is essential for our most difficult and challenging children because they have defined themselves as "bad" or "unworthy," incorporated this into their self-concept and live out this self-fulfilling prophecy in school.*

Imagine you are Mark, a 5-year-old child, sitting at a table with four others. Your kindergarten teacher places a tub full of toys in front of you. The teacher thinks she is putting down counting bears for a math lesson. You know differently! These are toys! You grab the bucket of toys and lock your arms securely around it. Your eyes dart to the other children, daring them to touch your toys.

Suddenly, events unfold that make little or no sense to you. The child beside you starts to cry and another screams for the teacher. The child opposite you folds her arms across her chest and glares, saying, "You're not my friend anymore." The remaining child leaves the table to go to another area. The teacher approaches and you sense an atmosphere of increasing fear. You hold the bucket tighter to safeguard your bears.

The teacher says, "Mark, the counting bears are for all the children. How would you feel if someone had all the bears and wouldn't give you any? Don't you want to share with your friends?" If you could talk to yourself in your head, you would probably say, "No, I want them all. Does it look like I want to share?" At age five, however, you have not developed mature inner speech and communicate mostly through actions. You turn your back on your teacher and hold the bucket even tighter.

Your teacher says with increasing irritation, "Mark, should you have all the bears? What should you be doing with the bears? What is our rule about sharing in this classroom?" Since you are well aware of the rule, you respond with "take turns." Of course, knowing the answer to the question and giving up the bears are two different issues, so you put the bucket in your lap for safekeeping.

Completely frustrated, the teacher exclaims, "Mark, give me the bucket." You ignore her. She becomes even more agitated and shouts, "Mark do you want your name on the board? Do you want to sit by yourself?" You don't care where you go as long as the bears go with you! So you walk off with the bucket. Your teacher grabs the counting bears from your arms. You try to hold on and end up hitting her in the struggle. The next thing you know, you are at the principal's office and your mother is coming to get you. A sense of doom prevails.

In this story, the teacher began each attempt to persuade Mark to share by unconsciously assuming his intent was negative. When we attribute negative intent to others, we subtly attack them. We create a feeling of danger every time we try to make others feel bad, wrong or responsible for our upset. The other person often becomes defensive in response to the danger, creating conflict. The conflict mounts if we advance our agenda without inspiring the other person to cooperate. When we learn to attribute positive motives to others, we transform opposition into cooperation by evoking willingness.

Assigning negative intent to children's behavior does three things:

- It defines the core of the child and his behavior as bad.
- It throws us into the lower centers of the brain where blame and punishment are our only options.
- It defines the child as bad in the eyes of classmates and fellow teachers.

Assigning positive intent to children's behavior also does three things:

- It defines the core of the child as good enough and the child's behavior as needing to change.
- It keeps us in the higher centers of the brain where solutions and change are possible, and we can wisely discern which executive skills the child is missing to begin the teaching process.
- It defines the child as one who makes mistakes and is willing to learn in the eyes of classmates and fellow teachers.

Children will oppose us. Their ongoing development dictates that they will violate the rules and limits at certain times and in certain situations. Children need to say "no" to test limits and social rules. Passive and aggressive adults unconsciously invite children to test limits more often than those who are assertive. At each stage of life through adulthood, people resist and oppose to clarify who they are and what they believe.

Our response to challenging behaviors is critical. Many teachers assume children's motives are negative. Negative intent always encourages children to be more oppositional, as shown in our example. Mark's teacher unconsciously encouraged him to fight instead of cooperate by assuming he had selfish motives. Our first task is to inspire children to cooperate so we can teach them how to behave within acceptable limits.

Negative intent always encourages children to be more oppositional.

When Mark's teacher first realized she had a problem, she said, "Mark, the counting bears are for all the children. How would you feel if someone had all the bears and wouldn't give you any? Don't you want to share with your friends?" Her statement tells Mark his perspective is wrong. The bears are not his. They are for everyone. The teacher also implies that Mark is selfish; a kind child would willingly share. Mark faces two choices: He can submit to her attack by admitting he is wrong and give up the counting bears, or he can defend his honor by resisting. Whether Mark submits or resists depends on his temperament, age and mood. One day he might have submitted by grumpily pushing the bucket towards the middle of the table. Another day he might have submitted by relinquishing the tub and refusing to participate. In either case, his joy in the learning process would be diminished or lost. In our example, Mark chose to resist the perceived attack by holding his bucket of bears tightly.

Even if we refrain from a direct verbal attack on a child, our nonverbal communication (implication and tone) can hurt him deeply.

Even if Mark didn't hear his teacher's initial attack message, he felt it. When her first attempts to influence Mark fail, the teacher steps up her unconscious attack. She says, "Mark, should you have all the bears? What should you be doing with the bears? What is our rule about sharing in this classroom?" Her negative messages have become more direct. On a deep level, Mark hears, "What's wrong with you? Are you a stupid kid? Don't you know anything?" Again, Mark is left with two choices: submit or defend. If Mark submits, he unconsciously accepts the hurtful labels (wrong, bad, stupid) and incorporates them into his self-concept. Mark again defends his position.

The teacher, now very frustrated, shouts threats, "Mark do you want your name on the board?" Her message is, "You are guilty and deserve punishment." She has upped her negative intentions to a punitive stance. You may be thinking, "But the punishment will teach him a lesson!" You may be thinking, "Doesn't he need to know his behavior was wrong?" Yes, he does need to adjust his behaviors. However, our goal is to communicate this information in a manner the child can hear and to create an environment he can maintain his dignity in while choosing to cooperate. If Mark hears repeatedly that he just wants things for himself and doesn't care about others, he will come to view himself as selfish. He will act in a way that confirms this self-image. This is called a self-fulfilling prophecy. Remember, what we focus on, we get more of. I would suggest that Mark is five years old, still learning how to share. He is trying to influence others and make the world go his way in the best way he can at the moment. If we believe our job is to equip Mark with the executive skills to do it differently next time, then a punishing approach will not serve our goal. Punishment will merely stall him in the lower brain states where learning is impossible and his skill set is limited. Rather than punish him, we need to assist Mark in regaining an executive state so he can learn that life won't always go his way, that he can handle that fact and that there are skills he can use to do it differently next time. He does not need the message that he is a bad, selfish, disrespectful little boy.

When the attack-defend process gets rolling, communication and connection break down.

The attack-defend process causes us to lose the ability to reach or teach others. It also leads us to punish ourselves when we make a mistake. The blame we heap on ourselves keeps us in the lower centers of our brain, believing the messages on our CD-Roms. We often feel bad about ourselves (limbic state) but seem paralyzed to resolve our problems (problem-solving is an executive state function). We cannot simultaneously feel bad about our situation and focus on what we must do to change it. It is our choice to bask in guilt or improve our lives.

There is a better way to help our children handle conflict. Since conflicts arise when we proceed without first winning cooperation, we must do something to confirm ourselves as allies at the very beginning of an exchange. We can do this by assuming that the child's motives are positive. Instead of seeing the child as bad or trying to make life difficult, shift that perception! Assume the child is simply trying to achieve a goal but lacks the appropriate skills to do so.

Activity to Determine Mark's True Intent

When Mark grabbed the bears, what do you think was his intention? Check one:

- ❏ He wanted to keep the other children from learning math.

- ❏ He wanted to humiliate the teacher in front of the other children.

- ❏ He wanted to disrespect the teacher's authority.

- ❏ He wanted to make sure he got enough counting bears.

Answer: The truth is we don't know Mark's intention. We make it up. If we are going to make it up, we might as well make it positive. When we define children positively, we hold them in high esteem, keeping both the child and ourselves in a higher brain state. The first three choices attributed negative intent, while the last response attributes positive motives to Mark.

> *If we are going to make up a child's intention, we might as well make it positive!*

When we attribute positive motives to a child's behavior, we position ourselves to teach and the child to learn. We also model respect and loving kindness. Picture yourself again as little Mark. You have just grabbed all the counting bears. Your teacher approaches and says, "Mark, you wanted to be sure you have enough counting bears. I want you to have enough, too. Count out 10 bears for yourself and 10 bears for each person at the table." Can you feel how beginning the interaction with positive intent is more likely to elicit cooperation? The following further illustrates the contrast between negative and positive intent:

Negative Intent:

Adam: "I don't want to hold your hand."
Dylan: "You're my partner and I need to hold your hand."
Adam: Pushes Dylan away roughly and screams, "No!"
Teacher: "Adam, what are you doing? Was that nice to push your partner? How do you think he feels when you push him and refuse to hold his hand? Would you want someone to treat you like that? Go to the end of the line. You will not have a partner today."
Adam: Screams, "No!" and runs down the hall.
Teacher: Sends two children to the office for help in covering the class and catching Adam.

Positive Intent:

Teacher: "Oh Dylan, Adam pushed your hand away like this and screamed, *No!* Did you like it?"
Dylan: "No."
Teacher: "Tell Adam, *I don't like it when you push my hand away and scream at me. Say, Let's walk side-by-side today without holding hands.*"
Teacher: "Adam, you wanted to walk without holding hands today and you wanted Dylan to understand this. When you want to walk side-by-side say, *Dylan, let's just walk side-by-side today without holding hands.*"
Teacher: Says to both boys, "Today you two will walk beside each other with your hands at your sides. You will be a different kind of partner."
Boys: Both boys walk quietly down the hall side-by-side.

In the first example, the teacher both implied and stated Adam's badness. Adam's reaction to this was predictable. In the second scenario, she attributed a positive motive to him. She stayed calm, helped the children be calm and taught them important new skills. Dylan learned to be assertive when he had been wronged. Adam learned to ask for help instead of lashing out physically when frustrated. The teacher learned to be flexible and open to new ways of being partners.

When we attribute positive intent to a child's behavior we are able to stay calm and help calm our children. We send children the message that their inner core and their essence are good enough. We also send the message that their choices of behavior are not helpful. With this frame as the backdrop, most children are willing and motivated to learn a new skill, comply with adult commands or choose a more appropriate behavioral response.

Building Bullies and Gang Readiness Through Negative Intent

As we've discussed, our intent shapes children's self image and the way others see them. Imagine you are in the classrooms below. What is your image of the aggressive child, the victimized child and the teacher? Who do you perceive to have control of the situation? What social skills are being modeled?

> Liam is working on math work at his desk. Mason stares off into space for a while, then grabs Liam's notebook and begins to write on it. Liam screams, "You stupid butt!" as he pushes Mason's shoulder and takes back the notebook.

Classroom A: Mrs. McGhee hears the commotion and responds, "Liam you know better than to call names and push people. You know the rules in this classroom. Liam tries to explain, "But, but he..." Mrs. McGhee replies firmly, "No excuses! Go turn your card to red. You will lose 10 minutes of recess today." Liam tries again to explain, "He took my math notebook and…" Mrs. McGhee raises her voice and says, "I don't care what he did. It's no reason to name call and push. One more word and you will get a discipline referral. Is that what you want to happen?" Liam knocks his desk over in frustration.

- What is your image of Liam? Would you want to sit next to him and continue being friends?

  _____

- What is your image of Mason? Would you want to sit next to him and continue being friends?

  _____

- What skills for dealing with conflict did you learn from Mrs. McGhee?

  _____

- Who do you think had control of the situation?

  _____

- Would you go to Mrs. McGhee in the future if you had a problem?

  _____

Classroom B: Mrs. McGhee hears the commotion and immediately takes a deep breath as she goes over to help with the problem. She enters the scene describing what she is seeing. "Mason, you're holding your shoulder like this." (Model the action.) Mason responds, "Liam pushed me!" Mrs. McGhee asks, "Did you like it?" "NO!" screams Mason. Liam snaps back, "Well, he took my notebook and wrote all over it!" Mrs. McGhee asks, "Did you like it?" Liam responds, "No! I was working." Mrs. McGhee reframes the situation with positive intent, "No wonder you're both feeling angry. Neither one of you knew the words to use to work things out. Take a deep S.T.A.R. breath with me." They all breathe. She continues, "Mason, you wanted to get Liam's attention. When you want his attention, tap him on the shoulder, wait for him to look at you and say, *Hey Liam*. Liam, you wanted your notebook back. When you want your belongings, hold out your hand like this and say, *Mason, please give me back my notebook*. Try a do-over using your new skills now."

Liam speaks assertively to Mason. Mason returns the notebook, but Liam's body slumps when he sees all the scribbles on it. Mrs. McGhee notices this aloud. Liam responds, "It is messed up with scribbles." Mrs. McGhee says, "That is a problem. Mason, what could you do to be helpful?" Mason says, "I was bored and wanted to play with Liam. I guess I could erase my stuff." Mrs. McGhee then turns to Liam and says, "Mason was bored because he is having trouble with math. What could you do to help him?" Liam says, "Once we get my paper clean, I could help him with the problems." "Both solutions would be helpful," responds Mrs. McGhee, "I will check on your progress as you both follow through on your commitments. You can do it."

- What is your image of Liam? Would you want to sit next to him and continue being friends?

  _____

- What is your image of Mason? Would you want to sit next to him and continue being friends?

  _____

- What conflict resolution skills did you learn?

  _____

- Who do you think had control of the situation?

  _____

- Would you go to Mrs. McGhee in the future if you had a problem?

  _____

Negative intent unconsciously labels and defines children as bad, mean, selfish or inconsiderate. Children usually accept these labels over time and become aggressive, withdrawn and/or exhibit bullying behaviors. Their peers quickly learn who the bad children are, and either exclude or befriend them. Those who choose to befriend them are generally other "bad" kids. With negative intent, we are leading kids to define themselves as bad, and helping the bad kids find each other and bond. Our negative intent promotes the formation of cliques and builds gang readiness. Offering positive intent to challenging children keeps them in an executive state so they are willing to learn how to solve problems and remain members of the School Family.

Bully Prevention Must Start Young

A meta-analysis of bullying intervention programs across a 25-year period from 1980 through 2004 showed the majority of programs evidenced no meaningful change (Merrell, Isava, Gueldner, & Ross 2008). Another study of 7,000 sixth through tenth grade students from 195 schools led researchers at Michigan State to conclude that bullying prevention programs actually contribute to an increase in bullying: "Contrary to our hypothesis, students attending schools with bullying prevention programs were more likely to experience peer victimization compared to those attending schools without bullying prevention programs (Jeong & Lee, 2013)."

Traditional bully prevention programs – often full of handy slogans and zero tolerance approaches – have no effect or actually increase bullying. Conscious Discipline approaches bullying differently, so our results are different. In Conscious Discipline, bully prevention begins with seeing both the victim and the bully through the Power of Love, embracing their calls for help, and bringing both back into the school community.

Bullying is a specific form of aggressive behavior that is intentional (designed to be physically and/or psychologically hurtful), threatening and persistent. It occurs within relationships where an imbalance of power exists. A bullying culture can develop anywhere people interact, including schools, families, workplaces and neighborhoods. Any culture that is competitive, autocratic and based on external controls can be a breeding ground for bully/victim relationships.

The overwhelming majority of school cultures are competitive, based on external and autocratic controls. They are primed to create the bully/victim relationships they seek to stomp out. Bullying will continue to flourish unless we change our approach from an autocratic power-over culture to an inclusive, compassionate, democratic School Family that utilizes positive intent to see the best in children who act out. These kids don't just show up in school one day and decide, "I think I'll be a bully!" It takes years to become a bully and all bullies actually start out as victims.

> The good news about bullying is that we are becoming conscious of it and the problems it creates. The bad news is we are now confusing all aggressive acts with bullying. Children come home from school and instead of saying, "He pushed me," they are saying, "He bullied me." Successful intervention requires that we differentiate between everyday aggression and bullying.

Becoming a bully is a journey of specific life experiences starting at birth. Conscious Discipline produced a video called "How to Make a Bully From Scratch" that examines the five road signs of a bully in the making. Watch this powerful piece on your web portal or on YouTube. Bullies are disconnected children and each road sign represents another form of disconnection. We can choose to intervene at any time using the Conscious Discipline skills you are learning in this book.

Road Sign 1: Attachment Difficulties (0-3 Years)

Some children who have experienced prenatal stressors will be born with difficult temperaments. Some children with difficult temperaments will have insecure attachments with their primary caregivers. Lacking a secure attachment, their behavior can be difficult to manage and some will receive harsh punishment. When this occurs by age three, we start to see two different types of victims emerging. One is aggressive, defiant and hot tempered. The other is passive, acquiescent and anxious.

Road Sign 2: Difficulty Playing With Friends (3-5 Years)

During this time, children find themselves in more complex social settings like school and childcare. The aggressive child grabs, hits and explodes when the world does not go her way. The passive child simply gives up. They both have trouble playing with others because they lack basic social skills and the ability to regulate behavior. Teachers may compound the problem by using exclusionary strategies such as timeout, suspension and expulsion.

Road Sign 3: Difficult Making Friends (6-8 Years)

The exclusion gets worse as both children move further into the world of friends. Both children (aggressive and passive) experience immense social pain. Social pain actually involves the same pathways in the brain as physical pain in the body. Somewhere during this time, the social pain of rejection becomes so great that the brain undergoes significant changes, and a bully and a chronic victim emerge.

Road Sign 4: Social Exclusion and Chronic "I Don't Care" Language (8-12 Years)

The part of the brain responsible for the motivation to care is now turned off in both the bully and the victim, so there is no punishment or reward that will help them. When children say, "I don't care," their brains are saying, "I don't feel cared for by anyone." Rewiring both the bully's and the victim's systems can only occur through intense connection with others.

Road Sign 5: The Brain's Empathy System is Offline (Teen Years)

At this age, the bully may join a gang of tough guys or hook up with a clique of mean girls. They perfect their craft through cyber bullying, spreading rumors, physical action and day-to-day threats. At this point, the bully is a dangerous teenager whose brain has changed in two very significant ways:

- The brain has become programmed to biochemically experience pleasure from hurting others. The bully's internal pharmacy provides him with opioids that act like morphine to deaden the pain of his life journey. The teenager is literally addicted to causing others pain.
- The brain is immune to rejection and ostracism. This teenager no longer feels a need to belong or care. Empathy is completely offline.

Our victim, on the other hand, lacks the internal pharmacy that a bully has to provide himself with relief. The teenage victim is prone to suffering quietly and then exploding. The pain can become so intense that the he may commit suicide or kill others, as we have seen play out in school shootings.

Bullying a bully with tough measures and excluding him with zero tolerance policies compounds the problem. We are systemically applying the exact treatment that created the bully and then expecting it to help. Bully prevention must start in the early childhood years. It involves creating a School Family, and teaching the self-regulation and social skills necessary to get along with others. None of this is possible unless we use all of our Conscious Discipline skills to help children access an executive state. Specifically, the Skill of Positive Intent will help us see the best in others so they can see the best in themselves. Watch videos of interventions for each road sign on your portal.

Reframing Our Intent From Negative to Positive

Committing ourselves to view the world through a different set of lenses doesn't mean we will automatically be successful. We will need to consciously choose to reframe situations over and over again until this new perspective becomes our pattern. Whenever we are upset, we are focused on what we don't want and have attributed negative intent. The easiest way to know if we need to reframe a situation is to ask ourselves if we're upset. If the answer is, "Yes," then it's time to reframe it:

- Notice if you are upset. Actively calm yourself. (S.T.A.R., "I'm safe, keep breathing, I can handle this," and wish well.)
- Focus on what you want to happen. Shift your attention and your intention will follow.
- Change your beliefs about the other person's motives from negative to positive.

Activity to Move From Negative to Positive Intent

Reframe the negative intent to a positive intent.

Negative Intent	Positive Reframing
Some children are just mean.	Some children need social skills.
They sure know how to push my buttons.	_____
He's being hurtful for no reason.	_____
He keeps others from learning.	_____
She is disrupting the whole class.	_____
She is plain old lazy.	_____

As you look over your answers, notice that negative intent leaves us stuck in the problem and positive intent opens the problem up for solutions. "Some children are just mean" leaves us powerless and hopeless. "Some children need social skills" puts us in a position to make a difference in children's lives. In the examples below, practice seeing what the child wanted instead of what the child did in order to set the situation up for problem-solving and teaching. Use the phrases "You wanted ___" and "You were hoping ___" to help make this shift.

Negative Intent	Positive Reframing
A child pushes another child.	You wanted _____.
A child ignores your direction to shut down the computer.	You were hoping _____.
Emma takes some of Elton's popcorn when he is not looking.	You wanted_____.
A child grabs a pencil from another.	You wanted _____.
A child says, "Move it, stupid."	You wanted _____.

Sample responses for both exercises can be found on the web portal.

Once we have attributed positive intent, all parties are more likely to be operating from an executive state. In an executive state, the child is asking, "What can I learn?" and we can ask ourselves, "How can I help the child be successful at _____?" We are now in a position to teach children the missing social skills needed to be successful. We might say, "You wanted her to move. When you want her to move, say, *Move please*."

Commitment: Breathe deeply, relax and affirm to yourself: "What I see in others I strengthen in myself. I cannot attack others without hurting myself. I am willing to see children's disruptive and aggressive behaviors as a call for help. I understand this does not get them off the hook, but it does unhook me to better guide them into using socially acceptable behaviors to get their needs met.

Signature: _____ Date: _____

Positive Intent, Hurtful Actions

Up until this point, we have focused on **seeing** the situation differently. It is also essential for us to **respond** to the situation differently. Positive intent is the second-to-last skill in the book because nearly all the other skills are needed to help us utilize positive intent. Here are the basic skills necessary:

- We must access composure by actively calming ourselves (S.T.A.R.).
- We must assertively focus on what we want.
- We must empower victims to use their BIG Voice.
- We must create a compassionate encouraging School Family culture so children are willing to learn a better way.
- We must offer empathy to upset children to help them access an executive state.

With these skills in mind, we are ready to address hurtful actions by teaching new skills to both victim and aggressor.

Teach the Victim Assertiveness Skills

Before we enter the conflict, we will upload calm, focus on what we want and offer positive intent to all parties involved. We will always go to the victim first unless violence is a concern. Approaching the victim first shows we value healing over hurting. It also empowers the victim to teach others how to treat him. As discussed in Chapter 5 (Assertiveness), ask the victim, "Did you like it?" Then provide the necessary assertiveness training through coaching. For example, "Tell Cameron, *I don't like it when you push me. Walk around me, please.*" The children's book *Shubert's BIG Voice* does an excellent job of showing this process. In many cases, you will then support the victim in teaching the aggressor new social skills by using the following six-step "Teach the Aggressor" process.

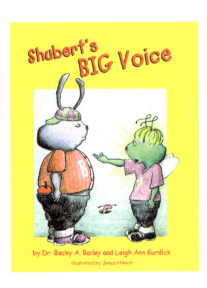

Shubert's BIG Voice

by Dr. Becky A. Bailey and Leigh Ann Burdick
illustrated by James Hrkach

 Watch videos of young people paying it forward by using their BIG Voices.

Teach the Aggressor a New Skill

Teach the aggressive child new skills using the six-step process below. Our intent as we approach the aggressor will foster the willingness to learn new skills or it will foster aggression and resistance. Therefore, it is essential to begin every interaction with positive intent.

Step 1: **Offer positive intent:** Restate the aggressive child's motive using positive intent. Do this by completing the sentence, "You wanted ____" or "You were hoping ____." This builds security and cooperation.

"You wanted Malik to move."

Step 2: **Notice the action without judgment:** State the skill the child used to achieve his goal. Make no judgment; simply notice the child's actions. Use a phrase like, "So you ____." This builds awareness, stimulating the frontal lobes.

"You wanted Malik to move, so you pushed him."

Step 3: **State the missing skill by giving the benefit of the doubt to the child:** The phrases, "You didn't know the words to use to ____" and "You didn't know what else to do," define the child as a good person who made a mistake.

"You wanted Malik to move, so you pushed him. You didn't know what else to do."

Step 4: **Set the limit:** State the limit and why it is needed. This gives the child a clear boundary. Do this by completing the sentence, "You may not ____. ____ hurts." Relate the undesired skill to hurtfulness or a lack of safety in order to tie the child's action back to the School Family commitment to help keep the classroom safe.

"You wanted Malik to move, so you pushed him. You didn't know what else to do. You may not push. Pushing is hurtful."

Step 5: **Teach a new skill:** To teach the child a new course of action, say, "When you want ____, say (or do) ____. Say (or do) it now."

"You wanted Malik to move, so you pushed him. You didn't know what else to do. You may not push. Pushing is hurtful. When you want Malik to move, say, *Move please*. Say it now for practice."

Step 6: **Offer encouragement:** Encourage both children for their willingness to try a different approach. Come up with a symbolic way to repair the relationship.

"You did it! You tried a new way. Are you both willing to work together to do things differently from now on? What can you do or say to recommit to being helpful friends?"

Activity to Practice Positive Intent for Hurtful Actions

Situation 1: Sydney pushes Caleb away from the water fountain.

Teach Victim Assertiveness First
Notice: "Caleb, Sydney just pushed you away from the water fountain because she was so thirsty. Did you like it?" (Pause for response.)
Teach: "Tell Sydney, *I don't like it when you push! Wait behind me.*"

Then Teach Aggressor a New Skill

Step 1 - Positive intent: "Sydney, you wanted _____."

Step 2 - Notice: "So you _____."

Step 3 - State the missing skill: "You didn't know _____."

Step 4 - Set limits: "You may not _____. _____ hurts."

Step 5 - Teach: "When you want _____, say (or do) _____."

Step 6 - Encourage: "You did it!"

Situation 2: Noah hits Angie for no apparent reason.

Teach Victim Assertiveness First
Notice: "Angie, Noah just walked over and hit you. Did you like it?" (Pause for response.)
Teach: "Tell Noah, *I don't like it when you hit me. If you feel mad, go to the Safe Place.*"

Then Teach Aggressor a New Skill

Step 1 - Positive intent: "Noah, you wanted _____."
(Take your best educated guess.)

Step 2 - Notice: "So you _____."

Step 3 - State the missing skill: "You didn't know _____."

Step 4 - Set limits: "You may not _____. _____ hurts. It is not safe."

Step 5 - Teach: "When you want _____, say (or do) _____."

Step 6 - Encourage: "You did it!"

 Possible answers: There are no right answers. Remember, the goal is to see the best in each moment and in each child. Examples of possible solutions are on your portal along with videos of the process in action.

A.C.T. When Time is Short

The previous process is for older children when time allows. Sometimes you must just act. Use the A.C.T. version of the previous strategy for younger children or when time is an issue.

A. <u>A</u>cknowledge the child's deepest desire and intent.
"You wanted _____" or "You were hoping _____."

C. <u>C</u>larify what skills to use.
"When you want _____ then say (or do) _____."

T. <u>T</u>ake time to practice.
"Say (or do) it now for practice."

Teach children the nonverbal actions that go with the social skills they are learning. For example, when a child is learning to ask for a turn, she would need to practice holding her hand out, palm up and saying, "Turn, please." When a child is learning to get another person's attention, she would practice tapping her friend on the shoulder, waiting for him to look and then calling him by name. The portal houses several videos of young children learning new skills through this process.

Activity to Practice A.C.T.

Two-year-old DeShawn is playing next to Garrett. He reaches to take the ball Garrett is holding.

"DeShawn, you wanted _____.

When you want _____,

say _____. Let's practice!"

Three-year old Savannah pats Emily on the head several times to get her attention.

"Savannah, you wanted _____.

When you want _____,

say _____. Let's practice!"

> Biting is a primal act that requires a different approach, especially for children younger than three years old in group settings. Children who bite after age three are sending a red flag that must be addressed. Visit your portal to access a biting program that helps navigate this difficult issue.

When We Don't Know What the Child Wanted

Sometimes we really don't have a clue what the child wanted. All we see is a child using a nonverbal communication strategy (hitting, pushing) to achieve a goal. We have two choices when this happens: take our best guess and let the child correct us, or notice the nonverbal actions and wait for a response. Noticing integrates the left and right hemispheres so the child will often begin to talk about what happened. If the child remains quiet we could add, "Something happened," in an inquiring tone of voice. Below is an example of what this looks like:

Situation: Child slams his math book shut and slumps down in his chair with arms crossed.
Notice: "You slammed your book and slumped in your chair with your arms like this. (Imitate the child and download calm.) Your body is telling me you might feel frustrated."
Child: "I can't do math. It's stupid."
Positive intent: "You wanted to let me know you need help with math, so you slammed your book. You didn't know what else to do. When you feel frustrated, raise your hand for help like this."
Practice: "Raise your hand now to show me how you will ask for help. There you go. Good for you!"

Positive Intent, Hurtful Words

Physical aggression is the hallmark of a survival state. When children are in an emotional state, they are likely to be hurtful with words. These children verbally exclude others. "Bug off, we don't like you!" They attack through name calling. "Beat it, lard bucket!" They disrupt the learning process with their inability to manage their emotions. Whether in a physical survival state or a mouthy emotional state, we can use positive intent to transform these moments of negativity into positive interactions where all parties learn a helpful means of expression.

Situation: "Go away, stupid."
Monica is talking with some friends when Sandra approaches the group. Monica turns to Sandra and says, "Go away, stupid." The teacher sees this occur.

Teach Victim Assertiveness First
Notice: The teacher approaches Sandra by saying, "Monica just called you a name. Did you like how she spoke to you?" Sandra replies, "No,"
Teach: Coach Sandra to assertively speak to Monica, telling her the exact words to use. "Sandra, tell Monica, *I don't like it when you call me names. My name is Sandra. Please use it.*"

Then Teach Aggressor a New Skill
Step 1 - Positive intent: "Monica, you wanted to let Sandra know you were busy talking to your friends."
Step 2 - Notice: "So you called her a hurtful name."
Step 3 - State the missing skill: "You seemed frustrated and didn't know any other way to get your point across."
Step 4 - Set limit: "You may not call people names, name calling is hurtful."
Step 5 - Teach: "When you want to let a classmate know you want privacy with your friends, say, *Sandra, this is personal. I would like to talk to my friends alone. We can talk later.* Say it now, so you can practice what to say that is helpful and not hurtful."
Step 6 - Encourage: "It's hard to do things differently when feelings have been hurt. Both of you gave it a try. Good for you both. Do you want to give high fives or pinky hugs to show you are still part of the School Family and respect each other."

Activity to Use Positive Intent for Hurtful Words

Role-play the following scenes with a partner. Address the victim first to teach assertiveness and then address the aggressor with positive intent to create a teaching moment. After the role-play, check in with each other using the questions below.

Scene 1: James calls Kareem "gay" when he shows up wearing pink socks.
Scene 2: Melissa calls Sheila "stupid face" when she answers a math problem incorrectly.
Scene 3: Several boys are chanting, "Girls suck!"

1. Did you go to the victim first? Did you ask, "Did you like it?" or did you Oops and say, "How did that make you feel?"
2. Did you empower the victim by giving the exact words to say or did you ask, "What could you say?"
3. Did you offer positive intent to the aggressor with, "You wanted ____?" or did you start with, "Why did you _____?"
4. Did you set the limit and relate the aggressor's actions to hurtfulness/safety or did you launch into a lecture?
5. Did you ask the aggressor to practice the skill right away?
6. Did you encourage both students at the end? What words did you say?

Flip and Reflect: Moving From Complaints to Solutions

There is a difference between the intensity of an upset emotional state and everyday complaining. Since the right prefrontal lobe processes negative emotions, it is the center of basic complaints and pessimism. Everyday complaining, "Can you believe the amount of paper work we have?" is different than emotional upset, "I hate this paper work. There is no time to teach. This is the most ridiculous policy ever!" Positive intent phrases "You wanted _____." or "You were hoping _____" are perfect for flipping everyday complaining into possible solutions.

When coping with complaining parents, co-workers or students, "So you _____" and "So you were hoping _____" help us flip the statement from what they don't want to what they do want and reflect it back to them. It's also helpful to use this phrasing to transform our internal speech when we're the ones complaining. The following are examples:

Complaining Parents
Parent: My child never brings home homework. I don't know what is going on in your classroom.
Teacher: So, you want to stay in touch with your child's progress.

Complaining Coworkers
Coworker: Parents today. I can't get them to return a call, sign papers or do anything!
Teacher: You were hoping the parents would work with you this year.

Complaining Children
Student: Do we have to do this? It's boring.
Teacher: You were hoping we could do more science.

Complaining Self
Self: What was I thinking? The politics in education will never change.
Self: I was hoping the focus would shift to the needs of the child.

By entering interactions attributing positive intent instead of judging the situation as bad, we lay the groundwork for teaching moments and goal-achievement. This promotes safety, connection and problem-solving in the classroom.

Positive Intent Embeds Problem-Solving in Your School Family

The following structure, ritual and routine help children internalize problem-solving as a lifelong skill as we utilize the Skill of Positive Intent to create teaching moments and the Power of Love to see the best in others.

Structure: Celebration Center

The purpose of this center is to celebrate children. Celebrate events of change such as losing a tooth, welcoming a new sibling, an older sibling's graduation or a great grandmother's birthday. Celebrate children's efforts in academics and efforts to be helpful. Celebrate things the children suggest and that are important to them. The Celebration Center is a way for children to honor each other, their achievements and their commitments. It is not a place to give rewards for special events or good behavior.

Younger Children

The Celebration Center for young children often consists of a special celebration chair and a prop box. I suggest using a chair the children have painted and decorated themselves. The prop box contains items that support the celebration and remains beside or beneath the chair. One teacher kept a large wooden tooth necklace in the celebration prop box. A child who had lost a tooth would sit in the celebration chair wearing the tooth necklace as the class sang the Tooth Song.

Tooth Song
Sing to the tune of "The Farmer in the Dell"

You lost a tooth.	New ones will grow.
You lost a tooth.	New ones will grow.
You are growing day by day.	You lost a tooth today.
You lost a tooth.	And new ones will grow!

Older Children

Children in older grades can help decide what will constitute their Celebration Center, what they would like to celebrate and how they will go about celebrating. A fourth grade classroom decided their Celebration Center would be on the computer. During designated times, students could go to the computer and make a certificate for a classmate. They would then share what they had done with the teacher and discuss their plan to present the certificate during the morning routine. If the teacher approved the plan, the event occurred. On the morning I visited this particular classroom, Douglas received a celebration certificate from the class in honor of his spelling achievements. He received a certificate for improvement and the following poem:

> *You couldn't spell,*
> *On the test you would fail!*
> *You could have given up! And you did a time or two,*
> *But you dug deep and worked harder, until you knew,*
> *How to spell a word or two!*
> *So, good for you! Good for you!*

Douglas' response was charming. He said, "Thanks for caring, spelled: K-A-R-I-N-G." The class laughed and the teacher looked nervous. Then he said, "Just kidding! Spelled: C-I-D-D-I-N-G." The laughter increased and this time the teacher joined in. Go to Shubert's School online to watch videos of all kinds of classroom celebrations.

Celebration Chair

Celebration Board

Ritual: Wishing Well

Hopefully, you have been wishing well in your classroom throughout the year, beginning with wishing absent children well. Now it is time, if you have not done so already, to extend wishing well to all the many situations children find difficult to understand and cope with. Children may want to wish well for a sick relative, a parent who lost a job or a big sister who is taking a test. Set up opportunities for this to happen during your morning routine, closing routine and other daily activities. Invite children to share and wish well, and do the same yourself.

Routine: School Family Assemblies

Add School Family Assemblies to your yearly calendar once a month, once every nine weeks or quarterly. The School Family Assembly has three goals:

1. To contribute to the School Family culture of safety, connection and problem-solving
2. To foster the school-wide implementation of Conscious Discipline
3. To link the school to homes and the community

Work with administrators and staff to model your assemblies after the Brain Smart Start discussed in Chapter 4. Ask for volunteers to plan and design them. As everyone becomes more confident, turn as much of the planning and organization of the assemblies over to the children as their age permits. Below is an outline for a School Family Assembly. The *Creating the School Family* book includes additional assembly plans, while the web portal contains assembly videos and a song list for each of the components below.

> **Entrance Song**
> **Activity to Unite:** Welcome announcement and uniting song
> **Activity to Disengage Stress:** These follow all high-energy activities
> **Activities to Connect:**
> * Welcome new students and faculty
> * Acknowledge birthdays
> * Celebrate
> **Mini Conscious Discipline Lesson** from the Principal or designated team
> **Activity to Commit**
> **Ending Song and Exit**

Entrance Song: Getting all the classes in and out of the assembly space requires planning, practicing and displaying expectations in picture form. M.A.P. out all expectations (**M**odel, **A**dd visuals and **P**ractice). Play a song as children enter. As each class sits down, coach them to do specific song movements in their seats.

Activity to Unite: Welcome children, staff, faculty, and any family or community members joining the event. "Welcome to the Little River School Family Assembly. At Little River, my job is to keep the school safe. Your job is to _____." Have attendees respond, "Help keep it safe." Then have attendees take three S.T.A.R. breaths. "We keep it safe by remembering our school-wide agreements (mission statement, etc). Let's say them together now. (Say them together.) Remember, an agreement is a promise we make to ourselves (point to self), to our friends (point to friends), to our teachers (point to a teacher) and to our communities (point to a guest). If you are willing to help keep Little River a safe school, give a thumbs up." Then conduct a uniting song that involves specific movements.

Activity to Disengage Stress: After each song or high-energy activity, instruct the children to S.T.A.R., Drain, Pretzel or Balloon.

Activities to Connect: Invite new students, families, staff or faculty members to stand up and be welcomed with a round of applause or silent cheering. Sing the song "Welcome" from *It Starts in the Heart*. (You may want to cut the songs down to around a minute to keep the assembly moving along.) Then invite all those who have had a birthday since the last assembly to stand and sing *On the Day You Were Born* by Red Grammar. Finally, invite children up to share celebrations. Be certain to have teachers preselect these students and encourage them to celebrate whatever they choose.

At Fern Creek Elementary School in Orlando, Florida, the school-wide celebration involves children marching across the stage, stopping at the microphone and announcing their celebrations. Some would say, "My name is Terrell. I am in Mrs. Robin's second grade classroom. I am celebrating my mom's new job." The crowd would cheer. On one occasion, 5-year-old D'Mario walked up to microphone and said, "I am celebrating I didn't hit nobody," and started walking away. The crowd cheered for his success. He returned quickly to the microphone and added, "All day!" The crowd roared.

We often imply what should be celebrated, like good grades or the number of books read. This dampens children's ownership of success and joy in their celebration. We must free children to celebrate what they find meaningful. When Fern Creek (a Title 1 elementary school) first started doing celebrations, most of the children chose non-academic accomplishments. By the second year of Conscious Discipline implementation, most of what the children chose to celebrate had to do with academics. They had learned the joy of learning for themselves.

Mini Lesson: Conduct mini lessons (no more than three to five minutes) that complement what you are learning about Conscious Discipline as a faculty. If you are doing a monthly faculty book study and monthly assemblies, create a lesson from each skill chapter. The first assembly would be about composure through belly breathing. The second assembly would be about assertively using your BIG Voice. Some schools have children act out the Shubert books as part of the mini lesson.

Activity to Commit: Pick one specific thing from the mini lesson and ask attendees if they are willing to commit to practicing that particular skill or have that specific focus. Have some kind of chant or motion (thumbs up) to signal the commitment. Follow up with morning announcements, hall bulletin boards and classroom activities that reinforce the concept.

Ending Song and Exit: Select an ending song and have the classrooms exit in preplanned ways. Use the M.A.P. process like you did for the entrance procedure. The goal is for all those who attend the assembly to feel more love, joy, connection and motivation in their hearts. This includes the staff! If teachers seem to feel like they are policing children instead of joining in the fun, invest additional time in planning and focus vigilantly on what you want to happen.

Student-led School Family Assembly

Practicing S.T.A.R. in School Family Assembly

Positive Intent Summary

Power:	Love: See the best in others.
Becoming Brain Smart:	Positive Intent integrates the brain and produces oxytocin, increasing trust, safety and moral behavior.
Skill:	"You wanted___," "You were hoping___," A.C.T., Reframing
School Family:	Celebration Center, Wishing Well, School Family Assemblies

Power of Love Reflection

We've explored how the willingness to see the best in others allows us to hold hope for the hopeless, safety for the fearful and encouragement for the discouraged. The Power of Love and the Skill of Positive Intent transform resistance into willingness, and set the stage to teach new skills to those who call for help through hurtful actions and words. Begin practicing the Power of Love by doing the following:

❏ **Reflect on what we unconsciously value.** What we see with our eyes, we value with our heart.

❏ **Attribute positive intent to ourselves.** Instead of chiding, "I can't believe I forgot to go to the store," reframe it. Say, "I wanted to get home in time to greet the children when they got off the school bus, so I will spend time with the children now and go to the store later."

❏ **Consciously notice how often we try to determine others' intentions.** How much energy does this occupy? Pay attention to how often we attribute negative intent to our selves, our partners, our colleagues and the children we teach. Who do we tend to give the benefit of the doubt to and who are we hardest in judging?

❏ **Continue wishing well.** Encourage children to wish well by providing ample opportunities throughout the day. Personally wish ourselves and others well when difficulty arises.

❏ **Practice reframing negative intent to positive intent.** Reframe upset! Take a deep breath and say, "I am willing to see this differently." Then ask, "Am I extending love or calling for help?" Obtain the help you need.

❏ **Watch the Power of Love video** on the portal to deepen your reflection.

Brain Smart Teaching Moments

Look for times when children are hurtful to each other with words or actions; do not wait for the victim to come to you. Proactively use these conflicts as teaching opportunities in your classroom. Work vigilantly on offering positive intent to the aggressor and going to the victim first (except in cases where a child may hurt many children at once).

Behaviors to Use as Teaching Moments

Physical Hurtfulness	Social/Emotional Hurtfulness
• Pushing	• Name calling
• Grabbing	• Exclusion
• Poking	• Racism
• Hitting	• Sexism
• Tripping	• Intolerance of physical differences

Skill Reflection: Common and Conscious

If possible, partner up with someone and say the two statements out loud. See if you can feel the difference. After each statement share, "The difference between Common and Conscious for me was…"

Common	Conscious
He keeps others from learning.	He needs more individualized work to be successful.
She is disrupting this class.	She needs help to stay on task.
She is just plain lazy.	She needs help to get started.

School Family Implementation Checklist

- ❏ **Attribute positive intent with the phrase "You wanted ___"** to teach social skills such as turn taking, asking for help and getting another person's attention.

- ❏ **Offer positive intent and/or use A.C.T.** to transform challenging and aggressive behaviors into teaching moments.

- ❏ **Notice instead of judge** when we cannot figure out what a child wants.

- ❏ **Trust children to correct "You wanted" statements** if our educated guesses are incorrect.

- ❏ **Create a Celebration Center.**

- ❏ **Establish School Family Assemblies.**

- ❏ **Use the website, including Shubert's School and the portal,** with a focus on positive intent, celebrations, wishing well and assemblies.

Chapter 10

CONSEQUENCES

Helping children learn from their mistakes

Consequences teach children to examine their behavior, reflect on the impact of their choices and make changes until they reach their highest goals.

Well, we've made it to the Skill of Consequences! This skill is last, not because it's less valuable than the others, but because it requires the other six skills to be effective. With the traditional approach to consequences, the same children end up with the same consequences day in and day out. What story have you told yourself about these children; are they hardheaded, stupid or purposefully defiant? Has your heart ached as you've marched them to the office and watched them fail to receive the rewards that come regularly to others? Ineffective consequences discourage children and teachers. Discouraged children are disconnected. Disconnected children are dangerous to themselves and others.

Generally, we use consequences as a punishment for undesired behavior. It's time for a change! This entire book has prepared us to create schools and classrooms that are based on **effective** consequences that foster permanent behavior change. The true consequence of an act isn't the physical result of the action, it is the way we feel about the result. Our feeling about the result motivates us to act. Without access to and ownership of our feelings, we will blame the consequences of our actions on others and external situations. This shifts our motivation from changing ourselves to trying to make others change so we feel safe and loved. There is a better way!

The icon representing this skill is a maze. Each turn in the maze gives us feedback as to our next wisest move. Taking a wrong turn does not make us bad; it simply asks us to choose again. Mistakes are opportunities to learn. As you reflect on this motto, think of the mistakes you have made. Take time to think how these events shaped who you are today. We've all made choices that yielded painful outcomes. Did those consequences motivate us to reflect and make life changes or did they pound us down with guilt, regret and shame, dooming us to repeat the same ineffective behaviors? **Motivate** is the key word here. Consequences do not teach new skills; they motivate us to repeat or stop using the skills we already possess. In order for a consequence to be effective, it must be applied to a connected child who already possesses the desired skill. In a non-Conscious Discipline classroom, the same children receive the same traditional consequences over and over again because they are disconnected ("I don't care") or lack the needed skills. The Seven Skills of Conscious Discipline teach us to build connection and coach children with the new skill needed. Then, when we introduce a consequence, it is effective. Watch a video on the Power of Intention on the portal for a more in-depth understanding.

The Power of Intention

The Power of Intention states that mistakes are opportunities to learn. Every action we take is preceded by an intention. Our intention as we approach a situation will influence the outcome in profound ways. Intentions can happen unconsciously, rolling wherever our emotions and impulses take us like a boat without a rudder, or we can set them consciously before we act. Conscious Discipline encourages us to become conscious of our intentions in order to reach our highest goals. Intention is a powerful energy. Deepak Chopra states, "Intention is directed consciousness that contains a seed form of that which you aim to create" (Chopra, 2011). We constantly plant seeds with our intent; some of our seeds carry intent to make children feel bad for their mistakes and some carry the intent to help children learn from them.

Our intention energetically enters the situation before we do. We know this to be true. If a person approaches us with the intention of attack, we can sense it and become guarded. If a person approaches us with an open heart and mind, we feel that, too! Intention has the invisible power to bond us together, enhance honest communication and foster goal achievement. Of course, the opposite is also true, as expressed in the saying, "The road to hell is paved with good intentions."

I learned early in life that people are senders and receivers of unseen energy. Back in the day, I was amazed that I could improve the television picture by holding the antenna. I eventually removed the antenna and stuck my finger in the hole to get an even better picture. I knew I was a transmitter and receiver of something I couldn't see or define, and that stuck with me. It was also fascinating to me how the energy in the room felt different when my father was home or my mother was grumpy. Today, research confirms my youthful observations. As mentioned in the Power of Unity, we live in a sea of energy and information, and are in constant communication with each other through this field. Researchers at the Institute for Noetic Sciences discovered that when one member of a couple sent healing intentions to the other member with cancer, a large number of physiological responses such as heart waves, brain waves, blood flow and respiration synched between them. This occurred even when secure metal walls separated them in different rooms (Radin & Schlitz, 2005). The energy of their loving intentions traveled from one to the other, linking them inextricably together.

Healthy communication occurs when our intent matches our impact. When our intent in a situation is to be helpful and the impact of our communication is perceived as helpful, then all goes smoothly. When our intent does not match the impact, communication can sour quickly. We must be conscious of our intent and its impact, especially during discipline moments. As mentioned throughout the book, all conflict begins with upset. If we do not manage the upset before we attempt to solve the problem, our attention will be focused on what we don't want and our intention will be hurtful (defensive, forceful, argumentative or deceiving).

We often misuse intention like a magic wand or a "get out of jail free" card. For example, I can be hurtful to others (intentionally or unintentionally) and justify it by saying, "That was not my intention." The implication is you have no right to feel hurt because I did not intend to be hurtful. Communication will improve when we take responsibility instead of justifying our actions. We must consider both the intention and the impact instead of relying on good intentions as a way to deflect responsibility. A helpful phrase would be, "I had no idea that was hurtful. I didn't intend to ____, but I can see the hurt it caused." Follow this up with concrete steps for more helpful communication or by making amends. The reason we often use intent to cover our tracks is because unintentional acts are viewed more favorably than intentional ones. Unintended actions are attributed to external factors such as fatigue, hunger or our jobs, while intentional actions are attributed to internal character.

Our intention is hurtful any time we are focused on what we don't want. Our intention is usually helpful when we focus on what we want. If communication goes sour, reflect by asking yourself the following four questions:

1. What occurred? Was the impact of what I communicated helpful or hurtful? (Forget about the intention and focus on the impact.)
2. How is the outcome different from what I intended? My deepest desire was to ____.
3. Where can I take responsibility? What part of the process would change for the better if I would be willing to honestly align my intent with its impact?
4. How do I clean this up? How can I work to do this differently the next time and share this information?

Activity to Determine Intent

Reflect on the following. Is Jonas' behavior disrespectful or does Jonas indicate he is missing a skill? Is one situation worse than the other? If so, why?

Scene 1: Jonas accidentally pushes Jennifer on his way to line up.

_____

_____

_____

Scene 2: Jonas deliberately pushes Jennifer on his way to line up.

_____

_____

_____

We often believe intentional acts deserve punishment, while accidental behaviors can be accepted as an Oops that requires teaching. The Power of Intention empowers us to see Jonas as missing a skill in both scenes. In the first, Jonas could be missing the executive skill of attention. In the second, Jonas could be missing the executive skill of impulse control.

Consciousness of our intent and impact can improve our communication skills. It also can improve our self-regulation and goal achievement. If you are like me, you often have the best intentions in regard to life goals but fail to act on them. Research indicates that implementation intentions are more helpful than goal intentions in supporting our commitments (Gollwitzer & Sheeran, 2009). Goal intentions use the formula "I want to reach X." "I want to weigh 135 pounds." Implementation intentions are more specific and procedural: "When situation X arises, I will do Y." "When I start craving sugar, I will eat an apple." Children, especially those who are struggling, will make broad commitments such as, "I will listen to my teacher all day." They will need help from us to create an implementation intention to be successful. You might suggest, "When I find myself talking to friends while the teacher is teaching, I will touch my ears and listen." When we set a clear and personally-compelling intention, we tend to respond, create supportive opportunities and make choices in harmony with our intention.

> Much of this book has focused on becoming conscious of our intent and its impact. Many educators start this journey with the intent to make children behave. Hopefully you have now begun changing that intention from "making children behave" to "helping children be successful." With that small but exponentially important shift, you will experience "be the change you want to see" more often than "do what I say, not what I do."

An Intention to Control Versus an Intention to Teach

Our intentions while delivering consequences will determine whether children grow to view mistakes as opportunities to learn or as personal failures reflecting innate flaws. Our intention will instinctively become defensive when we feel threatened by a child's behavior, leading us to act in hurtful ways. Our intention will be to stop a behavior when we feel frustrated by it, leading us to act in punitive or permissive ways. Our intention will become a conscious choice when we feel calm, composed and in control of ourselves. (Composure is always available to us through active calming.) There are three core intentions when it comes to consequences: the intention to punish, the intention to save and the intention to teach.

Intention to punish: The goal is to make children feel bad about themselves or guilty for what they have done. "You should have known better." "What has gotten into you?" "Can't you ever listen? If you had listened to me, none of this would have happened." The punitive position says the child should feel rotten, miserable, unworthy and guilty for his actions. It says, "Do not feel what you are feeling, feel what I tell you to feel." Remember our beach ball analogy in Chapter 8 — whoever is holding the ball has the power and the responsibility to change. In this case, the adult is smacking the child in the face with his own beach ball, trying to force him to take responsibility instead of gently giving the beach ball back so he can accept personal responsibility. When we use the intent to punish, children learn to use their intelligence and energy to blame, defend and deflect instead of taking responsibility for their actions.

> *At any given moment, we are either being responsible or offering blame. The choice is ours!*

Intention to save: The goal is to rescue children from intense feelings of discomfort by saving them from the consequences of their actions. Children often beg, "I won't ever do it again. I promise. Erica made me. Please don't call my parents. I will be good." As parents, we often rush forgotten homework or lunch money to school, saving our children from the consequences of their actions. Rescuing children from their feelings says, "Do not feel what you are feeling. Upset feelings are bad. I will save you this one time, but don't let it happen again." The adult takes the child's beach ball and holds it so he will not feel the distress created by his choices. Without access to his feelings, consequences will have no effective impact. The implied message is "Feelings are bad" or "You are incapable of handling your feelings." Children learn to use their intelligence and energy for manipulation and entitlement instead of responsibility.

Intention to teach: The goal is to help children reflect on how they feel about the impact of their choices in order to take responsibility for their actions. Their feelings provide the motivation to learn new skills and do things differently in the future.

> **Student:** "I did my homework. I just forgot to bring it in. I can bring it tomorrow."
> **Teacher:** "Homework was due today and it will not be accepted tomorrow."
> **Student:** "That's crap! I hate you. I did it. This isn't fair."
> **Teacher:** "You seem frustrated. It's disappointing to spend time doing your homework and not get the credit. Take a few deep breaths. Calm down and let's work together on a plan to make sure you bring it on time in the future."

When we hold the intention to teach, children learn to use their intelligence and energy to manage intense feelings, take responsibility for their actions and create healthier options for themselves in the future. There are four basic steps to teach children how to take responsibility:

1. Give children tasks and guidelines they can handle.
2. Stand back and allow them to blow it.
3. Apply liberal doses of empathy, and let the consequences motivate change and the learning of new skills.
4. Give the same task again with new skills in place.

We cannot teach responsibility by demanding or threatening children into admitting their mistakes; we teach it through creating the safety and connection needed for them to reflect and listen to the messages their feelings provide about their impact on the world. A classroom based on reward and punishment carries one intention with it; a classroom based on Conscious Discipline carries a different intention altogether. A phrase we often use in Conscious Discipline is, "It starts in the heart." The older I get, the more I realize the truth of this statement.

> It is vital we become conscious of both intent and impact. We tend to judge ourselves by our intentions and ignore our impact on others. We judge others by the impact of their behavior on us and ignore their intentions. School administrators must be particularly sensitive to their impact because there is a tendency to read more into behaviors of those in positions of authority. Often, well-intentioned leaders do not appreciate the impact of their behavior on others within their organization.

Becoming Brain Smart

In Chapter 3, the Conscious Discipline Brain State Model, we talked about the prefrontal lobes being the CEO of the brain, representing an integrated executive state. The prefrontal lobes are one of the most integrative areas of the brain, linking with the brain stem and limbic system (Ramnani & Owen, 2004). Like the CEO of a large corporation, the prefrontal lobes can only be as good as the flow of information and energy in and out of each department (the brain stem and limbic system). A decreased ability to self-regulate is a sure sign that integration is impaired. This shows up as behavior that is chaotic (overly emotional), rigid (controlling of everything and everyone) or both.

There are experiences that impair integration and experiences that enhance it. Children born with autism, bipolar disorder or schizophrenia are born with impaired integration. Trauma, poverty, malnutrition and environmental toxins are also associated with impaired growth or damage to integrative brain fibers (Siegel, 2012). Beyond these big categories, we have everyday interactions that enhance or diminish brain integration, especially during moments of conflict. When our intention is to help children be successful, we foster integration and the development of self-regulation. When our intent is to make (or get) children to behave, we impede integration as control and power replace connection and teaching.

The goal of Conscious Discipline is to become conscious and release the discipline practices that inhibit integration. We want to embrace skills and systems that foster integration. Higher degrees of integration are associated with positive emotions. We build integration into our lives and our brains when we feel peace, joy, love, delight and gratitude. That is why the School Family is an essential foundation for academic integration. In contrast, constant negative emotions (intense sadness, anger and fear) decrease integration. That is why the intent to shame children or make them feel bad through external punishments must change. Shame impairs the neural circuitry of integration. It promotes self-hatred and traps children in a state of isolation, despite their longing for connection (Siegel, 2012). Instead of blaming and shaming, we must help children reflect on what they are feeling and use those feelings to motivate behavioral changes. This occurs when we use effective consequences.

Our Executive Skills

Our integrated executive state gives access to our executive skills. These skills collectively enable us to:

- Direct our attention in order to set and achieve goals despite distractions
- Regulate our emotions and inhibit impulsive behavior
- Hold information in our heads, self-monitor and reflect
- Develop empathy and problem solve

The prefrontal lobes and our executive skills develop through problem solving in social settings. Almost everything we do in life, from running errands to going to work involves problem solving in social settings (social media and electronic games are among the exceptions). As educators, we know our job requires the capacity to multitask, organize, plan and prioritize, and then be flexible enough to shift our attention to an upset child and then return to the lesson without forgetting our place. We must manage and model self-control despite hundreds of interruptions, problems and distractions. Our executive skills work together to help us manage our classrooms, much like air traffic controllers manage the arrivals and departures of dozens of planes on multiple runways at busy airports (Center on the Developing Child At Harvard University, 2011).

A classroom can become chaotic and teaching a source of stress when children have underdeveloped executive skills. Executive skills are crucial building blocks for school readiness, academic and social success, even more so than early literacy or math (Barkley, 2001 and Blair, 2002). Look at the list of the executive skills introduced in Chapter 2 (A TOP WIFE Makes Good Tea). These skills begin developing shortly after birth, and require nearly two decades of caring, attuned relationships and prefrontal lobe lending from adults.

Executive Skills: A TOP WIFE Makes Good TEa

A = Attention
T = Time management
O = Organization
P = Prioritization
W = Working memory
I = Impulse control
F = Flexibility
E = Empathy
M = Metacognition
G = Goal achievement
T = Task Initiation
E = Emotional Regulation

 View additional information about each of the executive skills on the portal.

Children exposed to highly stressful early environments have impaired executive skill functioning. Attuned, responsive educators embedding resiliency into a school culture through safety, connection and problem solving will scaffold executive skill development for all children, even the most challenging ones. Research shows that the rate of executive skill development increases significantly from birth to three years of age, and advances even more dramatically from three to five years of age. The rate of development slows significantly after age six, but continues steadily through age 25 (Weintraub, Dikmen, Heaton, Tulsky, Zelazo, Bauer, Carlozzi, Slotkin, Blitz, Wallner-Allen, Fox, Beaumont, Mungas, Richler, Deocampo, Anderson, Manly, Borosh, Havlick & Gershon). The rapid rate of development during early childhood provides a critical window of opportunity for executive skill scaffolding. This scaffolding requires adults to commit to the shifts advocated in this book.

Contrary to popular belief, executive functions like controlling impulses, paying attention and retaining information do not unfold automatically as children mature. We are born with a potential for these skills, and we develop them (or not) depending on our experiences during infancy and childhood. Conscious Discipline utilizes findings from neuroscience and developmental research by creating learning environments based on safety, connection and problem solving to foster children's executive skill development. The combined tools for safety (N.A.R.C.S), connection (R.E.J.E.C.T.) and problem solving (S.P.A.C.E.) embed resiliency in schools through intentionally fostering the development of these vital life skills.

Lending our prefrontal lobe requires we use the A.B.C. approach.

A = Access our executive state through active calming.
B = Be willing to perceive misbehavior as a call for help.
C = Coach new skills as needed.

When a child behaves in challenging ways, it is our job to calm ourselves enough to see the call for help. Does he need help with willingness (answering the questions "Am I Safe?" and "Am I loved?" in the affirmative), or does he need help with scaffolding of executive skills ("What can I learn?")? Children who lack willingness also lack integration. They are oppositional, noncompliant, withdrawn, and hard to reach and teach. They are our most challenging children. Trying to scaffold executive skills with a child whose goal is self-defense will fail. These children need help with the integrative building blocks of life. They need help answering "Am I safe?" and "Am I loved?" with a resounding "Yes!" Helping these children requires the time and resources to offer them more opportunities to experience the combined safety tools (N.A.R.C.S.) and connection tools (R.E.J.E.C.T.). They need more **N**oticing throughout the day. They need consistent exposure to **A**ssertive adults and classmates. They need additional individualized social stories and **R**outines in pictures to clearly visualize the goal. They need **C**omposure from frequent downloading. They need to hear the language of **S**afety, and they need assistance in learning to use the Safe Place. They need additional individualized **R**ituals for connection, **E**ncouragement for every small increment of success, and **J**obs and opportunities to be of service to others. They need **E**mpathy when emotionally over-aroused, **C**hoices to focus and coaching to become an integral member of **T**he School Family.

Zoe needed additional help to feel safe and connected in Mrs. Beebe's prekindergarten class. She had very little ability to regulate herself. Mrs. Beebe looked at the skills needed for safety (N.A.R.C.S.) and started consciously giving Zoe twice as much as she typically would for other class members. Mrs. Beebe worked hard to stay calm and download calm into Zoe as often as possible. She decided to notice her at least 10 times a day. Zoe had several jobs in the classroom, most importantly the Safe Place Assistant in which she helped others learn to calm themselves.

Mrs. Beebe constantly prompted Zoe to focus on what to do using visuals routines and assertiveness. While visiting Zoe's classroom, I noticed a book titled, *Zoe's Day at School*. I picked it up and flipped through the photos showing exactly what would happen during every part of Zoe's day at school. When Zoe saw me, she bolted up from circle time, grabbed the book and yelled, "That's my book!" Clearly, the book and the felt sense of safety it provided were very important to her! A video of Zoe reading her book is on the web portal.

In addition, Zoe needed help answering the question "Am I loved?" Mrs. Beebe worked one-on-one to give Zoe more connection skills (R.E.J.E.C.T). She did I Love You Rituals with her twice a day. She encouraged her through noticing helpful acts. She gave her extra jobs in the classroom so she could be of service. She used empathy and choices extensively as limit-setting tools. She also framed Zoe's behaviors as calls for help, eliciting the School Family's help in the intervention plan.

Once Zoe had a strong foundation of safety and connection, Mrs. Beebe began scaffolding some specific executive skills to contribute to her success.

Mrs. Beebe consulted the Executive Skills Lending Library to discern what intervention would most likely be helpful. This library, available on the portal, provides suggestions and videos of specific ways to help children with each executive skill.

> Zoe's success created more positive emotions, strengthening her brain's integration and allowing her to become a safe, connected contributor to her School Family. The time Zoe spent in positive emotional states steadily increased while the time spent in negative emotional states decreased. There are thousands of children like Zoe who have seen their lives transformed by educators practicing Conscious Discipline.

Remember the following when creating intervention plans for children with behavior issues:

- Novel situations and stressed children require more scaffolding.
- Prefrontal lobe scaffolding is labor intensive. It requires a present, connected, attuned adult.
- The adult must possess the skill he is trying to scaffold.
- Self-regulation begins in the right hemisphere. Add play, music, movement, art and visuals to your interventions as much as possible.
- Disconnected children do not have access to their executive skills due to lack of brain integration. Safety and connection are key starting points.

 To help you scaffold missing or emerging executive skills, use the Executive Skill Lending Library on your portal. It is frustrating to attempt to lend others those skills that are our personal weak suits. The classroom structures of Conscious Discipline support executive skill practice in the social and emotional domain. Think of the Job Board or the Safe Place in terms of the executive skills they scaffold. If you have not begun implementing the classroom structures suggested at the end of each chapter, start now. If you implement three structures per year, within three years you will have achieved full implementation of the structures.

> Common school expectations require extensive executive skill use. When I think of school rules in terms of the executive skills required, I am amazed at how many children manage success daily and I feel deep compassion for the number of children who try hard yet fail each day because they lack the necessary integration to be successful. Think about your school's rules and expectations. How many "A TOP WIFE Makes Good TEa" skills are required for children to be successful with each rule? Check the list of executive skills required for each grade level on your portal.

Conscious Discipline and Multi-Tier Systems

There is growing momentum nationwide to develop systematic intervention models to identify and help children who are at risk for academic or behavioral issues. Instead of a "one size fits all" style of education, the goal is to meet the differentiated needs of students through a multi-tiered process. Students who struggle receive systematic assistance and increasingly intensive interventions to become successful learners. Originally called Response to Intervention (RTI), the process is now often referred to as Multi-Tiered System of Supports (MTSS).

RTI came from the world of special education as this education community recognized the need for a perceptual shift. At one point, disabilities were viewed as "within child" factors. Interventions were aimed at the child, a one-way street designed to fix the deficits. This belief was also held in the general public as parents took children to counselors for the counselors to fix them and teachers sent students to the principal to be fixed. The RTI movement highlighted the need to see interventions as a two-way street. It added the notion of reciprocity, linking adult action to child response. It asked us to be more conscious of the outcomes of our interventions. This is consistent with the mind-set shift of Conscious Discipline. "Do as I say, not as I do" thinking places the burden of change on the child's shoulders. Conscious Discipline teaches that the change occurs in the dynamic between the adult, the child and the environment.

We live and breathe in a social world. Discipline is relationship-specific. (We've known this since we were two years old: We can get way with nothing with Mom, a little with Dad and everything with Grandma.) We must translate this basic truth to the children in our care. Is my response to the child's upset helping him calm down or making matters worse? Are my executive skills a good match or a mismatch for the skills he is lacking? Many people familiar with RTI get caught up in the three-tiered pyramid design of interventions and largely overlook the fundamental perceptual shift to "Am I helping the child be successful?" Conscious Discipline places all of its focus on this essential question.

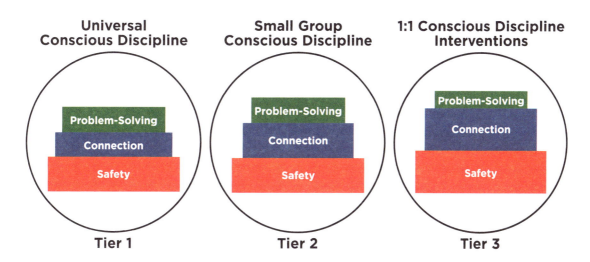

RTI for behavior includes the principle that behavioral supports at a universal level are intended to effectively address the needs of all students in a school (referred to as Tier 1). However, not all students will respond successfully to these universal behavioral supports. As a result, some students with identified needs receive supplemental intervention at Tier 2, like in Zoe's story earlier. At Tier 3, students with the most severe needs receive even more intensive and individualized behavioral support. This system allows educators to identify the needs of all students, match the level of support to the severity of the behavior or academic problems, and then assess the students' response to intervention. An example process and forms for assessing intervention success are located on the portal.

Research (Hoffman, Hutchinson, & Reiss, 2005) indicates that the majority of Tier 2 students can be brought back into a typical range of behavioral function in a classroom by implementing Conscious Discipline with high fidelity. The more challenging the child (Tier 3), the more intense the focus needs to be on developing safety and connection. Sadly, most interventions start with scaffolding the executive skills. The efficacy of RTI-type programs would be greatly increased by strengthening the foundation of safety and connection (fostering brain integration and willingness) before applying specific executive skill interventions.

The Skill of Consequences

We have all experienced the consequences of our actions. At some point, all of us have paid the price for drinking too much, eating too much, working too much or losing our temper. We have repeated these unproductive choices, sometimes habitually. Yet there have also been times when we've taken responsibility for our actions and the consequences we experienced, inspiring life changes. Reflect for a moment on the difference between repeating past mistakes and the motivation to change.

The motivation to change comes from owning the consequences of our actions, reflecting from the higher centers of the brain and consciously choosing a different action. It does not come from judging or blaming. Judging and blaming are lower brain activities that cause us to stagnate in the problem, creating habitual reactions instead of change. Learning from the consequences of our actions requires us to do two things:

1. Reflect on the choices and their outcomes in relation to our long-term goals.
    Was ordering a pizza in alignment with my desire to lose weight?
2. Take ownership of our choices and the feelings they generate within us.
    I feel disappointed that I've probably delayed reaching my goals.

Becoming conscious of consequences is the key to change. This consciousness comes from getting in touch with how we feel about the outcome of our choices and their impact. Pain is our body's signal that something is out of balance. It says, "Pay attention to this area and gather information; something is amiss." If we ignore the physical pain of a sprained ankle, we doom ourselves to worsening the injury. If we ignore our emotional pain or project it onto others ("Look how you made me feel!"), we doom ourselves to repeating the same choices. Our emotions signal us that something is out of balance. They are an internal guidance system that helps us discern right from wrong. Without access to how we feel, we are ships without navigational equipment; we cannot see the consequences of our behaviors or change course. Suffering is not a requirement of consequences, however, awareness of our feelings is essential.

As we've already discussed, reward and punishment systems impede higher-order brain function and do not teach children to self-regulate. Their goal is to make children feel a certain way about their actions: Feel good when you do good, feel bad when you do bad. The message is "do not feel your feelings; feel the ones assigned to you." In these systems, the adult judges the child's behavior as good or bad. If judged good, something good is given. If judged bad, something bad is given. These children are likely to develop an external compass for moral living. Their focus is external, with the ultimate outcome of believing it is their job to make others happy or make others change instead of changing themselves. They come to depend on the judgment of others as the basis for their moral decisions. This appears to work when children are young because the "other" is generally an adult. In the teenage years when the "other" is more likely other teenagers, this can be quite a dangerous arrangement.

> **Becoming conscious of consequences is the key to change.**

Effective consequences have a different mode of operation. They help children focus inward to reflect about their choices and then draw conclusions about the wisdom of their actions. By using effective consequences, teachers help children behave like scientists studying their own behaviors. "Did you achieve your desired outcome? If not, how did it feel and what other strategies could you try in a similar situation next time?" Consequences teach children to examine their behavior and make changes until they reach their goals. Children who learn to reflect on their feelings, choices and outcomes become conscious of their own actions. They grow up empowered to choose the wisest course of action for each situation and to solve problems. If their first attempt doesn't provide the results they'd hoped for, they try again. These children develop their own inner compass for moral living, learn self-regulation and become responsible citizens. Their focus is internally-based, with the ultimate outcome of believing they are in charge of their behavior and that happiness is an inside job (and therefore available to everyone). Let's look at the difference in real-life terms.

Common, External Focus: Jackson brings home his report card to get it signed by his parents. He has two Ds, and one of them is in art. He slowly hands his mom the paper and says, "You need to sign this." Mom opens the report card and sees the two Ds. She responds, "I knew it. You've been out with your friends, playing soccer and ignoring your schoolwork. You've been lying to us about your homework and everything! I can't believe these grades, especially a D in art. Who gets a D in art?

Jackson: Well, the teacher didn't like me.
Mom: I don't care if she is the devil himself. That's no excuse. We didn't raise you to be lazy and make excuses. You will no longer play soccer and you won't have those new friends of yours over to the house. You were making decent grades until you started hanging out with them. Do you understand me?

Conscious Use of Effective Consequences: Jackson brings home his report card to get it signed by his parents. He has two Ds, and one of them is in art. He slowly hands his mom the paper. She opens the report card and studies it quietly. Jackson's heart is beating so hard that he's sure she can hear it. Finally she speaks, "Jackson you got one B, three Cs and two Ds. How do you feel about your grades?"

Jackson: Well the art teacher hates me. Ask anyone at school.
Mom: That may be so, but how do you feel about your grades? Are you proud of them? Are you okay with them? Do you feel disappointed? How is this report card for you?
Jackson: I don't know. Not so good I guess.
Mom: You seemed hesitant to show me your report card and seem to have prepared a defense. Sounds like something is going on inside you.
Jackson: Well, I don't feel so good about the Ds, but I don't mind the other grades.
Mom: So it seems you feel a little disappointed with yourself and also afraid I would feel disappointed in you.
Jackson: Yeah, I blew it, he says as his body slumps.
Mom: So you feel disappointed like you messed up and want your grades to be at least a C or better?
Jackson: (Nods his head.)
Mom: Would you like some help coming up with a plan to raise your grades or would you like to make one yourself?
Jackson: I can do it but I might need help doing all my homework. I thought art would be easy.
Mom: Write up a plan and we will go over it after dinner. You can do this. (She closes the report card and heads into the kitchen.)

Reread the second scenario above and reflect: How does this dialogue differ from how you were raised? How do you think Jackson's inner speech might develop differently from yours? What about his confidence, self-esteem and ability to enact positive changes in his life?

You might be thinking, "But what if Jackson didn't care about his D grades?" In earlier chapters we explained that a child who repeatedly says, "I don't care," is essentially saying, "I don't feel cared for." When there is a relationship issue (Am I loved?), there is nothing we can do quickly to raise the grades (What can I learn?). We can only repair relationships by changing our intention and connecting. We've also discussed discipline as being a combination of slow-slow relationship building and quick-quick skill building in the moment. When a child chronically responds, "I don't care," our job is to provide more slow-slow safety and connection using our combined tools N.A.R.C.S. and R.E.J.E.C.T. In the meantime, we could link the report card to something he does care about as motivation. The interaction might go something like this:

> **Conscious Use of Effective Consequences for "I Don't Care":** Jackson brings home his report card to get it signed by his parents. He has two Ds, and one of them is in art. He slowly hands his mom the paper. She opens the report card and studies it quietly. Jackson's heart is beating so hard that he's sure she can hear it. Finally she speaks, "Jackson you got one B, three Cs and two Ds. How do you feel about your grades?"
>
> **Mom:** How is this report card for you?
> **Jackson:** I don't care. I hate school.
> **Mom:** (Mom inquires further) So the Ds don't bother you at all?
> **Jackson:** No, I don't care about them or the Cs or the B. Aren't you listening? I DON'T CARE!
> **Mom:** You seem hopeless and angry. You want school and maybe other things to just go away? (Jackson freezes in his spot, says nothing and just raises his eyebrows. Noticing this, Mom knows she has his attention.) With Ds on your report card, you will be suspended from the soccer team until you bring them up. Remember your agreement with the coach?
> **Jackson:** I don't care.
> **Mom:** It is hard to feel hopeless. Nothing feels like it really matters. (Mom breathes deeply and thinks of something that might seem important to him.) Isn't your best friend who moved to another school on the soccer team? It seems it would be hard not to see him anymore. (Jackson looks up, makes eye contact and seems shocked to hear this.)
> **Jackson:** Well, maybe, but you could take me to see him.
> **Mom:** Maybe, or you can work with me to get those grades up and then you will definitely see him every week. Then you would be in charge.
> **Jackson:** Okay. (Jackson rolls his eyes and walks away.)

Successful consequences truly require all seven powers and skills of Conscious Discipline. Note the way Jackson's mom used composure, assertiveness, encouragement, choices, empathy, positive intent and consequences to help Jackson be successful.

Now, think of the last mistake you believe you've made. How did you handle your error? Was your inner voice helpful? "Oops! I made a mistake. How do I feel about it? What can I learn from it? How can I forgive myself and improve?" Or did your mind work on the theme of worthlessness? "How could I have done this? I am horrible. This is all my fault." Perhaps your mind spun to the rottenness of others. "He should have told me. Some friend he is. I would never treat him like that." Punishment and blame don't facilitate the reflective learning process; they stop it. The inner dialogue (old preprogrammed CD-Rom) with which we bash ourselves over mistakes and build ourselves up over accomplishments is not human nature. It is a learned pattern. We have learned and internalized a value system that sets us up to feel good when we believe we are right and feel bad when we believe we are wrong. Seeking to feel good by being right sets us up for power struggles, not problem-solving. We can retrain ourselves to think differently and act differently in order to teach children a better way of handling big emotions and problems.

> *It is not human nature to feel we are bad based on our mistakes and good based on our accomplishments. We learn this mindset.*

Commitment: Take a deep breath and commit to the following: I am willing to make mistakes. Mistakes don't mean I am bad. Mistakes mean I have the courage to change. In removing my fear of making mistakes, I free myself to make lasting changes in my behavior.

Signature: _____ Date: _____

Myths and Realities of Consequences

Jackson and his mom have shown us that utilizing the Power of Intention when applying the Skill of Consequences allows children to feel the discomfort of their choices and utilize that discomfort as the motivation for change. Conscious Discipline is not void of consequences. It is about giving adults the mindset, skill set and cultural foundation to use consequences effectively so we can all take responsibility for our actions and learn from our mistakes. Natural, logical and problem-solving are the three core types of effective consequences we will use. Each type of consequence helps to motivate in different ways. Before we learn about these three essential consequences, we must first derail some basic myths. Read carefully and decide if you are ready for a shift in thinking.

Myth 1: Effective consequences are created by adults and imposed on children. Often during Q & A times at workshops, teachers ask what would be a good consequence for certain behaviors. The implication is there is a perfect consequence that would make a child stop a behavior once and for all (or repeat a desired behavior forever).

Reality 1: Consequences happen all the time. The shift needed isn't to discover the perfect consequence to impose, but to place more conscious attention to the consequences already embedded in the event. Conscious Discipline asks us to go back to a more basic concept of consequences as they relate to the world of cause and effect: All thoughts, feelings and actions already have consequences embedded within them. The goal is to become conscious of them.

Effectiveness 1: The effectiveness of a consequence is determined by our conscious awareness of them and their impact. A child who blames a teacher for being unfair is different than a child who sees his responsibility in the situation.

Myth 2: The consequence of an action is determined by the outcome. If a child chooses not to study for a test, the consequence is failing or doing poorly. If a child chooses to hit a friend, the consequence is removal from the class.

Reality 2: The consequence of an action is how we feel about the outcome. If a student chooses not to study for a test, the true consequence is how he feels about failing. If a child chooses to hit a friend and is removed from class, the consequence is how she feels about the removal. The shift needed is from focusing solely on the outcome to focusing on the inherent feelings elicited by that outcome.

Effectiveness 2: The effectiveness of a consequence is determined by our feelings about the outcome, not the outcome itself. A child who feels disappointed about failing is different than a child who does not care. A child who misses classroom friends when removed is different than a child who feels relief from the over-stimulation of a classroom environment.

Myth 3: "Consequence" is just a new name for "punishment." Over and over again at my workshops I hear, "When do we get to consequences?" or "What about consequences?" Most of the time, these attendees are actually asking, "When is enough, enough? At what point do we get to punish them for what they've done?"

Reality 3: Consequences and punishments are different. Punishments rely on judgment. "What is happening is bad. You are guilty, and you should feel bad about the damage you've inflicted." The degree of powerlessness we feel in a given situation will determine the intensity of our desire to punish. Effective use of consequences relies on reflection accessed through composure. Our intent must be for the child to reflect. Did his choice produce the desired outcome? How does he feel about the outcome of his choice? What could he change to achieve his long-term goals?

Effectiveness 3: Our intentions will determine the consequence's effectiveness. There is a difference in a child who is told he should feel bad (judgment) and one who actually feels remorse for the impact of his choices (reflection). We must approach the situation with a calm, helpful intent in order to foster reflection.

Myth 4: The severity of the consequence is equal to its effectiveness. If a certain consequence does not appear to achieve desired results, then it is important to increase the severity. One way to do this is to find out what truly matters to the child and then threaten the removal of that object, activity, etc.

Reality 4: Consequences do not teach, they motivate. For consequences to be effective, we must proactively teach children new conflict resolution skills, teach them how to manage intense emotions so they can access those skills, notice them each step of the way to provide feedback for success, and instill the sense of belonging and connectedness that supports their willingness to use the new skills. Each of these steps requires differentiation of instruction and scaffolding from the other six skills of Conscious Discipline. Increasing the harshness of a consequence only reinforces the child's feelings of alienation, worthlessness and hopelessness. Over time it teaches, "I am bad, I am unlovable and I don't belong." Children must believe "I am safe, and I am loved," so they can ask, "What can I learn from this?" in order to make life changes.

Effectiveness 4: The effectiveness of a consequence is determined by how well we **proactively teach** the social and emotional skills needed and how connected and valued children feel as a members of the School Family.

Myth 5: The hard part about consequences is coming up with ones that are reasonable, logical and related to the infraction.

Reality 5: The most difficult part of consequences is handling the backlash of children's reactions when we administer the consequence. If we say the consequence of a hurtful action is a referral to the office, the difficult part often happens when it is time to send a child out of the room. The child's reaction could be a verbal or physical outburst as she attempts to blame us for the emotions bubbling within her. (Referring back to our beach ball metaphor in Chapter 8, she throws her ball at us.) Gently return ownership by following consequences with empathy instead of lectures, admonishment or punishment.

Effectiveness 5: The effectiveness of a consequence is determined by how in touch children are with their feelings about what happened. Empathy provides that awareness. Effective consequences are followed by empathy, not lectures or condemnation.

> **Commitment:** I am willing to let go of the myths and outdated beliefs I hold about consequences. When I find myself reverting to my old ways of thinking and behaving (punishing, etc.), I will take a deep breath, renew my intent to teach and approach consequences more consciously.
>
> Signature: _____ Date: _____

Natural Consequences: Motivation to Learn New Skills

Natural consequences arise without any prearranged adult planning or control. As the name suggests, they happen naturally. They are one of the most powerful means for motivating future behavior change. A child who puts her hand on a hot stove is strongly motivated to do things differently in the future. The following are examples of natural consequences:

- A child who does not tie her shoes may trip and fall.
- A child who repeatedly treats her friends poorly may find herself friendless.
- A child who rides a roller coaster right after eating a chili cheese hotdog may throw up.

These types of natural consequences are possible (and sometimes probable) results of personal choices. Remember though, interactions with our environment yield a wide range of possible results. Adults tend to overdo the prediction of harm. "If you run around with your laces untied, you will fall and hurt yourself!" For young children, these types of statements can be hypothesis to be tested. At any age, these dire warnings send two messages: 1. Adults are all knowing and can read the future, and 2. Children have no control over the events in their lives.

Children who internalize these beliefs grow into adults who give their power away and feel victimized by life. A more accurate approach would be, "If you leave your shoes untied, you may trip and hurt yourself. My job is to keep you safe. Your job is to help keep it safe. Now tie your shoes so you can run safely."

As powerful as natural consequences are, they have been almost completely removed from the school environment, opting instead for heavy reliance on logical consequences that are prearranged and posted. Natural consequences are powerful motivators that provide instant teaching opportunities for new social and emotional skills; removing them creates problems rather than helping resolve them.

Traditional discipline views interpersonal conflict as something to be stopped at all cost, relying solely on logical consequences. Conscious Discipline uses these same conflicts as teaching opportunities that allow all children (victim, aggressors and bystanders) to learn from others' mistakes immediately. The consequence for using an ineffective social skill (pushing, name calling) in a Conscious Discipline classroom isn't a logical consequence like missing five minutes of recess; instead, a natural consequence teaches effective new social skills in the moment.

When we change our minds enough to see that social-emotional learning happens similar to academic learning, we will be more motivated to change how we manage our classrooms. Pretend a child has missed several words on his spelling test. We see this as feedback indicating more practice or additional instruction is needed. We do not turn a card from green to yellow; we coach the child and present him with additional opportunities to spell the word correctly. This is also how we must approach daily conflicts in the classroom. Attempting to remove daily conflicts through the application of logical consequences (either rewards or punishments) removes the opportunity for teaching social skills lessons in context. It forces schools and teachers to add a separate social-emotional curriculum to an already full workload.

> *Conscious Discipline is not void of consequences. It is about giving teachers the mindset, skill set and cultural foundation to use consequences effectively so we can all take responsibility and learn from our mistakes.*

The power of natural consequences as an agent of change is undeniable. They motivate us to want to learn a new skill. There are, however, plenty of circumstances where natural consequences are not appropriate. Our job description (as laid out in the School Family chapter) is to keep the classroom safe. It would be dangerous to allow a child to run into the street to experience the possible natural consequence of being hit by a car. It would be dangerous to use natural consequences for violent acts such as fistfights in school. Therefore, natural consequences are most useful for everyday teasing, pushing, poking, name calling and other small infringements between children. For these daily occurrences, natural consequences are unparalleled in their effectiveness when used with the other skills and powers in this book. When safety is not an issue, natural consequences provide powerful motivation to learn new strategies. Let's explore using natural consequences to help children who break rules or disregard routines, and to use tattling as a social skills teaching tool. Start by watching a portal video showing how one teacher handled a child pulling a chair out from under another.

Natural Consequences Help Children Who Break Rules or Disregard Routines

Students' daily life is scripted with numerous classroom routines. We must teach and reteach these routines and use visuals to scaffold their learning (Chapter 5). Children, for many reasons, will still forget the routines and fail to utilize the visuals to be successful. We often find ourselves reminding and warning students repeatedly instead of using natural consequences as they present themselves.

Ella has brought a delicate butterfly model to school for show-and-tell at science. To keep their items safe while in the classroom, the rule for the children is to store them in their cubbies until circle time. Mr. Evans always models putting his things in his cubby. Ella is so pleased with her butterfly that she walks around the room carrying her butterfly during centers. Mr. Evans calls on the seven skills of Conscious Discipline to help Ella become aware of and handle the natural consequences of her actions.

"Ella, I see you are carrying your butterfly. You seem excited to share it. Put your butterfly in your cubby so it will be safe until it is time for science. Remember, that is one of our class rules." He points to the picture rules on the wall showing this rule. "If you continue to carry your butterfly around, it may get broken."

Ella pretends to put her butterfly away but secretly keeps it in her pocket. The butterfly breaks as two children try to look at it at the same time. Ella begins to cry hysterically. Mr. Evans approaches the scene, takes a deep breath, resists the urge to lecture and instead says, "Oh Ella, your precious butterfly is broken. You seem sad. You were hoping to carry it around all day, show your friends and keep it safe."

Ella responds, "They broke it, I hate them," as she points to the two children. Mr. Evans says, "You seem so disappointed. That makes sense. The butterfly was important to you. You can handle this. It is hard. You have a choice. You can pick up the pieces yourself or you can ask your friends to help pick up the pieces and put them in a plastic bag in your cubby to take home. Which is better for you?"

We can all remember times when we've made decisions that resulted in painful outcomes. Which type of person was helpful during these times: One who predicts our future ("If you don't put that butterfly away right now, it will get broken"), one who blames us for not listening ("You knew the rule and you deliberately ignored it!"), one who proves how wise he is through our misfortune ("I told you this would happen but you wouldn't listen.") or one who is supportive, reflective and empathic ("You seem disappointed…")? Now, reflect on the changes required to become a supportive, reflective, empathetic person for the children in your care. Are you willing to make the needed changes?

> *Natural consequences motivate children to want to do things differently and therefore are excellent in fostering the learning of social skills.*

Natural Consequences Use Tattling as a Teaching Tool

In a Conscious Discipline, the natural consequence of tattling is assertiveness training. In early elementary school, tattling occurs so frequently that teachers often seek to eliminate it. In later elementary school years through high school, teachers and administrators spend enormous effort encouraging children who are being bullied or who witness acts of bulling to report the incidents. It seems we want to eliminate tattling in the younger years and support it later. We would be better served to use tattling as a teaching tool throughout the school years by perceiving it as a call for help and teaching children to see the wisdom in seeking adult assistance in times of need.

Activity to Reflect on Tattling

Reflect for a moment on how you respond to tattling and the preprogrammed CD-Rom messages that play in your head. Mark the thoughts that apply to you below, and write any additional false CD-Rom messages in the blanks.

❏ If it isn't serious, don't come to me.

❏ Is anyone bleeding or dying? Then get back to work.

❏ Did you use your words?

❏ It's not nice to tattle.

❏ If I have to get involved, then you will both be in trouble!

❏ Is this any of your business?

❏ Don't worry, honey, I'll take care of it. He had no right to hit you.

❏ I'm not listening. You need to learn to handle it yourself.

❏ Other: _____

❏ Other: _____

Tattling is a wonderful teaching opportunity, especially during the early childhood years. Developmentally, children up to eight years of age are genetically programmed to bring their distress to significant adults for assistance. Attempting to stop tattling during these years can skew their developmental path, inadvertently teaching children that authority is not be trusted, revenge is a helpful problem-solving tool and victimization is just part of life. Practice becoming conscious of what your current response to tattling teaches by completing the activity using the summary graphic on your portal. The three general types of tattling are intrusion, revenge and safety tattling. How we respond to these types of tattling is critical.

Intrusion Tattling

Intrusion tattling deals with some form of victimization such as physical aggression ("She pushed me!"), verbal aggression ("She called me a name!") or property infringement ("She wrote on my paper!"). How we respond to those who infringe on others teaches children to be assertive, passive, aggressive or passive-aggressive. Children who tattle in this manner are saying, "I don't have a clue how to handle this, could you help me?"

Responding to intrusion tattling requires children use their BIG Voice as taught in Chapter 5. The intrusion tattling example below reminds us how to teach assertive language with a focus on helping children flip from "Stop it!" to stating how they want the aggressor to treat them in the future. For example:

> **Child:** Ashely wrote on my paper!
> **Teacher:** Did you like it?
> **Child:** No!
> **Teacher:** Tell Ashley, "I don't like it when you write on my paper."
> **Child:** Ashley, I don't like it when you write on my paper.
> **Teacher:** What do you want her to do?
> **Child:** Stop it!
> **Teacher:** So you want her to write on her own paper. Tell Ashley, "Please write on your own paper."

Not all children will have the courage or confidence to assertively teach aggressive children how they want to be treated. Children with low confidence will need extra coaching and practice to be successful. The following demonstrates how to help these children.

> **Child:** Andrea took my sweater.
> **Adult:** Did you like it?
> **Child:** No (in a whiny, little voice).
> **Adult:** Go tell Andrea, "I don't like it when you take my sweater. Give it back." Remember to hold out your hand like this (demonstrate). Let's practice.
> **Child:** I don't like it when you take my sweater. Give it back (still in a small, whiny voice).
> **Adult:** Yes, that's it. Now say it again, matching your voice to mine. "I don't like it when you take my sweater. Give it back!" (Model a firm, confident voice with hand outstretched.)
> **Child:** I don't like it when you take my sweater. Give it back.
> **Adult:** That was much louder. I heard you that time. I will walk with you to tell Andrea.
> **Child to Andrea:** I don't like it when you take my sweater. Give it back.
> **Adult to Andrea:** I am here to let you know it is important to listen to others in your School Family. See her hand? Place the sweater in her hand.

In this example, the adult spent some time modeling an assertive voice for the passive child. This modeling and coaching will take time because the child has beliefs about herself or life that impede her confidence. The same coaching process is necessary for children who respond aggressively by screaming, "I don't like it!" instead of speaking assertively. We must teach children what an assertive BIG Voice sounds like, looks like and feels like to help them succeed.

Natasha was writing a morning message on the board when two girls started pointing, giggling and chanting, "You can't spell. You can't spell. You can't even read."

Mr. Lekes overheard these remarks and listened for Natasha's comeback. She says softly, "I'm telling," but does not move toward the teacher. Mr. Lekes approaches the situation. He starts by noticing so all parties involved could see the hurt that occurred.

Mr. Lekes: Natasha, your School Family members were teasing you about your spelling and reading. Your face is going like this (demonstrates) and is telling me how sad you feel. Your body is slumped like this (demonstrates) showing me you feel hopeless, like no one cares. (The two girls who were taunting stand still.) Did you like it when they were putting down your skills?
Natasha: No! I thought in our School Family we would help each other.
Two girls: (The girls hang their heads.)
Mr. Lekes: Natasha, tell the girls, I don't like it when you put me down.
Natasha: I don't like it when you put me down.
Mr. Lekes: What do you want them to do next time when you are having trouble writing the morning message?
Natasha: I want them to breathe and wish me well and ask if I need help.
Mr. Lekes: Tell the girls, Next time please be a S.T.A.R., wish well and offer help.
Natasha: I don't like it when you put me down. Next time S.T.A.R., wish well and offer help.
Mr. Lekes: Are you girls willing to do that?
Two girls: Yes, we are sorry, Natasha. Can we help you now?
Mr. Lekes: How are you three going to show you still care about each other and will treat each other with respect?
Girls: (Exchange pinky hugs.)

Revenge Tattling

Revenge tattling is often reported in hopes of getting others in trouble or out of a belief that others aren't doing what they should. "She's not cleaning up!" How we respond to this type of tattling will teach children that helpfulness or revenge is the better problem-solving tool.

We have all felt at a loss to persuade others to do our bidding. Children often have trouble persuading others to do something exactly as they envision it. One way children seek revenge is to try to get others in trouble. It often sounds like, "So-and-so is not doing what he is supposed to." The goal is to passive-aggressively get the other person in trouble. Another form of revenge tattling comes from children who know the rules and deem themselves assistant teachers. Regardless of intent and form, revenge tattling involves one child telling on others. To use revenge tattling as a natural consequence, begin the interaction with, "Are you telling me to be helpful or hurtful?" as is shown in the following examples:

> **Child:** Liam is not cleaning up!
> **Adult:** Are you telling me to be helpful or hurtful? (This fosters reflection.)
> **Child:** (Pauses to reflect) Hurtful.
> **Adult:** What could you do that would be helpful? (This sets up the teaching moment.)
> **Child:** I don't know.

Adult: You could say, "Liam, would you like some help cleaning up?" (Give the child the sentence and tone of voice to use.)

Notice how your response encourages both reflection and ownership, while also upholding the core School Family values of unity and helpfulness. Sometimes a child responds to the question, "Are you telling me to be helpful or hurtful?" with the answer, "Helpful." Our response will still focus on safety and unity, like this:

Child: Liam is not cleaning up!
Adult: Are you telling me to be helpful or hurtful?
Child: (Answers quickly) Helpful.
Adult: How is telling me about Liam being helpful to Liam?
Child: He is supposed to clean up. We all have to clean up!
Adult: So, you want Liam to be successful in our School Family and follow our agreements? How could you help him remember to clean up? (Positive intent is the key to setting up the teaching moment.)
Child: I don't know.
Adult: You could say, "Liam, would you like some help cleaning up?" (Give the child the sentence and tone of voice to use.)

Two things are likely to happen when an adult approaches tattling in this way: 1. The child who tattled will drop the whole event or 2. The child will offer Liam help in being a successful member of the School Family. Essentially, our job with revenge tattling is to act like a coach stationed inside a revolving door. If a child enters a revolving door from the street and stays in it long enough, he will make a complete circle and end up on the street again. Our coaching job inside the revolving door is to help the child transform the hurtful action into a helpful interaction. Children enter the revolving door with a perceived problem (often coupled with the intent of being hurtful or rescued). We coach them in flipping their intent to positive, teach them specific words and actions that are helpful, and then release them back into the classroom with new skills and a "we're all in this together" attitude.

Safety Tattling

Safety tattling involves reporting safety issues to the teacher. "Natalie fell off her chair." How we respond to these situations teach children to trust or mistrust authority.

When children see other children getting hurt, the natural response is to seek assistance in restoring safety by telling an adult. The adult's job is to assure children we will take care of it and reaffirm our School Family job description of keeping the classroom safe. When a child says, "Tomesia fell down the steps." Our response is, "I will take care of Tomesia. Telling me was helpful. I will keep her safe."

Activity to Practice Responding to Tattling

Below are four tattling situations. First, discern the type of tattling and the message the child is relaying. Then, respond to the underlying message through role-play with a partner.

1. Child comes to you and says, "Anna is not lining up."
2. Child comes to you complaining, "Sam wrote on my paper."
3. Child comes to you whining, "Avery pushed me."
4. Child comes to you and says, "Maya pushed Kevin off the swing. He's bleeding."

Three Types of Tattling

Type	Skill Needed	Message	Response
Intrusion: Child has been victimized. "She pushed me!"	Assertiveness	Powerlessness "I feel powerless to deal with this. Help me!"	"Did you like it?"
Revenge: Child wants to get someone in trouble or uphold rules. "She is not cleaning up!"	Helpfulness	Revenge "I'm angry at ___ for not ___. I don't know how to express myself directly."	"Are you telling me to be helpful or hurtful?"
Safety: Child sees someone getting seriously hurt. "She fell off her chair."	Trust in authority	Safety "I don't feel safe."	"I will take care of it."

Review: Benefits of using natural consequences in the classroom yield the following:

- Aggressive acts provide us with the opportunity to model and practice self-regulation, and the executive skills of impulse control, attention and empathy.
- Aggressive acts provide us with opportunities to teach the aggressor how to communicate verbally in socially acceptable ways (saying, "Move please," instead of pushing).
- Passive and passive-aggressive acts (tattling) provide us with the opportunity to teach emotional control and an assertive BIG Voice.
- School Family members witness ways to handle situations they may encounter later, learning new skills in meaningful real-life moments.
- School Family members see a call for help from their friends (rather than good guys and bad guys) and offer assistance by taking deep breaths.
- We receive many opportunities to practice and fine-tune our Conscious Discipline skills to help strengthen personal relationships.

Logical Consequences: Motivation to Use Skills We Already Possess

Often adults cannot allow children to experience natural consequences for safety reasons. At these times, logical consequences are useful to motivate connected children to use skills they already possess. Children who are disconnected or are missing social-emotional skills often become "frequent fliers" or "serial offenders" when we attempt to use logical consequences to motivate them to use skills they do not possess. These children need natural consequences or problem-solving that yields additional teaching, not logical consequences.

Before deciding to use logical consequences, ask yourself two questions: 1. Is the child a connected member of the School Family? 2. Does she already posses the skill we are motivating her to use? If the answer to both questions is "yes," logical consequences may be helpful. If the answer is "no," logical consequences may be hurtful.

The **three Rs** (**R**elated, **R**espectful and **R**easonable) help us structure a sound logical consequence, and the **big E** (**E**mpathy) helps the child reflect, claim ownership and feel motivated to change.

Related: A logical consequence is related to the child's behavior in a cause-and-effect relationship. It is also related back to safety, helpfulness or other class agreements.

Respectful: A logical consequence is given in an assertive voice of "no doubt." Verbal and nonverbal cues must reveal an intent is to teach.

Reasonable: A logical consequence is doable and makes sense in terms of duration and severity (no empty threats).

An effective logical consequence for a child who runs with scissors is to lose the opportunity to use scissors without supervision. An ineffective consequence would be to have him miss recess, call his parents or turn a card.

Empathy: When the child chooses to persist in hurtful behavior, enforcing the logical consequence may produce intense emotions and outbursts. Back talk, threats, begging, promises and more may come flying our way. It is essential to offer empathy during this time so the child can own her actions and be responsible for her choices. When the child starts mouthing off, it is easy to get triggered and begin lecturing or badgering the child into submission. If this occurs, the child's focus shifts from personal responsibility to a power struggle with the mean, unfair adult (us).

> **Consequences followed by empathy = Reflection and ownership**
> **Consequences followed by lectures = Blaming others**

When we've repeatedly taught a connected School Family member to say, "May I have a turn?" yet he persists in grabbing, it is time to give a logical consequence.

"Max you have a choice. You can say, *May I have a turn?* when you want an item your friend has and continue working in your small group, or you can grab again and you will work alone in this chair for the rest of the day so both you and your friends are safe. Max, tell me what will happen if you grab from your friends again so I know you understand."

Max repeats the consequence and the teacher checks for clarity. As soon as the teacher turns her back, Max grabs again.

"Max, I can see by your actions that you have chosen to sit at this table (point to the location) and work alone. Pick up your papers and move to the table."

Max pleads, "I won't do it again. I promise. He grabbed it first. I was just getting it back. I will be good. Give me one more chance. Please!"

Empathetically, help Max reflect and own his actions, "You seem disappointed. You were hoping you could stay with your friends and work together. You will have another chance tomorrow. Breathe with me. You're safe. Pick up your papers. You can handle this."

Let's break that scenario down into steps:

Step 1:   **Choices:** Present the choice to act helpfully or hurtfully with specific actions and outcomes for each.

"You have a choice! You can choose to ___ (helpful skill) and ___ (positive consequence), or you can choose to ___ (hurtful skill) again and ___ (negative consequence)."

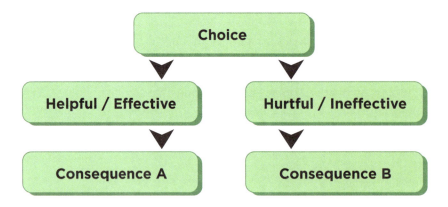

Step 2:   **Relate:** Relate the consequence for the ineffective or hurtful strategy to safety, class agreements or rules.

". . . so you are safe and so is everyone else."
". . . so you can be successful with our School Family agreements."

Step 3: **Reflect:** Check for understanding by asking the child to repeat what will happen if he chooses the hurtful action again. This step will vary depending on the child's age and language skills.

"Tell me what will happen if you ___ again."

Step 4: **Clarify:** Clarify if necessary to insure the child understands the consequence of the action.

Step 5: **Apply:** If the behavior persists, apply the logical consequence by restating it as a choice the child has made.

"I can see by your actions that you have chosen to ___." (Be specific with location and length of time.)

Step 6: **Empathy:** Provide empathy for the child's emotions, even if they are projected onto you or others. Resist the temptation to lecture or negate the child's upset. Use the Skill of Empathy (Chapter 8) combined with Positive Intent (Chapter 9).

"You seem ___. You were hoping for/wanting ___. It's hard. Breathe with me. You're safe. You can handle it."

End of the Day Checklist

	I wrote down the daily reminders from the board into my calendar
	Papers returned to me are in the "Papers to be filed" part of my notebook
	I completed the daily practice sheet ☐ Yes, and it's in the work completed basket ☐ No, it's in my bag to do for homework
	These things are in my bag to bring home: ☑ 3-ring binder ☐ Math Book ☐ Calendar ☐ Things to turn in folder ☐ Writing folder and flash drive

Scaffolding executive skills is essential for keeping School Family agreements

Activity to Apply a Logical Consequence

Emma, a connected member of the School Family, is poking her friends during group work time. She knows how to work as a team member and get her friend's attention by tapping her on her shoulder and calling her name.

Step 1: **Choices:** "Emma, you have a choice.

You can choose to _____ and

_____,

or you can choose to _____ and

_____."

Step 2: **Relate:** Relate to safety or agreements.

"_____"

Step 3: **Reflect:** Reflect back.

"Tell me what will happen if you _____ again."

Step 4: **Clarify:** Clarify if needed.

"_____"

Once you leave the work area, Emma continues to poke her friend.

Step 5: **Apply:** "I can see by your actions that you have chosen to _____

_____"

Step 6: **Empathy:** Emma shouts, "I wasn't doing anything. You always pick on me! I don't have to listen to you!"

Regain composure if needed and offer empathy.

"You seem _____.

You were hoping for/wanting _____.

You're _____. You can handle this. _____ with me."

The following response will help guide your answers. See if you can identify all six steps.

Teacher: "Emma, you have a choice. You can choose to work together with your group, tapping friends on the shoulder and calling them by name to get their attention, and work at the table until the project is completed. Or you can choose to poke your friends and you will work privately at your desk until the project is completed so everyone feels safe enough to focus on the task. Emma, tell me what will happen if you continue to poke your friends and distract the team?"

Emma: "I will work alone at my desk until the project is done."

Emma continues to poke once you leave.

Teacher: "I can see by your actions that you are choosing to work alone at your desk so everyone feels safe enough to complete the task."

Emma: "I didn't do anything. You always pick on me. I don't have to listen to you."

Teacher: "You seem angry. You were hoping you could stay with the group and finish the project. It is time to move back to your desk. You're safe. You can handle this. Breathe with me."

> **The short version of this process is:** "If you choose to _____ then you will _____," followed by empathy. The short version is easier to administer, but the long version contributes to the creation and maintenance of the School Family. I suggest using the six-step approach as a teaching tool earlier in the school year and shorten it to a prompt as the year progresses.

Creating Logical Consequences with Student Input

Some logical consequences can be created in class meetings involving the children. Begin with a discussion of how actions can be both helpful (positive) or hurtful (negative) depending on our behavioral choices. Give examples and ask children to predict if the outcome of the behavior would be helpful or hurtful to themselves or others. Discuss why they think so and how to change a hurtful outcome into a helpful one. The following examples will help with this discussion:

- "You have a choice to check your work carefully to correct any mistakes and raise your score, or you have a choice to hand it in without double-checking and possibly receive a lower grade. Which choice would support our agreement to do our best?"

- "You have a choice to use your BIG Voice or ask for help when you become frustrated so you can play with friends and have fun, or you can choose to hit and grab others and play by yourself so you and your friends are safe. Which choice is hurtful? Helpful? To whom?"

After you have helped children understand the above concepts, then you can involve them in coming up with the rules and the logical consequences needed. Without the above discussion, children tend to create harsh consequences or hurtful punishments.

Classroom Behavioral Charts

Traditional classrooms begin the year by posting rules and consequences. The first step with a misbehaving student is giving a warning, often followed by a second warning and then some form of loss of privileges. The loss of privileges is for all students breaking the rules, regardless of whether the child is a connected member of the class or possesses the necessary skills. If this is not effective, the school calls the child's parents in for assistance, imposes increasingly severe logical consequences and/or creates a behavioral plan.

In the School Family, children have the ultimate choice whether or not to keep the School Family safe through helpfulness. To be helpful, the child must keep his agreement to the School Family, keep his commitment to himself and follow procedures. **Step one** for children who choose not to be helpful in a School Family is the opportunity to choose again and be helpful. **Step two** is for us to encourage these children to go to the Safe Place to calm down. Once they return to learning, we prompt them to be helpful again. If they are still unwilling, this is an indication that they are disconnected. **Step three** involves creating a behavioral plan that increases the student's felt sense of safety and connection, fostering a greater willingness to cooperate with classroom procedures and agreements. Once it is clear the child is connected and knows the skill to use, we may apply logical consequences.

Problem-Solving: Motivation to use Executive Skills

Problem-solving is the third type of consequence used in Conscious Discipline. It motivates children to become part of the solution through the use of shared power. In many programs, problem-solving isn't viewed as a consequence; however, the consequence of many choices requires problem-solving. Simple examples of this are having a flat tire or running out of milk at breakfast. A wide range of problem-solving is required as a consequence of these experiences.

Many teachers say, "I can't think of a natural or logical consequence that makes sense and isn't a punishment." That is often an indication that problem-solving is in order. Problem-solving is particularly helpful for chronic problems (children who often say, "I don't care") and problems that involve the whole class (misbehaving with a substitute, excluding children, fighting, etc.). Watch a portal video showing how one principal uses problem-solving to address the chronic, school-wide problem of fighting.

Problem-solving is a tool best utilized when all parties are in a relaxed, alert executive state with access to their executive skill set. The state allows for the creative thinking necessary for brainstorming solutions and creating a plan. The following suggestions will help embed problem-solving into your school or classroom.

- When presenting a problem to the children, present it with positive intent and a focus on what you want the children to do. For example, two children may want to read the same book. To elicit suggestions, state the problem as, "Both of you want to read the same book at the same time. We have two people and one book. How can you solve this problem?"
- As children generate ideas that work for them, create a problem-solving class book showing visual images of various strategies that have been helpful.
- Conduct School Family class meetings.

Our job is to help keep it safe.

Choice to Be Helpful

Choice of Safe Place

Behavior Plan

Increase safety, connection and problem-solving (download available on portal)

Logical Consequences

Classroom Behavioral Chart

Consequences Create Problem-Solving Opportunities in the School Family

As you practice using the Power of Intention and the Skill of Consequences to reframe mistakes as vital opportunities to learn, the following structures and ritual will help children utilize problem-solving as a lifelong skill.

Structure: Class Meetings

> Ms. Gill's fifth grade class is going to have a substitute for four days. She reviews her expectations and how it's the students' job to help the substitute be successful. Upon Ms. Gill's return, the substitute reports that the students were unruly and disrespectful. The class had broken their agreements to Ms. Gill, each other and themselves, and the classroom was not safe. Ms. Gill shares her own frustration with the class and gives an assignment to reflect on the last four days. She asks the students to write which agreements they had broken, how they felt about it, and whether their behavior was hurtful or helpful and to whom. She calms herself in the Safe Place while the students work quietly. She comes out of the Safe Place upon completion of the assignment and begins a class meeting to discuss the consequences needed for them to make helpful choices next time.

Class meetings take many forms and are your core forum for solving problems like the one in Ms. Gill's class. Certainly, adults can problem-solve these issues on our own, but giving children a voice in the process provides the sense of ownership that is essential to following through on whatever goal, guideline, consequence or new skill is decided upon. Ms. Gill's class decided to write a letter of apology to the substitute, make a "Ways to Help the Substitute" class book, and create a new visual class signal to help each other to "Stop, Listen and Respect" next time they had a substitute.

Class meetings vary greatly depending on age and grade level. Young children tend to have circle time while older children go to morning meetings. At any age, structure these gatherings around a Brain Smart Start. As you recall from Chapter 4, the Brain Smart Start is a routine that consists of four activities:

1. Activity to **unite**
2. Activity to **disengage** the stress response
3. Activity to **connect** the children to the teacher and each other
4. Activity to **commit** oneself to learning

Within the framework of the Brain Smart Start, incorporate the P.E.A.C.E. process below for problem-solving:

P = <u>**P**</u>roblem and impact are stated
E = <u>**E**</u>ncourage the children to own their part of the problem
A = <u>**A**</u>ffirm the problem, restating it in terms of what you want to happen
C = <u>**C**</u>ollect solutions and come to a consensus
E = <u>**E**</u>valuate the effectiveness

> The following song is often used as the activity to unite in a class meeting where you intend to conduct the P.E.A.C.E. process.
>
> **It's Time to Solve Some Problems Song**
> *Sing to the tune of "Have You Ever Seen a Lassie?"*
> It's time to solve some problems, some problems, some problems.
> It's time to solve some problem, some problems today.

P = State the <u>P</u>roblem as you see it and its impact on you.

State what has happened that is of concern, without bias or judgment. "I've noticed that when children use their BIG Voices, some friends are not listening and continue with hurtful behavior instead." Follow this statement with how this is a problem from your point of view. "This is a problem for me because my job is to keep the classroom safe, and I can't do my job if you are not willing to listen to each other's BIG Voices. The classroom becomes unsafe, and learning suffers."

Key Skills: Make sure you are calm and can present the problem in a neutral tone. When you state how this is a problem for you, it must come from your heart and be authentic. This step is not about imposing guilt on students; it is about helping them see from your point of view.

E = <u>E</u>ncourage the children to own the problem.

"Have any of you noticed anything similar? For example you might have said, *I don't like it when you bump me in line, please walk carefully behind me*, and some children continue to bump you or say, *So what, get a life!*" This step allows the children to own part of the problem. With ownership, they are more likely to follow through on the plan devised.

Key Skills: Use specific examples (without names) you have seen in the classroom so children can identify with the problem. If children start to point the finger of blame at specific children, flip their negative intent into positive intent as discussed in Chapter 9.

> **April:** Parker always bumps me in line. She never listens to me!
> **Teacher:** So, you were hoping your friend would listen to your words.
> **Parker:** She's a liar. She bumps me and calls me names.
> **Teacher:** So you were hoping your friend would listen to your words, too. No wonder many children are feeling frustrated in our School Family. It seems we have an important problem to solve.

A = <u>A</u>ffirm the problem, restating it in terms of what you want to happen.

It is essential to flip the problem to what you do want to happen. Instead of saying, "As a School Family, we are not listening to our friends' BIG Voices," you would say, "So the problem is remembering to listen to each other's BIG Voices."

Key Skills: You must flip the problem from what you don't want to what you do want. Each phrasing produces very different results. In a classroom of young children, brainstorming solutions for not listening will produce many ideas for punishing those who don't listen. A classroom brainstorming how to remember to listen will produce a productive, solution-based conversation.

C = Collect helpful solutions to solve the problem.

"What would help you be more likely to listen to your friends' BIG Voices?" In this step, collect opinions and summarize solutions into common threads. Restate the common thread solution(s) into a new class agreement or rule. Role-play how to use the new skill so each child sees what it looks like, sounds like and feels like. You may want to make the new agreement into a chant with movements to help each person remember their commitment.

Key Skills: It is critical to listen when children express their opinion and then reflect back to the child the essence of what was said. This, at times, will require you to transform their idea from negative intent to positive intent and flip it from what they don't want to what they do want.

E = Evaluate to see if it is working.

End the problem-solving session with the question, "How will we know if our solution is working?" Work with the children to create a way to measure if their ideas are working. Meet again to check on the plan, and celebrate their success or do additional problem-solving if the issue persists.

Activity to P.E.A.C.E. Process Role-Play

In a small group (if possible) choose a chronic problem you are having in your classroom. Role-play a problem-solving session. Use each step of the P.E.A.C.E. process to guide you.

Structure: Conflict Resolution Time Machine

The *Conflict Resolution Time Machine* is your natural consequence structure for interpersonal conflicts in your classroom. The natural consequence of a hurtful encounter in a School Family is to redo the interaction in a helpful way. The Time Machine helps both teachers and children accomplish this "redo" by using their BIG Voices (discussed in Chapter 4). The Time Machine from Conscious Discipline has seven basic steps illustrated on it. It requires extensive coaching both in whole group sessions and individually as hurtful interactions occur; however, the ultimate goal is for children to use the Time Machine independently. Videos on the portal show children beginning to use the Time Machine on their own. There are seven basic steps for the Time Machine:

Step 1: **Roll back time.** Have the entire class roll their hands backwards or make some other unifying motion that represents going back in time preparing for a do-over.

Step 2: **Ask for willingness.** "Devon, are you willing to go back in time and solve your problem in a helpful way, teaching the whole class how it can be done?" Ask both parties. If the answer is, "Yes," then proceed.

Step 3: **Be a S.T.A.R.** Coach the entire class to Smile, Take a deep breath And Relax with the volunteers.

Step 4: **Wish each other well.** Coach all class members to place their hands on their hearts and extend their love outward as they extend their arms toward the problem solvers. The problem solvers wish each other well, too.

Step 5: **Focus on the goal.** Coach the class in saying "1- 2- 3." Then coach the problem solvers in chanting, "Let's do it." This step builds a sense of unity in the class and with the participants. Chanting together helps internalize the class values of respect, commitment and unity.

Step 6: **Coach the children to use helpful words.** Have the child who perceived him/herself as the victim speak first using the phrase, "I don't like it when you _____. Next time _____." Then help the children learn to teach others how they want to be treated. Most children will finish the sentence by saying, "Stop it," or "Don't do it anymore." Our job is to help reframe these thoughts to reflect what the child wants the other child to do, using phrases like, "Say, *Move please*, instead of pushing me," and "Tap my shoulder and say my name." The response from the aggressive child is, "Okay, I can do that."

If the other child feels he was intruded upon, the children change sides on the mat and repeat the process with the other child using an assertive voice.

Step 7: **Ask the children to show there are no hard feelings.** The children involved in the incident show there are no hard feelings by connecting somehow. They may choose a handshake, a hug, a high five or other connecting ritual. Encourage the children to come up with what feels most appropriate for them.

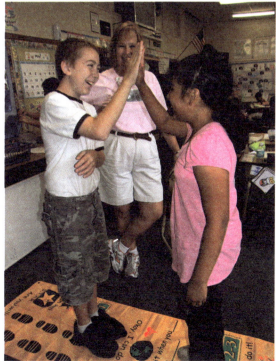

Younger students using the Time Machine   *Older students using the Time Machine*

Ritual: Relationship Repair

After a class meeting where you have undertaken problem-solving or used the Time Machine, it is important to conduct a ritual to bring it all together and repair possible relationship damage. End each session with a ritual that represents the following:

- We are all in this together.
- We commit to work the plan.
- We have repaired or are willing to repair any ruptured relationships that occurred during the problem-solving discussion.

The closing ritual could be as simple as standing in a circle facing inward, crossing arms, holding hands and uniformly raising hands overhead while turning to face outward. This movement uncrosses everyone's arms, leaving an intact circle. This could symbolize "We are ready to move forward as a School Family with each person having the other's back." Rituals are most meaningful when the class creates them as a group or they evolve spontaneously from class events.

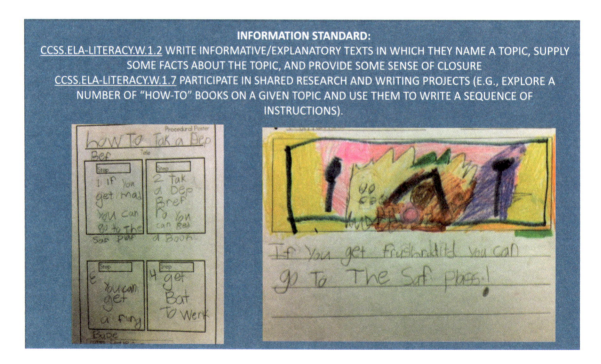

Tie Conscious Discipline to your standards

Consequences Summary

Power:	**Intention:** Mistakes are opportunities to learn.
Becoming Brain Smart:	The brain functions differently under threat.
Skill:	Natural consequences, tattling as a teaching tool, logical consequences, problem-solving, P.E.A.C.E. process
School Family:	Class Meetings, *Conflict Resolution Time Machine,* Relationship Repair Rituals

Power of Intention Reflection

Consciously notice if our intent and impact match. Notice how we treat conflicts, whether we deem them accidental or intentional. Let go of the pain associated with times we believe we've intentionally or unintentionally hurt others, and times we've been intentionally or unintentionally hurt. Start practicing the Power of Intention by taking the following steps:

❏ **Catch ourselves using intention as a deflection strategy.** Listen to how often we say out loud or in our heads, "Well, that wasn't my intent."

❏ **Use the four questions on page 288** to clear up miscommunications with loved ones and coworkers.

❏ **Stop punitive self-talk by focusing on these questions instead:** What was my choice? What happened as a result? How did it feel to me? Did it achieve what I wanted? What new strategies might serve me better?

❏ **Shift our intent when children act out** by asking, "Do I want my students to feel bad and pay for their crimes, or do I want to teach my students to reflect on their choices, change their choices and develop self-control?"

❏ **Become conscious of our typical intent in delivering consequences** (to punish, save or teach) and how it changes based on our level of upset.

❏ **Ask, do I rely too heavily on logical consequences?** If so, enact more problem-solving and focus on using natural consequences as a teaching tool.

❏ **Think about next year.** Tweak traditional first warning, second warning systems to be more effective. Discuss this issue with your grade level team and implement a plan for next year.

❏ **Watch the Power of Intention video** on the portal to deepen your reflection.

Brain Smart Teaching Moments

Every broken class agreement, refusal to follow a class routine or failure to comply with a rule is a teaching moment.

- Look for daily interpersonal conflicts like these as opportunities to use **natural consequences** to teach new skills:

  - Excessive talking
  - Off-task behaviors
  - Failure to complete work
  - Pushing and shoving
  - Name calling
  - Destruction of property

- Use **logical consequences** for connected children who possess the skills but lack the motivation to use them and for safety issues.

- Use **problem-solving** when natural and logical consequences don't seem to fit the situation and for chronic classroom issues.

- Create **behavior plans** for children with chronic issues by using the Executive Skills Lending Library.

Skill Reflection: Common and Conscious

If possible, partner up with someone and say the two statements out loud. See if you can feel the difference. After each statement share, "The difference between Common and Conscious for me was…"

Common	Conscious
That was not my intention. Do you think I'm that horrible of a person?	My intention was to be helpful. I can see by your face that it didn't come across that way. Are you willing for a do-over?
You should have thought about this before. You've made a mess for yourself.	You seem anxious. You are worried about staying on the basketball team.
That was a good choice.	You really thought that through. It seems it worked out for you.
Is someone bleeding or dying?	Are you telling me to be helpful or hurtful?
Use your words.	Tell him, "I don't like it when you _____. Next time please _____."

School Family Implementation Checklist

❏ **Determine whether a situation is best served by natural, logical or problem-solving consequences**, utilize the appropriate consequence, and follow up with the Skill of Empathy.

❏ **Differentiate between intrusion, revenge and safety tattling, and respond accordingly:** Did you like it (intrusion), are you telling me to be helpful or hurtful (revenge), I will take care of it; it's my job to keep the classroom safe (safety).

❏ **Ask, "Is this child a connected member of our School Family, and does he possess the skills needed to be successful?"** before administering logical consequences.

❏ **Discern what executive skill a child might be missing and create an intervention plan** by reviewing the Executive Skills Lending Library.

❏ **Teach the *Conflict Resolution Time Machine*** to children.

❏ **Practice the P.E.A.C.E. process** when solving problems in class meetings.

❏ **Create a Relationship Repair Ritual** for problem-solving class meetings.

❏ **Review additional helpful resources on ConsciousDiscipline.com**, including Shubert's School and the portal, with a focus on Class Meetings, the Time Machine and the Executive Skills Lending Library.

Only books have endings. Life is a journey! All our experiences, whether perceived as joyous steps or devastating missteps, have brought us to this time of transformation. Every situation and every choice—whether governed by insecurity, impulse, wisdom or reflection—has prepared us for this "now" moment.

May your journey with Conscious Discipline inspire you to inspire others by being the change you want to see in the world.

Becky A. Bailey

Conscious Discipline
Many problems. One solution.

Resiliency

Social Skills

Trauma Informed

Bully Prevention

School Climate

Be the change!

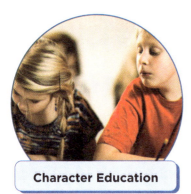

Character Education

Social-Emotional Learning

Classroom Management

13   The missing piece - Conscious Discipline provides one solution to many problems.

References

Anant, S. S. (1966) The need to belong. *Canada's Mental Health*, 14, 21-27.

Bailey, B. A. (2011) *Managing Emotional Mayhem: The Five Steps for Self-Regulation.* Oviedo, FL: Loving Guidance, Inc.

Bailey, B. A. (1997) *I Love You Rituals: Activities to Build Bonds and Strengthen Relationships With Children.* New York: Harper Collins.

Bailey, B. A., & Montero-Cefalo, E. (2012) *Baby Doll Circle Time.* Oviedo, FL: Loving Guidance, Inc.

Barfield, S., & Gaskill, R. (2005) *Positive impact of the Neurosequential Model of Therapeutics on high-risk children in a therapeutic preschool setting.* Lawrence, KS: University Press of Kansas.

Barkley, R. A. (2001) The inattentive type of ADHD as a distinct disorder: What remains to be done. *Clinical Psychology: Science and Practice*, 8:489–493.

Baumeister, R. F., & Tierney, J. (2011) Willpower: Rediscovering the greatest human strength. New York: The Penguin Press.

Behrends, A., Müller, S., & Dziobek, I. (2012) Moving in and out of synchrony: A concept for a new intervention fostering empathy through interactional movement and dance. *The Arts in Psychotherapy* 39: 107–116.

Belsky, J. (2008) Family Influences on Psychological Development. *Psychiatry*, 7, 282-285.

Berridge, K. (2004) Motivation concepts in behavioral neuroscience. *Physiology and Behavior* 81, 179-209.

Blair, C. (2002) School Readiness: Integrating Cognition and Emotion in a Neurobiological Conceptualization of Children's functioning at School Entry. *American Psychologist 57* Issue 2, page 111.

Burke, C. A. (2010) Mindfulness-Based approaches with children and adolescents: A preliminary review of current research in an emergent field. *Journal of Child and Family Studies*, 19(2), 133.

Caldji, C., Diorio, J., & Meaney, M. J., (2002) Variations in maternal care in infancy regulate the development of stress reactivity. *Biological Psychiatry*. Dec 15;48 (12):1164-74.

Center on the Developing Child at Harvard University (2011) Building the Brain's "Air Traffic Control" System: How Early Experiences Shape the Development of Executive Function: Working Paper No. 11. Retrieved from www.DevelopingChild. Harvard.edu.

Center on the Developing Child at Harvard University (2010) *The Foundations of Lifelong Health Are Built in Early Childhood.* http://www.developingchild.harvard.edu.

Chopra, D. (2011) *The Seven Spiritual Laws of Success: A Practical Guide to the Fulfillment of Your Dreams.* San Rafael, CA: Amber-Allen Publishing.

Cohen, J., & Geier, V.K. (2010) School Climate-Research Summary: January 2010. New York, N.Y. Retrieved from: www.schoolclimate.org/climate/research.php.

Colvin, G., Kameenui, E. J., & Sugai, G. (1993) School-wide and classroom management: Reconceptualizing the integration and management of students with behavior problems in general education. *Education and Treatment of Children*, 16, 361-381.

Cote, S. M., Borge, A. I., Geoffroy, M., Rutter, M., & Tremblay, R. E. (2008) Nonmaternal care in infancy and emotional/behavioral difficulties at 4 years old: Moderation by family risk characteristics. *Developmental Psychology*, 44, 153-168.

Cozolino, L. (2013) *The Social Neuroscience of Education: Optimizing attachment and learning in the classroom.* New York: W.W. Norton & Company.

Cozolino, L. (2006) *The Neuroscience of Human Relationships: Attachment and the Developing Social Brain* (2nd Edition): *Building and Rebuilding the Human Brain.* New York: W.W. Norton & Company.

Dawson, P., & Guare, R. (2009) *Executive Skills in Children and Adolescents: A practical guide to assessment and intervention* (2nd Edition). New York: Guilford Press.

Deci, E. L., & Ryan, R. M. (2008) Facilitating optimal motivation and psychological well-being across life's domains. Canadian Psychology, 49, 14-23.

de Waal, F. B. M. (2008) Putting the altruism back into altruism: The evolution of empathy. *Annual Review of Psychology* 59: 279-300.

Edwards, A., Shipman, K., & Brown, A. (2005) The socialization of emotional understanding: A comparison of neglectful mothers and their children. *Child Maltreatment*, 10, 293-304.

Emory University Health Sciences Center. (2002) Emory Brain Imaging Studies Reveal Biological Basis For Human Cooperation. *ScienceDaily*. Retrieved from www.sciencedaily.com/releases/2002/07/020718075131.htm.

Findlay, L. C., Girardi, A., & Coplan, R. J. (2006) Links between empathy, social behavior, and social understanding in early childhood. *Early Childhood Research Quarterly*, 21, 347-359.

Fruzzetti, A. E., Lowry, K., Mosco, E., & Shenk, C. (2003) Emotion regulation: Rationale and strategies In W. T. O' Donohue, J. E. Fisher & S. C. Hayes (Eds.), Empirically Supported techniques of cognitive behavior therapy: A step-by-step guide for clinicians (pp. 152-159). New York: Wiley.

Gerwin, C. (2013) Innovating in Early Head Start: Can Reducing Toxic Stress Improve Outcomes for Young Children? Center on the Developing Child at Harvard University. Retrieved from: http://developingchild.harvard.edu/resources/stories_from_the_field/tackling_toxic_stress/innovating_in_early_head_start.

Gollwitzer, P. M., & Sheeran, P. (2006) Implementation intentions and goal achievement: A meta-analysis of effects and process. *Advances in Experimental Social Psychology*, 38, 69-119.

Gluckman, P., & Hanson, M. (2006) *Mismatch*. New York: Oxford Press.

Huang, J., & Sekuler, R. (2010) Attention Protects the Fidelity of Visual Memory: Behavioral and Electrophysiological Evidence. *The Journal of Neuroscience*, 30(40):13461–13471.

Hoffman, L. L., Hutchinson, C. J., & Reiss, E. (2009) On improving schools: Reducing reliance on rewards and punishments. *International Journal of Whole Schooling* 5(1): 13-24.

Hoffman, L. L., Hutchinson, C. J., & Reiss, E. (2005) Training teachers in classroom management: Evidence of positive effects on the behavior of difficult children. *Strate Journal*. 14(1) p. 36-43.

Holt, D., Ippiloto, P. M., Desrochers, D. M., & Kelley, C. R. (2007) Children's Exposure to TV Advertising in 1977 and 2004: Information for the Obesity Debate. *Federal Trade Commission, Bureau of Economics Staff Report*. Retrieved from http://www.ftc.gov/reports/childrens-exposure-television-advertising-1977-2004-information-obesity-debate-bureau.

Ingvarson, L., Meiers, M. & Beavis, A. (2005) Factors affecting the impact of professional development programs on teachers' knowledge, practice, student outcomes & efficacy. *Education Policy Analysis Archives*, 13(10), 1-26.

Jensen, E. (1997) *Completing the Puzzle: The Brain-compatible Approach to Learning*. Del Mar, CA: The Brain Store, Inc.

Jeong, S., & Lee, B. H. (2013) A Multilevel Examination of Peer Victimization and Bullying Preventions in Schools. *Journal of Criminology*.

Jiang, Y., Ekono, M., & Skinner, C. (2014) Basic Facts about Low-Income Children: Children 6 through 11 years, 2012. National Center for Children in Poverty. Retrieved from: http://www.nccp.org/publications/pub_1090.html/.

Kaiser Family Foundation (2007) *Food for Thought. Television Food Advertising to Children in the United States*. Menlo Park, CA: Kaiser Family Foundation. Retrieved from http://kff.org/other/food-for-thought-television-food-advertising-to.

Keltner, D., Marsh, J., & Smith, J. A. (2010) *The Compassionate Instinct: The Science of Human Goodness*. New York: W. W. Norton & Company.

Kern, L., Gallagher, P., Starosta, K., Hickman, W., & George, M. L. (2006) Longitudinal outcomes of functional behavioral assessment-based intervention. *Journal of Positive Behavior Interventions*, 8, 67-78.

Klemm, W. R. (2010) Free will debates: Simple experiments are not so simple. *Advances in Cognitive Psychology*, 6, 47–65.

Kohn, A. (1999) *Punished by Rewards: The Trouble with Gold Stars, Incentive Plans, A's, Praise, and Other Bribes*. Boston: Houghton Mifflin.

Kosfeld, M., Heinrichs, M., Zak, P. J., Fischbacher, U. & Fehr, E. (2005) Oxytocin increases trust in humans. *Nature* 435, 673-676.

Kühn, S., & Brass, M. (2009) Retrospective construction of the judgment of free choice. *Consciousness and Cognition*, 18, 12-21.

LeDoux, J. E. (1996) *The Emotional Brain*. New York: Simon & Schuster.

Legault, L., & Inzlicht, M. (2013) Self-determination, self-regulation, and the brain: Autonomy improves performance by enhancing neuroaffective responsiveness to self-regulation failure. *Journal of Personality and Social Psychology*, 105, 123-138. doi:10.1037/a0030426.

Levin, D. E. (2013) *Beyond Remote-Controlled Childhood: Teaching Young Children in the Media Age*. Washington, D.C.: National Association for the Education of Young Children.

Ludington-Hoe, S. M., McDonald P. E., & Satyshur, R. (2002) Breastfeeding in African-American women. *The Journal of National Black Nurses Association.* July;13(1):56-64. Review.

Madigan, J. B. (2009) Action Based learning: Building Better Brains through Movement. Retrieved from: www. ActionBasedLearning.com.

McCraty, R., Deyhle, A., & Childre, C. (2012) The Global Coherence Initiative: Creating a Coherent Planetary Standing Wave. *Global Advances in Health and Medicine,* (1): 64-77. Retrieved from: www.gahmj.com.

McCraty, R., Tiller, W. A., & Atkinson, M. (1996) Proceedings of the Brain-Mind Applied Neurophysiology. *EEG Neurofeedback Meeting.* Conducted from Key West, FL.

McEwen, B. S. (2001) Plasticity of the hippocampus: adaptation to chronic stress and allostatic load. *Annals of the NY Academy of Science*s. 933:265-77.

McGonigal, K. (2012) *The WillPower Instinct: How self-control works, why it matters, and what you can do to get more of it.* New York: Penquin Group.

McKay, M., Fanning, P., Paleg, K., & Landis, D. (1996) *When Anger Hurts Your Kids: A Parent's Guide.* Oakland, CA: New Harbinger Publications, Inc.

Mehrabian, A. (1971) *Silent messages: Implicit communication of emotions and attitudes.* Belmont, CA: Wadsworth.

Merrell, K. W., Isava, D. M., Gueldner, B. A., & Ross, S. W. (2008) How Effective Are School Bullying Intervention Programs? A Meta-Analysis of Intervention Research. *School Psychology Quarterly.* Vol. 23, No. 1, 26-42.

Miller, S. (2011) *Energizing Brain Breaks 2.* Boulder, CO: Engaged Teaching Inc.

Muraven, M. (2008) Autonomous self-control is less depleting. *Journal of Research in Personality,* 42, (3) 763-770.

NICHD Early Child Care Research Network. (2003) Does amount of time spent in child care predict socioemotional adjustment during the transition to kindergarten? *Child Development,* 74, 976-1005.

NICHD Early Child Care Research Network (Ed.). (2005) *Child Care and Child Development: Results of the NICHD Study of Early Child Care and Youth Development.* New York: Guilford Press.

Nichols, M. P. (1996) *The Lost Art of Listening: How Learning to Listen Can Improve Relationships.* New York: Guilford Press.

Panksepp J. P., & Burgdorf J. (2003) The neurobiology of positive emotions. *Neuroscience and Biobehavioral Reviews,* 30: 173-187.

Pert, C. (1999) *Molecules Of Emotion: The Science Between Mind-Body Medicine.* New York: Scribner.

Radin, D. I. & Schlitz, M.J. (2005) Gut feelings, intuition, and emotions: An exploratory study. *Journal of Alternative and Complimentary Medicine,* 11(5): 85-91.

Rain, J. S. (2014) Final Report: Conscious Discipline Research Study. Comprehensive program evaluation conducted for Loving Guidance, Inc. February 24, 2014. Oviedo, FL: Loving Guidance.

Ramnani, N. & Owen, A. M. (2004) Anterior prefrontal cortex: insights into function from anatomy and neuroimaging. *Nature Reviews Neuroscience,* 5, 184-94.

Rizzolatti, G. & Craighero, L. (2004) The Mirror-Neuron System. *Annual Review of Neuroscience,* Vol. 27: 169-192. DOI: 10.1146/annurev.neuro.27.070203.144230.

Ryce, M. (1996) *Why Is This Happening To Me. . . AGAIN?! ...and What You Can Do About It!* Theodosia, MO: Dr. Michael Ryce.

Sansone, C., & Harackiewicz, J. (2000) *Intrinsic and Extrinsic Motivation: The Search for Optimal Motivation and Performance.* New York: Academic Press.

Sapolsky, R. M. (1998) *Why Zebras Don't Get Ulcers: An Updated Guide to Stress, Stress Related Diseases, and Coping* (2nd Edition) New York: W. H. Freeman.

Schwartz, J. M., & Begley, S. (2002) *The Mind & The Brain: Neuroplasticity and the power of mental force.* New York: HarperCollins.

Schwartz, J. M., & Gladding, R. (2011) *You Are Not Your Brain: The 4-Step Solution for Changing Bad Habits, Ending Unhealthy Thinking, and Taking Control of Your Life.* New York, NY: Penguin Group, Inc.

Seita, J. R., & Brendtro, L. K. (2002) *Kids who outwit adults?* Longmont, CO: Sopris West.

Siegel, D. J. (2012) *Pocket Guide to Interpersonal Neurobiology: An Integrative Handbook of the Mind.* New York: W. W. Norton.

Siegel, D. J. (2012) *The Developing Mind (2nd Edition): How Relationships and the Brain Interact to Shape Who We Are*. New York: Guilford Press.

Siegel, D. J. (2010) *Mindsight: The New Science of Personal Transformation*. New York: Random House.

Sunderland, M. (2006) *Science of Parenting*. New York, NY: Penguin Group, Inc.

Teper. R., Segal, Z., & Inzlicht, M. (2013) Inside the Mindful Mind: How Mindfulness Enhances Emotion Regulation Through Improvements in Executive Control; *Current Directions in Psychological Science*, 22:449-454.

Tolle, E. (2004) *The Power of Now: A Guide to Spiritual Enlightenment*. San Francisco, CA: New World Library.

Tronick, E. (2007) *The Neurobehavioral and Social-Emotional Development of Infants and Children*. New York: W. W. Norton & Company.

Turecki, S., & Tonner, L. (1985) *The Difficult Child: A New Step-By-Step Approach*. New York: Bantam Books.

Volling, B. L., Blandon, A. Y., & Kolak, A. M. (2006) Marriage, parenting, and the emergence of early self-regulation in the family system. *Journal of Child and Family Studies*, 15, 493-506.

Vygotsky L. S. (1986) *Thought and Language*. Cambridge, MA: The MIT Press.

Walker, H. M., Colvin, G., & Ramsey, E. (1995) *Antisocial behavior in school: Strategies and best practices*. Pacific Grove, CA: Brooks/Cole.

Weintraub S., Dikmen, S. S., Heaton, R. K., Tulsky, D. S., Zelazo, P. D., Bauer, P. J., Carlozzi, N. E., Slotkin, J., Blitz, D., Wallner-Allen, K., Fox, N. A., Beaumont, J. L., Mungas, D., Richler, J., Deocampo, J. A., Anderson, J. E., Manly, J. J., Borosh, B., Havlik, R., & Gershon, R. (In Press) *NIH Toolbox for the Assessment of Behavioral and Neurological Function: Cognition domain instruments. Neurology*.

Wesselmann, D., Schweitzer, C., & Armstrong, S. (2014) *Integrative Parenting: Strategies for raising children affected by attachment trauma*. New York: W.W. Norton and Company.

Zahn-Waxler, C., & Radke-Yarrow, M. (1990) The origins of empathic concern. *Motivation and Emotion* 14: 107-130.

Zanto, T., & Gazzaley, A. (2009) Neural Suppression of Irrelevant Information Underlies Optimal Working Memory Performance. *The Journal of Neuroscience*. 29: 3059-3066.

Zak, P. J., Stanton, A. A., & Ahmadi, S. (2007) Oxytocin Increases Generosity in Humans. *PLoS ONE*, Vol. 2, No. 11.

Zins, J. E., & Elias, M. J. (2006) Social and emotional learning. In G. G. Bear & K. M. Minke (eds.), *Children's needs III: Development, prevention, and intervention* (pp. 1-13). Bethesda, MD: National Association of School Psychologists.